HENRY CRABB ROBINSON

ON

BOOKS AND THEIR WRITERS

HENRY CRABB ROBINSON IN 1860

From a sketch by G. Scharf

HENRY CRABB ROBINSON

ON

BOOKS AND THEIR WRITERS

EDITED BY

EDITH J. MORLEY

VOLUME THREE

LONDON

J. M. DENT AND SONS LIMITED

APPENDICES

APPENDIX I

LETTERS FROM CARLYLE TO CRABB ROBINSON [1]

Haddington, 29th April 1825.

(1) My dear Sir,—Knowing by repeated experience [2] your readiness to oblige, I make no scruple of applying to you in the present emergency, more especially as it relates to a department of business in which you take a deep interest for its own sake.

I have been engaged with an Edinburgh Bookseller to prepare three or perhaps four volumes of Translations from the German intended as specimens of their chief novel writers, with Prefaces, Lives, and Criticisms, and all the addenda which may serve to procure them a good-natured reception from the English public. My acquaintance with this branch of German literature is small, for it does not stand by any means in the highest favour with me, yet I calculate pretty confidently on being able to select a handful of sound wheat from the loads of chaff which I have yet examined only on the surface; and being naturally anxious to effect this as perfectly as possible, I have determined on soliciting the benefit of your knowledge and taste to aid me in my choice. The Bookseller leaves me unlimited freedom; he has no information on the subject, and few counsellors by whose light it were safe to walk. So far as I can judge his chief dependence seems to be on the *Volksmärchen* and *Rittererzählungen* of our neighbours; on Musäus, La Motte Fouqué, Lafontaine, and the other 'mob of gentlemen' who wrote for the venerable *Plebs* of the reading community. I dislike these people, but must not altogether neglect them. For the sake of popularity independent of merit, I must try to get a specimen or two from each of these notable personages; but my chief dependence is placed on Tieck, Richter, Wieland, and Goethe. From the last I have already determined to take *Werter*, *Melusine*, and what you told me Schlegel called

---

[1] Carlyle's letters are printed exactly as he wrote them, his capitals, spelling, abbreviations etc., being retained.

[2] There had not been much time. Crabb Robinson first made Carlyle's acquaintance on June 22nd 1824.

the *Mährchen aller Mährchen*.[1] In Wieland, I think, I shall find
an article or two in the *Hexameron von Rosenhain* or elsewhere,
valuable more for its author's than its own qualities, but giving
room for some discussion on *that* topic and therefore useful for
me.   Of Richter I yet know little; I have looked into his *Herbst-
buminen* [*sic*], his *Flegeljahre*, and am now reading his *Fibel*.   It is
easy to see already that next to Goethe (and Tieck?) he is the
best man in Germany; but his extravagance and barbarism will
render the task of selecting from him one of some difficulty.
The *Phantasien* which you lent me are all I know of Tieck; but I
must if possible have him included in my list, and some of his
smaller tales I hope will give me the opportunity.   There is also
one Hoffmann whose *Elixiere des Teufels* was translated last year
in Edinburgh (with small success) concerning whom I could like
to have some further information.   As to Claurens [*sic*], with his
Scherz und Ernst, I have got the book beside me, but put no faith
in it.

Now, my dear sir, could you of your own knowledge, or by
consulting with any of your German friends, afford me advice in
this matter?   Could you learn for me which is Lafontaine's *best*
novel in one moderate volume?   I have read his *Raphael* (in
French), his *Rudolph von Werdenberg*, and his *Tinchen* (in
German): there is genius in all of these; but whether any of them
is among the best of his half-a-century of works, I have no means
of ascertaining.   Do you know the character of his *Sagen aus dem
Alterthüme* and his *Kleine Romane*?   What is Tieck's best novel?
La Motte Fouqué's best novel or novels of the small sort?   Is it
Ondine [*sic*]?   This they wish me to translate, thinking it badly
done at present, but after reading the original, I despise it a good
deal.   Can you tell me which is the Baron*ess* La Motte Fouqué's
best?   None of her little Tales are good: I must give a specimen
both of her and her husband, but I wish to make them very short,
for they are intrinsically very slender people.

In Edinburgh are several handsome collections of German
books, to most or all of which I have obtained or shall obtain
access, particularly to that in the Advocates' Library, one of the
most numerous if not the best selected in the Kingdom.   Still
the quantity of books I shall have access to, compared with the
quantity I should wish to read before making a final choice is
inconsiderable; and as buying on the great scale is out of the
question, I am anxious to have the range of my examination

---

[1] 'In what book or treatise does he so call it?'   [Carlyle translated
it in 1832.]

narrowed before commencing. For this purpose I put no small trust in you. I doubt not you will give me minutely your own thoughts on the matter; and transmit me those of your German friends in whose judgment you most rely. Has not Mrs. Aders (the lady who lent me *Wilhelm Meister*) great skill in such things? So great is my confidence in your goodness that if you could readily procure me a *loan* of any quantity of books likely to be of use to me, I should not hesitate to ask you to take the trouble of sending them for my perusal and criticism: consigned to a Bookseller in London, they might with the greatest ease and speed be sent to my Bookseller in Edinburgh, and thence to my abode. This seems a strange proposal, but when I look at your Don Quixote and Quevedo, I hardly think it stranger than your kindness of disposition. At all events, I count on your favouring me with your advice, the first hour you have leisure. I make no apologies for the trouble I am giving you, but I hope I shall not feel the obligation the less on that account. If you write within a week after this arrives (which would be very desirable), please to direct to No. 18 Salisbury Street, Edingh; if not till after that, it will be safer to say: Mainhill, Ecclefechan, Dumfries-shire, where I am to be all summer.

In a short while I mean to send you one of those *Schillers* that you may send it to Goethe: then I shall try to write less drily. At present I must stick to the naked point of business, and even this I can hardly yet handle in intelligible terms: crowds of people are about me. I must pray you to make the best of it, and to believe me always, with true esteem,

My dear sir,

Most faithfully yours,

THOMAS CARLYLE.

[Endorsed in Crabb Robinson's writing:]

La Motte Fouqué (Baroness) and Claurens [*sic*]—reprobated.
Wieland,[1] La Fontaine,[1] Familie von Halden [1] the best.
First collect[io]n of Moralische Erzählungen, Dankbarkeiten u. Liebe.
Messner, Der Hund des Melei. Tieck new ones lately transl[ate]d.
Richter, fragments from Titan. Reise des Feldpredigers Schmelzler a small work with (beautiful) notes. Neujahrsnacht.

[1] These also are 'reprobated,' i.e. omitted, from *German Romance*.

Klinger, Friederich Kind, small novelist.
Caroline Pickler.
La Motte. Der Zauber Ring. One volume. By far the best.
Franz Horn. Der ewige Jude. In an Almanach.
Hoffman.[1]—Serapions Brüder: in that Fräulein v. Scuderei u.
  Phantasiespielen in wch.
Der goldene Topf.
A Miss Nancy Mitchell.
Amatonda.
Volksmärchen v. Musaeus.

Hoddam Hill, Dumfries-shire, 25th April, 1826.

(2) My dear Sir,—It is long since I ought to have thanked you
for your friendly and prompt answer to my last inquiries: and I do
so now with no very good grace, when I have a new favour to ask
of you. The Book of *German Novelists*, concerning which I took
your advice last spring, is actually in the Press: after much
loitering, groping, consulting, and passive and active meditating,
I at last fixed upon my men, began printing last January, and am
in hopes of being rid of the affair, if you can help me out of this
strait in which I am for the present entangled.

I am to have four volumes; *two* names in each of the first three;
and Goethe's *Wilhelm Meisters Wanderjahre* is to occupy the
fourth. Of these, the first and the *last* and half of the second are
already printed. Musäus, Fouqué, Tieck: Goethe with lives and
so forth; Hoffmann, Jean Paul, and Maler Müller [2] are still
desiderated. And like to be so, unless you can lend me a hand;
for the original works are not to be had in any *shop* of this Island;
and though I have sent for them both to Leipzig and Hamburg,
and the *invoice* from Fleischer in the former of these book-marts
reached me about a month ago, no glimpse of the ware itself
has yet come to light, not even a probability when it is to be
looked for. You will conceive the *nodus* of the case when I tell
you that in ten days unless some *Deus intersit*, Ballantyne with all
his Devils will be at a stand.

Of Hoffmann, I have a piece besides me that would answer, one
of his *Fantasiestücke in Callots Manier*; but I want much to see
his *Leben und Nachlass*, or any even the slenderest account of his
life; being ignorant at present even of the date of its termination.

[1] 'It has been far the worst and the most troublesome of them all.'
Letter to John Carlyle, May 1826. *Early Letters*, Norton, 1887.
[2] His works remained unobtainable and were not included among
Carlyle's translations.

43505

With Jean Paul, also, I could contrive at a dead lift to 'help myself through'; on the faith of your recommendation I sent for *Schmelzle's Reise* and also for the *Leben Q[uintus] Fixlein*, with a Biography of the Illustrious Dead himself; the former works I suppose are on the road at present, but as for Biographies, Fleischer declares that though two *höchst interessante* Lives of Jean Paul are in the Press, no life whatever of him has yet come out of it. Nevertheless I have got the *Picnic und Dejeuner dansant zu Kuhschnappel* of Richter here, and if no better might be, with this I could serve my turn. The death of Richter, among many deep feelings of sadness which it excites in me, affects me likewise with this very mean inconvenience, that I should and cannot give some more precise account of his life. The date of his death even is not known to me. This, however, surely might be learned.[1]

But with regard to Maler Müller I confess myself totally helpless. This Müller is a person whom I do not recollect having heard you mention. Maler (Painter) is the *agnomen* by which he is commonly designated, though he has two Christian names besides. Richter, Horn, and other *Aesthetic* gentlemen speak in high terms of him; and an intelligent Hamburger [2] whom I met with last summer recommends him with panegyrics almost rapturous. In short, I have come to regard this Maler Müller as an indispensable personage; and to believe that I cannot with a safe conscience present my Seven Champions of Germany to the English unless he be among the number. It seems he was a contemporary of Goethe in early days, and published various choice pieces about the period of *Werter;* but afterwards forsook poetry for painting, in the but moderately successful pursuit of which he died some months ago at Rome. His Literary works (Maler Müller's *Sämmtliche Werke*, 3 Bände, 8°) are mentioned in Fleischer's catalogue, as published at Heidelberg in 1811; since which time it would appear they have met with quite a new reception; and says my Hamburg correspondent, 'it is even thought that had he continued to cultivate poetry, he might have all but equalled Goethe himself!'

Forgive me these horrid blots, it is a chance to which the finest Calligrapher is exposed when his pen has been six weeks on duty and his ink become a syrup.

Now you can easily figure how gladly I would buy these three

[1] 14th November 1825.
[2] Dr. Julius. See *Early Letters of Carlyle*, Norton, 1887.

volumes; borrow them, beg them, nay, almost steal them; so any one of these four modes of appropriation could bring them into my hand.   As I have no late catalogue of any London German Bookseller, it seems barely possible that Bonte, widow Boosey, Black, or some of these people may have the article in their possession.   Nay, failing this, who knows but your Mrs. Aders or some other of your German friends may have it in their library, and be prevailed upon for the sake of helping a disconsolate Author out of this Slough of Despond, to let him have it for a week or two in his extreme need ? If you can possibly do anything for me, I know you will do it; if not, why then we must just summon our Christian fortitude, and await in meekness and humility the chances of wind and weather.   I will tell you again what I want:

(1) Hoffmann's (C. T. A.) *Leben und Nachlass*, or any account of his life, even the date of his decease.

(2) Richter's *Schmelzle* and *Quintus Fixlein* and the same thing about *his* life.

(3) Maler Müller's *Werke*, with, if possible, the like appendage.

The first of these works would enable me to go on for the matter of four weeks; by which time, it is likely enough, the Leipzig package may have arrived; the last would enable me in some measure to make ends meet without its arrival; the whole three would elevate me on the 'Rock of Necessity,' from which I might snap my fingers in the face of all chances whatsoever.

I confess, my dear Sir, I have very little hope that it will be in your power to accomplish aught for me in this difficulty: yet when I have tried you, I am at the very end of my resources; at which point, as you know, it is much easier to rest in patience than at any nearer one.   So I trespass once more on your [good] [1] nature, still trusting, though feebly.   If you succeed in getting any of these books, and can leave them with C. Tait, Bookseller, Sign of Horace's Head, 63 Fleet Street, he will send them directly to his brother in Edinburgh, who is my Bookseller in this adventure.   The Fleet Street Tait will, of course, purchase, that is, pay the books, if purchasing or paying avail: but this I doubt much.

At all events I shall gain a letter from you, by this attempt I am making; and that will amply repay the trouble it costs me. I have not forgotten the still Temple, nor Alsatia, nor the kind Philosopher that dwells there.   When you see this book, I hope

---

[1] Torn by seal.

you will find that your advices have not been quite thrown away on me; and here and there a little trait will remind you of our dialogues over coffee and *Sally Lunns*. I have a note about Nicolai and *Philisters*, to which I would gladly have appended an acknowledgment to the proper quarter, had I been authorized.

Literary news, news of yourself, news of all kinds, are a scarcity with me here. For many months after leaving you I lay as if in the Castle of Indolence; stretched under whispering beeches reading German, smoking Orinocco, and one of the lordliest prospects in the world spread out at my feet; Skiddaw, Saddleback, Helvellyn, and all these everlasting hills for my background, the silver water of the Solway in front, my time slipped smoothly away, divided into two portions like Lafontaine's *l'une se passait à dormir, l'autre à ne rien faire*. I am grown a little healthier and much happier, but I am still as recluded as ever. If you can let me hear afar off the tumult of the Brick Universe, its sound will be welcome to me; for there is much in your Babylon that I like, and hope to revisit under kinder auspices. Believe me always,

My dear Sir,
Most faithfully yours,
THOMAS CARLYLE.

I have a long row of Spanish books now in my eye; for which my conscience many a time reproves me. I will send them when I go to Edinburgh; sooner if you require them.

What has become of Coleridge and his book of *Aids*? Where loiter the sweet singers of England, that no twang of a melodious string is heard throughout the Isle, nothing but the chink of yellow bullion? Alas! We are all Philistines together. But *veniet dies!*

Edinburgh, 21 Comel[e]y Bank, 14th May 1827.

(3) My dear Sir,—May I beg of you to accept this copy of my last Compilation in the furtherance of which you more than once showed yourself so ready to assist with *Rath und That*; a service which I would willingly convince you that I have not forgotten, however unable to do more than remember it. The Book has been out for some time, and your copy should have been sent sooner; but Late is better than Never; and I still hope you will accept the little gift in good part, and sometimes think of me with favour when you see it in your shelves.

I have got some Spanish books of yours, a *Don Quixote* and a

Quevedo, which I still keep in spite of the reproaches of my conscience, now really getting rather bored on the subject. The truth is the volumes are not by me at this moment, but in Dumfries-shire; and my only consolation is that they are safe, and that your need of them is not pressing. I am ashamed to say that I have yet read far too little of them, or indeed of any Spanish work, though some late German translations from that language (particularly one of Calderon) have not a little strengthened my wish to become immediately acquainted with it. One is so busy, so laboriously idle! It will be long before I write aught worth reading, and yet I must not let my pen grow altogether rusty, and so my reading is too much curtailed.

I have got wedded [1] since I wrote last: my wife also is a reader and a lover of German; and we have a pleasant cottage here with China roses and the like, and the towers of Edinburgh peering through the branches of our *tree*, at a safe distance. Would not the best way to get your books be to come hither in vacation time and seek them? I am sure it would be the surest; and we could form as pretty a *bureau d'intelligence* for the discussion of *aesthetic* matters here, as you would wish to see. There is a spare bed, too, and coffee worthy of King's Bench Walk itself. Oh, I would give a shilling to see one other Sally Lunn! But the Temple with its reverend alleys, and good inmates, is become a reminiscence; and London, huge, monstrous London itself, looks beautiful by distance. Surely I shall once more see it, and the chosen men that make it worth seeing.

A letter from you, full of news of all sorts, would be a treat to be remembered. Some sultry noon, when your streets approach the first degree of Wedgwood, and you cannot stir abroad, for being broiled, who knows but you may favour me? I really should receive it as a most kind service. At all events if I can assist you in aught here, or in *any* way manifest my sense of obligation to you, I shall *expect* to be applied to.

Believe me always, my dear Sir,
Most faithfully yours,
T. CARLYLE.

I have more than once meditated inquiring of you about that 'London University,' of yours. I learn from the Newspapers that the people have advertised for Professors; but never having seen the advertisement itself, the offers they have made, the persons to be applied to, in short, the whole aspect of this matter

[1] 17th October 1826.

is unknown to me. If you know, or can learn aught throwing light on it, I should be thankful to hear you; for certain of my friends are clear that I should make application for a post in that new Seminary; and, indeed to myself it seems that some Moral Philosophy or Rhetoric Professorship there would be no such unhandsome appointment. I can teach Mathematics also, and Physics (Physic, alas! I know practically) and touches of Metaphysics, the oddest mixture of Scotch and German, Dugald Stewart and Immanuel Kant! But the fittest place for me would be that of 'Jack of all Trades,' in case they wanted such a hand. Seriously I should like to know.

[Endorsed on letter by Crabb Robinson:]

14th May 1827 (received June). Carlyle with German book.

1864. The now famous Thomas Carlyle.

The book here mentioned and given to me was the first of his numerous works. Our acquaintance has long ceased.

APPENDIX II

EXCERPTS FROM LETTERS OF CRABB ROBINSON TO THE REV. JOHN
MILLER, BOCKLETON VICARAGE, TENBURY WELLS

[*By permission of Miss Emma Hutchinson*]

(1) JULY 4th 1850. [A leaflet about the meeting at Justice
Coleridge's which resolved to raise a subscription to do honour
to the memory of Wordsworth and determined the objects of
the subscription. It gives the names of the Committee and of the
Executive Sub-committee and a preliminary list of subscribers.
On the back is a letter to John Miller, written from Bury. Crabb
Robinson says he is on the sub-committee *not* by his own act.]
. . . I here content myself with saying that Dr. Chr. Wordsworth is now at Rydal, preparing under Mrs. Wordsworth's eye a
memoir of our departed friend, and that *The Recluse*, part one, is
to appear forthwith. . . . In the 5th volume of Southey's *Life*, there
is a brief notice of our old friend E[lton] H[amond] but without
anything to betray his name, and indeed very little to draw
attention to the fact.

(2) DEC. 1st 1850.

(3) OCT. 4th 1852. . . . There comes into play a sentiment
which dear Charles Lamb felt intensely and expressed as he did
every[thing] with an enriching humour. I carried him an invita-
tion to drive with a common friend. 'There will be only the
three Stansfelds.' 'How I *hate* those three Stansfelds.' 'Hate
them! Why, they are three Yorkshiremen. You have never seen *one*
of them.' 'That's the reason! I cannot hate any one I have ever
seen.' I used to say to Charles Lamb: 'I will adopt your pets,
but not your antipathies.' . . .

(4) NOV. 24th 1852.

(5) JAN. 14th 1853. . . . The better half of this letter . . . consists
of a copy and remarks on the most marvellous poem [*The Bridge of
Sighs* by T. Hood] I have met with of late years. . . .
. . . Of all the men of genius I ever knew, Charles Lamb was
the one I most intensely loved.—My love proves nothing, but he
was loved with equal warmth coupled with like admiration by

Thomas Clarkson and his wife, my dear friend; by Southey, Coleridge, Wordsworth, etc. . . .

(6) [Undated but placed here by contents.]

(7) APRIL 1st 1853. . . . In your estimate of the *Bridge of Sighs*— a disappointing title by the bye, and therefore to be regretted—I fully concur, even in censures which I would not have brought forward, but being uttered by you, or indeed any one, could not remove or contradict. Tho' as I am afraid, I have already said oftener than necessary, that I am infinitely more obliged to the critic who points out to me a beauty I might not have detected, than to him who makes me aware of a blemish I might have overlooked. Yet do not suppose me so *excessively* unwilling to see faults that I do not willingly receive and confess to be just, all the faults you find in Hood's marvellous poem. Far from it. I go further and think you have omitted just matter of reproach. . . . I agree with you that the *liberties* taken with the grammatical construction are excessive. The four lines commencing with 'Still for all slips of hers' want what is worse, I fear, than a grammatical construction—a logical connection. Why the lips are to be wiped 'for all slips' I do not see, and I have occasionally omitted those lines when reading. You have justly shown the *abuse* of the triple rhyme, and demanded for Wordsworth the preference to which he is entitled. . . .

. . . . Wordsworth himself in terms said that he thought he had more cause of complaint against the *Quarterly* than the *Edinburgh*. We can more easily forgive the open, rather ostentatious enemy, than the would-be-thought friend. . . .

(8) OCT. 10th–17th 1853. . . . A very amiable woman,[1] a *Calvinistic Dissenter*, who admiring the author nevertheless would not let her boys read it [*Mrs. Leicester's School*] till she had torn out *The Young Mahometan* and *The Witch Aunt*. When I told Lamb of this, he said: 'I am delighted to hear it; I wrote them both.' . . .

. . . As to Valentine Le Grice, I know a great deal more about him than I could bring within the compass of a letter. He is a remarkable man and so was his father before him. A native of my native town. . . . Val Le Grice is a strange man, one of those very clever unmanageable beings characterised in a couplet:

And some there are blessed with huge stores of wit
Who want as much again to manage it.[2]

[1] Mrs. Pattisson.
[2] For whan a man hath over greet a wit,
Full oft hym happeth to mysusen it.
Chaucer, *Canon Yeoman's Prologue*, ll. 648-9.

I have heard Lamb tell odd stories about Le Grice, of whom the best to be said is that he overflowed with kindness to his fellow creatures, and was warm-hearted. He and Lamb loved each other, but Lamb confessed that he saw him ever with apprehension. And well he might.—They used to go to debating societies together—the same which I frequented years afterwards, and there made some of my most valuable friendships. They attended when the question was: *Who is the greatest orator, etc.?* Le Grice rose: 'I was once in company, Mr. Chairman, when a lady was asked which she liked best, veal, mutton, or beef. She answered: Pork. So, sir, your question asks: *Who is the greatest orator, Burke, Pitt, or Fox?* I answer *Sheridan.*' Another time on rising he said: 'Mr. Chairman, the last time I entered this room, I had the honour to be kicked out of it.' 'I was present,' said Lamb, 'and certainly he deserved it.' . . .

[PS.] . . . Mrs. Wordsworth is here at Henry Taylor's. She does not know you personally, but as the friend of her nephew, desires to be kindly remembered. We shall be going soon, that is in November, to see Mrs. Clarkson, the widow of the Slave-trade abolisher.

Mrs. Wordsworth is in good health apparently and is making a visit to a dear friend, Miss Fenwick—two pious women who consider this is a solemn leave-taking. She will, in my oldest friend Mrs. Clarkson, see one of her most esteemed friends. She will not go to see the statue [of the poet] in the artist's studio. . . .

(9) Nov. 22nd 1856. . . . What I love myself I am most anxious that all those I esteem should love also, considering love and enjoyment as the same. This led me to be a sort of martyr (I incurred the martyrdom of ridicule) in the cause of Wordsworth, but I have been amply rewarded by witnessing in old age the triumph of his poetical school. . . .

(10) SEPT. 3rd 1857.   Bury St. Edmunds.
My dear Sir,—It will give you pleasure, I have no doubt, to read that on a recent visit to Rydal I found dear Mrs. Wordsworth all I could wish and more than I could hope. It would seem burlesque to refer in speaking of a blind old woman of 88 to such an image as the *phantom of delight*, yet the weightier couplet:

> A perfect woman, nobly planned
> To warn, to comfort, and command,

may still be brought to one's mind.

In her extreme old age she has attained an age not contemplated in those three stanzas to which I have referred, and

exhibits a phase of existence worthy to be the sequel of those.—
I spent nearly a week with her. During my stay I had frequent
walks with her on the well-known terrace and read to her from
her husband's poems—the reading in which she most delights.

During this stay, I never heard a syllable of regret pass her
lips. She is the *beau ideal* of resignation. I probably related to
you an anecdote. It is said that at the very last moment of *his*
life, she was heard to whisper in his ear, 'You are going to Dora.'
We may be sure therefore that in her calm submission she never
forgets that she is going to William. The faithful James is still
at Rydal and will not leave his mistress. She had her choice
between her carriage and him and she retains him. She enjoys
the perfect health of an octogenarian.

Not far from Rydal resides Mrs. Hutchinson and her daughters.
They all speak of you with gratitude and affection as the friend and
patron of their son and brother, the clergyman, and are expecting
from his Northern Mission the other brother.

The chief changes I remark in this district are made by death.
Those who depart have successors, but in the nature of things
these must be for the present at least, *inferiors*, whatever they
may become hereafter. The most remarkable of the residents is
Mrs. Fletcher. . . . Mrs. Fletcher, older than Mrs. Wordsworth,
has been eulogised by Lord Brougham with his characteristic
force, and after years of comparative poverty and threatened with
want, she became the leader of Edinburgh literary society, but in
the time of Jeffrey's triumph was the almost single avowed admirer of the *Lyrical Ballads*. She exhibits the remains of great
personal beauty, resembling Mrs. Barbauld, in whose house I
saw her sixty years since.

There, too, is the widow of Dr. Arnold. She scarcely belongs
to the same *age*—yet she has a son known as the author of a
military novel of which the scene is in India. He is the head of
the Educational Establishment in the Punjab, and Mrs. Arnold
read to me a letter written early in the spring, before any outward
symptom was exhibited of the catastrophe that has since burst out,
in which, however, his apprehensions are clearly announced, and
now assume the character of prophecy. Subsequent letters from
him show that he is aware of the full extent of the peril, tho' it
has not yet reached the district in which he lives. . . .

(11) JAN. 12th 1858. . . . You are aware probably that the
placing of the Wordsworth monument has given great disgust
to a large proportion of the most zealous promoters of the

III—B

subscription. . . . The Queen gave £50 on condition that the monument to William Wordsworth should be placed in the Abbey. Nevertheless the Dean and Chapter extracted the full fee, as if the party represented had been a calico printer or Indian nabob. The precise sum I cannot now remember, but it was several hundred pounds—while the fee was remitted to those who placed Campbell's monument, I suppose in recognition of his higher merit! This is not all, but I have said more than enough.

I should like to know your opinion of the *new edition*. Your friend Mr. Johnston has had the advantage of connecting his own name honourably with that of the poet as Editor. . . .

(12) JUNE 4th [1858].

APPENDIX III

LETTERS OF CRABB ROBINSON TO SAMUEL NAYLOR, JUNIOR

The following seventeen letters from Crabb Robinson to
Samuel Naylor, junior, are in the possession of S. Naylor's grand-
daughter, Mrs. Clifford Bax, who has allowed me to see and
make extracts from them:

Jan. 1st 1851	March 8th 1854
April 19th 1851	Dec. 11th 1854
Oct. 30th 1851	June 29th [1855]
Jan. 27th 1852	Sept. 14th [1855]
Aug. 5th [1852]	Nov. 21st 1855
Sept. 8th 1852	March 26th 1859
Nov. 16th [1852]	Dec. 28th 1859
Dec. 25th 1852	June 23rd 1869
Oct. 14th [1853]	

The years of the undated letters are proved by internal evidence.

(1) JAN. 1st 1851. . . . I need no motive beyond the mere love of
excitement. Therefore I never suffer ennui. I shall be glad to
hear that you can find as I can in mere reading a sufficient zest.
To me the periodicals would supply almost enough of excitement.
. . . Let me direct your attention to *Fraser's Magazine* . . . and in
the year 1849 you will find some very clever papers entitled
Yeast, a sort of novel—very like in character and perhaps better
in execution than *Alton Locke*. The author is Kingsley, who
fluctuates between sentimental religion and free-thinking. On
leaving your house I fell in with the younger J. W. Parker, of
West Strand, the publisher of *Fraser*—a clever young man. He,
like Kingsley, etc., being trained in the Church school has broke
bounds without being expelled the school. He belongs to an
anomalous set, of which Julius Hare, Frederick Maurice, etc., are
individuals. . . .

(2) SEPT. 8th 1852. . . . Here [Rydal] I came on Monday—
intending to lie by as much as possible during the week I meant to
spend here. But yesterday I could not help walking about eight

miles *not* to see the fine lake of Grasmere or the sweet Rydal Water
—here the scenery has always been subordinate to social feelings.
And the loss of the great poet, to which has been added that of his
son-in-law, Quillinan, renders this place in a great degree a place
for mournful recollections.   And here I have three most interesting persons all sharing my feelings concerning the departed, with
whom I spend my time: Mrs. Wordsworth, Mrs. Arnold, Mrs.
Fletcher, each in her own way most admirable.   Mrs. Fletcher, in
her eighty-third year, has the most vigorous nature of them
all. . . .

I envy you the pursuit of fine art.   It is that portion of it
especially which you cultivate, which I am least incapable of
relishing as it deserves—the art which in its highest form of
excellence gives

> To one brief moment caught from fleeting time
> The appropriate calm of blest Eternity.

Ruskin thanked me for communicating this sonnet to him.   I
have conceived a very high opinion of this man, and am quite
disturbed by his avowed disesteem of the greatest of landscape
painters, if this be a correct announcement of his highest function
—Claude Lorraine. . . .

(3) DEC. 25th 1852. . . . Mr. Rogers is now at Brighton.   He is
in his ninety-first year, and though a marvellous man in his way,
yet no one now asks anything of him, beyond the repetition of an
oft-repeated anecdote or joke.   In several instances, and some more
than a year ago, he undertook to do something which might be
fairly expected of him, and from the not doing of which a loss was
sustained in a cause in which he took an interest.   But he forgot
what he was to do, though the person to whom he was to speak
was often at his elbow! . . .

(4) DEC. 11th 1854. . . . Of literature I have nothing to say
within a writable or even readable compass.   And yet there is
much that is curious abroad.   The most remarkable books now
coming out are the collection of De Quincey's writings.   Even
his diseased malice cannot altogether take away the charm of his
writings. . . .

APPENDIX IV

[By permission of Mr. R. W. Gibson, Antiquarian Bookseller, Oxford]

Nov. 26th 1856. . . . I found on my table 5 vols. to be read—all new.—Yours [1] excites the most interest both on account of the author and the subject. I expect great pleasure from half of yours. The portion assigned to a reprint I pass over.—The Preface I must not speak of unread, but as I presume it is controversial and in self-vindication, I wish it unwritten, for even the successful defence implies the having suffered injustice. . . .

---

[1] *Seven Lectures on Shakespeare and Milton by the late S. T. Coleridge. A List of All the MS. Emendations in Mr. Collier's Folio, 1632; and an Introductory Preface.* 1856.

APPENDIX V

A LIST OF LETTERS FROM CRABB ROBINSON TO THE
PATTISSONS WITH EXCERPTS

[By permission of Mr. Martin Hardie]

Pattisson Correspondence

Volume 1, 1629–1805

(1) To Mrs. Jacob Pattisson, senior. Colchester, 6th April 1795.
H. C. Robinson has sent Mrs. Pattisson [1] a round Dozen of Novels
besides a Catalogue which Mrs. Pattisson will either purchase or
return when she sends a Parcel as she thinks proper. Out of the
List which Mrs. P. sent (which H. C. R. always carries in his
Hand and selects from it as many Books as he can find) H. C. R.
could only catch

> *The Emigrants.* 3 vols.[1]
> *Family Party.* 3 vols.[2]

In order to complete a Parcel he has sent

> *Theagenes and Chariclea.* 2 vols.[3]

which, in the Law Phrase, he Warrants Excellent, and recommends
to Mrs. P.'s particular Attention.—And

> Mrs. Inchbald's *Simple Story.* 4 vols.

which was considered as a Work superior to Common Novels by
the Reviewers. H. C. R. would have selected some Novels he
read about 7 years ago, but he was fearful that he might pitch
upon those Mrs. P. had read. He recollects *The Fool of Quality* [4]
was then esteemed an eccentric Work. And *Arundel* [5] was lately
recommended to him by a Young Woman of very distinguished
Talents, Amelia Alderson [Opie] as a work of first-rate Merit.

---

[1] *The Emigrants, A Gallic Tale.* 1794.
[2] 1791. Both these novels are mentioned in the *New Annual Register*.
[3] By Heliodorus. *An Æthiopian History*, translated by T. Underdowne. 1587. A fresh translation, anonymous, appeared in 1791.
[4] By Henry Brooke. 1766.
[5] By Richard Cumberland. 1789.

There are several Modern Novels which are now all the 'rage'—

Madeline.[1]
The Weird Sisters.[2]
The Cyprists.[3]

which perhaps Mrs. P. might desire to see, but H. C. R. cannot recommend them himself as he has not during some Months read any Work of the kind. H. C. R. takes the Liberty of reminding Mrs. P. that Johnson's *Rasselas* and the Continuation of it called *Dinarbas* [4] rank highly in this Species of Composition. . . .

(2) To William Pattisson.   Colchester, 4th May 1795.
. . . I suppose you have not yet seen *The British Critic* of the last Month which has reviewed the first Vol. of the *Cabinet*. [Here follows a summary of the criticisms which 'were in direct opposition to ours' as regards the essays, one by Charles Marsh. Crabb Robinson proceeds to give his own opinion on the various poems in the *Cabinet*, some of which he thinks 'would not disgrace Della Crusca.']

(3) To W. P.   25th April 1795.
[Consists in the main of an essay on *The Profession of a Barrister*, Section I: *Morality as a Principle of Action*. In a marginal commentary Crabb Robinson writes:] I claim no Originality of Idea. The greatest part of the reasoning is derived from Godwin and is an abridgement of his Morality; tho' I admit that my Ideas were received from him, I ought to observe that nothing has been taken from him *verbatim*. And tho' I had made an Analysis of the 1st vol. I did not refer to it when I wrote this Letter. There is also one point in which I differ totally from Godwin and he would be very severe upon the first part of my Letter. Godwin established the Origin of Moral Duty upon a Principle of Disinterestedness natural to Man (which by the bye appears to me consummate Nonsense.) He does not call to his Assistance a future State and is very severe upon the Self Love system.

(4) To W. P.   9th May 1795.
[2nd section of same essay: *On the Study of the Law*.]

(5) To W. P.   Bury, 24th August 1795.
[3rd section of same essay: *On the Practice of the Bar*.]

[1] By Isabella Kelley. 3 vols. 1794.
[2] 3 vols. 1794. *New Annual Register*.
[3] 2 vols. 1795. *New Annual Register*.
[4] *Dinarbas, a Tale, being a continuation of Rasselas*, by Ellis Cornelia Knight. 1790.

Volume 2, 1795–6

(6) To Mrs. J. Pattisson.   Colchester, 8 March 1795.

(7) To W. P.   Colchester, 26 May 1795.

. . . I will like a Knight Errant of the Days of Chivalry maintain that the fair beautiful and peerless System of Godwin is superior to all other systems. And I will defend with my Sword and Buckler its incomparable Worth. . . .

(8) To W. P.   Bury, 17th November 1795.

Dear Pattisson,

Without scruple I confess that I wrote *Philo-Godwin*. I thought you would have discovered me before, for I had written it when you were in Bury, but as it had not then appeared in the *Cambridge Intelligencer* I kept it a secret. . . . I bar your excepting to a very obscure Passage where I had compared Paine with Godwin and where the Printers by omitting a Line converted a decent Parallel into Nonsense. . . .

Volume 3, 1797–1800

(9) To W. P.   Savile Row, 29th September 1797.

. On Friday I began *Ossian*. I am indeed charmed [?] extremely beyond Expectation and considerably beyond Measure with his poems. At present *Carthor* is my favourite. . . .

(10) To W. P.   Bury, 3rd May 1798.

(11) To W. P.   Bury, 31st May 1798.

(12) To Thomas Amyot.   Bury, 3rd July 1798.

(13) To W. P.   Bury, 31st July 1798.

(14) To W. P. and to Mrs. Newton. Yarmouth, 8th Sept. 1798.

(15) To W. P.   London, 31st October 1798.

(16) To W. P.   London, 22 November 1798.

[Defence of Burke's consistency.]

(17) To W. P.   London, 19th February 1799.

. . . Of modern Literature I have nothing interesting to say but that Mackintosh has published an Introduction to a course of Lectures on the Law of Nature and Nations. It is one of the most exquisite Morsels both in Sense and Style that I have ever seen. . . .

(18) To W. P.   London, 27 June 1799.

(19) To W. P.   Devizes, 9th December 1799.

(20) To Mrs. W. P.   Devizes, 16 March 1800.

Volume 4.   1797–1831

(21) To W. P.   Bury, 26th March 1798.

(22) To W. P.   Bury, 22nd April 1798.

. . . I am labouring through *Zoonomia*,[1] which is too unlike the Books I have been used to read to be easy or pleasant, particularly the more medical chapters.   I have re-perused *The Mysteries of Udolpho* with Delight. . . .

(23) To W. P.   Bury, 18th May 1798.

(24) To W. P.   Bury, 14th February 1800.

(25) To W. P.   Grimma, 20th December 1801.

(26) To W. P.   Frankfurt, 6th July 1802.

(27) To W. P. and Mrs. W. P.   Jena, 25th October 1802.

(28) To W. P. and Mrs. W. P.

Hatton Garden, 31st January 1813.

. . . I have no doubt you have good nature enough to be pleased with the success of Coleridge's Tragedy.[2]   It is by no means probable that it will attain so advanced an old age as till your visit, but if it do, I shall use all my entreaties with you and William to go and see it. . . .

(29) To W. P. and Mrs. W. P.   13th December 1816.

(30) To W. P.   Bury, 13th April 1817.

(31) To W. P. and Mrs. W. P.   Rome, 27th December 1830.

Volume 5.   1802–4

(32) To W. P.   Jena, 7th May 1803.

(33) To Mrs. W. P.   London, 3rd December 1806.

Volume 6.   1805–6

(34) To W. P.   Bagshot, 22nd December 1805.

. . . Miss Hays lives in retirement, an highly respected character.   She pursues literature as a profession; she does not estimate her productions above their value; she is content to be a useful writer and does not lose feminine excellence and virtues while she seeks literary fame. . . . I dined . . . with Mrs. Barbauld and to my admiration of her as a writer there is now associated a great personal regard for her.   She is altogether without

---

[1] By Erasmus Darwin.   [2] *Remorse.*

pretension and at the same time without the affectation of modesty which I should censure more. She speaks with decision and discrimination. . . . Dr. Aikin is a man of sharp understanding, but still, compared with his sister, he is in company what his Writings are compared with hers. . . .

(35) To Mrs. W. P.   Bury, 12th February 1806.
                                              [Misdated 1867.]

(36) To W. P. and Mrs. W. P.   London, 4th April 1806.
    . . . I have been twice at Mrs. Barbauld's . . . and have every encouragement from her and Mr. B. to renew my visits. They both interest me exceedingly. I have seen her shew off. She reasons acutely tho' that is not her great excellence. The *suaviter in modo* is most peculiarly hers. She has the *fortiter in re* but in common with other superior persons of our Age. There is something repulsive in Dr. Aikin. . . . Lucy Aikin is the only member of the family I do not like. Every other person in it is on the whole amiable and interesting, for the something I have objected to in the Doctor, does not outweigh the conviction of his sense and integrity which every one will be persuaded of who sees the Doctor. . . .

(37) To W. P. and Mrs. W. P.   London, 5th August 1805.

(38) To W. P.   [torn edge] November 1806.

Volume 7.   1807-9

(39) To W. P.   Altona, 24th March 1807.

(40) To W. P.   London, 21st November 1807.
    . . . I have looked into W. Hazlitt's answer to Malthus. It is rich in good things without being itself a good thing. It is acute, but pert; argumentative, but the argument is directed more against unessential parts of the book he writes against than against the system itself. It has not changed my opinion in the least as to the great question, tho' it has given great force and clearness to a number of correcting and qualifying remarks which had before occurred to me. There are many very light and censurable things in it, yet it is an amusing book. The concluding 2 pages is a piece of masterly eloquence.

    I can at the same time recommend, however, another book of Hazlitt's from which you will all . . . receive great pleasure. It is his Abridgement of Tucker's *Light of Nature*, 1 vol. 8vo.[1] The preface has some of the best remarks I have ever seen on Kant's

---

[1] *The Light of Nature Pursued,* by Abraham Tucker.

philosophy.   Tucker's book itself is very curious indeed.   I have read the *Vision*, which in spite of its oddities, is highly interesting. . . .

(41) To H. Pattisson.   London, 24th November 1817.
   [Incomplete]

(42) To W. P.   London, 1st January 1808.

(43) To W. P.   London, 5th January 1808.

(44) To W. and H. P.   London, 14th April 1808.

. . . If you want books I can with confidence recommend *Plymley's Letters*.[1]   They will delight you, for they are on the right side and are written with great talent and humour.   Since the barbarous Gothamite taste you betray in matters of poetry, I despair [sic] must deprive you of all interest in the persons of my favourite Poet[s], I shall only say in general that I have made the acquaintance of Wordsworth.   He is an highly interesting man and has confirmed me in all my previous notions of the close connection of high moral excellence and the poetic character.   I had long conversations with him on the subject of poetry and I wish I could be with you for a week were it only to deliver a few lectures to you on a subject which would interest me.   I have also seen Southey and have been asked by Coleridge to go and see him.   You see I am in with all of them. . . .

(45) To H. P.   London, 21st May 1808.

(46) To W. and H. P.   Corunna, 31st August 1808.

(47) To H. P.   London, 5th April 1809.

. . . You may if you please think Locke a great metaphysician and Pope a great Poet, you may laugh in your ignorance at Kant and refuse to understand and feel that Wordsworth has deep moral feeling and high poetic conceptions of man . . . and for all these heresies against good taste and sound philosophy I shall never be a whit displeased. . . . I am delighted that you are so much pleased with Miss Lamb's book.   I shall give her your letter because it will give her pleasure.   She is a very worthy woman indeed—a prime favourite with me as you know. . . .

(48) To W. P.   London, 8th May 1809.

. . . Capel Lofft . . . tried late in the evening to gain a hearing in order to propose the memory of Charles James Fox, but he could not get a hearing.   He was pathetic and implored attention, but all in vain. . . . I breakfasted with him yesterday at Richard

[1] By Sydney Smith.

Taylor's and have seen a great deal of him to-day also. I have had great pleasure in his company notwithstanding all his oddities. . . .

(49) To W. and H. P.   London, 19th November 1809.

. . . I am at this moment rather in a hippish mood, having just finished, 1 a.m., *Ennui*.[1] You have read this useful and moral Tale and can tell what chords within me it strikes rather harshly. . . .

Volume 8.   1810–11

(50) To H. P.   Bury, 2nd January 1810.

. . . Coleridge's last *Friend* contains 4 Sonnets [2] by Wordsworth, so noble that I am sure you would be converted to high admiration of him.   Such real purity of moral sentiment, such heroic dignity of public feeling I never saw before clothed in poetic form so beautiful and exquisite. . . .

(51) To H. P.   London, 5th April 1810.

(52) To Mrs. Pattisson, senior.   London, 24th April 1810.

(53) To Mrs. W. P.   London, 5th June 1810.

(54) To W. P. and Mrs. W. P.   Bagshot, 25th July 1810.

(55) To Mrs. W. P.   London, 9th November 1810.

. . . In reference to my own work, I have to ask has William *The Diversions of Purley*?[3]   If so, I can spare my trunk weight and room. . . .

(56) To W. P. and Mrs. W. P. London, 26th December 1810.

. . . There is generally a reciprocity of feeling.   Love, esteem, friendship are mutual in most cases because they belong to the heart, while the opinion the judgment forms is self-subsistent. It does not follow that because I look upon any man, Coleridge for instance, as a genius that he must therefore think me a philosopher, tho' he will probably, if he is acquainted with my opinion, deem me a man of good sense and correct taste.   Poor Coleridge! the name awakens a number of interesting reflections.   How insufficient is mere genius for moral purposes, and what weakness and obliquity may not the finest and purest intellect permit the indulgence of, where the sedative of moral habits and severe

[1] By Maria Edgeworth.
[2] 'The land we from our fathers had in trust,'   'And is it among rude untutored dales,'   'O'er the wide earth, on mountain and on plain,' 'It was a *moral* end for which they fought.'
[3] By Horne Tooke.

principle are wanting!   Coleridge dined with us on Sunday.   He
was the delight of a large party from half-past three till 12 o'clock.
He discoursed of politics, metaphysics, and Shakespeare with
equal brilliancy, yet I fear he will with all his infinite powers
leave behind him no permanent record of a salutary exercise of his
talents, unless he is to be considered, as perhaps the Greek philosophers were, a public instructor, a desultory educator of adults.
And in this way he may, and I have no doubt does, scatter the
seeds of wisdom wherever he appears.—But I know not how I
have been led to digress on Coleridge. . . .

(57) To W. P. and Mrs. W. P.   London, 15th January 1811.

(58) To Mrs. W. P.   London, 16th April 1811.
   . . . I called yesterday on Mrs. Charles Aikin.   She has
promised to lend me *Thalaba* which she prefers to *Kehama*. . . .
   . . . I saw Godwin last night . . . Godwin by the bye, without
being attached to any sect of Christians, as you may suppose,
considers Sandeman as one of the most consistent of the leaders
of parties. . . .

(59) To Jacob Pattisson.   London, 16th April 1811.

(60) To W. P. and Mrs. W. P.   London, 9th May 1811.

(61) To Mrs. W. P.   London, 23rd July 1811.
   . . . I will call at half-past ten in Newgate Street and I will
thank you to give me or leave me *Thalaba* there.   Of course I
should be disappointed not to finish the poem on your return, but
the volume need not lie unused during your absence. . . .

(62) To Mrs. W. P.   London, 27th August 1811.

(63) To W. P.   Bury, 23rd September 1811.

(64) To Mrs. W. P.   London, 18th December 1811.

(65) To Mrs. W. P.   Bury, 27th December 1811.

(66) To W. P.   Bury, [?] December 1811.

Volume 9.   1812-14

(67) To Mrs. W. P.   London, [?] February 1812.

(68) To Mrs. W. P.   London, 24th March 1812.
   . . . I have been with Mrs. Barbauld but twice within six
months. . . . My evenings have been frequently spent in hearing
lectures by Coleridge, Hazlitt, and Flaxman. . . .

(69) To Mrs. W. P.   London, 16th September 1812.
   . . . I think of Miss Baillie's plays as you do, and Ellis's

Specimens [1] are better qualified to instruct than give immediate pleasure. . . .

(70) To W. P. and Mrs. W. P.   London, 26th October 1812.

(71) To Mrs. W. P.   London, 21st January 1813.

. . . It will be a sad result of my late adoption of a profession . . . should I be forced to forgo that kind of literary pleasure in which you have so frequently sympathised with me. *A propos* of this better kind of the pleasures of taste, I will copy, without apology, a sonnet I lately met with in the *Courier*. I pity those who will not feel and appreciate it. [Here follows Wordsworth's sonnet: 'Now that all hearts are glad, all faces bright.']

(72) To Mrs. W. P.   London, 30th March 1813.

. . . I told Mrs. T[hornthwaite] when I wrote last, to recommend for your book-club Disraeli on the *Calamities of Authors*. It has very much amused me. . . . You will not suspect any *insidious* design on my part in praising it. I have never read a book which exhibits in a more impressive manner the 'follies of the wise.' It is a truly *moral* work and may be commended as a specific to all young people who are in danger of being seduced by the vain and meretricious attractions of literary glory. . . .

(73) To Mrs. W. P.   London, 7th April 1813.

(74) To Mrs. W. P.   London, 5th May 1813.

(75) To Mrs. W. P.   Bury, [?] July 1813.

. . . I ought to have acknowledged the kind loan of Burns before. . . .

(76) To W. P. and Mrs. W. P.   Bury, 13th October 1813.

(77) To Mrs. W. P.   London,[2] [no date, P.M. 1813.]

. . . I shall be glad indeed to introduce you to Mrs. Barbauld. . . . You may tell me all you think and feel and all you love and hate in Madame de Staël without any fear of wounding any tender part about me. My admiration of her is great but very far indeed from being unqualified. . . . But nothing in her or her works fixes my love and admiration as the works of the Northern Poet continue to do. . . .

(78) To W. P.   Jena, 7th February 1804.

. . . I have discovered with great pleasure that our favourite Dr. Aikin and Mrs. Barbauld are worthy pupils of the Horatian School. Dr. Aikin indeed has not the delicate taste or sportive

[1] George Ellis. *Specimens of Early English Metrical Romances*. 1805.
[2] From internal evidence.

fancy of his Master. But Mrs. Barbauld has added a new charm
to the genuine Horatian grace of her mind and pencil by the gentle
corrections and qualifications arising from the purer and juster
morals of Christianity. By adding to the sober wisdom and
chaste pleasantry of the Roman (of course I do not refer to the 8th
and 12th Epodes [*sic*], etc.) the hopes and humane sentiments of
Christianity, she has, if I may use the phrase, sanctified Horace.
. . .

(79) To W. P. and Mrs. W. P. London, 15th February 1814.

Volume 10. 1814–16

(80) To Mrs. W. P.   Bury, 27th July 1814.

(81) To W. P.   Paris, 25th September 1814.
      . . . I visit Helen Maria Williams. . . .

(82) To W. P.   London, 8th December 1814.

(83) To W. P. and Mrs. W. P.   London, 6th February 1815.
      . . . My last Witham visit was in no respect uncomfortable and
the want of an entire sympathy in regard to the Poet and the Poem [1]
only served to stimulate to a salutary exercise of reasoning and—
forbearance. . . . To-day I received a letter from your friend Mr.
Fox [2] of Chichester. He had indirectly applied to me for information about German books. I wrote to offer him the use of mine
and I mentioned my late reading of the Poem to Hannah. In
return he speaks of Wordsworth in terms of praise so discrimi-
nating that a friend of W.'s has taken the letter away to copy a
part of it. I am satisfied with the progress the work is making.
Half of the impression is already sold. You will be interested
perhaps to hear that Montgomery is author of the *Eclectic* article.
This Josiah Conder informed me, who is now the Editor of the
review. I am glad that Montgomery did write that review. It
is pleasing to observe free and even exuberant eulogy from a
rival, who might be sooner than another tempted to 'damn with
faint praise.' Hannah [Mrs. W. H. Pattisson] will further be
amused by hearing that I have heard of Hogg, the author of the
Queen's Wake. He has been visiting Wordsworth, who entertains
great respect for his talents. Hogg is, like Burns, a genuine
peasant. But he is prudent. With all his simplicity of character and habits, still a Scotchman in the main. He thinks

---

[1] *The Excursion.*
[2] William Johnson Fox. The letter is No. 121 of the 1809–17 volume
of Crabb Robinson's correspondence.

Jeffrey the greatest living writer, and the late *Edinburgh* review of his work appears to have been an exchange of eulogy. Further I have to inform you that I have seen a proof sheet of Wordsworth's new edition of his Poems. It will be a very *beautiful* work as to its outward form and substance. He has condescended to *adorn* many of his poems, but has sturdily refused to *exclude* any one.

I hear from everyone so high a character of Southey's *Don Roderick*,[1] that I think you may venture to buy it for your bookclub: on the other hand, *The Lord of the Isles* is less talked of than I expected. The fact undoubtedly is that Lord Byron has put Scott's nose out of joint—and no wonder, for what is popularity but a system of favouritism? Possibly Scott's concealment of himself, if he be really the author of *Waverley*, is a prudent policy. Wordsworth, I hear, is a great admirer of *Waverley*, and he ascribes it also to Scott. . . .

My love to [the boys] when you write. I have been buying for them Miss Edgeworth's *Moral* and *Popular Tales*. . . . Perhaps with your usual precaution you may like to read them first. I would recommend *Forester* and *L'Amie Inconnue* as very excellent; but I think the moral of both somewhat equivocal. However, it is not the sort of doubtful morality you will censure. . . .

(84) To Mrs. Pattisson, senior.   [No date or address] 1815.

(85) To W. P. and Mrs. W. P.   London, 16th April 1815.

. . . I have, since I began this letter, been looking into the new edition of Wordsworth's Poems. There are two new Prefaces and a great number of new pieces. Wordsworth has done me the *honour*, and I truly feel it as such, to send me a copy of the work, in which I shall take a heightened and extended delight. But I have been so busy for these few days that I hardly know what the fresh treat amounts to. I have read some half dozen admirable sonnets on politics. . . .

(86) To W. P. and Mrs. W. P.   Amsterdam and The Hague, 20th August 1815.

(87) To W. P. and Mrs. W. P.   Bagshot, 4th October 1815.

(88) To W. P. and Mrs. W. P.   London, 8th April 1816.

(89) To Mrs. W. P.   Keswick, 17th September 1816.

[Consists of a detailed account, taken almost verbatim from his journal, of his visit with Torlonia and Walter to Rydal, and to

---

[1] *Roderick, the last of the Gothes*, by Southey, was published in 1814; Scott's *Vision of Don Roderick* had appeared in 1811.

Southey at Keswick, and of his own return to Rydal and journey with Wordsworth to Cockermouth, Calder Abbey, Ravenglass, and Eskdale.]

Volume 11.   1817–18

(90) To W. P. and Mrs. W. P.   London, 20th February 1817.

(91) To Mrs. W. P.   London, 8th May 1817.

. . . I take for granted you know that Talfourd is now a licensed special pleader. . . . Perhaps he is a little anxious about his success. I wish it were in my power to assist him. . . . I believe T. to be a very competent pleader. . . . It is much easier to recommend and bring forward a pleader than a barrister. . . .

(92) To W. P.   [? London], 20th June 1817.

(93) To Mrs. W. P.   London, 4th July 1817.

(94) To W. P.   London, 5th July 1817.

(95) To Mrs. W. P.   Bury, 27th March 1818.

(96) To Mrs. W. P.   Frankfurt, 15th September 1818.

(97) To Mrs. W. P.   Bury, 25th October 1818.

Volume 12.   1819–20

(98) To Mrs. W. P.   London, 1st February 1819.

. . . During my stay at Bury and on the Sessions journey I read a novel which pleased me very much indeed. If you have not read it I could recommend it to you confidently—*Pride and Prejudice*.[1] The merit lies in the perfect truth of the painting. The dialogue is exquisitely in character and the characters, tho' not ideal, are charming. The women especially are drawn after the life and Mrs. Bennet is a very jewel—equal to any of Ostade or Gerard Dou's portraits, and these you know are not prized for the beauty of the originals. Mr. Collins too, the sneaking and servile parson, is quite a masterpiece. The heroines (for there are a brace of them) are as natural as beauties can be and as beautiful as any successful portrait can be. . . . Since my return I have been reading, however, a still better book that you have probably already read—*The Heart of Midlothian*.[2] If not, read it directly. You were offended and with reason by the former *Tales of my Landlord*, for the tendency was not good certainly, tho' I think the author held up with perfect truth and impartiality at the same time the heroic virtue which religious feelings

[1] Published 1812.   [2] Published 1818.

III—C

produce, to our admiration, and the horrid crime to which religious fanaticism leads. But in this book he has made the *amende honorable* to the Scotch pietists or Cameronians. *Old douce David* may be put in comparison with the Reverend Mr. Primrose as a sort of Christian hero, and his exalted virtues are only thrown into relief by the human alloy. His narrow-mindedness and intolerance are rendered amusing only and excite no resentment in a character so scrupulously conscientious and upright. And I should have the lowest opinion of the understanding of a Unitarian who did not enjoy the fine characteristic speech in which *Socinian vermin* are spoken of with a contempt and horror quite boundless. Jeanie Deans too, the perfect heroine, loses none of our admiration because she, in the simplicity of her heart, doubts whether she can without sin enter a church where is an organ, or hear the word of God spoken by a man with a surplice on, and considers it as an 'awfu' thing' that there are so many prelatists in the city with the 'muckle kirk.' Swift said with truth, and I fear he was himself an instance, 'men have religion enough to hate and not enough to love each other,' and I think it one of the most laudable and useful of literary tasks to exhibit that excellence we all love and admire in combination with infirmities which we ought to learn to tolerate. This is not the only quality which renders this new *Tale of my Landlord* eminently moral. The conclusion of Effie Deans's history is very instructive. . . .

(99) To W. P.   London, 3rd March 1819.

(100) To W. P.   Bury, 26th April 1819.

(101) To W. P., junior.   [?] 1819.

(102) To W. P. and Mrs. W. P.   London, 31st October 1820.
    [Itinerary of tour with Wordsworth, etc.]
    . . . Such an excursion in fine weather and excellent company could not but be delightful, and I rejoice on reflection as I did while I was anticipating and actually partaking of the pleasures offered me. . . .

Volume 13.   1821–2

(103) To W. P.   London, 8th May 1822.

(104) To W. P.   London, 9th May 1822.

Volume 14.   1823–4

(105) To W. P.   London, 17th June 1823.

(106) To W. P.   London, 27th November 1824.

Volume 15. 1825–6

Nothing from Crabb Robinson.

Volume 16. 1827–30

(107) To W. P. (Hannah's death.)   Bury, 20th July 1828.
(108) To W. P.   Bury, 3rd August 1828.
(109) To W. P.   Bury, 17th May 1829.
(110) To W. P.   Rome, 15th December 1829.

. . . In the same house is a very agreeable woman of a certain age, Miss Burney, sister of Madame D'Arblay, and herself the author of several esteemed novels. . . .

(111) To W. P. and sons.   · Naples, 2nd April 1830.
(112) To W. P. and sons.   Florence, 17th July 1830.

[Asks for copies of *The Essays of Elia* and Coleridge's *Aids to Reflection* to be sent him.]

Volume 17. 1831–2

(113) To W. P. and sons.   Florence, 14th June 1831.
(114) To W. P. and sons.   Turin, 13th September 1831.

Volume 18. 1832–44

(115) To W. P.   London, 27th August 1837.

My dear friend,

I meant to send the accompanying Volumes long ago. But there has been blundering in their being forwarded to me. Mrs. Jacob Pattisson will find an autograph of the great poet in the last Volume. The Volumes of Lamb's letters will excite your pity as well as admiration, tho' Talfourd has shewn great skill in the throwing into shade what, in a prominent light, would have wounded the feelings of survivors and friends or provoked the sneers or reproaches of the unfriendly. Wordsworth says it is the only book of the kind he knows, executed with delicacy and judgment. Hereafter there may be large additions.—Mary Lamb, I rejoice to say, has been long in quiet good health. She shewed me her brother's grave a few days ago with composure and something like cheerfulness. . . .

(116) To J. P.   London, 19th June 1844.

Volume 19.   1845–50

(117) To Jacob P.   London, 22nd January 1846.
. . . I have heard Wordsworth speak very kindly both of the writings and person of Leigh Hunt. . . .

(118) To J. P.   Bury, 29th August 1846.

(119) To J. P.   London, 11th January 1847.
. . . I go to-morrow to Mr. Wordsworth (Rydal Mount, Ambleside) and mean to remain with him about three weeks. . . .

(120) To J. P.   Rydal, 1st January 1846.
. . . Here I have been enjoying myself in spite of very bad weather.   There is congregated here a variety of talent and moral excellence quite astonishing in a place of so small population.   To say nothing of the poet or any other males, the females alone form a singular delightful society.   Here are Mrs. Wordsworth and her pious and benignant friend Miss Fenwick, and Mrs. Arnold, the worthy helpmate and survivor of the Doctor; Mrs. Fletcher, for many years the most distinguished member of Edinburgh society . . . and her two daughters, Mrs. Davy . . . and Miss Fletcher, also an authoress, and of recent accession, Harriet Martineau, who by her benevolence and generosity and activity of mind has conciliated the friendship of everyone in spite of Unitarianism and Mesmerism. . . .

(121) To J. P.   London, 17th January 184[9].
. . . I have begun to read Macaulay's very eloquent history. He has not abandoned the principles of political philosophy in which he was brought up, nor lost his love of civil and religious liberty. . . . You will be glad to hear that I found Mr. Wordsworth's mind in a much healthier state than it was last year.   He has learnt to submit to the will of Providence in the loss of his daughter.   Both he and Mrs. Wordsworth are in good health. . . .

(122) To J. P.   London, 22nd July 1847.

(123) To J. P.   Bury, 30th July 1850.
. . . My wish has been to be at Rydal.   Mrs. Wordsworth has pressed my going to meet Miss Fenwick, and my intention is to go without losing a day the moment I am released from hence. . . .

(124) To J. P. (death of W. P.)   Leeds, 12th January 1848.
. . . Poor Wordsworth cannot bear up against the insupportable grief he feels for the death of his daughter.   I was with him three weeks, during which time I was seldom able to withdraw his mind from the moody abstraction in which it seems to be from all

present objects. This doubles Mrs. Wordsworth's affliction. But she is able to talk of this sorrow, the loss of her dear child. . . . I will, however, tell you an anecdote of Wordsworth's man-servant James, born a parish boy, who has lived all his days in servitude, a *character* of whom I will one day tell you more. Expressing my sorrow that Mr. W. was unable to *submit*, he said: 'Ah, Sir, so I took the liberty to say to him, and then master said: "Oh, but she was such a bright creature." And then I said: *"But don't you think she is brighter now than she ever was?"* And then he burst into a flood of tears.'

These could not have been tears of unmixed grief. But James's answer may match with any to be found in the sayings of eminent men. . . .

(125) To J. P.   London, 31st January 1848.
(126) To J. P.   London, 5th December 1847.
(127) To J. P.   Playford Hall, 20th September 1848.
(128) To J. P.   London, 28th March 1848.

[Of the French Revolution]
    . . . I should despair but for a vague hope which clothes itself in the words of our most spiritually-minded poets. The last of them has said that:
    All things are less dreadful than they seem.[1] . . .

(129) To J. P.   London, 10th October 1850.
    . . . I once said to Mrs. Arnold: 'I think your husband [2] was one of the best Christians and worst Churchmen I ever knew.' She smiled and said: 'There are many of that opinion.' . . .
    . . . She [Mrs. Rutt] looked so venerable and so happy—'with a sunny face' to borrow an epithet of Wordsworth's.[3] . . .

(130) To J. P.   London, 14th February 1848.
    . . . I have been looking over the volume of letters [from himself to the Pattissons] this morning.—It is not like the volume which I saw on Talfourd's drawing-room table—a bound collection of all the complimentary letters written on *Ion* and which therefore it was intended everyone should read. . . . I am surprised at the small number of letters from myself.[4] . . . There is no letter between 1802 and 1813, nor between 1817 and 1830. . . .

---

[1] Wordsworth, *Ecclesiastical Sonnets*, Part I, sonnet VII, last line.
[2] Dr. Arnold of Rugby.
[3] Used of his neighbour, Mr. Harden.
[4] He continues in comment on some of these, notably on that dated Rome, 27th December 1830 (number 31 in this list).

(131) To J. P.   London, 22nd January 1848.

(132) To J. P.   Bury, 9th July 1850.

. . . Having so little to say, I have thought it expedient to write on the back of the last circular [1] sent me, having a much greater number than I can distribute without the charge of obtru-[siveness], which there will not be from you under any circumstances and whether or not you rank your name among the admirers of the great Christian and moral poet.   The subscription now, I understand, amounts to little more than £600 which will never suffice for a full length.   Nor do I expect that the further subscriptions will be sufficient unless the Dean and Chapter remit the fee they usually demand for the licence to put up a full length—£300—which they probably will do out of respect to him. . . .

(133) To J. P.   Bury, 6th September 1848.

. . . My brother is very comfortable in health but—
            By sudden blast or slow decline
            Our social comforts die away.

(134) To J. P.   London, 4th May 1850.

. . . I did not go down to Westmorland to attend the funeral. Indeed the interment took place on the Saturday, and I should have scarcely had time.   But I find I was expected and therefore I regret my absence.   But in the first letter the time was not mentioned and I therefore inferred that I was not expected.

The grief of friends ought to be absorbed in the contemplation of the public loss, and yet the public of to-day will be the immediate gainers.   There will be published forthwith THE POEM [2] which perhaps for the earnest and contemplative few of the present and future generations will be the most precious of the great man's works.   In 14 books Wordsworth has recorded the formation of his character.   This was written when his mind was in all its strength.

Dr. Christopher Wordsworth is commissioned to prepare brief memorials in illustration of his poems, and a short biography.   I should have been better pleased had the task been given to Mr. Quillinan.   For I fear there will be an inclination to press the great poet into the service of High Churchism.   But this is not easy to do.   There is at all events the sonnet *Young England* which is a bar in the way.   Wordsworth henceforward will be classed with our English classics.

It will afford you satisfaction to know that Mrs. Wordsworth

---

[1] About the Wordsworth Memorial.   [2] *The Prelude.*

has sustained this great trial as a Christian heroine should.   She attended the funeral at which was a very large collection of the neighbours.   This is the custom of the country.   I am expected to go soon and I shall. . . . The notices of the public press have been creditable to the country['s] literature, at least as far as I have yet seen the papers.   The best I have yet seen has been that of the *Inquirer*.   I believe Mrs. Wordsworth will be gratified by it and acknowledge its Christian character though it is by a Unitarian.   It is a curious fact that the Unitarians and the High Church have been among his warmest admirers.   This power of uniting extremes in one common sentiment of love and admiration is an evidence of a *catholicity* of character. . . .

PS. I have had a letter from Mrs. Wordsworth since I wrote the above.   She writes with great composure.

APPENDIX VI

THE following anecdotes, most of which have already been published either by Sadler or elsewhere, relate to men of letters:

No.

2. Horne Tooke.
6. Lamb (First Cause).
7. Hogg.
10. Rogers.
16. Ayrton. (Dirt-trumps.) Lamb not the author.
17. Lamb. (Luke-warm Christian.)
18. Lamb. (Compounds and simples.)
19. Lamb. (Shakespeare's anachronisms.)
35. Wordsworth. (Saul.)
36. Lamb. (Bacon and Cabbage.)
38. Capel Lofft.
42. Lamb. (Unitarians.)
47. Coleridge. (Bible Societies.)
48. Coleridge. (Goodness.)
50. Lamb. (Churchyard.)
51. Coleridge. (Bowyer.)
59. Lady Blessington. (Mrs. Norton's Wife.)
60. Sydney Smith. (Rogers.)
61. Mme. de Staël. (Coleridge.)
67. Coleridge. (Scotchmen.)
75. Coleridge. (Grapes and Gripes.)
77. Hood.
81. Porson. (Southey.)
88. Sydney Smith and Landseer.
92. Horne Tooke.
98. Theodore Hook.
99. Sydney Smith.
101. Theodore Hook. (Croker.)
102. Theodore Hook.
103. Theodore Hook.

No.

104. Theodore Hook.
107. Aikin.   (Cowper.)
108. Coleridge.   (Wordsworth.)
120. Sydney Smith.
123. Sydney Smith.
124. Sydney Smith.
127. Sydney Smith.
129. Disraeli.
140.[1] Disraeli.
141. Theodore Hook.
155. Tom Taylor.
156. Sydney Smith.
159. Kenyon.
160. Douglas Jerrold.
170. Coleridge.

[1] Should be 130.   The numbers are all ten out from here onwards.

APPENDIX VII

INDEX TO MENTIONS OF (I) WRITERS AND (II) BOOKS IN THE
VOLUMES OF CRABB ROBINSON'S CORRESPONDENCE AT DR. WILLIAMS'S
LIBRARY

(This includes a List of Letters written to him by English Authors.)

I. WRITERS

CRABB ROBINSON's correspondence and papers are preserved at Dr.
Williams's Library (i) in thirty-two volumes arranged chronologically,
and (ii) in eight Miscellaneous Bundles.

The following index is therefore twofold in its method. In the case
of the bound volumes, references are arranged in four columns which
give: (1) the date of the letter — this indicates the volume in which it
occurs, except where otherwise stated (e.g. 1848 in 1847 volume);
(2) the number of the letter in that volume; (3) the page of the letter;
(4) the number of the line in the page, unless it is the last, when it is so
designated, 'last seq.' means 'last line subject continued overleaf.' In
references to the Miscellaneous Bundles the actual letters or figures
given conform to the Library numbering which is not consistent. In
the index the first column gives the date of the letter without any indica-
tion where it may be found. The second column gives the number of
the bundle and letter in accordance with the Library procedure whatever
that may be (e.g. 3 A 32 is Bundle 3 A, letter 32; 2 IV K is Bundle 2,
subsection IV, letter K). The third and fourth columns, as in the case of
references to the bound volumes, contain information as to page and line
in the letter. It should further be noted that under the sub-heading
LETTERS, i.e. where reference is to the complete letter, the third and
fourth columns are ignored, and in cases in which more than one letter
occurs in any one year the references run on across the columns, thus:

1836   100; 134
1839   10; 19; 23; 26; 42;
      49; 57; 69

The only references to Crabb Robinson's correspondence with the
Wordsworth family printed here are those found to have been accident-
ally omitted from *The Correspondence of Henry Crabb Robinson with the
Wordsworth Circle*, which contains a full index to the papers in this series
preserved at Dr. Williams's Library.

[ ] indicate information supplied by the editor.

⟨ ⟩ indicate a paraphrase in the text.

AGNEW, Eleanor C.
   Geraldine   1840   135   1   16
AGUILAR, Grace   1850   87   6   1
AIKIN, Anna Laetitia. *See* Barbauld,
   A. L.

AIKIN, John, M.D.
and Sir Richard Phillips	1806	52	1	23
quoted	1799	129	2	51
	1842	184 *b*	3	10
	1843	121	8	17
	1852	4	2	last
and Crabb Robinson	1806	44	2	21
and Wakefield	1801	34	4	6
other references	1796	77	4	3
	1802	51	1	41
	1803	103	4	9
	1804	42	3	2
	1805	4	3	11
	1805	30	3	9
	1806	52–53	5	16
	1806	67	1	11
	1808	105	4	2nd P.S.
	1850	6 *b*	1	16
	1854	61 *a*	3	2

WORKS:
Biographical Dictionary
	1801	38	3	35
	1807	78	2	1

Miscellanies
	1796	85	4	2
	1835	101	2	10

AIKIN, Lucy
	1844	8 *b*	5	6
	1844	60	3	2
	1846	12	4	15
	1846	14 *b*–15 *a*	8	7
	1848	31 *a*	8	3
[in 1847 vol.]
	1855	39	7	3

WORK:
Life of Addison
	1843	22	7	1
	1843	97	3	15

LETTERS:
to Crabb Robinson	1849	81 *a*		
from and to Crabb Robinson	1854	55 *b*		

AINSWORTH, William Harrison
	1844	78 *a*	3	21
	1846	34	5	10

WORK:
Jack Sheppard
	1844	78 *a*	3	23

ALISON, Archibald
Essay on the Nature and Principles of Taste
	1795	55	pp. 1–3

LETTER to R. E. Scott
	1809	8	18	1

ALISON, Sir Archibald
History of Europe
	1866	64 *b*		

ALLIES, T. W.
(*Journal in France in* 1845)
	1850	67	3	11

ALLINGHAM, William
LETTER to Crabb Robinson
	1854	56 *b*		

ALLSOP, Thomas
and a portrait of Coleridge	1853	21		
request for some of Crabb Robinson's books	1867	2 VII 25		

ALLSOP, Thomas—*contd.*
  copies skit on Southey's verse by
    [Coleridge ?]   1866   77 *b*
    mentioned   1847   27   7   12
  WORK:
    Letters, Conversations, and Recol-
      lections of S. T. Coleridge   1865   24 *a*
    LETTERS to Crabb Robinson   1865   24 *a*
                             1866   60
Arabian Nights   1798   119   3   23
ARBLAY, Francis Burney, Mme D'.   *See*
  D'Arblay
ARGYLL, Duke of.   *See* Campbell, G. D.
ARNOLD, Matthew
  and family   1852   52   7   last
                             1856   21   4   25
                 [in 1857 vol.]
                             1857   30 *a*   4   10
  inaugural lecture as Professor of
    Poetry   1858   5 *a*   3   8
  poetry   1849   42 *b*   6   22 seq.
    Quillinan on   1851   8   5   19 seq.
    W. Wordsworth [grandson] on   1858   5 *a*   3   8 seq.
  and E. Quillinan   1850   1 *b*–2 *a*   7   9
                           1850   1 *b*–2 *a*   8   3
  Crabb Robinson on   1850   39 *a*   2   10
  and Wordsworth   1851   8   5   19 seq.
  and Wordsworth's memorial   1850   37
  other references   1848   5 *b*   1   17
                 [in 1847 vol.]
                             1849   77   4   10
  WORKS:
    Essays in Criticism   1865   23 *b*   3   12
    Strayed Reveller   1849   22 *b*   4   12
    [*Wordsworth's Grave*]   1851   8   5   19
ARNOLD, Thomas, D.D.
  Fragment on the Church   1844   103 *a*   4   5
                             1844   106 *b*   2   10
                             1845   1   2   3
                             1845   4   3   7
                            N.D.   2 IV K   4   9
  History of Rome   1839   2 XI 6   2   18
  Life.   *See* Stanley, A. P.
  LETTERS:
    to Crabb Robinson   1836   100; 134
                          1837   8; 23–24
                          1839   119
    from Crabb Robinson   1837   17
ATKINSON, Henry George
  and H. Martineau   1846   92   8   13
                 [in 1864 vol.]
    See also her *Letters on the Laws*
      of Man's Social Nature and
      Development

AUSTEN, Jane
  mention   1843   17 *a*   4   22
  Wordsworth on   1847   17 *b*   4   6
         [in 1848 vol.]

AUSTIN, Sarah, *born* Taylor
  WORKS:
    Characteristics of Goethe   1833   100
                              1833   130   1   8
                              1834   33   1   13
                              1836   109   3   26
                              1844   8 *b*   3   1
    (*Germany from 1760 to 1814*)   1854   8 60 1   3   9
    tr. of Ranke's *History of the Popes*   1843   83 *b*   4   6
  LETTERS to Crabb Robinson   1832   76
                              1833   100; 165 *a*
                              1834   10 *a*; 46 *a*; 50
                              1841   32 *c*
                              1854   8 60 1
                              1855   33 *b*; 36 *b*

BAGEHOT, Walter   1852   27 *b*   5   4
                              1855   13 *a*   1   4
  LETTERS:
    to J. Martineau   1855   18
    to Crabb Robinson   1849   31
                              1851   69 *b*–70 *a*
                              1853   69 *b*
                              1854   41 *b*
                              1855   [in 1854 vol.] 1 *b*; 4 *a*;
                                       11; 15 *b*; 23; 25
                              1856   44

BAILEY, Samuel
  (*Essays on the Formation and
    Publication of Opinions and other
    subjects*)   1845   112 *b*   4   10
BAILLIE, Joanna
  mention   1835   120   3   16
  T. Robinson on   1804   11   2   24
  LETTERS:
    J. Masquerier   N.D.   8 27 III
    to Mrs. Masquerier   1830   8 27 I
                                1831   8 27 II
                              N.D.   8 27 IV

BARBAULD, Anna Laetitia, *born* Aikin
  E. H. Barker on   1828   57   1   21
  Mrs. Benecke on   1838   33   1   7
  and Mrs. Chapone   1802   44   1   44 seq.
                              1802   3 A 22   3   38
  and Children's Books   1801   38   4   7
                              1802   44   4   27
  Christianity   1801   35   3   2
  and Mrs. Clarkson   1808   132   2   11
                              1808   134   3   20
  and the Classics   1803   3 A 32   3   32
  and Coleridge   1808   134   2   32

BARBAULD, Anna Laetitia—*contd.*

death	1826	141	2	19
and R. Hall	1799	132	2	8
and her husband	1808	105	4	2nd P.S.
and Lamb	1808	134	3	32
and Malthus	1806	44	2	27
paraphrased	1801	38	2	33
quoted	1801	3 C (4)	1	26
	1804	3 A 36	2	4
	1807	89	4	12
	1848	29 *a*	4	19
	1852	2	2	8
	1853	1	1	9
and Crabb Robinson	1806	44	2	26
	1808	134	3	20
Crabb Robinson consulted about her	1866	62 *b*		
and Mme de Staël	1804	3 A 36	2	34
W. Taylor on	1809	71 *t*	3	16
and Women's Disabilities	1806	44	2	26
other references	1805	30	2	14
	1806	52	4	14
	1810	29	2	5
	1812	69	1	13
	1812	72	1	19
	1819	41 *a*	1	12
	1833	142	1	26
	1834	19	4	5 [ll. across]
	1835	137	3	8
	1839	113	1	30
	1844	4 *b*	4	12
	1844	42 *b*	2	7
WORKS:				
writings	1808	134	3	29
	1835	86	2	P.S.
	1835	100	1	9
	1835	132	1	24
	1835	137	3	8
	1843	22	7	8
Devotional Taste	1796	85	4	3
'Life! we have been long together' tr. into German	1804	77		
Crabb Robinson on	1825	139	1	15
	1826	141	2	last seq.
	1826	146	2	12
	1826	162	3	
On Inconsistent Expectations	1801	34	1	29
	1835	101	2	5
LETTERS:				
to Crabb Robinson	1809	1 *a*		
	1813	99 *b*		
	1816	126 *b*		
BARHAM, Richard Harris				
Ingoldsby Legends	1844	78 *a*	2	18

BARKER, Edmund Henry
  on *Junius* — 1828 — 57 — 2 — 17
  Parriana — 1829 — 115–117 — 2 — 14
  Index to Thesaurus — 1828 — 57 — 1 — 3
  LETTERS:
    to Crabb Robinson — 1828 — 47; 57
    — 1829 — 115–117
    from Crabb Robinson — 1829 — 95 *a*

BARRETT, Charlotte
  LETTERS to Crabb Robinson — 1831 — 1 II 30
  — 1842 — 174 *b*
  — 1848 — 14 *b*; 16 *a*
  — 1853 — 2 *b*; 11 *a*; 93 *a*
  — 1854 — 14 *b*; 42 *b*
  — 1855 — 19; 90 *b*
  — 1864 — 5 *a*

BARRETT, Elizabeth. *See* Browning, Elizabeth Barrett

BARTON, Bernard
  and Lord Byron — 1844 — 74 — 2 — 2 seq.

BEATSON, Robert
  Political Index to the Histories of Great Britain and Ireland — 1788 — 29 — 1 — 18

BEATTIE, James
  Amyot on — 1795 — 55 — 4 — 17
  — 1796 — 71 — 4 — 15
  and T. Gray — 1795 — 61 — 2 — last marginal note
  WORK:
    Minstrel, The — 1796 — 71 — 4 — 15

BEDDOES, Thomas
  Observations on the Nature of Demonstrative Evidence — 1801 — 34 — 2 — 13
  Pamphlet on Pitt — 1811 — 50 — 3 — 20

BEDDOES, Thomas Lovell
  Crabb Robinson on — 1851 — 64 — 5 — 10
  — 1854 — 1 *a* — 1 — 10

BELL, Andrew, D.D. *Life. See* Southey, Charles Cuthbert

BELSHAM, Thomas
  Elements of the Philosophy of the Mind — 1801 — 34 — 4 — 14

BELSHAM, William
  Memoirs of the Kings of Great Britain of the House of Brunswick — 1807 — 112 — 3 — 24

BENTHAM, Jeremy
  LETTERS to E. Hamond — 1809 — 71 *o*
  — 1819 — 71 *p*; 71 *q*; 71 *r*

BEVAN
  God in Christ — 1844 — 20 *a* — 4 — 8
  — 1844 — 22 *a* — 9 — 5

BLACKBURNE, Francis
  Confessional — 1852 — 21 — 7 — 13

BLACKSTONE, Sir William
   Commentaries   1795   57   1   22
                            1795   57   2   10
                            1795   59–60   2   20
                            1796   68   4   P.S.
                            1796   74   4   4

BLAIR, Hugh
   Lectures   1851   20 *b*   3   14
   WORKS:
     (*Lectures on Rhetoric and Belles*
       Lettres) Crabb Robinson on   1826   170   2   14
     Sermons quoted   1803   107   1   37
                            1803   3 A 35   2   10

BLAKE, William
   and Gilchrist   1855   41 *a*   1   5
                            1855   41 *b*
   intellect   1864   6 *b*   1   5
   Life. See Gilchrist, A.
   memoirs of   1864   14 *a*
   Monckton Milnes on   1852   43 *a*
   Quillinan on   1848   38 *b*   2   8
                            1848   43 *b*   1   13
   Crabb Robinson on   1826   142–143   5   14
   and Wordsworth   1826   142–143   3   13
                            1826   142–143   6   18
   other references   1826   169   4   11
                            1836   147   2   18
                            1853   106 *a*   1   5

   WORKS:
     Job, to be published in Germany   1834   46 *a*
                            1834   50 *a*
     MS. and note   N.D.   100–102
                    [in 1867 vol.]
     Poetical Sketches   1848   27 *b*   1   3

BLESSINGTON, Marguerite, Countess of
   and Landor   1835   94   3   9
   Landor's lines for   1835   94   4
   Crabb Robinson introduced by
     Landor   1832   52   3   13
   other references   1833   133   1   3
                            1833   174   1   10
                            1835   124–125   4   14
                            1836   168   1   25
                            1843   30 *a*   2   19
                            1843   87 *b*   5   P.S.
                            1843   93   5   10
                            1843   97   6   17
   LETTERS to Crabb Robinson   1834   6
                            1836   122

BLOOMFIELD, Nathaniel
   Honington Green, a ballad   1801   38   3   16
                            1802   44   4   1

BLOOMFIELD, Robert
   Crabb Robinson meets   1805   29   3   7

BLOOMFIELD, Robert—*contd.*
  WORKS:
    Farmer's Boy   1800   5   1   21 seq.
                            1802   54   2   8
                            1802   3 C II   3   18
                            1802   3 A 21   4   37
                            1802   3 A 25   4   26
    Lines on Pope's willow-tree   1801   38   3   12
    Rural Tales   1802   41   3   28
BORROW, George   1843   49   2   1
    (*Zincali; or an Account of the Gypsies in Spain*)
    Crabb Robinson on   1848   23 *a*   5   11
BOSWELL, James   1829   115–117   7   25
    Life of Samuel Johnson, Crabb
       Robinson on   1797   92   3   9
                            1843   83   3   12 seq.
BOWLES, Caroline Anne. *See* Southey, R.
BRIGHTWELL, C. L.
    Memorials of Amelia Opie   1854   68 *b*   4   P.S.
BRITTON, John
  LETTERS to Masquerier   1836   8 21 II
                         1845   8 21 I
BRONTË, Charlotte
    Crabb Robinson on   1853   26   6   15
  WORKS:
    Jane Eyre   1850   2 *a*   8   P.S.
    Villette   1853   26   6   15
BROOKE, Stopford A.
    Life and Letters of the late Frederick
       W. Robertson   1865   33   2   6
                            1866   67 *a*   1   3
                            1866   68   2 seq.
                            1867   83 *a*   3   13 seq.
                            1867   83 *b*   2   4
                            1867   87   1   3
  LETTER to Crabb Robinson   1805   33
BROUGHAM, Henry Peter, Baron Brougham and Vaux
    on Lady C. Bury's *Diary* in the
      Edinburgh Review   1838   65   7   13
    Enquiry into the State of the Nation at the Commencement of the Present Administration. Pamphlet   1806   46   1   P.S.
  LETTERS:
    to Crabb Robinson   1838   40; 41 *a–b*
                           1842   116 *a*
                           1845   103 *b*
                           1848   84 *a*
                           1849   13 *a*
    from Crabb Robinson [copy]   1836   167
                           1842   115 *a*
BROWN, Thomas
    Observations on Zoonomia   1798   113   4   4

III—D

BROWNING, Elizabeth Barrett
   modernisation of Chaucer 1843 132 *b*–133 *b* 6 15
   and H. Martineau 1843 131 *b* 1 10
   other references 1842 151 *b* 4 15
   1842 172 *a* 2 19
   1845 84 *b* 4 1
   1851 59 4 last
   1852 59 6 5
   LETTERS to Crabb Robinson 1845 51 *b*
   1846 18 *b*
BROWNING, Robert
   Crabb Robinson on 1844 5 XVI *d* 1 20
   1851 59 4 last
   1852 59 6 5
   WORK:
     Colombe's Birthday 1853 39 *b*–40 *a* 6 23
BRUCE, James
   Travels to Discover the Source of
     the Nile 1796 69 2 15
BRYANT, William Cullen
   1845 87–88 *a* 5 13
   1845 91 4 9
BUCKSTONE, John Baldwin
   Ascent to Mount Parnassus 1853 39 *b*–40 *a* 7 2
BULWER, E. G. E. *See* Lytton
BURKE, Edmund
   and Anti-Catholic Legislation 1829 95 *a* 4 21
   and E. H. Barker's book on *Junius* 1828 47 3 2
   1829 95 4 3
   1829 115–117 4 1
   1829 115–117 7 19
   Correspondence 1845 48 *b*–49 *a* 8 16
   1845 51 *a* 4 5
   Letters; article on, in the *Athenæum* 1844 93 8 7
   the *Monthly Review* on 1796 85 3 8
   T. Paine on 1828 47 2 7
   Pattisson on 1798 119 3 4
   his pension 1796 80 3 18
   quoted 1796 79 1 23
   1796 80 3 3
   1797 94 2 4
   1826 170 1 last
   and Crabb Robinson 1805 3 A 44 2 52
   1806 60 3 8
   1808 136 4 9
   1844 53 *b* 2 12
   Crabb Robinson on 1797 96 2 13
   1829 95 *a* 1 23
   1829 95 *a* 4 2
   1842 124 *b*
   1853 26 2 10
   Schelling on 1802 3 A 28 2 22
   compared with Shaftesbury 1804 3 A 41 3 24
   his style 1809 15 1 10
   1810 20 *b* 2 23

Burke, Edmund—*contd.*
    and Thelwall   1796   77   3   33
                                                  1797   95   3   16
    and Weishaupt   1804   3 A 38 2   38
    other references   1799   126   2   5
                                                  1799   136   1   41
                                                  1801   3 A 12 3   21
                                                  1804   11   2   32
                                                  1830   44   1   25
                                                  1835   118   3   10

WORKS:
    *Enquiry into our Ideas of the Sublime
        and Beautiful*   1795   55   1   23
                                                  1795   55   3   10
                                                  1803   96   10   5
    *Letter to the Rt. Hon. H. Dundas
        with the sketch of a Negro Code*   1796   72   2   6th
                                                                   marginal
                                                                   note
    Letter to a Noble Lord   1853   26   2   11
    Letter to the Duke of Portland   1797   91   1   32 seq.
    Memorials on French Affairs   1797   100   4   11 seq.
    Pamphlet [? *The Regicide Peace* and
        the *Letter to the Duke of Portland*
        were both published in 1797]   1797   90   3   P.S.
    Reflections on the Revolution in France   1796   79   1   23
                                                  1796   80   3   3
Burn, Richard
    Justice of the Peace   1795   61   3   3rd
                                                                   marginal
                                                                   note

Burnett, George
    W. Taylor on   1810   7 1 u
Burney, Frances.   *See* D'Arblay
Burney, Sarah Harriet
    Geraldine Fauconberg and *Country
        Neighbours*   1843   17 b   1   12 seq.
    (*Romance of Private Life*)   1838   19   2   9 seq.
                                                  1840   141   1   8
    LETTERS to Crabb Robinson   1830   10; 19; 23; 36; 42;
                                                          49; 78
                                                  1831   98; 114
                                                  1832   33; P.2
                                                  1835   87
                                                  1838   19
                                                  1839   84
                                                  1840   141
                                                  1842   201 b
                                                  1843   17 a; 87 b
Bury, Lady Charlotte Susan Maria
    *Diary Illustrative of the times of
        George IV*, review by Brougham   1838   65   7   13
Byron, George Gordon, Lord
    and M. Arnold   1851   8   2   P.S. 18
    and B. Barton   1844   74   2   9

BYRON, George Gordon, Lord—*contd.*

and Lady Byron	1842	191 *b*–192 *a*	6	19
	1843	9 *b*–10 *a*	4	last
	1843	22	6	1 seq.
and Calvinism	1855	14 *a*		
and Coleridge's lectures	1849	84 *b*	7	4
and criticism	1842	125 *b*	1	15
death	1834	49	1	4
	1834	69	3	2
	1840	35	1	
epigram, by Lamb	1825	133–134	8	P.S. upside down
and Goethe	1823	95	3	3
	1829	151	1	last seq.
	1829	152	3	34 seq.
	1829	152	2	P.S.
	1829	154	1	17
and Kennedy's *Conversations on Religion*	1855	14 *a*	1	3
and Knebel	1827	12	6	last
	1828	51	2	5
and W. S. Landor	1830	60	4	1
	1836	172	1	11 seq.
	1843	25	2	7
lecture by Cooper	1847	29 *b*	5	25
Life. See Moore, T.				
and H. Martineau	1841	2	6	16
on T. Moore	1853	58 *a*	2	3
on religion. *See also* Kennedy	1821	8 19 11	1, 2	
Crabb Robinson on	1833	115	3	16 seq.
	1836	168	1	29 seq.
	1836	172	1	11 seq.
	1836	174	1	2 seq.
and Rogers. See *Question and Answer*				
and Southey	1836	168	1	29 seq.
and Southey's poems	1836	172	1	14
Tieck on	1829	154	2	5
and Wordsworth	1817	142	4	12
	1833	117	4	8
	1836	168	1	29 seq.
	1836	172	1	12 seq.
	1850	54 *b*–55 *a*	7	14
	1851	37	4	3
	1853	18	4	17
Wordsworth on	1833	117	4	8
other references	1816	135	2	10
	1828	47	4	3
	1829	94	2	5
	1832	49	2	8
	1844	80 *b*	1	22
	1851	37	4	3
	1851	37	5	2
	1859	29–30 *a*	8	19
	1866	39 *a*	4	9

BYRON, George Gordon, Lord—*contd.*
  WORKS:
    Charity Ball, The   1843   9 *b*–10 *a*   5   4
    Childe Harold's Pilgrimage   1817   142   4   13
                             1837   55   2   11
    Don Juan   1833   115   4   8
                             1836   168   2   20
                             1836   172   1   11 seq.
    Fare thee Well   1842   191 *b*–192 *a*   7   28
                             1843   9 *b*–10 *a*   5   6
    Heaven and Earth   1829   152   2   P.S.
                             1834   62   2   23
    ⟨*Manfred*⟩   1817   142   4   12
    [*Question and Answer*]   1833   115   3   16
    Sardanapalus   1853   61   6   1
    Werner   1847   29 *b*   8   13
  LETTER [to Masquerier ?]   1821   8 19 II
BYRON, Lady Noel
  LETTERS:
    to Masquerier   N.D.   8 19 IV
    to Crabb Robinson   1853   76; 86 *a*; 101 *b*; 102 *a*;
                                  118 *a*; 119; 123
                         1854   23 *b*; 28 *a*; 67 *b*; 69 *a*;
                                  75 *a*; 78 *a*; 80 *a*; 82 *b*
                         1855   3 *a*; 10 *b*; 12 *b*; 14 *a*;
                                  17 *a*; 20 *b* [in 1856
                                  vol.]; 26 *b*;   29 *a*;
                                  32 *a*;   42 *b*;   57 *a*;
                                  72 *b*;   1 II 4;   1 II 5;
                                  1 II 6
                         1856   42 *b*; 1 II 7
                         1858   6 *a*; 25 *b*
                         1859   12 *a*; 38 *a*
                         N.D.   1 II 8
    from Crabb Robinson   1853   77 *a*

CALDWELL, Anne.   *See* Marsh
CAMPBELL, George Douglas, 8th Duke
    of Argyll
    On the Natural and Supernatural   1864   23 *b*   3   9
CAMPBELL, John, 1st Baron
    Lives of the Lord Chancellors and
    Keepers of the Great Seal of Eng-
    land   1848   19 *a*   6   13
                               1850   12 *b*–13 *a*   6   3
CAMPBELL, Thomas
    and Lady Byron   1842   191 *b*–192 *a*   6   16
                               1842   207   1   11
    J. P. Collier on   1829   164   2   12
    death   1844   65   5   last
    and W. S. Landor   1836   172   1   30
    and the laureateship   1843   135   3   1
    lectures   1812   80   3   14
    and the *New Monthly Magazine*   1831   124   4   5
                               1842   191 *b*–192 *a*   6   16

CAMPBELL, Thomas—*contd.*

and the *New Monthly Magazine*	1842	207	1	11
poems, Quillinan on	1851	37	3	22
and Wordsworth	1826	155 *a*	1	18
	1836	172	1	30
mentioned	1826	153	3	P.S.

WORKS:

Hohenlinden	1851	37	4	1
Life of Mrs. Siddons	1834	53	1	12
	1834	56	4	11
	1840	141	2	2
Pleasures of Hope	1844	65	6	6
LETTER to Crabb Robinson	1833	99		

CAREY, Henry Charles

Essay on the Rate of Wages	1836	102	2	5

CARLYLE, Thomas

and Mrs. Aders	1825	123	3	12
Sara Coleridge on	1846	56	1	3
	1847	17 *b*	3	12 seq.
[in 1848 vol.]				
	1849	2 1 K		
and copyright petition	1839	85	1	9
	1839	90	3	8
and Emerson	1839	85	1	9
	1848	22 *a*	2	6
and Goethe	1829	94	1	20
influence	1847	17 *b*	3	12
[in 1848 vol.]				
in the Lake District	1826	151	4	3
on London	1826	151	4	7
on Macaulay's *History of England*	1849	26	2	5
marriage	1827	13	1	last seq.
and Mazzini	1844	65	3	15
and R. M. Milnes	1844	5 XVI *f*	4	19
and Nicolai	1826	151	3	30
and a Professorship	1827	13	2	P.S.
and the *Quarterly Review*	1840	170 *b*	3	17
Quillinan on	1850	11	4	17 seq.
and Crabb Robinson	1848	23 *a*	2	last seq.
	1848	63 *a*	2	P.S.
Crabb Robinson on	1849	21	5	14
	1856	67 *a*	4	29
T. Robinson on	N.D.	2 IV xxiv	1	5
and A. J. Scott	1848	67 *b*	1	last
Southey on	1839	2 XI 6	2	12
and W. Taylor	1844	8 *b*	3	11
and Whewell	1840	148	8	15
Wordsworth on	1839	85	1	9
	1839	2 XI 6	2	12
other references	1824	112 *b*	2	P.S.
	1837	30	1	2
	1837	39	2	5
	1840	132	1	11
	1842	161 *a*	2	1
	1849	42 *b*–43	8	19

CARLYLE, Thomas—*contd.*
  other references   1849   47   4   8
     1849   82 *b*   1   P.S.
     1862   49 *b*   1   7

  WORKS:
  Chartism   1840   148   8   15
  (*German Romance*)   1826   151
  History of the French Revolution   1839   2 XI 6   2   5
     1846   56   1   9
  Latter Day Pamphlets   1850   11   4   17
  Past and Present   1843   83 *b*–84 *a*   11   8
  LETTERS to Crabb Robinson   1825   123
     1826   151
     1827   13
     1838   9

CARR, Sir John
  Northern Summer Trip round the Baltic   1807   100   2   15
CARRUTHERS, Robert
  on Coleridge, Southey, and Words-worth in *Chambers's Encyclopaedia*   1844   37 *b*–38 *a*   5   14
     1850   40 *b*–41 *a*   2   last
  Quillinan on   1850   40 *b*–41 *a*   2   14
CARY, Henry Francis
  tr. of *Pindar*   1833   174   2   33
CARY, John
  County Maps   1807   112   3   21
CARY (CAREY), John
  Prosody   1807   112   3   22
CAVENDISH, George
  Life of Wolsey   1829   95 *a*   2   16
CAWDRY, Robert
  Treasurie or Storehouse of Similies   1799   147   2   10
CHALMERS, Alexander
  (*General Biographical Dictionary*)   1833   155   1   2 seq.
     1833   164   1   2
     1834   39   3   7
CHAMBERS, Robert
  Vestiges of the Natural History of Creation   1845   2 IV *w*   3   8 seq.
     1846   41   1   17
CHESTERFIELD, Philip Dormer Stanhope, 4th/Earl
  Letters to his Son   1799   145   1   50
     1799   147   3   25
CLARK, Emily
  LETTER to J. Masquerier   N.D.   8 1 II 14
CLARKE, The Rev. Adam, LL.D.
  LETTERS to Professor R. E. Scott   1808   8 9 1
     1810   8 9 II
CLARKSON, Thomas
  Essay on the Impolicy of the African Slave Trade   1820   45   4   12
  Essay on the Slavery and Commerce of the Human Species, Latin trans.   1821   57   1   23

CLARKSON, Thomas—*contd.*

History of the Abolition of the Slave Trade	1808	132	3	24
	1808	143	1	1
	1808	155	4	4
	1808	156	1	last seq.
Memoirs of the Private and Public Life of William Penn	1811	50	1	21
Portraiture of Quakerism	1804	42	3	40
	1805	4	2	18

LETTERS:

from W. Jay	1846	48 *a*	
from B. Montagu	1810	22	
from Crabb Robinson	1818	4	
to Crabb Robinson	1808	143	
	1811	49	
	1818	6; 7, 3, P.S.	
	1819	32; 36	
	1837	66	
	1838	37	
to Thomas Robinson	1818	10	
	1822	88	
	1830	74 *a*	
	1838	60	

CLARKSON-WILBERFORCE controversy
  See Miscellaneous Bundle 6 x [1]

CLOUGH, Arthur Hugh

Dr. Arnold on	1848	I VIII 71	1	12
Mrs. Arnold on	1848	77 *a*	1	5
	1848	80 *a*		
Crabb Robinson on	1851	29	5	21
	1852	3 *b*	3	10
	1852	26	5	16
Dean Stanley on	1848	54 *b*	1	7
	1848	I VIII 71		
and University College	1848	I VIII 71		
and University Hall	1848	74	5	8
	1848	79 *a*	8	6
	1848	82	6	18
	1849	6	7	2
	1849	7	4	10
	1849	2 IV XIII	6	14
	1850	5	8	4
	1850	66–67 *a*	5	20
	1850	83 *b*–84 *a*	5	22
	1851	80 *b*–81 *a*	2	10
	1852	4 *b*–5 *a*	6	12
other references	1850	39 *a*	2	15
	1851	78 *b*	3	10

WORK:

Bothie of Tober-na-Vuolich	1848	80 *a*	2	2
	1849	4	1	12

[1] Miscellaneous Bundle 6 x consists of letters on this subject by various writers; as the letters are unnumbered, and are devoted entirely to the one subject, they are not included in the LETTER lists of this index.

CLOUGH, Arthur Hugh—*contd.*
    LETTER to Crabb Robinson

COBBETT, William
    Letters
    Parliamentary History of England

COLERIDGE, Derwent

1849	70 *b*		
1836	113	3	27
1807	78	1	6
1813	95	2	9
1817	145	3	12
1826	171	4	ll. across
1830	14	3	5
1843	56–57	4	P.S.
1843	67–69	6	last
1844	42 *a*	2	4
1848	83	2	4
1848	2 IV vii (*a–b*)	1	14
1848	2 IV vii (*a–b*)	4	12
1849	1 *a–b*	2	1
1849	1 *a–b*	5	8
1849	4	1	7
1849	16–17	7	last
1849	37	6	9
1849	82 *b*	1	9
1849	88	6	10
1851	74 *a*	1	16
1852	3 *b*–4 *a*	8	10
1852	6	1	6
1852	15 *b*	2	14
1852	85	2	7

[in 1849 vol.]

1852	26	6	11
1856	1 II 25		
1857	6 *a*	3	15

    Life of Hartley Coleridge. *See*
        Coleridge, Hartley. *Poems*
    LETTERS to Crabb Robinson

1832	4
1852	28
1853	21
1855	1 II 26; 1 II 28
1856	1 II 25; 1 II 27
1857	34 *b*; 39 *b*
1858	5 *b*
1861	26 *b*; 34 *b*

COLERIDGE, [Mary] Mrs. Derwent
    LETTERS to Crabb Robinson

1854	72 *a*
1857	41 *b*

COLERIDGE, Hartley
    and *Blackwood* and the *Annuals*
    character

1830	14	3	last
1813	95	2	11
1826	171	5	ll. across
1830	14	3	last
1840	157	6	9
1843	67–69	6	16
1844	7 *a*	4	18
1849	1 *a–b*	1	14 seq.
1849	1 *a–b*	5	20
1849	2–3	4	3

COLERIDGE, Hartley—contd.

Mrs. Clarkson on	1813	95	2	11
death	1848	2 IV vii (a–b)	1	15
	1848	2 IV vii (a–b)	4	1
	1848	2 VII vi (a–n)	8	13
	1849	2	1	4
[notice in the *Athenæum* weekly gossip, 13th Jan. and 20th Jan. 1849]	1849	16–17	7	3 seq.
	1849	16–17	14	P.S.
and *The Examiner*	1851	24 a	3	23
funeral	1849	4	1	3
health	1848	37 b	3	16
	1848	83	3	6
	1849	1 a	1	14
and the *London Magazine*	1821	69	3	10
	1822	76	3	39
memorial cross to	1856	47 b	2	12
and the Montagus	1821	69	3	10
	1822	75	4	6
Crabb Robinson on	1849	1 a–b	1	14 seq.
	1849	1 a–b	5	20
	1849	2–3	4	3
Wordsworth on	1840	157	6	9
other references	1817	145	3	9
	1842	172 a	3	20
	1844	7 a	4	18
	1849	16	7	3
[in 1850 vol.]		39 b	7	4
	1852	7–8	6	1
WORKS:				
writings	1821	69	3	10
	1822	76	3	39
	1830	14	3	last
	1848	2 IV vii (a–b)	4	13
	1849	1 a–b	2	14
	1851	23	7	18
	1851	24 a	3	23
	1853	29 a	1	3
Poems of Hartley Coleridge with Life by his brother	1848	2 IV ii (a–b)	4	12
	1849	2–3	4	1 seq.
	1849	39 b	7	4
[in 1850 vol.]				
	1851	22 b	1	17
	1851	23	7	18
Uses of the Heathen Mythology in Poetry in the *London Magazine*	1822	76	3	39
Worthies of Yorkshire and Lancashire [*Biographia Borealis* published]	1849	1 a–b	2	17
COLERIDGE, Herbert	1847	17	8	3
[in 1848 vol.]				
	1848	24	2	11
	1848	59 b	2	23

COLERIDGE, Henry Nelson
death

	1843	9 *a*	1	3
	1843	18 *b*	2	14
	1843	33–34	4	10
and family	1843	2 IV *s*	4	10 seq.
health	1842	172 *a*	3	21
	1842	180	6	16
	1842	185 *b*	4	11
	1842	196 *b*	3	4
	1842	206 *b*	4	4
	1843	2 IV *s*	4	10 seq.

marriage. *See* Coleridge, Sara
marriage
and Crabb Robinson

	1840	144	3	6
	1841	69 *b*	2	12
	1842	157 *a*	6	14
	1842	157 *b*	1	8
and the Wordsworths	1835	111	2	P.S.
	1840	140	2	6
as a prose writer	1859	17	5	6
other references	1841	10–11–25	7	P.S.
	1848	26 *a*	1	8
	1852	15 *b*	2	13

WORKS:
  eds. of S. T. Coleridge's works
    See Coleridge, S. T., *Literary
    Remains*, and *Table Talk*
  Introduction to the Study of the
    Greek Classic Poets   1859   17   5   7
LETTERS:
  to Crabb Robinson   1836   164 *b*
  from Crabb Robinson   1836   165

COLERIDGE, Samuel Taylor
and the Aders

	1813	100 *b*	2	5
	1828	74	1	2 seq.
	1828	81	3	11
	1830	2	3	3
advertises for pupils	1822	76	3	last
on personal advertisement	1811	62	3	10

on the Aristotelian and the Platonic
  Schools   1820   101   1   21
                    [placed as 1814]

on Mrs. Barbauld	1812	69	1	12
	1812	69	4	7
and Benjafield	1811	44	2	14

and *Blackwood's Magazine* and
  the *Edinburgh Magazine*

	1817	145	2	10
	1821	69	3	6
	1821	70	1	9
	1821	71–72	6	20
	1822	75	3	18
	1840	145	2	1

inquiries concerning Jakob Boehmen   1817   141   2   8
and Dr. Brabant   1847   17 *b*   1   4 seq.
                    [in 1848 vol.]

Coleridge, Samuel Taylor—*contd.*

inquiries concerning Giordano Bruno	1817	141	2	14
at Cambridge	1833	151	2	23
	1835	120	1	16 seq.
Carlyle and	1826	151	4	3 of P.S
in *Chambers's Encyclopaedia*	1844	37 *b*–38 *a*	5	14
	1850	40 *b*–41 *a*	2	last
on the Church.　*See* religion				
and Clarkson	1808	132	3	19
	1851	25 *b*	1	15
on Clarkson	1808	129	2	11
and Mrs. Clarkson	1811	39	6	5
	1813	100 *b*	3	13
	1816	133 *b*		P.S.
	1817	140	3	13

See also her correspondence with Crabb Robinson, i.e. Letters 1811, 42 50, 63, 64, 65, 68; 1812, 69, 76, 80, 86 *a*; 1813, 88 *b*, 89, 90, 95
Sara Coleridge on.　*See* Coleridge, Sara.　Letters

and Cottle's *Early Recollections*	1835	146	3	10
	1836	153	3	10
	1836	163	2	1 seq.
	1839	103	1, 2	
letter to Cottle on opium eating	1836	151	2	5
	1836	153	3	15
	1837	59	1	23
and the *Courier*	1811	42	1	10
	1811	63	2	6
	1847	17 *b*	2	5
[in 1848 vol.]				
	1849	88	2	5
and the Rev. Mr. Curtis	1818	2	1	8
and Mrs. Dashwood	1832	48		
and Sir H. Davy	1849	84 *b*	2	last
death	1834	48	1	15
	1834	49	1	
	1834	53	3	25
	1834	69	3	4
and De Quincey	1834	67	3	16
	1849	84 *b*	1	P.S.
	1849	84 *b*	5	6
on Dryden	1820	101	3	3
[placed as 1814]				
	1817	140	2	25
and the *Eclectic Review*	1812	76	2	5
on Miss Edgeworth	1808	133	2	last seq.
epigram on Rhine wine	1836	160	3	lines upside down
	1836	163	3	8
on factory conditions	1818	8 *a*		
and his family	1817	145	3	
	1834	48	1	18 seq.

COLERIDGE, Samuel Taylor—*contd.*

and his family	1839	103	1	21
	1849	9 *b*–10	5	23 seq.
and Fichte's works	1811	85 *b*	1	11
	1813	100 *b*	2	8
Barron Field on .	1845	18	2	4
financial affairs	1817	145	3	1
	1831	135	3	28
and Frend	1835	120	1	16 seq.
and Hookham Frere	1817	140	1	19
	1817	141	1	13
visits Germany [1828]	1828	74		
	1850	85	1	7
	[in 1849 vol.]			
	1852	7	3	14
and Godwin's *Caleb Williams*	1852	10 *a*	3	1
and Goethe	1816	133 *b*	2	15
	1812	85 *b*	1	5
and *Faust*	1829	94	2	7
	1834	62	3	19
grave in Highgate Cemetery	1843	56–57	4	P.S.
	1851	34	2	5
and J. H. Green	1817	141	1	12
	1848	57 *b*	4	10 seq.
imitated by [Hancox]	1838	5 IX 13		
and Hazlitt	1816	133 *a*	2	last
	1845	86 *a*	2	18 seq.
	[in 1849 vol.]			
	1849	9 *b*–10 *a*	5	15
health	1808	122	1	7
	1811	60		
	1811	62	1	3
	1830	2	3	3
	1830	14	3	37
	1831	154	1	25
	1832	36	3	22
	1833	89	2	12
	1833	91	2	12
	1833	151	2	23
	1834	34	4	2
and hexameters	1840	145	2	8 seq.
	1840	146	2	20
at Highgate	1830	14	3	37
and Jacobi's works	1811	85 *b*	1	11
Jeux d'Esprit, by Southey [?]	1866	77 *b*		
and Johnson	1830	83	2	38
and Kant	1802	3 A 23	3	4
	1802	42	4	15
	1802	51	2	22
	1820	101	2	
	[placed as 1814]			
	N.D.	1 II 35		
and Klopstock	1810	17		P.S.
	1817	141	2	17
and C. Lamb	1811	58	4	8

COLERIDGE, Samuel Taylor—*contd.*

and C. Lamb	1818	18	3	33
	1818	2	1	4
and Mary Lamb	1811	38	4	2
	1818	2	1	4
and W. S. Landor	1834	69	3	4
lectures	1808	119	4	2
	1808	124	1	
	1808	129	1	6 seq.
	1808	130	3	22 seq.
	1808	132		
	1808	133		
	1808	134	1, 2	
	1808	138	2	8 seq.
	1811	58	2	22
	1811	59		
	1811	63		
	1811	64	2	19
	1811	65	1	8 seq.
	1811	66	1, 2 and P.S.	
	1812	68		
	1812	69		
	1812	79	2	26
	1812	87 *a*		
	1818	2		
	1818	18	3	36
	1849	84 *b*		
and Le Grice	1841	75 *b*	2	2
cfed. with Archbishop Leighton	1842	135 *b*	1	2 seq.
	1842	136 *b*	4	1
letters. *See also* Allsop	1836	113	3	27
	1838	36	3	15
and Library of Northern Literature	1820	101	1	14
[placed as 1814]				
Capel Lofft on	1810	17		P.S.
J. Miller on	1850	58 *b*	3	22 seq.
	1850	75	3	6 seq.
	1852	45–46 *a*	2	21
on Milton	1808	133	3	25
	1812	69	1	8
and T. Monkhouse's dinners	1823	93	3	
	1853	55	2	16
and the Montagus	1810	32	2	8
and Thomas Moore's *Lalla Rookh*	1817	140	2	13
and the *Morning Chronicle*	1841	107 *b*	5	16
and the *Morning Post*	1812	68	3	10
	1838	36	3	15
and opium	1813	89	1	18
	1836	153	3	15
on Paley	1843	2 IV *t*	4	1
M. Paravey on	1827	32		
at Penrith	1812	76	1	16
accused of plagiarism	1840	145	1	last seq.
	1840	146	2	10
	1843	70 *b*	2	14

COLERIDGE, Samuel Taylor—*contd.*

accused of plagiarism	1849	9 *b*		
	1852	10 *a*	2	8
	1859	17 *b*	4	22
on politics	1808	123	2	5 seq.
portrait of	1836	153	3	23
	1853	21	1	9
	1854	75 *b*	1	7
and the *Quarterly Review*	1834	62	3	17
on religion and the churches	1836	164 *b*	1	14
	1836	165		
	1839	2 XI 6	1	25
	1843	27 *b*	4	20
	1843	119 *a*	6	3
	1843	119 *b*	3	9
	1845	77	8	13
and Richter's works	1813	100 *b*	3	7
A. Robinson on	1809	15	3	1 seq.
and Crabb Robinson	1808	129	2	9
	1811	38	3	6
	1843	70 *b*	2	14
See also estrangement from Words- worth				
Crabb Robinson on	1797	95	3	18
	1808	156	2	7
	1810	35	1	19
	1811	58	1	12
	1836	165		
	1838	5 IX 13		
	1842	134 *b*	4	12
	1842	135 *b*	1	2 seq.
	1847	30	7	

See also Crabb Robinson's letters
   to Mrs. Clarkson under Cole-
   ridge, S. T., and Clarkson, Mrs.,
   and lectures				

T. Robinson on	1842	133 *a*	1	14
	1842	133 *a*	3	10
	1842	134 *a*	3	4 seq.
	1842	136 *b*	3	18
and Schelling's works	1813	100 *b*	2	14
and Schiller. *See* accused of plagiarism				
and Schlegel	1811	59	2	4
	1849	9 *b*	2	6
on Shakespeare. *See* lectures				
and Mrs. Shelley	1836	131	1	9
and Southey	1808	123	2	5
	1813	88 *c*	1	19
and Spinoza	1801	3 A 14	1	50
	1813	100 *b*	2	1
on Dan Stuart	1848	74	7	13
and Dan Stuart	1849	88	2	6
and William Taylor's *Letter concern- ing the two first chapters of Luke*	1811	41	3	2

COLERIDGE, Samuel Taylor—*contd*.

Thelwall on	1797	95	3	18
and Tieck	1817	140		
	1817	141		
	1829	154	2	7
and *The Times*	1811	59	1	17 seq.
Tupper and	1850	11–12 *a*	4	5 seq.
and Wade	1836	153	3	15
and Wagenroder	1817	141	2	22
and Wall's *Amatonda*	1811	38	3	6
	1811	39	1, 2, 3	
and the Wellesleys	1811	50	1	3
and Wordsworth	1808	122	1	7
	1818	1	2	30
	1836	153	3	23
	1847	30 *a*	7	14
	1850	58 *b*	3	23
	1850	75	3	6
estrangement	1811	42	1	17
	1811	63	2	13
	1811	64	4	1
	1812	76	1, 2	
	1812	79	2	
	1812	80	1	
	1813	88 *b*		
	1813	90	1, 2	
on Wordsworth	1836	153	4	1
and the Wordsworths	1808	129	2	9 seq.
other references	1802	46	1	42
	1812	82 *c*	2	18
	1813	95	2	6
	1822	77	2	6
	1830	83	2	13
	1835	101	1	10
	1835	119	3	21
	1836	103	1	19
	1836	109	4	3
	1836	113	3	27
	1836	168	1	30
	1841	55 *b*	1	7
	1841	107 *b*	5	16
	1842	183	3	1
	1850	11	4	15
	1850	58 *b*	3	23
	1850	75	3	6
	1852	10 *c*	2	4
	1853	55	2	16
	1854	30	5	15
	1856	30 *a*	2	7
	1859	29	3	10
	1866	39 *a*	4	10
WORKS:				
Aids to Reflection	1825	125–126	6	P.S.
	1826	151	4	P.S.

COLERIDGE, Samuel Taylor—*contd.*
  WORKS—*contd.*

Aids to Reflection	1842	130 *b*	2	2
	1842	133 *a*	2	1
	1842	134 *a*	3	last
	1842	135 *b*	1	2
	1842	136 *b*	3	18
	1843	119 *a*	5	24
	1845	78 *b*	2	2
Ancient Mariner	1859	17 *b*	4	last
Biographia Literaria, ed. Coleridge, Sara	1846	32 *b*	3	
	1846	41	5	23
	1847	30 *a*	7	10
	1847 [in 1848 vol.]	17 *b*	1	ll. across
	1847 [in 1849 vol.]	82 *a*		
Christabel	1850	11	4	16
Confessions of an Inquiring Spirit	1842	133 *a*	3	10
Friend, The	1809	4	3	
	1809	9	2	13
	1809	15	3	3
	1811	63	2	8
	1811	64	2	25
	1812	76	2	5
	1821	69	3	8
	1859	17 *b*	4	14
〈Hints towards a formation of a more comprehensive Theory of Life〉, ed. Watson, S. B.	1849	82 *b*–83	1	3 seq.
Literary Remains, ed. Coleridge, H. N.	1836	160	2	14
	1836	163	2	26
	1836	181	3	24
	1848	62 *b*	1	5
	1849	34 *b*–35 *a*	6	16
	1854	2 XI 7	3	13
Notes and Lectures upon Shakespeare ed. Coleridge, Sara	1849	9 *b*		
〈Remorse〉	1812	85 *b*	2	10
Table Talk, ed. Coleridge, H. N.	1836	164 *b*	1	11 seq.
	1836	165		
	1836	181	3	27
	1842	120	1	7
	1859	17 *b*	4	18 seq.
To an Unfortunate Woman	1852	10 *a*	1	
tr. of Wallenstein	1801	22	3	5
	1801	3 A 8	3	35
	1802	46	1	43
	1802	3 A 22	4	10
	1843	70 *b*	2	14
Youth and Age	1852	7	4	11 seq.
	1852	10 *a*	2	2
	1852	10 *c*	2	4

COLERIDGE, Samuel Taylor—*contd.*

LETTERS:

to J. Gooden	1820 [placed as 1814] 101			
to E. Hamond	1812	86 *b*		
to Crabb Robinson	1808	129		
	1811	39; 59; 60; 61 *a*; 62		
	1812	85 *b*		
	1813	100 *b*		
	1816	133 *b*		
	1817	140; 141; 145		
	1818	2; 8 *a*		

COLERIDGE, Sara, Mrs. H. N., on Dr.
Arnold. *See* on Mozeley's review

at Bath	1847	18 *b*–19 *a*	5	19
birth of a son—Herbert	1830	83	3	11
and Dr. Brabant	1848	17 *b*	1	4
on Carlyle and Hare	1849	2 1 K		
and Mrs. Clarkson	1848	73 *a*	3	4
	1852	15 *b*	4	10
See also at Playford				
and S. T. Coleridge and his works	1846	31 *a*	4	7
	1846	32 *b*	1	22 seq.
	1846	41	5	21
	1846	42–43 *a*	9	16
	1847	30 *a*	7	10
	1847	17 *b*	1	ll. across
	[in 1848 vol.]			
	1846	82 *a*		
	[in 1849 vol.]			
	1849	16	7	9
	1849	34 *b*–35 *a*	6	16
death	1852	28		
	1852	29	6	4
and A. De Vere	1852	85	7	15
	[in 1849 vol.]			
and seventeenth-century dramatists	N.D.	2 1 *c*	2	7 seq.
eyesight	1824	137	2	26
and Miss Fenwick	1847	17 *b*	5	6
	[in 1848 vol.]			
financial position	1843	66	2	12
on Froude	1844	122	4	5
	1844	122	1	P.S.
on Hare. *See* on Carlyle and				
health	1825	135	4	12
	1833	91	2	18
	1843	12 *a*	3	1
	1844	7 *a*	4	6
	1845	17 *a*	4	9
	1845	27 *a*	3	15
	1846	42–43 *a*	9	16
	1851	74 *a*	1	10
	1851	74 *b*–75 *a*	7	4
	1851	75 *b*–76 *a*	8	12
	1852	3 *b*–4 *a*	8	12
	1852	6	1	10

COLERIDGE, Sara, Mrs. H. N.—*contd.*

and Landor's works	N.D.	21 *c*	1	4
marriage	1829	158	3	39
	1830	14	3	41
	1833	151	2	27
and her husband's illness	1842	206 *b*	4	10
	1843	5 *b*	3	last
and her husband's death	1843	9 *a*	1	8
on Mozeley's review of Arnold's *Life*	1844	122		
at Playford	1822	86–87	5	P.S.
and Mrs. Plummer	1867	83 *a–b*		
portrait by Lawrence	1852	11	2	10
	1852	12	6	10
and Quillinan	1843	125	1	3
	1846	40 *a*	2	6
	1850	11	8	6
	1850	64	4	19
on religion and church matters	1849	9 *b*–11	6	8 seq.
	1849	21 *b*	4	12 seq.
	N.D.	21 *c*	4	2 seq.
	N.D.	21 *c*	2	P.S.
and Crabb Robinson	1841	69 *b*	2	12
	1843	77 *b*	4	8
	1843	112 *a*	2	20
	1844	5 XVI *d*	2	13
	1846	28	1, 2	P.S. at top
	1847	9 *b*–10 *a*	7	1
	1848	24	2	8
Crabb Robinson on	1843	77 *b*	4	14
	1843	119 *a*	5	18
	1843	119 *b*–120 *b*	5	3
	1843	129 *c*	3	10
	1848	29 *a*	2	5
	1849	1 *a*–1 *b*	6	2
and the Southeys	1841	26	1	11
	1841	31		
	1841	55 *c*	3	4
	1843	33	4	11
	1843	56–57		
	1851	27	2	1
and Dora Wordsworth	1824	106	2	20
	1840	140	2	6
	1845	111 *b*–112 *a*	1	8
	1846	40 *a*	2	3
and the Wordsworths	1829	118	3	11
	1843	85	3	7
	1843	85	4	18
	1847	10 *b*–11 *a*	7	P.S.
	1848	5 *b*–6 *a*	5	7
	[in 1847 vol.]			
	1849	43 *a*	4	9
	1850	11	8	6
on the Wordsworths	1847	17 *b*	3	9 seq.
	[in 1848 vol.]			

COLERIDGE, Sara, Mrs. H. N.—*contd.*

on Wordsworth's poetry	1843	56–57	4	3
	1848	17 *b*	3	9 seq.
	1852	3	4	4 seq.
	[in 1851 vol.]			
Wordsworth on	1846	35	2	7
Mrs. Wordsworth on	1849	16	7	9
other references	1825	136	2	20
	1826	171	4	17
	1840	175	3	28
	1841	10–11–25	7	P.S.
	1841	19 *a*	1	last
	1848	30	1	10
	1849	38	8	7

WORKS:
  ed. *Biographia Literaria.* See
    Coleridge, S. T.
  tr. *Memoirs of the Chevalier Bayard* 1824   137   2   26

LETTERS:
  to J. Kenyon   1845   86 *a*
                        [in 1849 vol.]
  to Crabb Robinson   1840   162 *b*
                        1841   31; 71 *b*; 85 *a*
                        1843   56–57
                        1844   122
                        1846   40 *a*; 56 incomplete
                        1847   [in 1848 vol.] 17 *b*; [in
                               1849 vol.] 82 *a*
                        1848   59 *b*; 62 *b*
                        1849   9 *b*–11; 21 *b* incom-
                               plete; 21 K
                        1851   48; 49
                        1852   3
                        [in 1851 vol.]
                        1852   7; 8; 10*a*; 10*c*; 11; 22*a*
                        N.D.   21 *c*

COLERIDGE, Sara, Mrs. S. T., *born* Fricker   1817   145   3   2
                        1822   86–87   5   P.S.
                        1826   171   4   18
                        1829   118   3   14
                        1829   158   3   39
                        1830   14   3   44
                        1842   206 *b*   4   12
                        1843   12 *a*   3   2 seq.
                        1843   112 *a*   2   19
                        1844   42 *a*   1   20
                        1845   27 *a*   3   14
                        1845   17 *a*   4   8
                        1845   86 *a*   2   17
                        [in 1849 vol.]

COLERIDGE FAMILY   1841   55 *c*   2   12
                        1842   208   3   3
                        1848   26 *a*   1   14
                        1850   74 *a*   1   18

Collier, John Payne

and the Duke of Devonshire	1830	24	2	21
	1830	58	2	47
	1831	92	2	27
	1831	143	1	P.S. upside down
	1832	66	3	21
and family	1830	58	1	40
	1832	66	3	16
	1845	58 *b*	1	20
	1846	10	5	3
	1846	71 *b*–72	5	12
	1848	64	2	21
	1850	67	6	16
	1851	71 *b*	4	1
	1853	33	4	last
	1853	86 *b*–87 *a*	6	11
becomes an F.S.A	1831	92	3	9
and Barron Field	1835	131	2	21
	1836	113	3	12
health	1807	76	1	12
	1844	5 XVI N	8	14
	1855	58 *b*	3	19
and Italian literature	1830	86	2	20 seq.
	1831	92	3	20
move to Kensington	1843	124 *b*	6	9
and Murray	1830	24	2	14
	1830	58	2	43
and the Proctors	1850	66	4	5
and Crabb Robinson	1828	49–50		
	1844	4 *b*	2	12
	1854	3	4	14
Crabb Robinson on	1826	141	2	2
on Tieck	1829	164	1	30
and John Walter	1847	32 *a*	2	27
and Wordsworth	1842	166	3	9
and Wordsworth's poems	1826	141	2	2
	1837	45	2	9 seq.
other references	1829	150	3	1
	1829	150	4	6
	1842	179 *b*	2	11
	1844	19 *a*–20 *a*	6	25
	1844	22 *a*	8	21
	1846	16 *b*–17 *a*	6	1
	1847	29 *a*	5	2
	1848	23 *b*	2	13
	1848	61 *b*–62 *a*	6	4

WORKS:

History of English Dramatic Poetry	1831	92	3	11
	1831	140	2	1
	1831	143	2	21
edn. of Shakespeare	1842	132 *b*	3	11
	1844	50 *a*	1	8
	1844	97 *b*–98 *a*	6	3

COLLIER, John Payne—*contd.*
  WORKS—*contd.*
    edn. of Shakespeare

1845	115 *b*	3	14
1852	7–8	5	17

    LETTERS to Crabb Robinson

1829	164		
1831	92		
1833	149		
1835	83		
1837	45; 54; 61		
1838	2; 24		
1842	166		
1850	20		
1854	83 *a*		
1857	42 *a*		
1859	13 *a*		
1860	6 *b*		

CONSTABLE, John. *See* Leslie
CORNWALL, Barry, pseud. *See* Procter, B. W.
COTTLE, Joseph
    and S. T. Coleridge's letter on
      opium-eating

1836	151	2	5
1836	153	3	13 seq.
1837	59	1	23

    mentioned

1836	147	2	24

    his portraits of Lamb, Southey, and
      Wordsworth

1836	163	1	27

    Crabb Robinson on

1836	151	2	2
1836	152	2	7
1836	153	3	11

    and Talfourd's request for Lamb's
      letters

1836	153	3	12

    The Times and

1847	47 *b*	4	10

    WORKS:
    Alfred

1836	151	2	2
1836	152	2	8

    (*Early Recollections chiefly relating
      to the late S. T. Coleridge*)

1835	146	3	10
1836	153	3	13 seq.
1836	160	3	2
1836	163	2	1 seq.
1836	181	3	17
1839	103	1	2
1847	47 *b*	4	10

    LETTER to Crabb Robinson

1839	103

COWPER, William
    his *Crazy Kate*

1800	5	1	30

    Life. See Hayley
    C. Lofft on

1808	115	3	20

    condition of his mind

1820	7 1 *i*	3	5

    T. Robinson on his works

1803	100	2	20

    other references

1799	136	2	16
1799	146	1	4
1821	62	3	7

CRABB, George
    German and English Dictionary

1804	51	3	3 seq.

CRABB, George—*contd.*
German Grammar

1798	108	1	31
1798	139	4	14
1800	13	3	8
1800	3 A 6	3	1
1801	3 A 11	3	20
1801	22	3	46
1803	3 A 32	4	9

Order and Method of Instructing Children

1801	30	1	34
1801	34	4	27
1801	38	2	41
1803	3 A 32	4	9 seq.

(CRAIK, G. L., and MACFARLANE, C.)
Pictorial History of England   1848 2 IV vii (*a–b*) 8   3
CROSS, Mary Ann (George Eliot).   *See* Evans, Mary Ann
CUDWORTH, Ralph
  mention   1835   101   1   18
  True Intellectual System of the Universe   1806   33   1   1
CUNNINGHAM, Allan
  on Blake in his *Lives of the Most Eminent British Painters*

1848	38 *b*	3	last
1848	43 *b*	1	17

  other references

1827	1	2	6
1841	66 *b*	2	21

D'ARBLAY, Frances [Fanny Burney]
  and S. H. Burney   1843   17 *b*   1   12
  her legacies   1840   141   3   15
  other references

1806	50	4	10
1833	104	3	8
1835	87	2	6

  WORKS:
  Diary and Letters

1842	174 *b*		
1842	201 *b*	1	24

  Evelina   1780   26   1   5 and note
  LETTERS:
  from J. Bryant   N.D.   8 55 IV
  from Mrs. Chapone   N.D.   8 55 II
  from Mrs. Montagu   N.D.   8 55 I
  to Mrs. Thrale   N.D.   [in 1867 vol.] 98; 99; 8 55 III
  from Mrs. Thrale

1780	26
1781	25

DARWIN, Erasmus
  Crabb Robinson on his poetry   1803   28   4   3
    [in 1804 vol.]
  mentioned   1798   113   4   5
  WORKS:
  Botanic Garden

1802	3 A 23	3	44
1802	3 A 24	4	15
1802	3 A 28	3	25

DARWIN, Erasmus—*contd.*
  WORKS—*contd.*
    Temple of Nature   1801   39   2   last seq.
                                    1804   16   1   22
DAVY, Sir Humphry
  Life.   See Paris
  Memoirs of.   See Davy, John
DAVY, John, M.D.
  Memoirs of the Life of Sir Humphry
    Davy, Bart.   1849   84 *b*   3   5
  LETTER to Crabb Robinson   1851   15
DE MORGAN, Augustus
  Rhymes on numbers   1866   77 *a*
  LETTERS to Crabb Robinson   1851   81 *b*
                                    1856   48 *b*
                                    1857   42 *b*
                                    1858   1 *b*
                                    1863   100 *b*; 101 *b*
                                    1866   69 *b*
DE QUINCEY, Thomas
  and *Blackwood's Magazine*   1829   91   3   1
  Mrs. Clarkson on   1854   57 *a*   2   6
  gift to S. T. Coleridge   1836   153   3   18
                                    1839   103   2   5
  and Coleridge's lectures   1849   84 *b*   5   7
                                    1849   88   7   2
  and Lamb   1835   104   1   35
  Crabb Robinson on   1816   135   1   9
                                    1821   69   2   20
                                    1846   23 *b*   1   11
                                    1854   2 XI 7   3   10
  T. Robinson on   1834   67   3   18
  and *Tait's Magazine.*   See *Auto-
      biography*
  and the Wordsworths   1816   135   1   9 seq.
                                    1825   127   4   13
                                    1829   91   4   1
                                    1836   120   1   last
                                    1854   57 *a*   2   6
  on Wordsworth in *Chambers's Journal* 1853   37 *a*   4   2
  WORKS:
    writings   1851   17 *b*   2   3
                                    1854   29   1   7
                                    N.D.   2 1 *i*   2   16
                                    N.D.   2 1 *i*   4   13
    Autobiography in *Tait's Magazine*   1850   2 IV xxvii   8   P.S.
    *Confessions of an English Opium
      Eater*   1821   69   2   21
    Plagiarisms of S. T. Coleridge [as-
      cribed to De Quincey]   1840   145   1   last seq.
    tr. of *Richter*   1821   69   3   1
  LETTERS to Crabb Robinson   1816   128 *a*
                                    1823   94

De Vere, Aubrey Thomas
and Sara Coleridge   1852   85   7   15
                 [in 1849 vol.]
  works:
    Crabb Robinson on   1850   64   5   16
    Letters on the Poor Law in Ireland   1849   88   8   17
    Travels in Turkey   1850   64   6   2
Dickens, Charles
  writings   1852   23 *a*–24 *b*   7   13
                  1855   61 *a*   3   1
                  1855   62   2   15
  other references   1843   135   4   1
                  1847   2 IV x   7   19
                  1848   20 *a*   8   4
                  1849   6   8   17
                  1850   38   5   12
  works:
    (*American Notes for General Circu-
      lation*)   1842   191 *b*–192 *a*   8   4
                  1842   2 1 *j*   3   15
    Barnaby Rudge   1842   134 *a*   3   6
    Bleak (*House*)   1852   23 *a*–24 *b*   7   13
    David Copperfield   1855   61 *a*   3   1
                  1855   62   2   22
    Memoirs of Joseph Grimaldi   1840   141   1   21
Disraeli, Benjamin, Earl of Beacons-
    field
    T. Paynter on   1855   68   5   8
    his politics   1839   100   3   12
                  1846   34   4   4
    Wordsworth on   1839   100   3   12
    mention   1853   26   4   11
  work:
    Sybil   1845   48 *b*–49 *a*   8   19
Disraeli, Isaac
  and Godwin   N.D.   1 VI 2
  works:
    Curiosities of Literature   1835   138   5   11
    Essay on the Literary Character   1837   6   3   20
    Vaurien or Sketches of the Times   1797   102   3   16
Doane, George Washington
  writings   1842   180   6   18
Donaldson, John William
  introduction to Wordsworth   1847   2 IV xxv   1   18
  letters to Crabb Robinson   1847   11 *b*; 21 *a*
                  1848   57 *a*
                  1849   68 *b*; 70 *a*
                  1853   27 *a*; 97
                  1856   16 *b*
                  1858   24 *b*; 1 VIII 20
Donne, William Bodham
  letters to Crabb Robinson   1850   70 *b*; 82 *a*
                  1852   30 *a*; 78 *b*
                  1855   1 VIII 19
                  1866   58 *a*

DUBLIN, Archbishop of.   *See* Trench
 and Whately

DUPPA, Richard
 *Life and Literary Works of Michael
  Angelo Buonarotti*   1807   88   1   7
                                          1808   115   4   12
  LETTERS from Southey   1807   88
  See also Southey letters for publi-   1814   IV 12 [copy]; N.D. IV 6
   cation   [copied extracts only]

DWARRIS, Sir Fortunatus
  LETTERS to Crabb Robinson   1855   29 *b*   32 *a*

DYCE, Alexander
 and Wordsworth   1840   157   5   18
                                          1840   177   1   P.S. at
                                                                   top
  other references   1846 16 *b*–17 *a* 5   7
                                          1848   9 *a*   6   2
                                          1852   74 *b*–75   7   15
                                          1853   26   3   7

  WORK:
  *Remarks on Mr. J. P. Collier's and
   Mr. C. Knight's Edition of Shake-
   speare*   1844   50 *a*   1   12
                                          1844   73 *a*   2   7
                                          1844 97 *b*–98 *a* 6   2

DYER, George   1796   72   1   2nd
                                                                 marginal
                                                                   note
                                          1796   77   4   6
                                          1806   56   1   7
                                          1841   50 *a*   3   7
                                          1854   2 *a*   3   P.S.
  subscription for his widow   1841   50 *a*   3   7
                                          1841   5 *a*   3   7
                                          1841   54
                                          1841   102
                                          1841   103

  WORKS:
  *History of the University and Col-
   leges of Cambridge*   1822   76   2   40
  Life and Writings of Robert Robinson 1796   73   4   P.S. 7
  Poet's Fate   1797   95   3   22 seq.

DYER, John
 Grongar Hill   1800   5   1   28
                                          1835   113

EATON, Charlotte A.
 Rome in the Nineteenth Century   1829   163   1   45
EDEN, Robert.   *See* Philpot
EDGEWORTH, Maria
 Children's books   1802   44   4   28
 Mrs. Clarkson on   1813   95   2   25
 Coleridge on   1808   133   2   last seq.

EDGEWORTH, Maria—*contd.*

description of	1844	24 *a*	3	18
quoted	1804	26	2	17
Crabb Robinson meets	1844	5 XVI *a*	5	12
	1844	5 XVI *b*	3	18
	1844	24 *a*	3	18
T. Robinson on	1844	25 *a*	5	5
other references	1844	42 *b*	4	7
	1850	52	3	4

WORKS:

Helen	1842	184 *b*	1	13
Practical Education	1798	106	3	9
	1802	44	4	28
Tales	1808	111	2	2

EDGEWORTH, Richard Lovell

T. Robinson on	1844	25 *a*	5	9

WORK:

Practical Education	1798	106	3	9
	1802	44	4	28

EDWARDS, Bryan
*History of the British Colonies in the
West Indies*

	1807	78	1	9

EDWARDS, Jonathan

mentioned	1852	45	4	19

WORKS:

Doctrine of Original Sin Defended	1835	101	1	23
	1835	136	1	22 seq.
	1845	124 *b*	2	10
Essay on the Freedom of the Will	1835	89	2	9

ELIOT, George, pseud. *See* Evans, Mary Ann

EMERSON, Ralph Waldo

and the Camden Society	1848	23 *b*	1	4
lectures	1843	65	8	11
	1848	28	8	15
	1848	32	4	17
	1848	33	6	2
H. Martineau on	1848	31 *b*	1	5
and Crabb Robinson	1844	60	4	12
Crabb Robinson on	1848	31 *a*	3	15
	[in 1847 vol.]			
	1848	20 *a*	8	13
	1848	22 *a*	2	1
	1848	32	4	17
	1848	33	6	2
	N.D.	2 IV *q*	2	15
	N.D.	2 IV *q*	4	20
and J. J. G. Wilkinson	1848	27 *b*	1	last
	1849	5 *a*	4	4
other references	1848	24	4	16
	1855	81 *b*	2	10

WORKS:

article on: *Slavery*, in the *Prospective Review*	1845	2 IV *w*	4	15
Essays	1842	125 *a*	4	9 seq.

EMERSON, Ralph Waldo—*contd.*
WORKS—*contd.*
   Representative Men   1849   5 *a*   4   4
                              1850   11   6   P.S.

ENSOR, George
   Independent Man   1826   170   1   27 seq.

ERSKINE, David Stewart, Lord Buchan
   LETTER to Mrs. Masquerier   1822   8 16 11

ERSKINE, Thomas
   Pamphlet: *Causes and Consequences*
      of the War with France   1797   90   3   P.S.
                              1797   91   2   15
                              1797   91   4   1

EUSTACE, John C.
   Tour through Italy   1822   75   2   10

EVANS, Mary Ann, later CROSS, pseud.
   George Eliot
   and Lewes   1859   19   2   4 seq.
                    1859   23 *a*   2   17
   WORKS:
    Adam Bede   1859   19   2   4
                    1859   23 *a*   2   10
                    1863   104   2   4 seq.
    Silas Marner   1863   104   2   4 seq.

FABER, Frederick William   1841   82–83 *b*   6   17
                                  1842   199   2   12
                                  1843   1 *b*   1   16
                                  1843   2   1   11
                                  1843   60   4   11
                                  1843   79–81   1   26
                                  1843   2 VI *s*   1   9
                                  1845   130   2   last
   WORK:
    Sights and Thoughts in Foreign
       Churches   1842   173 *b*   1   10
                    1842   180   4   4
                    1842   209 *b*   2   last seq.

FERGUSON, W.
   History of the Speculative Society
      of Edinburgh   1844   8 *b*   3   16
                    1844   32 *b*   3   6

FERRIER, Susan Edmonstone
   Inheritance   1843   17 *a*   4   20
FIELD, George   1846   19 *a*   2   18
                1846   34   5   20
   WORKS:
    writings   1846   21–22
               1846   2 IV *b*   3   14
    Words of Christ   1851   29   3   12
    LETTERS to Crabb Robinson   1845   86 *b*
                                    1846   7; 17 *b*; 21; 22
                                    1851   26 *b*; 28

FIELD, John
   Treatise on Prison Discipline   1848   78

FLETCHER, Mrs. *See* Jewsbury, M. J.
FONBLANQUE, Albany
   and Copyright Bill

	1839	82 *a*	2	8
	1839	83	2	4

   and W. S. Landor

	1835	94	2	12

   on Landor's *Pericles and Aspasia*

| 1836 | 121 | 4 | 2 |

   W. S. Landor on

| 1834 | 49 | 2 | 1 |
| 1834 | 49 | 4 | 11 |

   and Phillips

| 1849 | 77 | 3 | 11 |

   on Crabb Robinson's *Exposure of*
     Misrepresentations contained in a
     Life of William Wilberforce

| 1840 | 174 | 2 | 8 |

   Crabb Robinson on

| 1844 | 5 XVI *a* | 4 | 7 |
| 1852 | 3 *a* | 4 | P.S. |

   T. Robinson on

| 1844 | 45 *b*–46 | 7 | 6 |

   other references

1842	134 *b*	3	14
1844	38 *b*	2	14
1845	6 *b*	2	12
1846	3 *b*	2	1
1846	47	7	14
1847	48 *a*	7	14
1852	43 *b*–44	10	last
1853	112	7	15
1866	55	1	10

   LETTER to Crabb Robinson

| 1831 | 150 | | |
| 1840 | I VIII 91 | | |

FORBES, John
   Pamphlet. *Mesmerism true, mes-*
     merism false

| 1845 | 27 *a* | 3 | 9 |

FORSTER, John
   and *The Examiner*

| 1835 | 102 | 2 | 2 |

   at Mary Lamb's funeral

| 1847 | 27 | 7 | 9 |

   and W. S. Landor

| 1866 | 37 *a* | 3 | 4 |
| 1866 | 40 *b* | | |

   on Crabb Robinson's *Exposure of*
     Misrepresentations contained in a
     Life of William Wilberforce

| 1840 | 174 | 2 | 6 |

   other references

| 1835 | 86 | 2 | 13 |
| 1846 | 34 | 5 | 7 |

   WORKS:
   article on Charles Churchill in the
     Edinburgh Review

| 1845 | 5 | 3 | 9 |
| 1845 | 7 | 5 | 20 |

   Essays in a Series of Letters to a
     Friend

1805	29	2	17
1828	47	1	19
1828	57	3	8

   LETTERS to Crabb Robinson

1852	32 *a*		
1855	I VIII 79		
1856	19 *b*		
1866	37 *a*; 40 *b*		

FRASER, Peter
   death

| 1852 | 61 | 8 | 1 |

   and Crabb Robinson

| 1842 | 161 *a* | 3 | 12 |
| 1848 | 42 *a* | 6 | 15 |

FRASER, Peter—*contd.*
and Crabb Robinson	1850	12 *b*–13 *a*	7	16
	1850	22	6	21
	1852	21	6	21
	1852	22 *b*–23 *a*	7	14
	1852	23–24 *a*	6	5
Crabb Robinson on	1808	118	3	13 seq.
	1809	3	1	20
	1847	20 *a*	2	22
	[in 1849 vol.]			
	1851	32	2	8
and *The Times*	1808	156	1	20
other references	1848	39 *b*–40	7	5
	1850	22	6	21
LETTER to Crabb Robinson	1851	39		

FROUDE, James Anthony
Sara Coleridge on	1844	122	1	P.S.
	1844	122	4	5
and his family	1849	34 *b*–35 *a*	6	10
	1849	35 *b*	3	16
financial difficulties	1849	32 *a*		
	1849	36	2	12
	1849	44 *b*–45 *a*	8	8
and the Hobart professorship	1849	7	7	5
See also *Nemesis of Faith*				
and the *National Review*	1854	4 *a*	1	6
	1855	18	4	7
and Crabb Robinson	1849	46 *a*	2	12

WORKS:
History of England	1857	26 *b*	3	26
	1857	31	1	13
Nemesis of Faith	1849	21	7	16
	1849	23 *b*–24 *a*	3	7 seq.
	1849	24 *b*		
	1849	32 *a*		
	1849	32 *b*–33 *a*	5	12
	1849	53	2	17
review by Crabb Robinson	1849	35 *b*	3	14
	1849	44 *b*–45 *a*	7	last
	1849	53	2	17

FULLERTON, Lady Georgiana
Ellen Middleton	1844	40	1	27

GALLENGA, A. C. N., pseud. Mariotti
Italy Past and Present	1849	68 *a*	1	13

GARRICK, David. *Life*. See Murphy

GASKELL, Elizabeth Cleghorn Stevenson
meets Wordsworth	1849	2 IV *w*	3	16
mentioned	1849	47–48	1	22 seq. and P.S.

WORKS:
Mary Barton	1853	16 *b*–17 *a*	7	9
Ruth	1853	16 *b*–17 *a*	7	8
Wives and Daughters	1864	23 *b*	3	19

GILCHRIST, Alexander
  and Blake   1855   41 *b*   1   9
                                  1862   49 *b*   1   6
  LETTERS to Crabb Robinson   1855   41 *a*
                                  1860 1 VIII 48
GLADSTONE, William Ewart
  (*State in its Relations with the Church*) 1839   90   3 last seq.
                                  1839   2 XI 6   1   16
GLASSFORD, James
  tr. of Italian *Sonnets*   1835 121–122   1   5
GODWIN, Mary Jane Clairmont   1836   131   1   2
                                  1842   154 *a*   1   7
                                  1845   77   3   8
GODWIN, Mary Wollstonecraft   1803   107   4   3
                                  1804   3 A 36   2   34
                                  1804   3 A 38   1   37
                                  1807   112   2   13
GODWIN, William
  T. Amyot meets   1796   78   2 24 seq.
  attack by I. Disraeli in *Vaurien* 1797   102   3   18
  bankruptcy   1828   57   2   21
  E. H. Barker on   1828   47   4 3 seq.
  death   1836   131   1   3
  on Donne's poems   1810   27
  and Mrs. Fenwick   1807   112   2   22
  and Mrs. D. Gaskell   1843   36 *a*   5   2
  and German philosophy   1802   3 A 26   4   29
                                  1803   3 A 34   1   47
                                  1805   3 A 43   2   17
  and Robert Hall.   *See also* Works:
    Enquiry concerning Political Justice 1804   11   2   44
  and E. Hamond   1819   7 1 *d*   1   19
                                  1850   18   4   16
  and Hartley   1797   89   1 20 seq.
                                  1802   43   1 16 seq.
  Fanny Holcroft on   1797   99   2   26
  and Holcroft   1797   91   1   29
  on Human Perfectibility   1801   38   2   22
                                  1803   115   4   8
  and the *Illuminati*   1801   3 A 8   3 P.S.
  influence waning   1802   51   2   25
                                  1802   51   4 14 seq.
  and Lamb's *Tales*   1807   81
  and Mackintosh   1835   118   2   7
  and Malthus. *See also* and Dr. Parr 1802   3 A 20   4   26
                                  1804   42   2   27
  on marriage   1805   8   4   18
  and Dr. Parr. *See also* and Malthus 1801   3 A 15   3   27
                                  1801   30   1   36
                                  1801   34   4 20 seq.
                                  1828   47   4   3
  portrait   1842   154 *a*
  charge of plagiarism   N.D.   1 VI 2
  quoted   1803   3 A 32   1   21

GODWIN, William—*contd.*

quoted	1847	24	1	21
and Crabb Robinson	1795	61	4 II	7
	1795	86	3	9
	1797	92	2	27
	1797	94	1	2nd marginal note
	1801	25	1	24 seq.
	1801	3 A 10	2	50
	1801	3 A 11	1	48
	1802	3 A 19	4	27
	1804	3 A 36	3	32
	1815	124 *a*	3	5
Crabb Robinson on	1831	138	1	16
	1836	131	4	endorsement
visits T. Robinson	1803	107	4	3
and Rousseau	1804	51	2	37 seq.
and Schelling	1803	3 A 29	1	35
on social conditions	1800	3 A 7	4	6
subscription for	1823	8 43 1		
and Thelwall	1796	78	2	28
and Wakefield	1799	124	1	last seq.
and Weishaupt	1804	3 A 38	2	28
other references	1796	68	4	marginal P.S.
	1796	72	2	4th marginal note
	1796	80	2	7
	1796	84	3	35
	1796	89	3	13, 22
	1797	100	2	18, 29
	1800	11	4	1
	1801	30	1	49
	1803	107	3	30
	1805	4	2	24
	1809	3	1	17
	1811	61	3	17
	1813	100 *a*	1	21
	1819	31	3	11
	1826	164	2	12
	1845	110 *b*	3	9

WORKS:

Antonio	1802	46	1	34
Caleb Williams	1852	10 *a*	2	9
	1852	11 *b*	2	8
Enquirer, The	1797	91	3	9 seq.
	1797	92	3	32 seq.
	1797	94	3	6th marginal note

GODWIN, William—*contd.*
WORKS—*contd.*

Enquirer, The	1797	95	2	P.S. in margin
	1797	96	3	4
	1797	99	1	30 seq.
Enquiry concerning Political Justice	1795	50	2	12
	1795	54	3	last
	1795	64–65	5	marginal note
	1796	70	1	3 seq.
	1796	70	3	7th marginal note
	1796	77	1	22
	1798	116	1	last seq.
	1798	118	1	9 seq.
	1802	51	2	25
	1804	3 A 36	3	28
	1805	8	4	20
Fleetwood	1805	8	4	15 seq.
	1805	3 A 43	4	34
Letter in the *British Critic*	1795	59–60	3	1 and marginal note
Life of Geoffrey Chaucer	1803	74	4	16
	1804	11	2	46
	1804	24	10	4
	1804	26	3	27
St. Leon	1844	97 *b*–98 *a*	4	last
Thoughts on Man	1831	135	4	1
LETTERS to Crabb Robinson	1809	13 *a*; 13 *b*		
	1810	27		
	1823	97; 103; 8	43	1
'Godwinian Style, The'	1795	64–65	1	7
'Godwinism'	1802	61	2	30
'Godwinites'	1796	69	1	last seq.
	1796	70	1	8 seq.
	1796	77	1	15
	1797	101	1	5
	1801	35	4	30
GRANT, Anne, Mrs.				
Letters from the Mountains	1847	3 *b*–4 *a*	6	6
GRAY, John				
Essential Principles of the Wealth of Nations	1797	102	3	15
	1798	110	2	2
GREEN, Joseph Henry				
LETTERS to Crabb Robinson	1836	73 *b*		
	1844	104 *a*		
GREENHOW, T. M.				
(*Medical Report of the case of Miss H. M.*)	1844	7	6	18

GREENHOW, T. M.—*contd.*
  (*Medical Report of the case of Miss*
    H. M.)   1845   9   6   21
                                1845   13   6   1
GROTE, George   1838   110   1   8
                     [in 1836 vol.]
                               1853   40   6   7
                               1853   104 *a*   3   6
                               1853   109 *b*   2   5
                               1866   61 *b*   4   10
  LETTER to Crabb Robinson   1854   36 *b*

HALDANE, James Alexander
  Man's Responsibility   1842   158 *a*   1   16
                               1842   159
                               1842   1 VIII 81

HALL, Samuel Carter
  and the Flaxman Gallery   1851   6 XVIII *n*
HALLAM, Henry   1835   119   2   8
                               1852   78 *a*   3   last
                               1855   69 *a*   2   22
  WORK:
    Constitutional History of England   1827   34–35   5   9

HAMILTON, Captain Thomas
  marriage   1833   164   2   21
                               1834   46 *b*–47   5   4
  mentioned   1836   76   4   5
                               1836   97 *a*   2   1
                               1842   169 *a*   1   12
  WORK:
    Men and Manners in America   1833   117   3   11
                               1833   130   3   17
                               1834   13   1   59
                               1834   34   2   15

HANCOX
  M.S. poems, Crabb Robinson on   1838   5 IX 13
HARDWICK, Earl of.   *See* Yorke
HARE, Julius Charles, Archdeacon
  LETTERS to Crabb Robinson   1832   3
                               1848   46 *a*   67 *b*
                               1850   33 *a*

HARE-NAYLOR, Francis
  (*Theodore or the Enthusiast*)   1805   12   3   16
HARRIS, Thomas Lake
  Herald of Sight   1861   36 *a*
  Lyric of the Golden Age   1856   30 *a*   2   2
                               1856   31 *b*   1   4
                               1856   31 *b*   2   6
                               1856   63 *a*   3   1

HARWOOD, Philip
  German Anti-supernaturalism: six
    lectures on Strauss' *Leben Jesu*   1841   112 *a*   4   5
                               1842   121 *b*   4   2
                               1842   128 *a*   3   1
                               1842   130 *a*–131   4   6

HARWOOD, Philip—*contd.*
Materialism in Religion 1841   55 *b*   1   6
  1841   63 *b*   3   16

HASTED, Edward
History of Kent 1849   42 *b*–43 *b*   2   10

HAYDON, Benjamin Robert
Autobiography, ed. Taylor, T. 1853   82 *b*   3   17
  1853   84 *b*–85 *a*   6   10
  1853   88   7   6

HAYLEY, William
Life of Cowper 1803   94   2   27 seq.
  1804   51   2   28
Memoirs of, ed. Johnson, J. 1825   124   4   P.S.
Triumphs of Temper 1780   26   1   1

HAYS, Mary
Female Biography: or Memoirs of
  Celebrated and Illustrious Women 1801   39   4   6
Historical Dialogues 1806   37   4   P.S.
Memoirs of Emma Courtney 1797   91   1   24 seq.
LETTERS to Crabb Robinson 1802   42
  1804   55
  1806   37
  1807   103
  1842   148 *b*; 154 *a*
from Crabb Robinson 1802   6 XIII *b*; 6 XIII *c*; 6 XIII *d*

HAZLITT, William
T. Amyot on 1806   51
autograph sought 1847   I VIII 54   8   13
character 1805   3 A 43   3   55
and Mrs. Clarkson 1811   48   1   last seq.
  1811   65   4   7
and Coleridge 1816   133 *a*   2   17 seq.
  1845   86 *b*   3   18
  [in 1849 vol.]
  1849   9 *b*–10   5   15
death 1830   58   3   28
  1831   138   1   28
  1831   141   2   3
and the Edinburgh Review 1814   117   3   10
proposed Essays 1810   20   2   6
and the Examiner 1816   135   3   19
and his family 1799   136   4   29
edits Holcroft's Memoirs 1809   16   1   12 seq.
  1809   16   2   7
and E. Irving 1828   57   2   26 seq.
and the Lambs 1809   16   2   19
  1816   135   3   19 seq.
  1823   66–68   11   13
lectures 1811   57   2 seq.
  1811   58   4   9
  1811   65   4   4 seq.
  1811   66   3   4
on Malthus 1808   133   3   11
and B. Montagu 1828   57   2   26 seq.

HAZLITT, William—*contd.*
 and Mrs. Opie   1809   16   1   14
 and Patmore. *See* Patmore, P. G.,
  Personal Recollections
 and Crabb Robinson   1816   133 *a*   2   13 seq.
    1828   57   2   26 seq.
    1836   172–174   5   27
 Crabb Robinson on   1811   65   4   7
    1811   66   3   3
    1811   133 *a*   2   17
    1831   138   1   28
 and T. Robinson   1812   78 *a*   4   P.S.
 on Southey   1816   135   3   19
 Tagart on   1856   17 *b*   2   14
 and Tieck   1829   154   2   9
 and Wordsworth   1816   133 *a*   2   13 seq.
 other references   1799   125   1   29
    1801   3 A 12   4   7
    1805   12   2   23
    1807   76   2   9
    1808   142   2   P.S.
    1827   47   3   25
    1835   134   3   10
    1836   168   2   10

 WORKS:
  Abridgment of The Light of Nature
   Pursued, by Abraham Tucker   1807   85   2   17
  Eloquence of the British Senate   1803   130   3   31 seq.
  Essay on the Principles of Human
   Action   1855   45 *b*   5   3
  Lectures on the Dramatic Literature
   of the Reign of Queen Elizabeth   N.D.   5 IX 9
 LETTERS to Crabb Robinson   1809   16
    1810   20
    1811   48; 57

HEMANS, Felicia Dorothea
 Crabb Robinson on   1836   160   3   11
 Mrs. Wordsworth on   1836   163   2   28
 mentioned   1859   21   6   3
HENNEL, Charles
 Inquiry concerning the Origin of
  Christianity   1845   2 IV *w*   4   4
HENRY, Robert
 History of Great Britain   1796   82   2   44
HERVEY, Lord Arthur
 Genealogies of our Lord and Saviour
  Jesus Christ   1853   97   3   7
HINCKS, W. *New Testament.* *See*
  Taylor, Edgar
HINTON, G. P.
 Apostacy of the Church Established
  by Law   1846   29 *b*
    1846   36
    1846   59
 LETTERS to Crabb Robinson   1846   36; 59

HOBHOUSE, Sir John Cam
   Essay on Italian Literature   1860   20   4   10
HOLCROFT, Thomas
   T. Amyot on   1795   56   3   20
   and Mrs. Collier   1806   64   2   1
   and his family   1799   152   2   22
   and German translations   1803   103   4   1
   visit to Germany   1803   74   4   19
   and Godwin   1797   102   3   18
   and Crabb Robinson   1797   99   2   25
                     1799   125   2   22
                     1800 3 A 2 2   22
                     1806   52   2   last
   on Mme de Staël   1805 3 A 43 4   3
                     1805   8   3   6
   and Wakefield   1799   124   1   17
   WORKS:
   Adventures of Hugh Trevor 1797   96   3   6
                     1801 3 A 11 3   5
   Anna St. Ives   1797   91   1   28
                     1801 3 A 10 4   10
   Autobiography. See Hazlitt, W.
   Hear Both Sides   1803   74   4   22
   Herman and Dorothea tr. 1803 3 A 31 3   34
                     1803   74   2   44
                     1803   74   2   6
                     1803   84   1   19
                     1803   88   2   33
                     1803   100   2   42
                     1803   116   1   45
                     1829   94   1   25
   Road to Ruin   1850   5   8   14
                     1852   61   7   7
   Travels   1805   8   2 11 seq
HOLFORD, M.
   Gresford Vale and Other Poems 1799 136   3   51
HONE, William
   visits Lambs   1811   37 *a* 1   8
   subscription for   1841   20
   his trial, Crabb Robinson on 1817   146   1 11 seq.
     Mrs. Clarkson on   1818   1   1   28
HOOD, Thomas
   and H. Martineau   1844   2 *a* 2   2
   poems   1855 49 *b* 1   6
   WORKS:
   writings   1844   2 *a* 2   2
                     1853   18   2 15 seq.
   Bridge of Sighs   1853   2 *a* 3   12
                     1853   18   1   last
HORNE, Richard Henry
   New Spirit of the Age   1850 2 IV V 1   12
HORNER, Leonard
   Memoirs and Correspondence of
     Francis Horner   1843 24 *b* 4   5

Howitt, William and Mary
  Crabb Robinson on   1852   9   5   4 seq.
Howitt, William
  Rural and Domestic Life of Germany   1843   19   2   32
Hunt, James Henry Leigh
  and Mrs. Clarkson   1811   50   4   6
  C. Lamb on   1823   66–68   11   13
  subscription for   1839   130
  other references   1807   88   1   21
                                              1835   94   2   5
                                              1835   107   1   7 seq.

  WORK:
  Ode to the Queen   1844   37 *b*–38 *a* 5   8
Hunt, Thornton
  and Wordsworth's death   1850   2 IV v   1   12
Hunter, Joseph
  History of Hallamshire   1849   66 *b*–67 *a* 8   7
Hurd, Richard
  mentioned   1795   56   3   33
  Letters on Chivalry and Romance   1796   82   1   note
Hutton, Richard Holt
  LETTERS to Crabb Robinson   1853   121 *a*
                                              1854   58 *a*
                                              1855   32 *b*; 38 *b*; 51 *a*
                                              1856   45 *a*
                                              1859   14 *b*
                                              1864   9 *b*

Inglis, Henry David
  Journey throughout Ireland in 1834   1836   86   3   4
Irving, Edward
  LETTERS to Crabb Robinson   1824   112 *b*
                                              1833   110
Irving, Isabella, Mrs.
  LETTERS to Crabb Robinson   1837   29; 30
Irving, Washington, pseud. Geoffrey Crayon
  *Life and Voyages of Christopher
    Columbus*   1834   45   4   11
Irwin, Eyles
  *Series of Adventures in the course of a
    Voyage up the Red Sea, in Letters
    to a Lady*   1782   27

James, Henry
  Church of Christ not an Ecclesiasticism   1855   81 *b*   2   2
Jameson, Anna Brownell
  Mrs. Aders on   1853   99 *a*   3   25
  and Frau von Goethe   1836   102   2   33
  and H. Martineau   1842 191 *b*–192 *a* 5   29
                                              1843   38 *a*   7   4
  and S. Naylor   1844   105 *b*   4   14
  and Crabb Robinson   1844   5 XVI K   6   8
  Crabb Robinson on   1845   77   2   last seq.
                                              1847   48 *a*   7   17

JAMESON, Anna Brownell—*contd.*
other references   1834   46 *a*   1   10
                                1834   50 *a*   2   1
                                1842   168 *a*–169 *a* 3   2
                                1845   64 *b*–65   7   6
                                1853   86 *b*–87 *a* 7   2
                                1853   116   8   5
                                1857   32 *b*   4   15

WORK:
Celebrated Female Sovereigns 1837   6   4   2
LETTERS:
to Crabb Robinson   1843   137
                                1847   57
                                1848   49 *a*
to George Scharf   1849   18 *a*
JAMIESON, Robert
Popular Ballads   N.D.   5 IX 9
LETTER to Professor Scott   1810   8 25 1
JERROLD, Douglas William   1845   5   3   last
                                1847   2 IV X   7   19
                                1849   15   6   16
JERROLD, William Blanchard   1845   122 *b*–123 10   1
JEWSBURY, Maria Jane
contributions to periodicals   1825   136   2   23
and Alaric Watts   1825   136   2   31
and the Wordsworths   1825   136   2   23
                                1826   144

WORK:
*Phantasmagoria, or Sketches of Life
and Character*   1825   136   2   34
JOHNSON, J.   *See* Hayley
JOHNSON, Samuel.   *Life.   See* Boswell
JONES, Sir William
tr. of *Sakuntala or the Fatal Ring*   1804   3 A 38   3   37

KENNEDY, James
(*Conversations   on   Religion   with
Lord Byron*)   1855   14 *a*   1   3
KENNEY, James   1845   15   2   16
                                1848   29 *a*   2   11
LETTERS to Crabb Robinson   1843   78
                                1846   29 *a*; 30 *a*
KENNEY, Louisa
LETTER to Crabb Robinson   1843   78
KENYON, John
poems   1838   27   3   7
                                1838   36   1   10
Rhymed Plea for Tolerance   1861   32 *a*   3   25
LETTERS to Crabb Robinson   1833   169
                                1835   99
                                1836   125
                                1838   25
                                1839   129 [addressed to Cap-
                                            tain Jones]
                                1840   138

KENYON, John—*contd.*
  LETTERS—*contd.*
    to Crabb Robinson   1841   75 *a*
                     1842   168 *a*; 169 *a*; 172 *a*
                     1843   129 *b*; 133 *a*
                     1845   7; 84 *b* [incomplete]
KINGLAKE, Alexander William
  Eöthen   1847   9 *b*–10 *a*   6   10
KIRBY, William.   *See* Spence
KNIGHT, Charles
  and the *Penny Encyclopaedia*   1842   172 *b*   2   4
                     1844   48 *b*–49 *a*   4   5 seq.
  and the Society for the Diffusion of
    Useful Knowledge   1844   48 *b*–49 *a*   1   4 seq.
    (*Weekly Volumes*)   1844   39 *b*–40   3   23 seq.
                     1844   48 *b*–49 *a*   4   26 seq.
                     1844   86–87 *a*   6   last seq.
  History of the Thirty Years' Peace.
    See Martineau, H.
  Land We Live In   1848   31 *b*   7   last
LAING, Malcolm
  History of Scotland   1801   38   2   49
LAING, Samuel
  Journal of a Residence in Norway   1838   2 IV F   2   1
LAMB, Charles
  and the Aders   1830   51   2   26
  and the *Athenæum*   1835   86   2   6
                     1848   43 *a*   2   9
  autograph   1832   75   1   11
                     1843   103–104   5   19
  and W. Ayrton   1829   142   2   6
  and Mrs. Barbauld   1808   134   3   32 seq.
  and Mary, joint biography sug-
    gested   1835   86   2   1 seq.
  and the British Museum   1827   5 *b*   4   20 seq.
  on Sir Thomas Browne   1829   95 *a*   2   12
  epigram on Byron   1825   133–134   8   P.S.
  character. *See also* opinions of
    particular people   1838   19   3   8 seq.
                     1838   33   1   16
                     1844   31 *b*–32 *a*   6   15
                     1852   56 *a*   1   12
                     1852   64–65
                     1852   67
                     1853   9 *b*–10 *a*   5   8 seq.
                     1867   83 *b*   3   7
  and Mary, and C. Clarkson   1818   18   2   10
                     1818   18   3   30
                     1835   104   1   10 seq.
  and Sara Coleridge   1841   71 *b*   4   9
  and Coleridge   1818   18   3   33
  and J. P. Collier   1826   141   2   4
  J. P. Collier on   1837   45   3   4
  death   1834   78
           1834   79   1   3

LAMB, Charles—*contd.*

death	1835	94	1	2
	1835	101	4	P.S.
	1835	104	1	10
and De Quincey	1835	104	1	33
and the East India House. *See also* Lamb, Mary, and her brother's work	1825	121		
	1825	124	1	8
	1825	125–126	1	15 seq.
	1825	125–126	5	21
	1825	127	3	3
and Mary, move to Enfield	1827	29		
	1827	34–35	6	16
and Mary, leave Enfield for Southampton Buildings	1830	58	3	38
and old English drama	1829	154	1	53
	1829	154	2	4
his epitaph	1835	143	2	19
	1835	146	2	7
and the *Examiner*	1835	86	2	5
and Mary, and Barron Field	1835	86	2	1 seq.
	1835	131	2	13 seq.
Final Memorials. See Talfourd				
financial affairs	1825	120	1	P.S.
	1834	79	3	3
on German literature	1811	38	3	9
and Godwin	1823	97	1	14
and Mrs. Godwin [2nd]	1845	77	3	8
and Mary, on Hazlitt	1811	65	4	6
health	1815	125	3	6
	1816	135	3	13
	1822	75	3	13
	1825	125–126	5	13
	1825	133–134	7	15
	1825	136	1	17
	1826	142–143	1	14
	1826	150	3	11
	1829	5 *b*	4	20
	1832	36	3	22
and W. Hone	1811	37 *a*	1	8
	1835	86	2	6
epitaph on Hume [by C. L. ?]	1830	20	3	53
and Mary, and the Hutchinsons	1825	127	4	23
his insanity	1847	42 *a*	6	8
	1847	47 *b*	3	15
and Mary, move to Islington	1823	66–68	11	4
and E. Isola	1833	135	4	12
and Jeffrey	1861	32 *a*	4	5
and Miss Jewsbury	1825	136	2	39
Dr. W. King on	1853	94 *a*	3	26
	1853	95	1	19
and Mary, and the death of John Lamb	1821	69	1	11
	1821	71–72	4	23
	1822	76	2	23

Lamb, Charles—*contd.*

and Mary, and their mother's death	1840	134		P.S. 16 seq.

and Mary, W. S. Landor and	1831	153	1	17
	1831	154	2	2
	1833	133	1	7
	1833	174	2	25
	1834	11	2	6 of note
	1834	69	3	5
	1834	80	1	5
	1835	94	1	2 seq.
and W. S. Landor's verse	1831	153	1	17
Le Grice on	1839	127	3	2 seq.
letter on a memorial for Clarkson	1827	96		

[in 1867 vol.]

	1835	104	2	5
	1866	60	2	2
letters				
to J. Cottle	1836	153	3	12
	1836	163	2	17
collected for publication. *See also*	1835	86	2	4
Talfourd as Lamb's biographer	1835	104	1	26
	1835	131	2	16
	1835	141	3	16
	1835	143	2	14
	1835	145	3	12
	1835	146	2	14
	1835	148	2	18
	1836	121	2, 3	P.S. upside down
	1836	147	2	26
	1836	153	3	12
	1835	163	2	17
	1836	175	3	6 of P.S.
	1848	13 *b*	4	6
	1848	53 *b*	2	4
Life and Letters. See Talfourd				
position in literature	1847	30 *a*	7	21
C. Lofft on	1810	18		
and C. Lofft's use of C.L. as a signature	1850	84	5	16 seq.
and the *London Magazine*	1821	59	3	20
	1821	69	3	2
	1822	75	3	15
	1832	76	4	1
	1825	120	4	3
	1835	86	2	5
Memoir of. See Procter, B. W.				
and T. Monkhouse	1823	93	3	10
	1824	116	1	4
	1824	116	1	12
	1825	124	3	2

Lamb, Charles—*contd.*

and Moore	1853	39 *b*–40 *a*	8	12
article by Crabb Robinson in the *Athenæum*	1853	54	1	5
	1853	55	1	13 seq.
Moxon suggested as a biographer	1835	86	2	1 seq.
and the *New Monthly Magazine*	1821	59	3	20 seq.
	1826	142–143	1	10
and the *New Times*	1835	86	2	6
and Norris	1827	7 *a*	3	11
(petitions the Benchers for Mrs. Norris)	1827	8 48 1		
obituary in *Longman's* by B. Field	1835	131	2	14
	1836	113	3	25
and Mary, W. H. Pattisson on	1837	50	1	6
personal habits. *See also* and the East India House	1810	35	1	16
	1810	35	3	10
	1830	51	2	29
	1837	59	1	20 seq.
taste in poetry	1861	32 *a*	2	26
portrait by Cary	1858	7		
by Hancock	1836	153	3	25
and *The Reflector*	1811	58	4	7
	1835	86	2	5
religion	1844	31 *b*–32 *a*	6	15
	1852	56 *a*	2	10 seq.
and Crabb Robinson	1817	146	1	7
	1825	139	1	3
	1830	51	2	26
	1834	48	2	8
	1850	85	5	16
and Mary, Crabb Robinson's gift to	1829	103		
	1836	121	2, 3	P.S. upside down
	1846	32 *b*	1	16
Crabb Robinson on. *See also* Lamb and Moore	1847	30 *a*	7	21
and Mary, Crabb Robinson on	1847	47 *b*	3	15 seq.
	1848	42 *b*	1	last
and Mrs. T. Robinson. *See also* verses to	1833	135	4	11
and Mr. Rooper	1847	45	6	12
	1847	47 *a*	4	4
and R. Southey. See *Letter of Elia*				
Southey on	1844	31 *b*–32 *a*	6	15
lends Stoddart the *Excursion*	1814	110	3	8
suppers in Great Russell Street	1865	24 *a*	1	10
and Talfourd. *See* letters for publication, and Talfourd, *Final Memorials* and *Letters of Lamb*				
L. Tieck and	1829	154	1	53 seq.

LAMB, Charles—*contd.*

and Mary, dislike of travelling	N.D.	37 *a*		
	[in 1810 vol.]			
	1825	125–126	5	16 seq.
will	1834	79	3	4
and N. P. Willis	1834	80	1	8
	1835	146	3	20
and Wordsworth's works	1814	110	3	8
	1826	142–143	1	18
	1825	147	4	9
	1826	152	3	27
and the Wordsworths	1808	122	1	2
	1816	135	3	19
	1822	76	2	1
	1822	76	4	16
	1825	127	3	21
	1835	43	2	11 seq.
and Mary, and the Wordsworths	1810	32	2	17 seq.
	1821	71–72	4	24 seq.
	1822	77	4	8
	1822	86–87	4	28 seq.
	1824	115	3	1
	1825	124	1	11
	1825	136	1	17
	1826	171	3	23
	1829	118	4	4
	1830	14	3	32
	1833	91	2	22
	1833	164	4	5
	1835	145	3	10 seq.
and Mary, Wordsworth on	1835	143	2	14 seq.
	1835	148	3	9
	1840	134		P.S.
other references	1810	32	1	last
	1827	1	1	20
	1830	83	3	15
	1836	109	4	3
	1847	27	6	15
	1847	28 *b*	2	P.S.
	1848	61 *a*	2	5
	1866	60	2	P.S.
and Mary, other references	1808	132	3	P.S.
	1812	86 *a*	2	20
	1814	110	3	8
	1821	54	4	5
	1821	55	1	P.S.
	1821	59	3	18
	1824	116–117	8	7
	1825	120	3	last
	1825	165	4	1
	1828	104	3	7
	[in 1818 vol.]			
	1829	127	3	3
	1833	89	2	10
	1833	115	2	1

Lamb, Charles—*contd.*

and Mary, other references	1834	65	3	15
	1834	69	2	21
	1849	44 *b*	4	12

works:

writings:

American appreciation	1833	98	1	8
new edition	1836	101	1	4
sale of	1837	69–70	5	last
unpublished poems	1835	131	2	19
and Mary, writings	1828	42		
	1833	98	1	8
	1838	4 *a*		
	1838	33	1	12
	1848	38 *b*	2	13
	1852	58	3	7 seq.
	1852	64	1	3 seq.
	1853	54	1	7
	1859	7	1	18
	N.D.	2 1 *g*	2	3
Adventures of Ulysses	1853	54	1	12
Album Verses	1830	51	2	last seq.
	1830	75	3	43
Dissertation upon Roast Pig	1852	58	3	14 seq.
Essays of Elia	1822	86–87	4	28
	1833	174	2	28
	1853	55	1	15

Letter of Elia to Robert Southey, Esq.

and the attack which occasioned it	1823	66–68	11	7
	end 1821			
	1852	67	2	15
	1857	1	5	P.S.
Mr. H—	1806	71	3	P.S.
Mrs. Leicester's School	1809	4	2	20
	1811	42	3	12
	1828	42	1	13
	1833	133	1	9
	1835	86	2	7
	1835	101	4	P.S.
	1851	63	5	14

On the Genius and Character of Hogarth

Hogarth	1811	58	4	7
South Sea House	1838	4 *a*	1	10
and Mary, *Tales from Shakespeare*	1807	81		
verses	1827	34–35	7	
to Sarah Robinson	1831	105		
	1831	120	4	19
(Wife's Trial)	1829	118	4	6 seq.

letters:

to Mrs. Montagu	1827		96
	[in 1867 vol.]		
to Crabb Robinson	1808	122	
	1809	5	

LAMB, Charles—*contd.*
  LETTERS—*contd.*

to Crabb Robinson	1820	44; 47	
	1824	118	
	1825	121	
	1827	8 48 1; 6; 7 *a*; 25 *b*; 29	
	1828	44 *a*	
	1829	95 *b*; 103; 111 *a–b*	
to T. Robinson	1822	84	
to Talfourd	1828	75 *a*	
to Wordsworth	1807	81; N.D. [in 1810 vol.]	
		37 *a*	

LAMB, Mary Ann. *See also* Lamb,
  Charles and Mary

and her brother's death	1834	79	2	2
	1835	143	13	10
arrangements for, after her brother's				
death	1834	79	3	4
	1835	93		
	1836	181	2	27
	1839	73	1	6 seq.
	1842	132 *a*	2	4
	1844	7 *a*	5	10
and her brother's work at the East				
India House	1835	146	2	11
	1835	148	3	9
and Sara Coleridge	1841	71 *b*	3	19
	1841	85 *a*	4	17
and Coleridge	1811	38	4	1
	1813	90	1	3
death	1847	26 *b*	3	5
funeral	1847	27	6	9
	1847	28 *b*	2	P.S.
health	1809	16	2	19
	1810	32	2	17
	1810	35	1	14
	1810	35	3	12
	N.D.	37 *a*	1	4
[in 1810 vol.]				
	1811	38	4	1
	1815	125	3	6
	1816	135	3	13
	1821	69	2	9
	1821	70	1	5
	1822	75	3	13
	1822	86–87	4	last
	1823	66–68	11	5
endorsed 1821				
	1825	120	1	P.S.
	1825	125–126	2	8
	1825	125–126	5	19
	1825	133–134	7	17
	1825	135	1	19
	1825	136	1	20
	1826	150	3	11

LAMB, Mary Ann—*contd.*

health	1827	29	1	4
	1827	34–35	6	14
	1829	5 *b*	4	20
	1829	142	2	6
	1830	20	3	53
	1830	58	3	40
	1830	83	3	17
	1832	36	3	22
	1833	115	2	2
	1833	125	1	21
	1833	133	1	7
	1833	151	2	29
	1833	174	2	25
	1834	34	4	1
	1834	65	3	15
	1834	78	1	last
	1834	79	2	2
	1835	118	1	13
	1835	141	2	15
	1835	146	2	2
	1836	104	4	17
	1836	106	4	P.S.
	1836	121	3	P.S. upside down
	1836	160	2	9
	1837	67	3	10
	1837	69–70	5	18
	1839	107	2	7
	1840	164 *a*	2	18
	1840	179 *b*	2	17
	1841	69 *b*	2	13
	1842	180	6	14
	1842	185 *b*	4	9
	1844	103 *a*	1	P.S.
	1845	129	4	12
	1846	42–43 *a*	10	12
	1846	164 *b*	4	1
	[in 1840 vol.]			
	1847	10 *b*	2	8
	N.D.	8 1 1	2	2
and housekeeping	1830	14	3	32
Landor's verses to	1835	94	1	18
religion	1844	31 *b*–32 *a*	6	14
and Crabb Robinson	1829	111 *b*	3	P.S.
	1834	48	2	8
	1839	107	2	7
	1839	121	1	16
	1842	132 *a*	1	last
	1844	31 *b*–32 *a*	6	11
and the Talfourds	1828	75 *a*	1	2
	1830	58	3	40 seq.
and the Wordsworths	1813	90	1	3
	1835	118	1	13
	1835	105–106	5	15

LAMB, Mary Ann—*contd.*

and the Wordsworths	1835	111	2	last of P.S.
	1835	146	2	2
	1838	67–68	4	21
	1843	47–48	5	6
	1845	126 *b*	4	11
	1845	129	4	17
other references	1843	5 *b*	5	12
	1843	112 *a*	4	12

LANDOR, Walter Savage

and Lady Blessington	1832	52	3	13
	1835	94	3	9
	1836	122	1	last
	1836	123	3	15 seq.
and Byron	1830	60	4	1
and H. F. Cary	1833	174	2	34
on contemporary poets	1831	154	1	19 seq.
	1834	49	1	1
	1834	69	3	1
and the Copyright Bill	1831	154	1	21
	1839	85	1	10
on Dryden	1834	80	1	12
and John Forster	1866	37 *a*	3	4
	1866	40 *b*		
and Goethe	1834	69	3	3
	1836	168	1	25
and Archdeacon Hare	1832	3		
and T. J. Hogg	1836	130		
and John Kenyon	1833	169		
	1834	25	1	9 seq.
	1836	123	3	15 seq.
	1836	125	2	1
and Charles and Mary Lamb	1831	153	1	17
	1831	154	1	2
	1833	133	1	7
	1833	174	2	25
	1834	11	2	6 of note
	1834	69	3	5
	1834	80	1	5
	1835	94	1	2 seq.
letters to be published	1866	40 *b*		
and the Hon. Frances C. Mackenzie	1831	94	3	11 seq.
	1831	125	2	17
on politics	1834	49	1	23 seq.
	1835	107	2	12
and his publishers	1831	149	2	19
	1831	153		
	1832	3		
and the Pyrenees	1828	81	1	7
attack by Quillinan (*Imaginary Conversation between W. S. Landor and the Editor of Blackwood's Magazine*)	1843	8	1, 2	
	1843	11	3	

LANDOR, Walter Savage—*contd.*

attack by Quillinan, etc.	1843	24	1	5
	1843	25		
	1843	26	1, 2	
	1843	27 *b*	2	
	1843	28 *a*	2	9
	1843	29		
	1843	30 *a*	2	1
	1843	23–34	6	1
	1843	47–48	3	21
and Crabb Robinson	1830	45	4	19
	1830	60	3 seq.	
	1830	70	2	26
	1830	86	3	10
	1831	133	1	17
	1831	133	3	46
	1831	151	3	13 seq.
	1832	52	3	13
	1833	169	1	2
	1835	146	3	21
	1837	39	2	17
	1839	90	1	16
	1844	16 *a*–17 *a*	8	1
	1846	68	6	13
	1847	15	2	6
	1850	32	5	24
	1851	59	4	14
	1851	65	6	4 of P.S.
Crabb Robinson on	1830	60	3 seq.	
	1831	98	3	3 seq.
	1831	151	3	13 seq.
on Crabb Robinson	1831	94	3	11 seq.
and Sir James Ross's Arctic crew	1849	77	3	16
on Sir Walter Scott	1834	69	3	3
on Spenser	1834	80	1	20
and Southey	1830	60	3	32
	1831	149	3	22
	1840	144	4	7
	1851	8	2	last seq.
on the sonnet	1833	174	2	39
	1834	19	3	19
and Mrs. Southey (Caroline Bowles)	1843	47	3	14
and the Southeys	1851	8	2	last seq.
and Miss Spender	1853	16 *b*–17 *a*	8	10
and N. P. Willis	1834	80	1	2
	1835	146	3	21
	1836	121	3	14 seq.
and Wordsworth	1830	60	3	31, 40
	1831	149	3	21
	1831	151	3	27
	1831	151	4	2
	1832	15	4	4

LANDOR, Walter Savage—*contd.*

and Wordsworth	1833	174	2	37
	1834	19	3	5, 19
	1834	80	1	10
	1835	107	2	8
	1836	121	3	14
	1836	123	3	15
	1839	90	1	16
	1847	16	1	18
	1851	8	2	last seq.
	1866	40 *b*	2	5
Wordsworth on	1836	119 *b*	2	16

WORKS:

writings:	N.D.	21 *c*	1	4
lines for Lady Blessington	1835	94	4	
Citation and Examination of William Shakespeare	1834	69	3	6
	1835	94	2	13
	1835	107	1	35
article on the Copyright question	1839	85	1	10
Four Willies	1835	107	1	9
(*Gebir*)	1836	172–174	4	4
	1836	172–174	6	11
	1843	47–48	4	19
High and Low Life in Italy	1831	149	2	3 seq.
Imaginary Conversations	1830	60	3	9 seq.
	1830	70	2	26
Imaginary Conversation between Southey and Porson	1842	200 *b*	4	1
	1843	8	1, 2	
	1843	24	1	5
	1843	25		
verses to Mary Lamb	1835	94	1	18
Letter to Cuthbert Southey	1851	8	2	last
Pericles and Aspasia	1836	119 *b*	2	16
	1836	121	3	15
Satire upon Satirists	1836	168		
	1836	172		
	1836	174		
	1843	11	3	7
Ode to Southey	1833	169		
	1834	11	2	1 of note
	1834	19	3	23
	1834	25	1	18 seq.
Ode to Wordsworth	1834	11		
	1834	19	3	21
	1834	25	1	7 seq.
	1843	30 *a*	2	12

LETTERS:

to Crabb Robinson	1831	109; 121; 149; 153–154
	1832	59
	1833	133; 175
	1834	11; 49; 80
	1835	94; 107

LANDOR, Walter Savage—*contd.*
  LETTERS—*contd.*
    to Crabb Robinson   1841   72
                               1844   16 *a*
                               N.D.   I II 32
    from Crabb Robinson [copies]   1834   25
                               1836   168; 172; 174
LANE, Edward William
  Manners and Customs of the Modern
    Egyptians   1838   19   3   24
LAYARD, Sir Austen Henry
  Nineveh and its Remains   1849   12   6   13 seq.
                               1849   16–17   5   7
                               1849   29   1   9
                               1849   75   7   9
  LETTERS to Crabb Robinson   1840   183
                               1842   198
                               1846   38–39
                               1851   82 *a*
                               1853   I VIII 7
                               1854   I VIII 11
                               1864   I VIII 9; I VIII 10
                               N.D.   I VIII 8
LE GRICE, Charles Valentine
  and the Bishop of Exeter   1844   113   5   21
                               1844   114   2   18
  and his father's affairs   1843   101 *b*   6   9 seq.
                               1843   105 *b*   5   12 seq.
                               1843   107 *b*   4   5
  and C. Lamb   1853   55   1   18
  Quillinan on his poetry   1850   I *b*–2 *a*   6   24
  Crabb Robinson on   1841   55 *b*   4   11
  mentioned   1841   78 *b*   1   20
                               1849   39   4   4
  LETTERS to Crabb Robinson   1837   32
                               1839   124; 127
                               1841   68 *a*; 75 *b*
LE GRICE, Charles Vœux [Valentine?]   1866   60   2   P.S.
LESLIE, Charles Robert
  Memoirs of John Constable   1847   20   4   8
LEWES, George Henry
  and Mary Ann Evans [G. Eliot]   1859   23 *a*   2   17
  family affairs   1859   19 *a*   2   last
  WORKS:
    article on Goethe in the *British and*
      Foreign Review   1842   207   1   2 seq.
    Life of Goethe   1856   12 *b*   3   last seq.
  LETTER to Crabb Robinson   1855   90 *a*
LEWIS, Matthew Gregory
  Ambrosio, or the Monk   1802   3 A 20   2   17
  Tales of Wonder satirized, in *More*
    Wonders by Moonshine [pseud.]   1801   23   3   3
LEWIS, Miss
  Woman's Mission   1847   I *a*–2 *a*   6   2

LINDLEY, John
  LETTER to Crabb Robinson   1834   33
LINGARD, John
  History of England   1837   41   4   8
LITTLEWOOD, W. E.
  Essentials of English History   1866   39 *a*
LLOYD, Charles
  Edmund Oliver   1798   133   4   2
LOCKHART, John Gibson
  and J. W. Donaldson   1847   21 *a*   1   4
  his publication of Scott's letter to
    W. Smith   1838   39 *a*   2   17
        1838   65   6   9
        1838   69   3   6
  and Wordsworth's sonnet   1845   16 *b*   1   13
LOFFT, Capel
  Autobiography   1802   61   4   8
  epitaph for Sarah Lloyd   1800   14
  Sonnets *To the Comet*   1807   68   2   14
        1807   102   3   18 and P.S.
        1807   104
  and sonnet writing   1809   8   1   21
  LETTERS [1]:
    to Crabb Robinson   1806   33
        1807   68; 75; 104
        1808   115; 117
        1809   8; 14 *a–b*
        1810   17; 18; 23
        1811   47, 3; 54
        1812   73; 75
        1813   88 *a*
        1814   106
        1817   139 *a*
    to T. Robinson   1808   150
        1812   77
LOFFT, Capel, jun.
  Ernest   1839   86
        1839   100   4   13
  his edition of the *Self Communion*
    of Marcus Aurelius   1862   70
  LETTERS to Crabb Robinson   1838   29 *a*; 44 *a*
        1839   86
        1862   70; IV 6
LYTTON, Edward George Earle Lytton
  Bulwer, Lord
  character   1843   73   3   1
  W. Wordsworth on   1852   19 *b*–20 *a*   7   12
  WORKS:
    writings: Barron Field on   1843   70 *b*   3   1 seq.
    articles on Schiller in *Blackwood*   1843   70 *b*   3   1
    Last Days of Pompeii   1835   121   3   2

[1] Owing to the difficulty of the handwriting, Capel Lofft's letters are very imperfectly indexed.

MACAULAY, Thomas Babington, Lord

L. Aikin and	1843	22	7	1 seq.
health	1853	40 *b*–41 *a*	2	3
reforms in India	1844	107 *b*	1	20
on Locke	1856	17 *b*–18 *a*	5	8
on Penn	1858	1 *b*	4	2
E. Quillinan on	1843	79–81	2	27 seq.
	1843	79–81	5	1 seq.
	1849	42 *b*–43 *b*	6	20
Crabb Robinson on	1843	83 *b*–84 *a*	2	11 seq.
	1843	83 *b*–84 *a*	5	last
	1853	47 *b*–48 *a*	6	13
T. Robinson on	1844	36	5	2 seq.
	1845	74 *b*	3	9
	1850	16	6	13
speech on the Scotch Church	1845	74 *b*	3	9
other references	1838	58 *a*	1	9
	1843	83 *b*–84 *a*	10	6
	1843	119 *b*–120 *b*	7	18
	1847	46	2	13
	1850	67	2	16

WORKS:

History of England	1849	2 1 *b*	4	3
	1849	26	1	11
	1850	16	6	13
	1850	17	3	2
	1850	65	4	8

Articles in the *Edinburgh Review*:

Addison	1843	22	7	3
	1843	79–81	2	27 seq.
	1843	79–81	5	1 seq.
(*Barère*)	1844	36	5	2 seq.
Clive	1843	79–81	5	27
Gladstone's, *State in its Relations with the Church*	1839	90	3	19 seq.
Machiavelli	1827	11 *a*	1	13
Ranke's *History of the Popes*	1843	83 *b*–84 *a*	5	last seq.
	1843	87 *a*	3	8

MacDONALD, George

syllabus of his lectures	1859	5 X 28		
Unspoken Sermons	1867	83 *b*	4	6
Within and Without	N.D.	5 IX 9		
LETTERS to Crabb Robinson	1859	5 X 28; 14 *a*; 20 *b*		
	1863	82 *b*		
	1865	28*a*		

MacFARLANE, C. *See* Craik

MACKINTOSH, Sir James

and Sara Coleridge	1849	88	7	last seq.
Life. See Mackintosh, R. J.				
Memorandum of his Lecture on the British Constitution	1799	122		

MACKINTOSH, Sir James—*contd.*
 WORKS:

Discourse on the Study of the Law of Nature and Nations	1799	152	2	9
History of England	1832	46	3	3
LETTER to [?]	1807	8 22 II		

MACKINTOSH, R. J.

Life of Sir James Mackintosh by his Son	1835	118	2, 3	
	1835	131	3	1
	1836	101	3	4

MAITLAND, Samuel Roffey

Dark Ages, The	1844	111 *a*	3	17
	1845	10	5	18

MALTHUS, Thomas Robert

Essay on the Principle of Population	1801	22	3	50 seq.
	1801	34	4	22
	1803	115	4	7

MANNING, James

Inquiry into the nature and character of the Possessive Augment	1864	17 *a*	4	5

MANTELL, Gideon Algernon

(*Fossils of the South Downs*)	N.D.	8 44 III	I	7
LETTERS to Masquerier	N.D.	8 44 III		
	N.D.	8 44 IV		

MARIOTTI, pseud. *See* Gallenga

MARSH, Anne Caldwell

Two old Men's Tales	1844	9 *b*–10 *a*	7	6

MARSH, Charles

Clubs of London [attributed also to J. Adair]	1828	47	3	7

MARTIN, Frances

Springtime with the Poets	1866	50 *b*	2	2
LETTER to Crabb Robinson	1866	50 *b*		

MARTINEAU, Harriet

at Ambleside	1845	78 *b*–79 *a*	7	25
	1846	28	3	3
	1846	46	I	17
	1847	56	7	9
	1848	2 IV vii (*a–b*)	7	10
	1849	16–17	11	4
and American affairs	1843	9 *b*–10 *a*	5	18 seq.
	1843	117 *b*	1	14 seq.
	1843	119 *a*	8	8
	1844	39 *b*–40	9	
	1844	48 *b*–49 *a*	5	21
	1847	6 *b*–7 *a*	6	6
	1850	50 *b*–51	2	18
American view of	1838	30	4	4
and Mrs. Arnold	1842	174 *a*	1	5
	1842	175 *a*	3	19 seq.
	1842	180	3	last
	1844	91 *a*–92 *b*	3	10
	1845	13	5	13 seq.
and the Arnolds	1845	61 *b*–62	8	15
	1850	50 *b*–51	9	7

MARTINEAU, Harriet—*contd.*

and the *Athenæum*	1845	23 *b*	6	19
	1845	24	1	23
	1845	27 *a*	2	12
	1849	16–17	14	P.S.
and H. G. Atkinson	1846	92	8	13
	[in 1864 vol.]			
	1851	21 *b*–22 *a*	7	11
and C. Brontë	1850	1 *b*–2 *a*	8	P.S.
on Brougham	1843	37	10	8
on Lord and Lady Byron	1842	191 *b*–192 *a*	5	27 seq.
	1843	9 *b*–10 *a*	4	11 seq.
and Lady Byron's pamphlet	1842	207	1	10
	1843	9 *b*–10 *a*	4	11
on Mrs. Chapman	1850	50 *b*–51	1	7
Mrs. Clarkson on	1843	124 *a*	1	3 seq.
	1844	24 *b*	1	12
	1845	134	4	12
	1851	70 *b*–71 *a*	1	last
and Hartley Coleridge	1849	16–17	14	P.S.
and the Copyright Bill	1837	67	1	9
and Craik's *Pictorial History of England*	1848	2 IV vii(*a–b*)	8	3
her ear-trumpet	1846	51 *a*		P.S. 5
visit to Egypt	1846	57 *a*	2	8
	1847	30 *a*	4	13
and Emerson	1848	22 *a*	2	8
on Emerson	1848	31 *b*		
31 *b* quoted	1848	32	5	4
on factory conditions	1844	39 *b*–40	10	7
and her family	1845	61 *b*–62	3	4 seq.
	1845	80 *a*	2	16
	1846	33	2	1
	1846	50	4	12
and Miss Fenwick	1845	10	1	15 seq.
	1845	61 *b*–62	8	11
	1845	64 *b*–65	7	18
	1845	77	2	last
	1845	117 *b*	5	2
	1850	50 *b*–51	8	8
on Mrs. Follen	1850	50 *b*–51	1	7 seq.
Mrs. Follen on	1851	40 *b*–41 *a*	2	2
on Lady G. Fullerton	1844	39 *b*–40	5	28
and T. M. Greenhow's (*Medical Report on the case of H. M.*)	1844	7	6	18
	1845	9	6	21
	1845	13	6	1
visit to the Gregs	1845	9	6	2
	1845	14	6	3
health. *See also* her letters to Crabb Robinson	1842	172 *b*	4	21
	1844	88	5	15
	1844	90	2	4
	1844	91 *b*–92 *a*	3	10
	1844	93	7	13

MARTINEAU, Harriet—*contd.*

health, etc.

1844	100 *b*–101	6	18
1844	104 *b*	3	6
1844	106 *b*	3	last
1844	109	5	3
1844	113	3	18 seq.
1844	114	1	14
1844	115	2	13
1844	116	3	8
1844	118 *a*	4	10
1844	118 *b*	2	13
1845	8	4	17
1845	9	6	4 seq.
1845	10	1	15
1845	14	2	4
1845	20 *a*	3	11
1845	91	3	16
1845	110 *a*	3	1
1845	130 *b*–131 *a*	5	11
1849	51	3	6
1852	51	6	8
1855	67	8	8

and Hood's review of *Life in the Sick Room*

1844	2 *a*	2	2

building a house

1845	87 *a*–88 *a*	6	2
1845	91	3	1 seq.
1845	110 *a*	2	13
1846	92	1	18

[in 1864 vol.]

lets her house

1846	54	1	3
1850	50 *b*–51	7	5
1851	33	2	13

and *Household Words*

1850	57 *b*–58 *a*	5	15

and Mrs. Jameson

1842	191 *b*–192 *a*	5	30

and Jardine

1844	86–87 *a*	5	4

on Knight

1844	48 *b*–49 *a*	1	4 seq.

and Knight's ⟨*Weekly Volumes*⟩

1844	39 *b*–40	3	23 seq.
1844	48 *b*–49 *a*	4	26 seq.
1844	86–87 *a*	6	last seq.

lectures

1848	29 *b*	5	8

on the privacy of letters

1843	9 *b*–10 *a*	1	16 seq.
1843	37	4 seq.	
1843	65	1	21 seq.
1843	128 *b*	5	17
1844	2 *a*	6	11
1845	61 *b*–62	9	9
1845	77	6	9

and C. Lofft, jun.

1838	29 *a*	1	8

in London

1849	77	4	12

and James Martineau

1844	22 *a*	4	9
1844	39 *b*–40	10	27

and Maria Martineau [niece]

1864	6 *b*	4	6

and mesmerism. *See also* health, and *Letters on Mesmerism*

1845	2 IV *w*	1	23

Martineau, Harriet—*contd.*

and mesmerism, etc.	1846	1	3	4
	1846	25 *a*	3	16
	1846	92	5	4
[in 1864 vol.]				
and Mme Mohl	1850	45	3	8
on Newman's *Phases of Faith*	1850	50 *b*–51	3	16
pension	1842	172 *b*	4	17
	1842	191 *b*–192 *a*	9	27
	1842	195 *b*	4	15
	1842	199	3	
and politics	1843	65	8	23
	1843	117	6	6 seq.
	1845	132 *b*–133 *b*	4	2
	1846	1	5	17
	1850	50 *b*–51	7	14
Richmond's portrait of	1849	2 1 *b*	3	3
and E. Quillinan	1848	29 *b*	4	8
	1848	37 *b*–38 *a*	6	3
	1848	38 *b*–39 *a*	4	21
	1849	44 *a*	2	25
	1849	51	3	6
	1850	74	4	8
E. Quillinan on	1842	199	3	
and Mrs. Reid	1841	2	4	1
	1841	79 *a*	1	23
	1841	170	2	1
	1842	169 *c*	3	11
	1842	191 *b*–192 *a*	9	17
	1843	65	5	4
	1843	128 *b*	3	1
	1844	86–87 *a*	9	6
on Robberd's *Memoirs of W. Taylor*	1844	5 xvi *a*	7	2
and Crabb Robinson	1846	164 *b*	1	7
[in 1850 vol.]				
	1841	4 *a*	4	9
	1841	9 *a*	1	5
	1842	169 *c*	3	11 seq.
	1842	181 *a*	1	5 seq.
	1844	3 *b*	5	25
	1846	2	5	10
	1846	28	3	3
	1847	29 *a*	8	19
	1850	57 *b*–58 *a*	5	9
	1855	67	8	8
	1864	84	1	2
Crabb Robinson's gift to	1846	28	3	11 seq.
	1846	33	1	8
	1846	51 *a*	1	15
	1846	57 *a*	1	5
	1846	92	3	21
[in 1864 vol.]				
Crabb Robinson on	1841	170	2	3 seq.
	1842	172 *b*	4	
	1843	119 *b*–120 *b*	5	last

MARTINEAU, Harriet—*contd.*

Crabb Robinson on	1844	5 XVI 4	2	10
	1845	17 *a*	4	14
	1845	27 *a*	2	12
	1845	77	2	last
	1845	77	4	6
	1845	87 *a*–88 *a*	6	2
	1845	87 *a*–88 *a*	9	8
	1845	130 *b*–131 *a*	4	25
	1846	1	3	4 seq.
	1846	2	5	10
	1846	8	3	6
	1851	61	6	19
	1852	2 IV *p*	7	12
	1853	102 *b*	2	6
T. Robinson on	1848	76	5	14
on Mrs. Sigourney	1843	37	8	23
on slavery. *See* and American Affairs				
and Julia Smith	1841	2	1	4
	1842	121 *a*	4	P.S.
	1844	2 *a*	1	2
Julia Smith on	1844	55 *b*	2	11 seq.
and Sydney Smith	1845	61 *b*–62	9	8
social activities:				
charity to Mrs. Dakin	1837	58		
charity to Polish children	1837	64	1	5
	1837	68	1	6 seq.
	1843	9 *b*–10 *a*	9	14 seq.
	1844	19 *b*–20 *b*	5	7
charity to Mrs. Stoker	1842	121 *a*	1	7
charity to Mr. ——	1844	19 *b*–20 *b*	3	23
charity to German girl	1844	19 *b*–20 *b*	5	23
	1844	39 *b*–40	1	11
	1844	86–87 *a*	1	7
building cottages at Ambleside	1849	16–17	11	4
	1850	2 IV *p*	3	3
social position affected by her views	1845	132 *b*–133 *b*	2	10
	1845	135	3	3
	1851	61	6	19
	1852	7–8	6	6
on Southey	1844	19 *b*–20 *b*	9	10
on Mrs. Southey (Caroline Bowles)	1843	37	8	31
subscription for	1843	21 *a*–*b*		
	1843	108	4	13
on William Taylor	1844	19 *b*–20 *b*	7	6
and Sir John Walsham	1846	2	3	10
visit to Windermere	1844	111 *a*	1	2
	1844	113	4	1
and Wordsworth	1845	9	6	last
on Wordsworth	1843	65	1	13
	1846	4 *b*	1	1
	1848	31 *b*	3	1
on Wordsworth's death	1850	1 II 24		
on Wordsworth's sonnet on the American repudiations	1842	180	6	8

MARTINEAU, Harriet—*contd.*

Mrs. Wordsworth on	1845	91	3	1 seq.
	1848	30	9	last
and the Wordsworths	1837	67	1	9
	1839	77	1	3
	1841	2	6	12
	1843	128 *b*	2	17
	1845	12	2	9
	1845	14	1	last
	1845	16 *b*	2	4
	1845	61 *b*–62	8	4
	1845	14	6	7
	1845	77	6	8
	1845	80 *a*	2	16
	1845	132 *a*	2	21
	1846	164 *b*	1	7
[in 1840 vol.]				
	1849	16–17	11	4
	1850	50 *b*–51	5	15
	1850	50 *b*–51	7	last
and H. C. Wright	1846	11	1	7
other references	1842	179 *b*	2	9
	1842	175 *b*	3	22
	1843	124 *b*	3	10
	1843	134 *b*	6	9
	1844	117	4	13
	1845	12	1	12
	1845	13	1	12
	1845	26	3	29
	1845	64 *b*–65	7	7
	1845	130 *b*–131 *a*	3	last
	1845	131 *b*	2	2
	1845	132 *a*	2	8
	1848	53 *b*	5	24
	1848	83	6	15
	1849	47–48	5	21
	1849	74	6	15
	1850	78	2	5
	1851	37	7	10
WORKS:				
writings	1842	23 *b*	4	6
	1844	48 *b*–49 *a*	8	19
article on Newcastle in the *Penny Encyclopaedia*	1842	172 *b*	2	4
(*Complete Guide to the English Lakes*)	1848	29 *b*	5	3
	1848	30	10	11
	1848	31	7	20
	1861	43 *a*	2	8
(*Eastern Life Past and Present*)	1847	52	7	2
	1847	53	3	13
	1847	56	7	12
	1848	29 *b*	5	17
	1848	30	10	16
	1848	31 *b*	4	14
	1851	70 *b*–71 *a*	2	1

MARTINEAU, Harriet—*contd.*

WORKS—*contd.*

letter on the Factory Bill	1844	19 *b*–20 *b*	10	
Forest and Game Law Tales	1845	130 *b*–131 *a*	5	1
	1845	132 *b*–133 *b*	4	16 seq.
History of England during the Thirty Years' Peace	1848	29 *b*	5	4
	1848	31	8	2
	1849	51	3	19
	1849	2 1 *b*	4	1
	1850	50 *b*–51	7	9
	1850	57 *b*–58 *a*	4	17
Hour and the Man	1841	2	5	1
			and endorsement	
	1843	9 *b*–10 *a*	1	15
Household Education	1848	2 IV vii (*a*–*b*)	8	6
Illustrations of Political Economy	1862	49 *a*	2	5
(*Letters on the Laws of Man's Social Nature and Development*)	1851	21 *b*–22 *a*	7	11
	1851	22 *b*	3	8
	1851	23	2	10
	1851	25 *b*	2	6
	1851	33	2	17
	1851	40 *b*–41 *a*	2	5
	1852	7–8	6	9
(*Letters on Mesmerism*)	1844	109	5	5
	1844	110	5	12
	1844	110	8	3
	1844	112	3	21 seq.
	1844	116	3	12
	1844	120	6	25
	1845	2 *a*	2	last
	1845	9	6	10 seq.
	1845	11	1	5 seq.
Life in the Sick Room	1843	23 *b*	4	6
	1843	117 *b*	8	5 seq.
	1843	124 *b*	3	14
	1843	125	1	last
	1843	128 *a*	2	5
	1843	128 *b*	1	9
	1843	129 *c*	1	18 seq.
	1843	131 *a*	1	5
	1843	131 *b*	1	9
	1843	132 *b*–133 *b*	6	18
	1843	133 *a*	4	10
	1843	136	2	11
	1844	2 *a*	2, 3, 4	
	1844	7 *a*	5	13
	1844	19 *b*–20 *b*	1	21
	1844	19 *b*–20 *a*	9	22
	1844	88	5	8
	1844	5 XVI *a*	6	2
	1848	53 *b*	6	3
Philosophy of Comte	1853	102 *b*	2	8

MARTINEAU, Harriet—*contd.*

WORKS—*contd.*

(*Playfellow, The*)

Crofton Boys   1842   172 *b*   4   25 seq.
                                           1862   49 *a*   3   6
   Feats on the Fjord   1842   172 *b*   4   27
   Settlers at Home   1862   49 *a*   3   6
Poor Laws and Paupers Illustrated   1844   86–87 *a* 5   15
Retrospect of Western Travel   1843   9 *b*–10 *a* 5 27
Rioters   1842   191 *b*–192 *a* 9 20
'Sanitary Tales' from *Household*
  Words   1850   57 *b*–58 *a* 5 15
(*View of Society in America*)   1838   18 *b*
LETTERS to Crabb Robinson   1837   58; 64
                                           1841   2
                                           1842   121 *a*; 191 *b*–192 *a*
                                           1843   9 *b*; 37; 65; 117 *b*; 128 *b*
                                           1844   2 *a*; 11 *b*; 19 *b*–20 *b*;
                                                   39 *b*–40; 48 *b*–49 *a*;
                                                   86–87 *a*; 89
                                           1845   61 *b*–62
                                           1846   extract copied 4 *b*; 33 *a*;
                                                   47 *a*; [in 1867 vol.] 92
                                           1848   31 *b*
                                           1850   50 *b*–51; I II 24; I VIII 5

MARTINEAU, James

WORKS:

writings, Crabb Robinson on   1851   11 *a*   4   5
Discourses   1843   2 IV *e*   3   11

LETTERS:

to W. Bagehot   1855   16 *a*
from W. Bagehot   1855   18
to Crabb Robinson   1855   1 *b*; 7 *a*; 20 *b*; 36 *b*
                                           1856   I II 37
                                           1857   I II 2
                                           1861   [in 1860 vol.] 26 *a*
                                           1863   97 *a*; I II 38
                                           1864   5 *b*
to T. Robinson   1843   38 *b*

MATHEWS, Charles

Memoirs of, by his wife   1840   141   1   19

MATHIAS, Thomas James

Pursuits of Literature   1797   94   1   25

MAURICE, John Frederick Denison

Theological Essays   1853   68 *a*   2   6
                                           1853   73   8   13
                                           1853   74   6   14
                                           1853   75 *a*   3   1
LETTERS to Crabb Robinson   1856   I VIII 4
                                           1857   I VIII 73
                                           1859   12 *b*
                                           1862   I VIII 3
                                           1864   9 *a*

MELLISH, Joseph Charles
translations from the German

1801	3 A 12	1	20
1801	3 A 15	4	1 across
1801	26	1	27, 36
1801	35	4	14
1802	46	1	34
1803	3 A 31	4	3 seq.
1803	88	2	37
1804	14		
1804	81		
1806	43	4	2
1806	44	2	7
1806	47	2	3

MILMAN, Henry Hart
article on Newman's *Essay on the
Development of Christian Doctrine*
in the *Quarterly Review*

1846	41	1	12

History of Latin Christianity

1842	186 a	2	2
1842	196 a	3	12

LETTERS to Crabb Robinson

1839	108 a; 120

MILNER, Isaac, Dean
Life of, by Mary Milner

1844	14	5	5

MILNER, John
End of Religious Controversy

1830	8	2	30

MILNES, Richard Monckton
breakfast party

1849	21	4	14

and Carlyle

1844	5 XVI f	4	19

and W. B. Donne

1852	78 b	2	7

literary taste

1838	1	2	23
1838	1	4	P.S. 5 seq.

Crabb Robinson first meets

1838	1	2	22
1838	1	4	P.S. 5

and Crabb Robinson

1844	5 XVI f	4	3
1844	5 XVI h	7	3

and Sydney Smith at Rogers's breakfast

1846	13	4	1

and the Wordsworths

1838	27	3	7 seq.
1838	36	1	10
1838	110	1	3

[in 1836 vol.]
other references

1842	198	3	42
1844	48 b–49 a	7	13
1853	26	4	9
1853	40 b–41 a	6	7
1859	28 a	2	9

WORKS:
writings: (*Memorials of a Residence
on the Continent and Historical
Poems;* or, *Poems of Many Years*)

1838	27	3	7
1838	36	1	10

LETTERS to Crabb Robinson

1838	29 b; 1 VIII 74
1852	43 a

MITCHELL, Forbes
and the British Museum

1810	8 9 11	1	6

MITFORD, John
    literary work 1852 36 3 17
    1852 74 *b*–75 *a* 7 9
MITFORD, Mary Russell
    her death and W. Harness 1855 I VIII 89
    and Mrs. Niven's trust 1852 39 *b*–40 *a* 6 18
    1852 39 *b*–40 *a* 7 9
    1852 40 2 12
    1852 41 4 10
    mentioned 1840 138 4 31
    LETTERS to Crabb Robinson 1843 6 *b*
    1852 47 *a*
MONTAGU, Basil
    LETTER to T. Clarkson 1810 22
MONTGOMERY, James
    and Crabb Robinson 1849 66 *b*–67 *a* 7 15
    POEMS 1806 52 4 16
    1829 95 *a* 1 13
MOONSHINE, MAURITIUS, pseud:
    More Wonders 1801 23 3 3
MOORE, John, M.D.
    View of Society and Manners in
    France, Switzerland, and Germany 1800 3 A 5 4 6
    1800 11 4 18
    1851 20 *a* 1 19
MOORE, Thomas
    W. S. Landor on 1836 172 1 30
    Life. See Russell, Lord John
    at T. Monkhouse's 1823 93 3 9
    and Crabb Robinson 1829 152 4 32
    1843 24 *b* 3 3
    1843 28 *b* 4 4
    1853 39 *b* 7 16
    Crabb Robinson on 1833 115 3 8
    1853 75 *a* 4 14
    at Rogers's 1843 24 *b* 3 3
    1843 28 *b* 4 4
    1843 135 4 4
    1848 29 *a* 2 12
    WORKS:
    writings translated into Italian 1837 55 2 12
    Lalla Rookh 1817 140 2 13
    1817 142 4 12
    Letters and Journals of Lord Byron 1829 152 4 32
    1831 124 4 3
    1833 115 3 13
    1842 207 1 13
    Meeting of the Waters, The 1826 167–168 5 22
    Memoir of Sydney Smith 1845 61 *b*–62 9 12
    (*Travels of an Irish Gentleman in*
    search of a Religion) 1833 115 3 8
    LETTER to Crabb Robinson 1828 61
MORE, Hannah
    Practical Christianity 1828 57 1 15
MORGAN, Sir Charles 1838 32 3 14
    1843 49 2 3

Morgan, Lady, pseud. Sydney Owenson
pension 1842 188 *b* 1 13
1842 189 *b* 4 14
Crabb Robinson on 1838 32 2 3 seq.
1842 188 *b* 1 13
1842 189 *b* 4 14
mentioned 1826 153 1 last
WORK:
Princess, The 1836 81 3 13
LETTERS:
to Captain B. N.D. 8 36 I
to Masquerier N.D. 8 36 II
Moultrie, John. *See* 'Moutray'
(Mountfield, David), Mountford in M.S.
Two Hundred Years Ago [pamphlet
2nd edition, first published as
Church and Nonconformists of 1662] 1862 55 *b* 4 14
'Moutray'
verses in the *Etonian*[1] 1821 55 3 21
Mozley, Thomas
Review of Stanley's *Life of Dr.
Arnold* 1844 122
Murphy, Arthur
All in the Wrong 1847 33 *b* 16
Life of David Garrick 1804 70 3 P.S.
Way to Keep Him 1852 74 *b* 4 2

Napier, Lieut.-General Sir William
Francis Patrick
Conquest of Scinde 1844 16 *a* 2 16
Naylor, Samuel
Reynard the Fox 1844 95 7 18
1844 98 *a* 1 11
1844 105 *b*
1844 108 *b*
1844 113 6 12
1844 116 7 21
1844 117 5 14
1845 1 5 17
1845 5
1845 29 *b*–30 *a* 6 20
1845 39–40 8 1
1846 16 *b*–17 *a* 6 1
1847 29 *b* 6 6
LETTERS:
to Crabb Robinson 1829 124; 136 *a*
1830 77
1831 156
1832 16
1834 1
1842 117–118
1844 105 *b*; 108 *b*
1845 5

[1] Cf. *Correspondence of Henry Crabb Robinson with the Wordsworth Circle*, p. 100, note 1.

NAYLOR, Samuel—*contd.*
  LETTERS—*contd.*
    to Crabb Robinson   1848   8 *b*; 61 *a*; 69
                               1853   3 *b*; 33; 84 *b*–85 *a*
                               1854   80 *b*
                               1855   54 *b*
                               1862   47 *b*; 50
    from F. Thompson   1863   78
NEWMAN, Francis William
  and the editorship of the *Inquirer*   N.D.   2 IV *z*   2   2
  WORKS:
    History of the Hebrew Monarchy   1848   15 *a*   4   3
                                     1848   24   7   18
    Phases of Faith   1850   50 *b*–51   3   15 seq.
    Soul: Her Sorrows and Her Aspira-
      tions   1849   40   8   17
                                     1849   53   3   7
                                     1862   56 *a*   4   14
  LETTERS:
    to Crabb Robinson   1848   6 *b*; 67 *a*
                                 1849   32 *a*
                                 1854   13; 17 *a*
    from Crabb Robinson   1854   14 *a*
                                 1855   37 *b*
NEWMAN, John Henry, Cardinal
  WORKS:
    Apologia pro Vitâ Suâ   1864   12 *b*–13 *a* 8   1
    Essay on the Development of
      Christian Doctrine   1846   14 *b*–15 *a* 5   6
                                     1846   41   1   9
                                     1846   43 *b*–44 *a* 7   7
    Sermons before the University of
      Oxford   1843   28 *b*   7   9
                                     1843   32 *a*   3   2
                                     1843   33–34   8   6
NORTH, Christopher, pseud. Wilson, John
NORTON, Caroline Elizabeth Sara
                                   1843   49 *b*   1   last
                                   1845   15   3   2 seq.
                                   1845   84 *b*   4   7
OLIPHANT, Margaret O.
  Son of the Soil   1864   23 *b*   3   19
OPIE, Amelia, *born* Alderson
  Mrs. Clarkson on   1802   45   3   10
                                     1843   46   4   4 from end
  death   1853   117 *b*   1   10
  visit to the Exhibition   1851   40 *b*–41 *a* 8   2
  Memorials of. See Brightwell, C. L.
  and music   1801   40   2   last seq.
  in Paris   1831   89   1   8 seq.
  and J. C. Richmond   1831   89   1   8 seq.

OPIE, Amelia—*contd.*
and Crabb Robinson

and Crabb Robinson	1806	52	2	20
	1847	35 *b*–36 *a*	7	5
	1847	36 *b*	4	19
and T. Robinson	1836	148	3	2
on *Utopia*	1802	47	2	25
other references	1809	16	1	20
	1838	65	6	3
	1843	53 *b*	2	19
	1843	97	7	P.S.
	1851	40 *b*–41 *a*	8	P.S.

WORKS:
writings	1801	40	3	29
	1802	47	3	18 seq.
	1802	47	4	5
Father and Daughter	1801	30	1	41 seq.
	1801	40	3	21
	1802	45	3	13

LETTERS:
to R. E. Garnham	1801	40		
	1802	47		
to Crabb Robinson	1833	126		

OWENSON, Sydney, pseud.   *See* Morgan

PAINE, Thomas
epigram on Burke	1828	47	2	7
other references	1796	71	1	12
	1801	22	2	46
	1802	3 A 21	3	49

WORK:
Agrarian Justice	1797	94	4	27
	1797	95	3	27 seq.

PALEY, W.
View of the Evidences of Christianity	1796	84	2	20
	1806	36	1	14

PALFREY, John Gorham
in London	1856	41	4	16
	1856	52 *b*	2	7

WORK:
*Relation between Judaism and
Christianity*
Relation between Judaism and Christianity	1855	12 *b*	3	6
LETTER to Crabb Robinson	1866	51 *a*		

PARIS, Dr.
Life of Sir Humphry Davy, Bart.	1849	82 *b*–83 *a*–*b*	8	8

PARKER, Theodore
(*Discourse on Matters pertaining to
Religion*)
(*Discourse on Matters pertaining to Religion*)	1845	47	3	20

PARR, Samuel
E. H. Barker and	1828	47	3	22 seq.
on religion	1828	57	3	13
sermon	1801	30	1	40
	1801	34	4	17
and G. Steevens	1828	57	3	7
and G. Wakefield	1805	4	2	34
	1805	4	3	18

PARR, Samuel—*contd.*
other references 1801 34 4 24
1803 3 A 29 2 12
1849 26 3 5
1853 94 *a* 2 26
1855 29 *b* 3 14
LETTER to J. L. Fenner, senior 1819 21
PATMORE, Peter George
Personal Recollections of W. Hazlitt 1845 86 *a* 2 18
[in 1849 vol.]
PENNANT, Thomas
Tour in Wales 1799 131 3 68
1799 135 4 4
1799 136 3 67
PENROSE, John
Moral Principle of the Atonement 1844 5 *b* 2 10
1845 110 *b*–111 *a* 4 9 seq.
1845 112 *b*–113 *a* 2 14
1845 120–121 *a* 7 last
LETTERS to Crabb Robinson 1848 48; 55; 56 *a*; 73 *b*
1849 53
1854 16 *a*
1857 15 *a*
PHILPOT, John
(*Examinations of the Constante
Martir of Christ, John Philpot*),
edited by R. Eden 1845 107 *b*–108 *a* 8 1
1845 109 4 2
1846 10 2 20
PINDAR, Peter, pseud. Wolcot, John
PLUMPTRE, Edward Hayes
Lazarus, and other poems 1864 20 3 6
LETTER to Crabb Robinson 1856 47 *b*
PORTER, Jane
Thaddeus of Warsaw 1806 37 4 P.S.
LETTERS to the Masqueriers N.D. 8 35 I
N.D. 8 35 II
PRAED, Winthrop Mackworth
on the Norfolk circuit 1830 5 3 41
1830 29 2 31
[in 1850 vol.]
LETTER to Crabb Robinson 1836 129 *a*
PRIESTLEY, Joseph
*Comparison of the Institutions of
Moses with those of the Hindoos,
etc.* 1801 24 2 21
PRIOR, Sir James 1829 115–117 8 13
LETTER to Crabb Robinson 1849 5 *b*
PROCTER, Bryan Waller, pseud. Barry
Cornwall
engaged to Anne Skepper 1822 75 4 5
health 1822 75 4 3
1822 77 4 12
at Mary Lamb's funeral 1847 27 7 15
style of living 1843 135 3 13

PROCTER, Bryan Waller—*contd.*
commission in lunacy	1845	84 *b*	2	18
and the Montagus	1822	75	4	5
	1822	77	4	16
and the Wordsworths	1822	77	4	11
other references	1846	24	6	5
	1851	59	5	2
	1851	74 *b*–75 *a*	1	20

WORKS:
Charles Lamb, a Memoir	1866	58 *a* ˙	3	7
(*Mirandola*)	1821	54	4	1
	1821	55	2	24

QUILLINAN, Dorothy, *born* Wordsworth
LETTER to Crabb Robinson	1841	19 *a*		

RADCLIFFE, Ann Ward
and Mme de Staël compared	1804	3 A 36	2	34
mentioned	1799	145	1	17
	1826	167–168	8	12
	1866	39 *a*	2	17

WORKS:
Italian, The	1856	58	1	14
Romance of the Forest	1794	48	1	17

RANDALL, Edward
Juridical Essays	1795	61	3	last marginal note

REED, Henry (of Philadelphia)
death	1854	72 *a*		
and the Wordsworths	1839	99	1	6
	1844	23 *b*	2	2
	1844	81 *a*	3	11
	1845	80 *a*	1	12
	1845	91	4	15
	1853	56 *a*	2	11
	1854	51 *b*	1	7
LETTER to Crabb Robinson	1854	57 *b*		

REID, Elizabeth Jesser, *born* Sturch
LETTERS to Crabb Robinson	1842	181 *a*
	1843	38 *a*; 2 1 *d*; 131 *b*
	1854	61 *a*
	1855	28 *a*; 67
	1856	15 *b*; 37 *a*; 49 *b*; 61 *b*; 2 1 *a*
	1858	6 *b*

RITSON, Joseph
Ancient Songs	1803	102	1	12

ROBBERDS, John Warden
Memoirs of the Life and Writings of
William Taylor of Norwich	1843	23 *b*	3	1
	1843	23 *b*	4	19
	1843	39	1	8
	1843	40 *a*		
	1843	134 *b*	4	16

Robberds, John Warden—*contd.*
   Memoirs, etc.

1844	1 *a*	3	14
1844	2 *b*	2	3
1844	3 *a*	2	7
1844	3 *b*	6	13
1844	4 *a*	4	3
1844	7 *a*	6	8
1844	8 *b*	1	16 seq.
1844	13 *b*	1	last
1844	19 *b*–20 *b*	7	14
1844	22 *a*	5	6
1844	32 *b*	1	12
1844	42 *b*	2	23
1844	5 XVI *a*	6	1
1844	5 XVI *a*	7	6

   Letters to Crabb Robinson   1844   8 *b*; 32 *b*

Robertson, Frederick William
   Lady Byron on. *See also* memoir

1853	75 *b*–76 *a*	6	12
1853	86 *a*		
1853	89	6	8
1853	95 *b*	3	29

   Lady Byron's stanzas

1854	84 *b*		
1855	56 *b*		

   contemporary opinion of   1856   67 *a*   4   35
   death

1853	68 *b*	1	2
1853	73	2	8

   health

1848	26 *a*	5	18
1848	36 *b*–37 *a*	8	2
1853	68 *a*	1	4

   and Dr. King

1853	123	5	3
1854	11 *b*	2	11

   Life and Letters. See Brooke,
      Stopford A.
   memorial   1861   34 *a* 1, 2, and en-
                                       dorsement
   memoir

1853	76 *b*		
1853	77 *a*		
1853	100 *a*	1	5
1853	101 *b*	3	9
1853	102 *a*		
1853	102 *b*	4	6
1853	110 *b*	1	7
1853	115 *b*	1	14
1853	118 *a*	1	4
1853	118 *b*–119 *a*	1	13 seq.
1853	119 *b*		

   obituary by Crabb Robinson in
      Christian Reformer

1853	15 *b*–16 *a*	4	10
1853	74	1	7
1853	77 *a*	1	11
1853	77 *b*	3	1
1853	75 *b*–76 *a*	7	4
1853	86 *a*		
1853	87 *b*	1, 2	
1853	89	6	2

ROBERTSON, Frederick William—*contd.*

obituary by Crabb Robinson, etc.	1853	90 *a*	1	2
	1853	90 *b*	2	last
	1853	94 *a*	1	4
	1853	95 *b*	4	2
	1853	96 *a*	2	1
	1853	113 *b*	1	3
	1854	1 *a*	1	4
	1854	14 *b*	1	12
	1854	17 *b*		
sermon [endorsed, Dr. King and Robertson]	1849	72		
sermons. *See also* WORKS	1846	62	4	5 of P.S.
	1848	18	2	14
	1853	95 *b*	4	6
	1853	98 *b*	2	11
	1854	75 *a*	3	11
and Crabb Robinson	1847	1 *b*	3	16
	1849	71	6	17
	1851	20 *a*–19 *b*	3	18
	1851	20 *a*–19 *b*	5	7
	1851	2 IV R	1	5
	1852	2 IV H	2	16
Crabb Robinson on. *See also* obituary	1846	63	1	14
	1847	43 *a*	6	15
	1847	45	5	5
	1847	47 *a*	6	19
	1848	66 *a*	7	1 seq.
	1849	74	2	11
	1850	65	3	8
	1851	76 *b*–77 *a*	7	11
	1852	70 *a*	2	3 seq.
	1853	10	7	14
and his vicar	1853	73	2	8
address to the Working Men's Association	1848	66 *a*	7	5
lectures on Wordsworth	1847	17 *a*		
	1853	17 *b*	2	1
other references	1847	47 *a*	6	1
	1848	24	8	10
	1848	37 *b*–38 *a*	5	22
	1848	38 *b*–39 *a*	5	last
	1848	45 *b*	4	6
	1850	64	8	16
	1850	65	1	18
	1850	76	3	1
	1852	71	3	8 seq.
	1853	18	2	5
	1854	16 *a*	1	last
	1856	66 *b*		
WORKS:				
to be published	1853	15 *b*–16 *a*	4	8
Sermons	1855	29 *a*	1	3
	1855	38 *b*	1	11

ROBERTSON, Frederick William—*contd.*

Sermons

1855	72 *a*	1	2
1856	2 *a*	1	15
1856	9 *a*	1	6
1856	29	1	14
1856	54	2	6
1856	58	1	16 seq.
1856	65 *a*	2	2
1857	5*a*		
1859	7	1	24
1861	35 *a*	1	4
1863	95	1	9
1866	40 *a*	3	8
1867	87	1	4

LETTERS:

to Crabb Robinson

1847	17 *a*; 50 *b*	
1850	84 *b*	
1853	17	

to Miss Roscoe   1849   49

ROBINSON, Anthony

and the *Analytical Review*	1798	108	2	3
and the *Monthly Magazine*	1801	22	2	35
	1801	3 A 10	3	37
and the *Monthly Review*	1800	8	1	P.S.
and the *Monthly Repository*	1808	130	2	28
			and endorsement	

WORKS:

writings

1827	2 *b*	1	31
1827	10	and endorse-ment	

A Pair of Portraits, Crabb Robinson's handwriting, endorsed, 'My correction A.R.'   1797   97

[*An Examination of a Sermon preached at Cambridge by Robert Hall on Modern Infidelity*]

1800	3 A 5	2	36
1800	8	1	P.S.
1800	8	3	27
1800	22	2	34

LETTERS:

from John Hollis	1800	9
to Crabb Robinson	1806	34
	1807	85
	1808	92
	[in 1803 vol.]	
from Crabb Robinson	1801	25
to T. Robinson	1809	15
	1813	97
	1814	104; 111
	1821	53 *a*
	1823	101

ROBINSON, John

Proofs of a Conspiracy

1797	101	4	P.S.
1804	3 A 38	1	42

[ROBINSON, Mary]

    Vancenza; or the Dangers of Credulity   1792   40   2   15

ROBINSON, Robert.   *Life.*   *See* Dyer, G.

ROGERS, Samuel

    and his bank's notes   1846   46   4   8

                                  1846   47   4   3

                                  1846   164 *b*   3   4

                   [in 1840 vol.]

    and the bank robbery   1844   107 *a*   1   4

                                    1844   107 *b*–108 *a*   2   9

                                    1844   107 *b*–108 *a*   6   2

    Behne's medallion   1856   42 *a*   1   3

    breakfast parties   1845   67 *a*   2   18

                                    1846   13   3   17

                                    1846   16 *b*–17 *a*   5   4

                                    1846   19 *b*–20   7   4

                                    1846   23 *a*   4   8

                                    1846   24   2   8

                                    1848   29 *a*   2   11

                                    1851   9   6   6

                                    1851   16 *b*–17 *a*   5   last

                                    1851   32   8   12

                                    1853   26   3   5

    Byron's verses (*Question and Answer*)   1833   115   3   17

    annoyed by beggars, and Doyle's

      caricature [1]   1842   196 *b*   3   12 seq.

                                    1842   199   2   1 seq.

                                    1842   200 *b*   3   15

    death and funeral   1855   89 *a*

                                    1855   89 *b*

    dinner party   1845   15   2   15

    and J. W. Donaldson   1847   1 *b*–2 *b*   2   11 seq.

                                    1847   1 *b*–2 *b*   2   9

                                    1847   1 *b*–2 *b*   5   1

                                    1848   68 *b*   4   1

    and the Flaxman Gallery   1847   29 *b*   6   3

                                    1847   43 *b*   2   12 seq.

                                    1847   45   2   19

                                    1847   48 *b*   3   17

                                    1848   31 *a*   4   7

                   [in 1847 vol.]

                                    1848   26 *b*   5   2

                                    1849   2 IV xiii   6   4

                                    1853   64–65   6   5

    and Gervinus   1846   16 *b*–17 *a*   5   4

    health   1844   9 *b*–10 *a*   7   14

                                    1845   111 *b*–112 *a*   7   2

                                    1849   35 *b*   4   1

                                    1850   53 *b*   3   2

                                    1850   63   4   19

                                    1851   60 *b*   2   16

                                    1851   76 *b*–77 *a*   2   13

                                    1853   26   3   5

[1] Cf. H. C. R. Diary, 5th Nov. 1842, and *Correspondence of Henry Crabb Robinson with the Wordsworth Circle*, p. 470, note 1.

ROGERS, Samuel—*contd.*

and old age	1838	56	4	9
	1838	58 *a*	1	last seq.
	1846	68	5	10
	1848	26 *b*	5	2
	1850	34 *b*–35 *a*	5	last
	1852	34	8	5
	1853	82 *b*–83 *a*	6	2
and Kenyon	1845	84 *b*	3	24
	1846	3 *a*	3	16
J. Masquerier's note on	1846	8 2 III		
dinner at Monkhouse's	1823	93	3	11, 16
in Paris	1838	56	4	9
	1838	58 *a*	2	last seq.
	1844	83 *b*–84 *a*	7	18
F. Pollock on	1866	63 *b*	2	5
E. Quillinan on	1850	74	4	P.S.
and Crabb Robinson	1841	71 *a*	3	P.S. up-side down
	1842	132 *a*	1	8
	1842	140 *b*	1	15
	1842	179 *b*	1	10
	1842	194 *a*	3	18
	1842	195 *a*	3	6
	1842	205 *b*	3	15
	1843	24 *b*	3	3
	1843	28 *b*	4	4
	1849	71	3	4
	1851	56	3	1
	1851	60 *b*	2	16
	1852	2 IV H	3	6
Crabb Robinson on	1835	146	3	6
	1837	12	3	8
	1839	90	4	14
	1842	169 *c*	1	17
	1843	12 *b*	4	16
	1843	75 *b*	1	17
	1845	39	6	25
	1846	68	5	10
	1848	66 *a*	6	14
	1850	5	7	22
	1850	65	5	3
	1852	12	6	16
	1853	75 *b*–76 *a*	4	5
and Crabb Robinson's *Exposure of Misrepresentations contained in a Life of William Wilberforce*	1838	49	3	2nd P.S
and the sonnet	1839	90	4	14
	1846	19 *b*–20	7	4
and H. M. Williams	1819	31	3	12
and the Wordsworths	1835	90	2	15
	1835	143	4	P.S. 2
	1836	104	4	19

Rogers, Samuel—*contd.*

and the Wordsworths	1836	126	1	8
	1838	110	3	P.S. 5
	[in 1836 vol.]			
	1840	146	1	7
	1842	132 *a*	1	15
	1842	164 *b*	2	14
	1845	111 *b*–112 *a*	7	2
	1846	3 *a*	3	17
	1848	30	7	2
and publication of Wordsworth's poems	1826	153	2	12
Wordsworth on	1838	67	1	18
and the Wordsworth Memorial committee	1850	2 IV *v*	4	19
other references	1839	107	2	4
	1839	121	2	8
	1840	143	3	2
	1840	156 *a*	1	17
	1843	5 *b*	5	9
	1843	12 *a*	3	16
	1852	70 *a*	2	4
	1853	55	2	16
	1854	14 *b*	2	17

WORKS:

Italy	1836	113	1	17
Poems	1859	37 *a*		

LETTERS:

to the Masqueriers	1834	8 2 1	
	N.D.	8 2 II	
to Crabb Robinson	1836	126	
	1838	I II 12; I II 15; I II 22	
	1839	I II 14; I II 21	
	1840	I II 23; I VIII 22	
	1841	I II 17; I II 40; I II 41	
	1842	I II 13; I II 19	
	1844	7 *b*; 57 *a*	
	N.D.	I II 16; I II 18; I II 20; I II 39	

Rollaston, Miss

A. Swanwick meets	1859	29 *a*–*b*–30 *a*	8	9

Roscoe, William

election	1806	69	1	6
Southey on	1808	123	2	4
criticized in *The Times*	1808	119	1	22 seq.
	1808	121	2	last
mentioned	1799	138	2	3

WORK:

Life of Lorenzo de Medici	1796	73	4	P.S. last

Ruskin, John

and G. Street's lecture	1859	I VIII 42	2	6

RUSSELL, Lord John
  Memoirs, Journals, and Correspon-
    dence of T. Moore   1853   39 *b*–40 *a* 7   16
                                   1853   54   1
                                   1853   54   4   endorse-
                                                              ment
                                   1853   55   2   7
RUTT, John Towil, and Wainewright, A.
  (*New Edition and Continuation of*
    Gilbert Wakefield's Memoirs)   1802   44   3   41
                                     1803   98   4   5
                                     1804   42   1   25
                                     1804   67   1
                                     1805   4   2   30
                                     1805   8   3   1
                                     1805   3 A 43   3   18
                                     1805   3 C V 1, 2

ST. DAVID'S, Bishop of. *See* Thirlwall, C.
SAYERS, Frank   1795   55   2   19
  WORK:
  Disquisitions, Metaphysical and
    Literary   1806   52–53   5   marginal
                                                              P.S.
SCARGILL, William Pitt
  death   1836   87   4   11
  Crabb Robinson on   1835   134   3   9
                                1850   68   4   15
                                1853   8 *b*   2   last
  Thomas Robinson on   1835   130   2   20
                                1842   197   2   9
  WORK:
  Autobiography of a Dissenting
    Minister   1834   73   2   12
SCOTT, Robert Eden
  Alexander Haldane on   1842   200 *a* 3   12 seq.
  his papers   1851   20 *b*   3   10
  WORKS:
  writings   1806   8 23 11
                                1810   8 23 1
  article on Ossian in the *Edinburgh*
    Review   1808   8 9 1   3   8
  LETTERS:
  from Alison   1809   8 18 1
  from Adam Clarke   1808   8 9 1
                                  1810   8 9 11
  from Jamieson   1810   8 25 1
  from D. Stewart   1806   8 23 11
                                  1810   8 23 1
SCOTT, Sir Walter
  Landor on his death   1834   49   1   4
                                1834   69   3   3
  health   1832   26   2   7
  in Italy   1832   26   2   5

Scott, Sir Walter—*contd.*

Crabb Robinson introduced by Wordsworth	1821	63	
letter to William Smith	1838	39 *a*	2	16
	1838	65	6	7
	1838	69	3	6
and Southey. *See also* letter to W. Smith	1807	88	1	7
and Weber's 'Antiquarian Miscellany' (*Illustrations of Northern Antiquities*)	1810	8 25 1	1	9 seq.
and Wordsworth	1832	26	2	11
	1833	124 *b*	2	last
mentioned	1833	140	3	16

WORKS:

writings	1834	41	1	last
	1835	121	3	6
read in Germany	1824	107	2	24
tr. into Italian	1837	55	2	13
Mrs. Wordsworth on	1833	163 *a*	2	4 seq.
Lay of the Last Minstrel	1806	48	4	16
	1833	163 *a*	2	6
Life of Dryden	1808	155	4	3
Life of Napoleon Buonaparte	1827	34–35	5	12
Marmion	1808	8 9 1	3	16
Peveril of the Peak	1833	140	3	20
Redgauntlet	1834	41	2	5
Rokeby	1833	163 *a*	2	7

LETTERS:

from Wordsworth	1821	63	
to Wordsworth	N.D.	[in 1867 vol.]	104

Sedgwick, Adam

article on Chambers, R., *Vestiges of the Natural History of Creation*	1846	41	1	17

Sharp, Richard

Crabb Robinson on	1829	163	3	last seq.
and the Wordsworths and Crabb Robinson	1829	91	2	18
	1829	97	3	8
	1829	100	1	15
	1829	118	1	24
	1829	122	1	1
	1829	122	4	13
	1833	115	1	15
	1833	115	2	13

Sharpe, Samuel

retires from banking	1861	28 *a*	
and the *Christian Reformer*	1850	61	2	20
	1851	75 *b*–76 *a*	7	5
and J. W. Donaldson	1847	21 *a*	1	9
and W. B. Donne	1848	34 *b*–35 *a*	7	18
epigram on	1847	16	3	1 seq.
and the Garnham MS.	1845	119	4	11
and Layard	1851	54 *b*–55 *a*	8	10

SHARPE, Samuel—*contd.*

lectures on Egypt	1852	66	6	16
	1853	112	4	11
	1859	5 *b*–6	7	12
and Crabb Robinson	1843	89	5	5
	1843	116	2	11
	1844	110	3	10
	1845	23 *b*	5	25
	1845	67 *a*	3	7
	1845	75 *b*	2	16
	1846	26	7	8
	1846	71 *b*	4	17
	1848	57 *b*–58 *a*	6	12
	1852	2	6	8
	1852	17 *b*–18 *a*	5	9
	1852	19 *b*–20 *a*	1	12
	1853	112	4	8
	1854	85	7	3
Crabb Robinson on	1847	16	3	1 seq.
	1850	61	2	17
	1850	83 *b*–84 *a*	7	1
	1851	54 *b*–55 *a*	8	8
	1851	60 *a*	4	P.S. 6 seq.
	1851	75 *b*–76 *a*	7	5
and Rogers's funeral	1855	89 *a*		
	1855	89 *b*		
and Rogers's *Poems*	1859	37 *a*		
and University College	1841	65		
	1844	15 *a*		
	1844	81 *b*		
	1866	59 *a*		
and his wife's death	1851	54 *b*–55 *a*	8	8
other references	1848	9 *a*	6	3
	1854	64 *a*	1	11
	1858	19 *a*	2	8
	N.D.	I II 41		
WORK:				
History of Egypt	1848	34 *b*–35 *a*	7	20
	1848	57 *b*–58 *a*	6	16
LETTERS to Crabb Robinson	1841	65 ; I VIII 10		
	1844	15 *a* ; 81 *b*		
	1848	6 XIII *g*		
	1855	89 *a* ; 89 *b*		
	1859	2 *b* ; 37 *a*		
	1861	28 *a*		
	1865	32 *a*		
	1866	59 *a*		

SHARPEY, W.

LETTER to Crabb Robinson	1863	I VIII 63		

SHELLEY, Mary Wollstonecraft

and American copyrights	1837	67	1	last
and Mrs. D. Gaskell	1843	36 *a*	5	3
and the Godwins	1836	13	1 and endorsement

SHELLEY, Mary Wollstonecraft—*contd.*
    at Rogers   1845   67 *a*   2   19
    WORK:
      Frankenstein   1818   22   4   P.S.
    LETTER to Crabb Robinson   1836   131
SHELLEY, Percy Bysshe
    Christian Teacher on   1849   87 *a*   4   4
    Crabb Robinson on   1845   67 *a*   2   20
    WORK:
      Fragment from Faust   1829   94   2   4
SIDDONS, Sarah, *Life*. *See* Campbell, T.
SIGOURNEY, Lydia, *born* Huntley
    [*Pleasant Memories of Pleasant Lands*]
      Mrs. Clarkson on   1843   9 *a*   3   15
                               1843   27 *a*   2   26
      Miss Fenwick on   1843   18 *a*   5   16
      H. Martineau on   1843   37   8   24
      E. Quillinan on   1843   11   1   16
                               1843   47   3   11
SINGLETON, Archdeacon
    Letter from Sydney Smith.   Pamphlet 1838   65   8   3
SMITH, Albert Richard
    lectures   1852   22 *b*–23 *a* 7   9
                       1859   22   4   12
⟨SMITH, Charlotte⟩
    Emmeline, or the Orphan of the Castle 1792   40   2   9
    novels discussed   1794   47   1   3 seq.
                       1794   48   1   4 seq.
SMITH, Horatio [Horace]
    Crabb Robinson on   1845   124 *b*   4   12 seq.
    on Crabb Robinson's *Exposure of
      Misrepresentations contained in a
      Life of William Wilberforce*   N.D.   107
                        [in 1867 vol.]
    other references   1835   131   1   7
                        1840   166 *b*   3   13
                        1841   104   1   16
                        1842   196 *c*   1   21
                        1844   97 *b*–98 *a* 5   6
                        1847   45   5   19
    WORK:
      Brambletye House   *c.* 1835   8 20 II
    LETTERS:
      to J. Masquerier   1832   8 20 I
                     c. 1835   8 20 II
                     N.D. [in 1867 vol.] 107
      to Crabb Robinson   1840   I VIII 66
SMITH, James [brother of Horace]
    position of family on his death   1857   6 *b*   3   6
SMITH, James
    *Divine Drama of History and Civili-
      zation*   1854   55 *a*
                        1854   59 *b*
                        1854   61 *a*   4   19
                        1855   2 *b*   2   3

SMITH, Sydney
   letters to H. Martineau   1843   9 *b*–10 *a*   4   8
      1845   61 *b*–62   9   9
   and R. M. Milnes   1846   13   4   3
   Memoir of, by Moore   1845   61 *b*–62   9   9
   on Pusey   1843   49   5   11
      1843   51 *a*   4   8
      1846   43 *b*–44 *a*   7   16
   on Whewell   1840   156 *a*   2   2
   mentioned   1829   98   2   18
      1838   65   7   11

   WORKS:
     articles; in the *Edinburgh Review*   1843   120 *b*   3   18
       on American affairs in *The Examiner*   1843   116   5   10
      1843   120   3   note
      1843   129   3   7
     Letter to Archdeacon Singleton   1838   65   8   3
     pamphlet; on *The Ballot*   1839   74   3   16
     on *Deans and Chapters*   1840   140   3   2
SMITH, Sir William
      1850   66   6   13
      1851   4   5   17
      1851   30   7   11
   LETTER to Crabb Robinson   1855   1 VIII 67
SMYTH, William
   (*Memoir of Sheridan*)   1844   57 *a*   1   3
SOUTHEY, Caroline Anne, *born* Bowles
      1839   122   3   6
      1840   50 *b*   1   9
      1840   166 *a*   1   last
      1840   166 *b*   4   16
      1840   174   2   2
      1840   179 *b*   2   22
      1841   5 *b*   2   9
      1843   17 *b*   1   17 and P.S.

   LETTERS:
     to Mrs. Hughes [copied extract]   1841   30 *a*
     to Crabb Robinson   1841   5 *a*
SOUTHEY, Charles Cuthbert
   and Miss Aikin   1855   39   2   12
      1855   39   7   3
   appointed to a benefice   1851   8   2   1
   and the Coleridges   1843   112 *a*   3   6
   Sara Coleridge on   1841   55 *c*   3   5
   early promise   1824   137   2   30
   and his father's executors   1843   26   4   17
   and his father's friends   1846   164 *b*   8   1
      [in 1846 vol.]
   tours with his father   1836   163   2   10 seq.
      1838   25   1   9
      1838   51   1   20
      1838   54   1   3 seq.
      1838   58 *a*   2   19
      1838   65   5   3

SOUTHEY, Charles Cuthbert—*contd.*

health	1841	19 *b*	3	1
Landor's *Letter* in *Fraser's Magazine*	1851	8	2	last seq.
Oxford career	1841	19 *b*	2	6 seq.
	1841	50 *b*	1	2
Quillinan on	1843	47	3	4
	1843	60	3	16
other references	1850	9 *b*	1	5
	1850	18	6	5
	1850	22	3	last
	1853	110 *a*	2	2

WORKS:
Life and Correspondence of Robert Southey

	1848	45 *b*–46 *a*	4	10

[in 1856 vol.]

	1848	29 *b*	1	last
	1850	9 *b*	1	8
	1850	58 *b*	4	13
	1850	70 *b*	2	7
	1850	74	4	6 P.S.
	1851	8	3	9
	1851	22 *b*	2	12 seq.
	1851	39 *b*	2	6
	1852	67–68 *a*	1	16
	1856	53 *a*	3	11

ed. Southey, R. *Life of the Rev. Andrew Bell, D.D.*

	1841	34		
	1841	36 *b*		
	1841	38		
	1841	41 *b*		
	1841	45 *c*	1	4
	1841	55 *c*	3	5 seq.
	1841	64 *a*	1	4
ed. Southey, R. *Life of Wesley*	1845	84 *b*	2	last

LETTERS to Crabb Robinson | 1850 | 7 1 letters *j* to *n*

SOUTHEY, Robert

article in *Chambers's Encyclopaedia*	1850	40 *b*–41 *a*	3	1
and Mrs. Austin's, *Characteristics of Goethe*	1833	130	1	8

and Sir E. Brydges. *See* letters for publication

bust	1845	27 *b*	1	13
by Lough	1844	7 *a*	5	6
and Byron	1836	168	1	30 seq.
	1836	172	1	14 seq.
	1836	174		
on Carlyle	1839	2 XI 6	2	12
R. Carruthers on	1850	40 *b*–41 *a*	3	1
and the Clarksons	1811	42	2	34
	1850	9 *b*	1	8

and Mrs. Clarkson. *See also* Southey Family

letters	1841	16; 23 *b*; 29 *a*; 95 *a*–96 *b*

SOUTHEY, Robert—*contd.*
and the Clarkson-Wilberforce controversy

1839	2 XI 6	4	12
1840	50 *b*		
1840	158	2	5 seq.
1840	159 *a*	1	14 seq.
1840	160 *a*	2	9
1840	160 *b*	1	16
1840	161 *a*	2	11
1840	161 *b*	1	12
1840	163	1	9
1840	164 *a*	1	16
1840	165 *b*	1	6
1840	166 *a*	2	1
1840	166 *b*	4	17
1840	174	2	2
1840	177	1	last
1840	179 *b*	2	24
1857	1	4	10

and Coleridge

1808	123	2	5
1866	77 *b*		

Coleridge on

1817	140	2	3

Sara Coleridge on. *See also* Southey
Family
letters

1841	31
1843	56–57

and Cottle's *Early Recollections,
chiefly relating to the late S. T.
Coleridge*

1836	160	3	7
1836	163	2	3 seq.

death

1843	27 *a*	2	21
1843	135	1	11

and R. Duppa. *See* letters for publication
and the *Edinburgh Annual Register*

1810	32	4	17
1810	33	1	5

and the *Edinburgh Review*

1810	33	1	8
1836	174	5	last

epitaph for

1843	23 *b*	4	18
1843	125	1	19
1843	129 *b*	1	9
1843	134 *b*	4	13

Barron Field on

1835	86	2	7
1845	114 *a*		
1845	115 *b*	1	6

funeral

1843	24 *a*	3	16
1843	26	4	9

and Greta Hall

1807	88	4	15 and 1 P.S.
1817	142	2	21

and Elton Hamond

1819–20	7 1	letters *a* to *i*	
1820	43		
1821	60	3	6
1821	62	2	9
1850	18	4	8
1850	22	4	2

SOUTHEY, Robert—*contd.*

and Major and Mrs. Hawker	1838	54	2	14
and Hazlitt	1816	135	3	20
	1836	174	5	28
health. *See also* Southey Family	1837	69	3	29
	1839	106	1	3 seq.
	1839	122	3	6
	1839	123 *b*	4	P.S.
	1839	134	4	11
	1839	138	3	45
	1840	141	2	14
	1840	144	4	5
	1840	148	8	20
	1840	157	6	16
	1840	167	2	17
	1840	172	4	9
	1840	175	3	29
	1841	4 *a*	3	last
	1841	4 *b*	2	5
	1841	5 *a*	1	7
	1841	5 *b*	2	11
	1841	50 *b*	1	15
	1843	11	1	7
	1843	12 *b*	2	7
	1843	12 *c*	3	4
	1844	114 *a*		
	1844	115 *b*	1	7
and hexameters	1802	46	1	42
	1821	54	3	11
	1839	90	4	18
and J. Kenyon. *See* tour in Normandy				
J. Kenyon on	1856	12 *a*	3	7
	1856	53 *a*	3	11
and C. Lamb. *See also* Lamb, C. *Letter of Elia to Robert Southey,* and the *Quarterly Review*	1835	86	2	7
	1835	143	3	9
Landor on	1831	154	1	22
	1835	94	3	19
	1851	8	3	3
Landor's *Ode*	1833	169		
	1834	11	2	1 of n.
	1834	19	3	23
	1834	25	1	18 seq.
and Landor's *Satire upon Satirists*	1836	168	1	32 seq.
	1836	172	1	3
	1836	174	5	3
letters for publication	1843	170 *a*	3	2
	[in 1840 vol.]			
	1843	33–34	2	11
	1843	39	1	8
	1843	40 *a*		
	1843	67–69	7	4
	1843	99	2	last seq.

SOUTHEY, Robert—*contd.*

letters for publication	1843	106 *b*	4	13
	1844	7 *a*	7	3
	1850	9 *b*	1	8
	1850	22	4	2
sale of his library	1843	33–34	8	10
	1843	60	3	10
	1844	37 *b*		
	1844	45 *a*	4	9
and Lord Lonsdale	1821	64	4	2
marriage to Caroline Bowles. *See*				
also Southey Family	1838	58 *a*	2	12 seq.
	1838	67	2	14
	1838	84	2	last
	1839	106	1	7
	1840	27 *a*	2	21 seq.
	1840	141	2	17
	1843	28 *a*	3	18
	1845	114 *a*		
	1845	115 *b*	1	6
	1845	117 *b*	2	4 seq.
H. Martineau on	1844	19 *b*–20 *b*	9	10
and Miller's sermons	1850	23 *b*	1	18
J. K. Miller on	1850	56 *b*	3	last
	1850	67–68 *a*	1	16 seq.
on Mont St. Michel	1838	54	2	8
	1843	57	2	16
	1844	10 *b*–11 *a*	6	14
	1844	12 *b*–13 *a*	3	6
monument to	1846	164	7	16
	[in 1840 vol.]			
motto	1849	2 1 *b*	2	12
and Robert Owen	1822	85	2	23
election to Parliament	1826	156	4	P.S.
and the periodicals. *See also*				
under separate titles	1809	7 1 *t*	1	7 seq.
on poetry	1850	75	2	17
and politics	1808	123	2	2
	1817	137	1	6
	1823	89	2	23 seq.
	1831	98	1	10
	1833	130	2	28
	1833	144	1	8 seq.
	1838	56	3	14
portrait	1836	153	3	30
on Puritans	1849	18 *b*	3	2
and the *Quarterly Review*	1823	66–68	11	23
	endorsed 1821			
	1844	22 *b*	1	3
	1844	61	6	5
	1851	9	7	16
	1851	22 *b*	2	12 seq.
	1852	56 *a*	1	P.S.
	1852	67–68 *a*	1	16 seq.
religious feeling	1843	23 *b*	4	18

SOUTHEY, Robert—*contd.*

rhymes for children	1841	5 *b*	4	1 seq.
and J. C. Richmond	1834	26	2	20
	1834	26	4	3
	1834	34	2	11
Crabb Robinson first meets	1808	123	1	last
and Crabb Robinson. *See also* tour in Normandy and Brittany, and Southey Family	1810	35	1	8
	1833	130	1	8
	1833	164	1	11
Crabb Robinson on	1797	95	3	18
	1806	2	2	17
	1810	35	2	9
	1816	135	3	20
	1816	135	4	15
	1833	130	2	28
	1833	144	1	8 seq.
	1836	168	1	30 seq.
	1836	172		
	1836	174		
	1838	56	3	14
	1841	5 *b*	2	8 seq.
	1844	3 *b*	6	16
	1847	30 *a*	7	20
and T. Robinson	1832	25	2	8
	1833	146	1	last
	1844	3 *a*	2	11
and Scott's correspondence	1838	69	3	4
and Mrs. Southey (Edith Fricker) her health	1834	49	1	17
	1834	68	1	19
	1834	69	3	4
her death	1837	67	4	5
	1838	54	2	16 seq.
and Dr. Sprague	1836	128	3	1
and C. Taggart's poems	1834	26	4	3
	1834	34	2	11
and Sir H. Taylor. *See also* letters for publication	1843	26	4	15
and W. Taylor	1802	3 A 27	3	47
	1823	89	1	10
letters to W. Taylor. *See* Robberds, *Memoirs of W. Taylor,* and letters for publication				
Thelwall on	1797	95	3	18
tour with his son. *See also* tour in Normandy	1836	163	2	9 seq.
tour in Normandy and Brittany	1838	25		
	1838	32	1	6
	1838	51	1	18
	1838	54	1	10 seq.
	1838	58 *a*	2	12
	1838	65	4	11
tour in Switzerland	1817	137	1	11

SOUTHEY, Robert—*contd.*

on Blanco White	1811	67	1	2 seq.
and Henry Kirke White	1807	88	2	11 seq.
and N. P. Willis	1835	143	4	5 of P.S
and Wordsworth. *See also*				
epitaph, and Southey Family	1823	89	4	4
	1836	168	1	30 seq.
	1836	172	1	14 seq.
	1836	174	1	3 seq.
	1838	54	4	10
	1843	24 *a*	3	16
	1843	26	4	9
on Wordsworth	1808	123	2	10
Wordsworth on	1817	142	2	21
	1821	54	3	3
	1835	143	3	9
	1838	67	3	1
and C. W. W. Wynn. *See* Southey Family				

WORKS:

Album Verses, 'Birds of a feather'	1841	5 *b*	3	1
Book of the Church	1824	109	1	3
appendix to *The Cid*	1817	140	2	3
Commonplace Book, ed. by J. W. Warter	1849	42 *b*	4	6
	1849	44 *a*	1	6 seq.
	1850	18	5	9
Curse of Kehama	1811	46	2	10
	1811	68	3	1
	1836	174	6	11
Doctor, The	1843	28 *a*	4	9
	1839	2 XI 6	2	1
History of the Peninsular War	1823	89	1	16
Jeux d'Esprit	1866	77 *b*		
Joan of Arc	1803	88	2	13
Letters from England, by Don Manuel A. Espriella	1807	88	4	1
Letter to William Smith, Esq., M.P.	1817	142	2	26
	1844	3 *b*	6	21
Life of the Rev. Andrew Bell. *See* Southey, Charles Cuthbert				
Life of Wesley	1845	84 *b*	2	last
Poetical Works	1836	168	2	24
	1837	41	4	6
Thalaba	1806	2	2	17
	1836	174	6	11
(*Vision of Judgment*)	1821	54	3	7

LETTERS:

to Abeilla	1810	33
to Duppa	1807	88
	1814	I V 12 [copy]
	N.D.	IV 6 [copied extracts]
to Hamond	1810	34
	1819	7 I *a*; 7 I *b*

SOUTHEY, Robert—*contd.*
  LETTERS—*contd.*

from Hamond	1819	7 1 *c* ; 7 1 *d*; 7 1 *e*;		
		7 1 *f* [copy]		
to Rickman, copied extract	N.D.	1 VI 47		
to Crabb Robinson	1811	67		
	1817	137		
	1818	3		
	1820	43 [copy]; 7 1 *h*		
	1823	89		
	1838	39 *a*		
from Crabb Robinson	1820	7 1 *g*; 7 1 *i* [copy]		
SOUTHEY FAMILY	1841	1–2 *b*		
	1841	4 *a*	4	1
	1841	7		
	1841	8 *b*		
	1841	10–11–25		
	1841	12–13		
	1841	14 *a*		
	1841	16	1	last seq.
	1841	19 *a*		
	1841	19 *b*		
	1841	23 *b*	3	8
	1841	24		
	1841	26		
	1841	29 *a*	2	15
	1841	30 *a*		
	1841	31		
	1841	35		
	1841	53 *c*		
	1841	64 *a*		
	1841	91 *b*	3	15
	1841	95 *a*–96 *b*	4	25 seq.
	1842	2 IV *l*	3	13
	1843	11	1	7 seq.
	1843	17 *a*	4	11
	1843	26	4	9 seq.
	1843	33–34	1	last seq.
	1843	39	2	6
	1843	46	4	15
	1843	47	2	25
	1843	56–57		
	1843	60	3	10
	1843	60	3	14
	1844	16 *a*	1	17
	1844	84 *b*	2	28

SPEDDING, James

	1841	19 *a*	1	5
	1845	15	2	19
LETTER to Crabb Robinson	1839	1 VIII 52		

SPENCE, William, and Kirby, W.
  Introduction to Entomology

	1819	8 26 II	2	last
	1826	8 26 I	1, 2	

Spence, William, and Kirby, W.—*contd.*
 Introduction to Entomology 1830 79 2 25
Spence, William
 LETTERS :
  to J. Masquerier 1819 8 26 II
           1826 8 26 I
  to Mrs. Masquerier 1834 8 26 III
  to Crabb Robinson 1834 I VIII 53
           1835 I VIII 51
           1844 26 *b*
           1848 6 XVIII *w*

Stanley, Arthur Penrhyn
 and the Archaeological Association 1847 35 *b* 4 25
 on Clough 1848 54 *b* I 7
      1848 I VIII 71
 mentioned 1856 67 *a* 4 31
 WORKS :
  writings 1864 6 *b* 4 11 seq.
  Great Opportunities 1864 6 *b* 4 13
  Life of Dr. Arnold 1842 2 IV *k* 4 2
         1844 5 XVI 5 8 8
         1844 65 4 11
         1844 67 *a* 4 12
         1844 70 *b* 2 12
         1844 86 8 5
         1844 91 *b* I last seq.
         1844 122
         1845 7 5 18
         1845 18 6 17
         1845 20 *a* I 7
         1845 52 *b*–53 *a* 6 15
         1845 77 7 5
         1849 25 *b* I 4
  Religion of the Nineteenth Century 1864 23 *b* 3 7
  Sinai and Palestine 1864 6 *b* 4 12
 LETTERS to Crabb Robinson 1848 54 *b*; I VIII 71
         1857 9 *a*; I VIII 49
         1861 I VIII 47

Stephen, Sir George
 and the *Athenæum* 1846 22 3 2
      [in 1841 vol.]

Stephen, Sir James
 Lady Byron on 1853 101 *b* 3 3
 and the Clarkson-Wilberforce
  controversy 1835 104 2 19
        1838 36 2 13
        1838 44 *b* 3 4
        1838 49 2 12
        1838 58 I 10
        1838 65 4 7
        1838 69 2 9
        1844 60 3 9
        1844 61 4 22
        1844 68 *a*

STEPHEN, Sir James—*contd.*

and the Clarkson-Wilberforce controversy	1844	112	7	19
	1849	41 *a*	1	13
	1849	41 *b*–42 *a*	4	7
	1849	42 *b*–43 *b*	4	22
	1849	47–48	4	17
	1849	56	2	last
	1856	67 *a*	2	19
and W. B. Donne	1852	69	8	4
on Macaulay	1827	11 *a*	1	13
and Crabb Robinson	1849	54 *b*–55 *a*	5	17
	1850	35 *b*	2	10 seq.
	1852	61	8	13
	1852	69	8	2
	1853	1	4	16
	1853	1	5	15
	1853	6 *b*–7 *a*	4	7
	1853	32 *b*–33 *a*	8	8
and Crabb Robinson's *Exposure of Misrepresentations contained in a Life of William Wilberforce*	1838	43 *b*		
and slavery abolition	1847	46	2	13
inquiry concerning Tucker	1834	28		
and Wordsworth	1838	36	2	13
	1848	38 *a*	6	7
mentioned	1846	22	3	5
[in 1841 vol.]				
	1856	65 *b*	3	7

WORKS:

article on the Clapham Sect in the *Edinburgh Review*	1844	XVI *r*	5	18
(*Essays in Ecclesiastical Biography*)	1849	41 *a*	1	5
	1849	41 *b*–42 *a*	4	11
	1850	35 *b*	2	19
Lectures on the History of France	1852	43 *b*–44	12	3

LETTERS:

to Crabb Robinson	1827	11 *a*
	1834	28
	1844	68 *a*
	1849	41 *a*
	1854	59 *a*

STEWART, Dugald

	1810	36	1	22
	1851	20 *b*–21 *a*	3	17

WORK:

Elements of the Human Mind	1804	3 A 39	4	5
	1804	3 A 41	3	28
	1804	51	2	26

LETTERS to Professor Scott on his

writings	1806	8 23 II
	1810	8 23 I

STODDART, Sir John

and Sara Coleridge	1849	82 *b*	2	14
and Hazlitt	1816	133 *a*	2	17
Crabb Robinson on	1816	134 endorsement		

STODDART, Sir John—*contd.*
  and slavery abolition   1814   109
                          1814   110
  LETTERS:
    to Masquerier   1844   8 44 1; 8 44 II
    to Crabb Robinson   1814   109; 110
                          1816   134

STOWE, Harriet Elizabeth Beecher
  Bunsen on   1856   65 *a*   2   19
  C. Clarkson on   1853   49   1   9
  Crabb Robinson on   1853   42   8   1
                          1853   47 *b*–48 *a*   8   6
  charity to the Warburgs   1856   61 *b*   3   8
  WORKS:
    Dred   1856   65 *a*   2   19
    Uncle Tom's Cabin   1852   70 *b*   3   10
                          1853   2 *a*   3   3
                          1853   14 *a*   1   14
                          1853   44   2   4
                          1853   49   1   last

STRONG, Charles   1844   73 *a*   2   11
                          1846   19 *b*–20   5   8
                          1846   23 *a*   4   10

STUART, Daniel
  and Coleridge   1838   36   3   17
                          1848   62 *b*   5   last
                          1848   74   7   14
                          1849   88   2   6
  and *The Courier*   1811   49   1
  and *The Morning Post*   1812   68   3   8

SWANWICK, Anna
  visit to the Lake District   1859   21
                          1859   29 *a*-*b*–30 *a*
  on the 'Lake Poets'   1859   29 *a*-*b*–30 *a*   3   8
  and Miss Langham   1859   21   2   7
  Crabb Robinson on   1853   61   6   15
  meets Miss Rollaston   1859   29 *a*-*b*–30 *a*   8   9
  on Wilkinson's [*War, Cholera, and*
    the Ministry of Health]   1855   2 *b*
  and Mrs. Williams   1857   17 *b*
                          1857   39   2   1 seq.
  and working-class Sunday schools   1855   83 *b*   1   14
  LETTERS to Crabb Robinson   1854   1 *a*
                          1855   2 *b*
                          1857   17 *b*
                          1859   21; 29 *a*-*b*–30 *a*
                          1860   3 *a*
                          1864   20

TAGART, Edward
  WORKS:
    articles:
      in the *Inquirer*   1847   33 *b*   7   19
      in the *Westminster Review*   1847   27   5   14
    Locke's Writings and Philosophy   1855   45 *b*–46 *a*
                          1855   17 *b*–18 *a*

TAGART, Edward—*contd.*
LETTERS to Crabb Robinson

1845	56		
1846	6		
1853	11 *b*; 36 *b*; 37 *b*; 43; 96 *a*		
1855	45 *b*–46 *a*; 17 *b*–18 *a*		

TAGGART, Cynthia
Poems

1834	21	2	13
1834	21	4	3
		draft of answer	
1834	26	3	15
1834	34	2	10
1834	37	1	17
1834	60	2	19
1834	60	4	8
1834	61	3	42
1835	103	3	24

TALFOURD, Francis
and Oxford University

1854	21 *a*	4	5

WORKS:
Mackbeth Travestie

1848	10 *a*	8	13

plays, produced privately by the family

1846	3 *b*	3	1 seq.
1848	10 *a*	8	12 seq.

TALFOURD, Sir Thomas Noon
at Ambleside

1844	29 *b*–30 *a*		P.S.
1844	37 *b*–38 *a*	6	7
1844	78 *b*–79 *a*	8	20
1844	81 *a*	3	21
1844	5 XVI 5	5	last

and Barron Field
Barron Field on

1835	131	2	17
1835	86	2	11
1835	113	3	12 seq.
1839	80	2	7
1844	50 *a*	3	11

call to bar
the *Copyright Bill* and petition

1821	55	1	P.S.
1837	67	2	12
1837	69–70	1	4
1837	69–70	2	5
1838	23	1	11
1838	27	1	4
1838	36	4	12
1838	44 *b*	4	6
1838	65	5	9
1838	67–68	4	15
1838	110	1	4

[in 1836 vol.]

1839	77	2	1
			and P.S.
1840	148	2	3

death

1854	25 *b*	1	8
1854	27 *b*		
1854	28 *b*	1	3 seq.

and Lord Denman. *See* sonnet on
entertaining in London

1847	2 IV *x*	7	12
1847	32 *a*	2	13

TALFOURD, Sir Thomas Noon—*contd.*

entertaining in London	1848	35 *b*–36 *a*	6	14
	1850	30	2	11
	1850	87	4	17
family affairs	1846	3 *b*	3	7
	1849	69	7	11
	1854	21 *a*	4	5
	1854	27 *b*		
	1854	28 *b*	4	12
and Jeffrey	1861	32 *a*	4	4
made a judge	1849	50	3	12
as Lamb's biographer. See also *Letters of Lamb, Final Memorials*, and Lamb, C., letters collected for publication	1835	86	2	11
	1835	131	2	17
	1835	146	2	14
	1836	113	3	27
	1836	121	2, 3	P.S. upside down
	1836	147	2	26
	1836	153	3	12
	1836	160	2	10
	1836	163	2	18
	1836	181	2	24
	1839	127	2	13 seq.
	1847	42 *a*	5	last seq.
	1848	13 *b*	4	6
and Lamb's epitaph	1835	143	3	9
at Mary Lamb's funeral	1847	27	6	20
and W. S. Landor's *Satire upon Satirists*	1836	172	1	5
	1836	172	3	8
	1836	174	2	15
and Valentine Le Grice	1839	127	1	15 seq.
J. Miller on	1853	55	1	26
and Parliament	1841	57 *b*	3	last
and Mrs. Pattisson	1822	74	2	22
introduced to Crabb Robinson by J. T. Rutt	1813	87 *b*		
and Crabb Robinson	1835	146	2	14
	1836	147	2	26
	1836	153	3	12
	1846	3 *b*	3	7
	1847	42 *a*	5	last seq.
	1854	28 *b*	1	3 seq.
Crabb Robinson on	1849	69	7	11 seq.
and *The Times*	1845	113 *b*	2	11
on a university education	1854	21 *a*	3	14
and the Wordsworths. *See also* the *Copyright Bill*	1821	54	4	5
	1821	55	1	P.S.

TALFOURD, Sir Thomas Noon—*contd.*

and the Wordsworths, etc.	1836	123	3	14
	1836	139	1	P.S.
	1840	134	1 of P.S.	
	1841	63 *a*	2	7
	1842	140 *b*	2	7
	1844	29 *b*–30 *a*		P.S.
	1845	121 *b*–122 *a*	5	15 seq.
	1846	25	8	7
and the Wordsworths	1848	37 *b*–38	3	18
	1848	53 *b*	2	2
	1849	4	3	P.S.
and Wordsworth at *Ion*	1836	172	3	8 seq.
	1836	174	2	15
other references	1836	109	4	7
	1839	80	2	7
	1842	164 *b*	3	2
	1844	5 XVI *l*	3	19
	1846	34	5	8
WORKS:				
⟨*Athenian Captive*⟩	1839	80	2	12
⟨*Castilian*⟩	1853	46 *b*		
Final Memorials of Charles Lamb	1847	42 *a*	6	2
	1847	45	6	12
	1847	47	3	11 seq.
	1848	37 *b*–38 *a*	3	18
	1848	38 *b*	2	8
	1848	42 *a*	8	2
	1848	42 *b*	1	2 seq.
	1848	43 *a*	2	8
	1848	53 *b*	1	26
	1848	53 *a*	6	1
	1848	53 *b*	3	17
	1848	61 *a*	2	12
	1852	67	1	13
	1853	55	1	15
⟨*Glencoe*⟩	1840	156 *a*	4	8
Ion	1835	131	2	21
	1835	137–138	5	19
	1836	172	3	20
	1836	174	2	15
	1836	181	2	29
	1839	80	2	13
	1848	10 *a*	8	12
	1849	68 *a*	1	6
Isle of Wight	1844	50 *a*	3	14
Letters of Charles Lamb with a Sketch of his Life	1836	113	3	27
	1837	50	2	4
	1837	59	1	19
	1838	19	3	8
	1838	33	1	14
	1840	134	1 of P.S.	
preface [unidentified]	1835	113	3	12 seq.
sonnet on Denman	1850	1 V 2		

TALFOURD, Sir Thomas Noon—*contd.*
  WORKS—*contd.*

(*Vacation Rambles and Thoughts*)	1845	18	7	13
	1845	121 *b*–122 *a*	5	15
Visit to the Alps	1844	50 *a*	3	11 seq.
LETTERS:				
from C. Lamb	1828	75 *a*		
to Crabb Robinson	1834	78–79		
	1835	93		
	1839	73		
	1853	46 *b*		
from Crabb Robinson	1848	42 *b*		

TAYLER, John James

taste in books	1859	17 *b*		
and Bunsen	1853	19	3	1
and Lady Byron	1854	82 *b*	2	13
and Germany	1849	62	2	7
	1858	21 *a*		
	1862	63 *b*		
health	1860	19 *a*	4	P.S.
lectures	1854	15	6	16
G. Long on	1857	16 *b*	2	4 seq.
	1857	26 *a*	1	11
	1857	28 *b*	2	4
	1857	30 *b*	1	8 seq.
and Manchester New College	1853	48 *b*–49 *a*	7	7
	1853	74	4	15
	1853	89	8	11
	1853	112	6	17
	1854	58 *b*	1	7
and the (*National Review*)	1854	82 *a*	1	4
	1855	11	1	21
	1855	18	1	7
	1855	21 *a*	1	18
	1855	23	2	8
	1855	24 *a*		
and the *Prospective Review*	1846	9		
	1846	10	2	21
	1855	13 *a*		
on Crabb Robinson's *Etymology of*				
the Word Mass	1854	50 *b*		
Crabb Robinson on	1845	75 *b*–76	9	6
	1846	14 *b*–15 *a*	5	last
	1847	35 *a*	4	11
	1848	4 *a*	6	last
	1851	64	2	21
and the sale at Rydal Mount	1859	17 *b*		
and Martin Schunck	1847	7 *b*–8 *a*	6	17
and A. J. Scott	1848	68	4	13
	1848	72	1	14
sermons	1846	3 *a*	4	13
	1847	35 *a*	4	11
	1852	29	8	9
and Sunday schools	1855	83 *b*		
	1866	58 *b*	2	10 seq.

TAYLER, John James—*contd.*

tour in Switzerland	1864	17 *b*	
	1865	29 *a*	
	1866	61 *b*	
and (University Hall)	1847	7 *b*–8 *a*	5	8
	1848	4 *a*	7	2
	1848	72	1	9
	1853	90 *b*–91 *a*	2	7
other references	1849	65	3	17
	1849	65	8	7
	1851	64	5	4
	1852	29	8	8
	1852	30 *b*–31 *a*	4	5
	1853	104 *b*	2	4
	1854	5 *a*	2	7

WORKS:

articles in the *Christian Teacher*	1846	19 *b*–20	1	10
Christian Aspects of Faith and Duty	1851	63	7	17
	1851	64	3	2
	1854	73	3	9 seq.

Retrospect of the Religious Life of England

	1845	95 *b*–96 *a*	8	9
	1845	96 *b*–97 *a*	2	14
	1845	102 *a*	2	12
	1845	107 *b*–108 *a*	6	4
	1845	109	2	2
	1845	120	4	13
	1845	132 *b*–133 *b*	7	8
	1846	3 *a*	4	18
	1846	92	3	5
[in 1867 vol.]			
	1856	65 *a*	2	8

LETTERS:

to Crabb Robinson	1846	9
	1848	72
	1854	50 *b*; 81; 82 *a*
	1855	1 *c*; 13 *a*; 24 *a*; 83 *b*
	1858	21 *a*
	1859	17 *b*
	1861	44 *b*
	1862	48 *a*; 63 *b*
	1864	17 *b*
	1865	29 *a*
	1866	56 *a*; 58 *b*; 61 *b*
from Crabb Robinson [copy]	1854	51 *a*

TAYLER FAMILY	1845	75 *b*–76	9	6
	1859	23 *a*	1	12
	1859	29	4	12
	1860	13 *b*	2	7
	1860	19 *a*	4	P.S.

TAYLOR, Catherine, later Whittler

Letters from Italy to a younger Sister	1848	26 *b*	7	7

TAYLOR, Edgar

Ewald and	1838	20 *b*	1	5
and family	1846	58	2	18

TAYLOR, Edgar—*contd.*

and Hessel	1845	54 *b*–55	7	14
and Lady Hewley's trust	1836	180		

WORKS:

⟨*New Testament revised from the Authorized Version*⟩	1842	148 *a*	2	9
Suffolk Bartholomeans : A memoir of John Meadows, ed. by Emily Taylor	1844	26 *a*	4	21
LETTERS to Crabb Robinson	1836	180		
	1838	8 *a* ; I VIII 37		

TAYLOR, Emily

books obtained from Dr. Williams's Trust	1862	49 *a*		
	1864	7 *a*		
	N.D.	5 XI 9		
and W. B. Donne	1850	70 *b*	1	2

WORKS:

writings : S. A. Miller on	1863	100 *a*	3	8
Ball I Live On, The	1862	49 *a*	2	3
	1863	100 *a*	3	12
Suffolk Bartholomeans. See Taylor, Edgar				
LETTERS to Crabb Robinson	1855	I VIII 18		
	1862	49 *a*		
	1864	7 *a*		
	1865	30 *a*		

TAYLOR, Sir Henry

and A. De Vere	1850	64	5	15
health	1843	47–48	1	9
	1844	23 *b*	2	17
and mesmerism	1845	20 *a*	3	17
and the *Quarterly Review. See* on Wordsworth's sonnets				
and Crabb Robinson. *See also* Taylor Family and Miss Fenwick	1842	180	6	18
Crabb Robinson on	1850	63	7	14
	1850	64	5	6 seq.
	1850	69 *b*–70 *a*	5	13
as Southey's executor	1843	26	4	15
	1843	135	1	17
	1844	29 *a*	4	3
and Southey's letters	1843	170 *a*	3	4
	[in 1840 vol.]			
	1843	33	2	11
	1843	39	1	8
	1843	40 *a*		
	1843	46	4	33
	1843	47–48	5	12
	1843	72	3	10
	1844	8 *b*	4	20
	1844	16 *a*	2	1
	1844	I VIII 36		
and the Southey family	1841	14 *a*	2	6
move to Wandsworth	1844	67	4	2

TAYLOR, Sir Henry—*contd.*
and Wordsworth's bust	1846	2 IV *y*	2	13
on Wordsworth's *Sonnets*	1842	121 *b*	3	7

WORKS:
Edwin the Fair	1842	172 *b*	5	8
(*Eve of the Conquest and other Poems*)	1847	53	3	10
(*Notes from Life*)	1850	69 *b*–70 *a*	5	last
Philip Van Artevelde	1834	62	3	23
	1835	120	3	20
	1835	121	2	19
	1847	50 *a*	6	11
	1848	I VIII 41	1	6

LETTERS to Crabb Robinson	1843	40 *a*	
	1844	I VIII 36	
	1848	I VIII 41	
	1854	11 *a*	

TAYLOR FAMILY and Miss Fenwick	1840	157	6	28
	1843	47–48	1	9
	1843	60	2	12
	1843	66	2	7
	1844	103 *a*	2	12
	1844	113	6	23
	1845	64 *b*–65	6	16
	1845	80 *b*–81 *a*	4	20
	1847	40 *b*	4	2
	1848	32	3	15
	1850	63	7	8
	1851	54 *b*–55 *a*	2	1
	1853	85	1	9
	1853	86 *b*–87 *a*	7	20
and Dorothy Wordsworth	1853	89	4	15
TAYLOR, Henry, of North Shields, *Life*	1827	10		

TAYLOR, Isaac
and the Puseyites	1840	140	3	8
	1843	46	2	31

WORKS:
writings	1839	2 XI 6	2	22
Ancient Christianity and the Doctrines of the Oxford Tracts	1839	101	2	16
	1839	106	4	7
	1839	115	4	6
	1839	121	4	4
	1839	122	2	last seq.
	1840	182	4	18
	1843	46	2	25
	1844	14	6	22
Natural History of Enthusiasm	1839	2 XI 6	2	last
Physical Theory of another Life	1839	2 XI 6	3	21
Saturday (*Evening*)	1839	122	2	29

TAYLOR, John Edward
LETTER to Crabb Robinson	1840	[in 1842 vol.]	116 *b*

TAYLOR, Richard	1803	84	1	4
	1805	27	4	6
	1827	31	3	18

TAYLOR, Richard—*contd.*

	1839	89	1	7
	1841	57 *b*	1	11
	1851	73	8	10 seq.
	1852	56 *b*	7	8

TAYLOR, Tom

and S. Naylor	1853	84 *b*–85 *a*	6	4
	1855	54 *b*–55 *a*	5	18
and *Punch*	1850	81 *a*	1	8 seq.
and (Quillinan's) verses	1850	81 *a*	1	8
	1850	82 *b*	1	2
Crabb Robinson on	1850	38	7	17
	1850	83 *b*–84 *a*	6	14

WORKS:
  ed. *Autobiography and Memoirs of
    B. R. Haydon. See* Haydon, B. R.

Diogenes' Lanthorn	1850	38	7	last
(*Our Clerks*)	1852	19 *b*–20 *a*	6	3
Vicar of Wakefield	1850	38	7	13

LETTERS to Crabb Robinson

	1823	1 VIII 40		
	1850	81 *a*		
	1851	6 XVIII *n*		

TAYLOR, William

on Diderot	1805	28	1	8
financial affairs	1810	7 1 *w*		
	1811	7 1 *x*		
	1812	7 1 *y*	3	21
	1813	7 1 *z*		
on Germany	1798	115		
	1798	117	1	10
and Godwin	1795	64–65	5	marginal note
	1796	78	2	25

and Goethe. *See Iphigenia in Tauris*

on Goethe	1805	28	1	8
	1810	31 *a*		
	1810	31 *a*	1	10
and hexameters	1802	49	3	18
	1802	54	1	32
	1802	74	2	35
and Rev. P. Houghton	1804	11	4	3
on Junius	1829	95 *a*	1	20
on Klopstock	1801	3 A 10	3	38
	1801	35	3	23
	1801	3 A 15	4	4 across
	1802	49	3	6
	1802	3 A 23	3	50
	1802	3 A 25	4	1
	1802	3 A 27	2	17
	1803	3 A 31	3	48

and Lessing. *See Nathan the Wise*

| and Marsh's *Clubs of London* | 1828 | 47 | 3 | 14 |
| H. Martineau on | 1844 | 19 *b*–20 *b* | 7 | 6 |

Memoirs of. See Robberds, J. W.

III—K

TAYLOR, William—*contd.*

and the *Monthly Magazine. See also* on Klopstock   1802   3 A 27   3   47, 57

                                   1804   3 A 27   4   3

and his mother's death   1812   7 I *y*

and Crabb Robinson   1797   98   I   24

                        1797   99   4   9

                        1798   113   2   14

                        1798   115

                        1798   117   I   6

                        1805   27   3   25

                        1806   39–40   6   P.S.

                        1808   121   2   5

on Crabb Robinson   1810   7 I *v*   3   7

and Southey. *See also* Robberds, J. W., *Memoirs*   1823   89   I   9

other references   1801   3 A 12   3   43

                        1801   3 A 12   4   7

                        1804   42   2   41 seq.

WORKS:

writings   1802   74   2   38

article on Kant in the *Monthly Review*   1801   3 A 8   I   48

Historic Survey of German Poetry   1828   57   4   P.S.

                        1835   121   2   15

tr. of *Iphigenia in Tauris*   1801   3 A 12   I   40

                        1802   3 A 20   2   11

                        1829   94   I   11

(*Letter concerning the Two First chapters of Luke*)   1811   41   I   8

                        1811   42   I   27

tr. of *Nathan the Wise*   1802   3 A 28   4   38

tr. of Plato   1802   3 A 28   3   17

LETTERS:

to E. Hamond   1808   7 I *s*

                 1809   7 I *t*

                 1810   7 I *u*; 7 I *v*; 7 I *w*

                 1811   7 I *x*

                 1812   7 I *y*

                 1813   7 I *z*; 7 I *i*; 7 I *ii*

                 1814   7 I *iii*; 102 *a*

to Thomas Martin   1798   115

to Crabb Robinson   1805   28; I VIII 35

                        1810   31 *a*; 31 *b*

TENNYSON, Alfred, 1st Lord

autograph sought   1847   I VIII 54   8   11

and the laureateship   1843   135   3   1

Quillinan on   1849   4   2   2

                 1851   37   4   5

at Rogers's   1845   15   2   21

Crabb Robinson on   1843   135   3   1

                        1845   15   2   21

WORKS:

writings   1851   37   4   5

           1859   25   7   1

TENNYSON, Alfred, 1st Lord—*contd.*
  WORKS—*contd.*

Idylls of the King	1859	25	7	2
In Memoriam tr. into German	1854	64 *a*	2	12

THACKERAY, William Makepeace
  lectures   1852   5 *b*–6 *a*   7   8
  WORKS:
   Crabb Robinson on *Esmond*   1852   69   6   14
    on *Vanity Fair*   1852   69   6   18

THIRLWALL, Connop, Bishop of St.
  David's
   Lady Byles on   1860   10 *b*   3   20
   and Dr. Hook   1846   84 *a*   2   6
     [in 1849 vol.]
   and London University   1836   103   3   13
   and Crabb Robinson   1848   14 *a*   8   4
   Crabb Robinson on   1852   69   2   6
  WORK:
   History of Greece   1835   121–122   5   4
        1835   137–138   5   6

TICKNOR, George
  History of Spanish Literature   1850   1 *b*–2 *a*   7   16

TOOKE, John Horne
  Amyot on   1796   77   3   11
  and Junius   1829   95 *a*   1   23
        1829   115–117   4   9
  politics   1796   76   3   29
        1796   77   3   11
        1801   24   1   30 seq.
        1801   40   2   10
        1803   3 A 32   3   43
  Crabb Robinson on   1796   76   3   29
        1797   97
  (trial)   1794   47   21   last
  other references   1801   3 A 9   3   12
        1801   33   2   last
        1802   43   1   26
        1802   49   3   30
        1802   3 A 22   1   27, 42
        1802   3 A 23   2   37
        1806   34   1   P.S.
        1844   76 *b*–77 *a*   3   11
        1845   41 *b*–42 *a*   3   3
  WORK:
   Diversions of Purley. ῎ΕΠΕΑ ΠΤΕΡ-
    Ο΄ΕΝΤΑ   1796   77   3   13
        1811   36   1   17

TOWNSEND, Charles [rector of Kingston]   1846   19 *b*–20   5   11
TOWNSEND, George
  Armageddon   1844   5 XVI *j*   7   last
TRAILL, Catherine Parr
  Letters from Canada   1862   49 *a*   3   3
TRENCH, Richard Chenevix, Archbishop
  of Dublin

TRENCH, Richard Chenevix—*contd.*
Lady Byron on   1854   78 *a*   I   II
and W. B. Donne   1852   78 *b*   I   9
Hulsean Lectures   1864   18 *a*   3   15
WORK:
(*Sabbation; Honor Neale and other
Poems*) sent to Wordsworth   1838   27   3   7
    1838   36   I   II

TUPPER, Martin Farquhar
WORKS:
writings: Quillinan on   1850   II   3   II seq.
J. C. Richmond on   1848   56 *b*   I, 2
    1850   II   4   II seq.

TWINING, William
LETTER to Crabb Robinson   1843   I VIII 39

TWISS, Horace
Public and Private Life of Lord Eldon   1844   71 *a*   3   II
    1845   18   6   14
    1849   37   7   16 seq.

TWISS, Sir Travers
LETTER to Crabb Robinson   1852   31

URQUHART, David
Spirit of the East   1841   112 *a*   I   16

VAVASOUR, Lady
(*My Last Tour and First Work; or,
A Visit to the Baths of Wildbad
and Rippoldsau*)   1843   87 *b*   3   15

WAINEWRIGHT, Arnold.   *See* Rutt, J. T.
WAKEFIELD, Gilbert
and Burke   1796   73   4   5 of P.S.
death   1801   33   I   8 seq.
    1801   34   4   4
    1801   3 A 17   4   18
    1801   3 C III   I   I
and M. Dodson   1799   149   I   35
    1799   149   3   35
reputation in Germany   1804   9   I, 2, 3
imprisonment   1799   130   2   3, 49, 55
    1799   130   4   18
    1799   134   I   30
and Jacobs of Gotha   1802   3 C IV   I   P.S.
    1804   6   I   14
    1804   3 A 38   I   27
and Knebel   1804   3 A 41   3   47
and Crabb Robinson.   *See also*
imprisonment   1797   95   3   22
    1805   3 C II   4   36
Crabb Robinson on   1804   9   I, 2, 3
    1805   3 C V   I, 2
    1827   34   I   23
and Rutt   1799   130   4   18

WAKEFIELD, Gilbert—*contd.*

and Jeremy Taylor	1805	4	3	21
trial	1798	108	2	14
	1799	125	1	33
	1799	135	3	P.S.
	1799	152	1	15
other references	1796	72	1	2nd marginal note
	1796	77	4	5
	1799	129	4	22
	1799	143	3	23
	1801	28	2	8
	1801	39	2	15 seq.
	1801	39	4	11
	1802	42	4	8
	1803	3 A 29	2	17
	1806	2	2	15
	1806	43	4	36

WORK:
Lucretius

	1804	3 A 41	3	46
	1804	3 A 37	1	16
	1805	3 A 42	3	18

Memoirs.   See Rutt, J. T.

LETTER to Crabb Robinson	1799	124

[WALKER, George]

Theodore Cyphon	1797	91	1	28

WALTER, John [1784–1847]
LETTERS:

from Crabb Robinson	1807	91; 92
to Crabb Robinson	1815	124 b
	1816	134
	1828	48
	1832	79
	1843	123 a

WALTER, John [*b.* 1818]

LETTERS to Crabb Robinson	1843	16 a; 35 b
	1844	27 a; 52 a
	1857	18 a
	1860	24 b

WARD, Robert Plumer

Tremaine	1843	18 b	4	26
	1845	37 b	4	2

WARNER, Richard

Walk through Wales	1799	132	1	5, 27
	1799	137	3	51

WARREN, Samuel

Crabb Robinson on	1847	27	8	2

WORK:
*Passages from the Diary of a Late
  Physician*

	1832	66	3	22

WARRINGTON, William

History of Wales	1799	145	2	7
	1799	145	3	37

WARTER, John Wood
  See Southey, R., *Commonplace Book*,
  and Southey Family

WATSON, Hewitt C.

and the *Westminster Review*	1845	61 *b*–62	8	22

WATSON, Dr. Seth B.

ed. Coleridge, S. T., *Hints towards a Formation of a more Comprehensive Theory of Life*	1849	82 *b*–83	1	3 seq.

[WEBER, Henry William]

Battle of Flodden Field	1808	8 9 1	3	16
(*Illustrations of Northern Antiquities*)	1810	8 25 1	1, 2	

WHATELY, E. Jane

Life and Correspondence of Archbishop Whately	1866	71 *a*		

WHATELY, Richard, Archbishop of Dublin

and Mrs. Arnold	1844	106 *b*	2	4
	1846	25	3	1
	1849	44 *a*	2	28
and Calvinism	1842	158 *a*	3	10
Mrs. Clarkson on	1842	158 *a*	1	26
	1848	158 *a*	3	10
	1842	164 *a*	1	2
H. Martineau on	1845	61 *b*–62	7	7
	1845	77	7	15
	1846	92	7	20 seq.
[in 1864 vol.]				
and mesmerism	1845	61 *b*–62	7	7
	1846	2	4	2
	1846	2	5	21
Crabb Robinson on	1842	209 *b*	4	3 seq.
	1844	4 *b*–5 *a*	5	8
	1847	18 *b*–19 *a*	6	24
and Blanco White's *Life*	1845	61 *b*–62	7	16
	1845	77	7	15
	1866	71 *a*	1	
Wordsworth and	1846	92	7	20 seq.
[in 1864 vol.]				
Mrs. Wordsworth on	1846	25	3	1
other references	1841	81	2	27
	1844	78 *a*–79 *b*	8	23
	1848	5 *b*–6 *a*	4	8
[in 1847 vol.]				

WORKS:

writings:

Crabb Robinson on	1843	2	2	1
and J. W. Donaldson	1847	11 *b*	4	9 seq.
Errors of Romanism traced to their Origin in Human Nature	1841	82 *a*	4	11
Essays	1841	108	2	2
	1841	109	3	9
	1842	158 *a*	1	26
	1842	158 *a*	3	10
	1842	164 *a*	1	2
Use and Abuse of Party Feeling in Matters of Religion [Bampton Lectures]	1841	108	2	6
View of the Scripture Revelations concerning a Future State	1841	108	2	3

WHATELY FAMILY
  and the Arnolds   1836   134   2   7
     1844   81 *a*

WHEWELL, William
  on Carlyle's *French Revolution*   1846   56   1   9
  Sara Coleridge on   1846   56   1   9 seq.
  and Robberds   1844   32 *b*   4   4
  and Crabb Robinson   1839   90   4   16
     1856   67 *a*   3   10
  Sydney Smith's epigram on   1840   156 *a*   2   1
  other references   1836   151   2   16
     1836   152   2   2
     1847   36   6   20
     1854   61 *a*   4   11
  WORKS:
    tr. of *Herman and Dorothea*   1839   90   4   16
     1840   142 *b*
    Isle of Sirens   1840   148   8   1
     1840   156 *a*   1   15
  LETTERS to Crabb Robinson   1840   142 *b*
     1847   26 *a*

WHITE, Joseph Blanco
  E. B. Browning on   1846   18 *b*   1   6 seq.
  Sara Coleridge on   1846   56   3   9
  insanity   1866   71 *a*
  Long on   1843   113 *a*
  J. Penrose on   1849   53   3   5
  Quarterly Review on   1845   71   6   9
     1845   72 *b*   3   11
     1845   74 *b*   4   18
  Crabb Robinson on   1843   93   3   20 seq.
  T. Robinson on   1843   102 *a*   2   2
     1846   2 IV *b*   4   10
  Southey on   1811   67   1
  WORKS:
    (*Life of the Rev. Joseph Blanco White, Written by Himself, with portions of his Correspondence,* ed.: Thom, J. H.) See also
    Quarterly Review on   1845   48 *b*–49 *a*   8   6
     1845   50 *b*–51 *a*   8   8
     1845   54 *b*–55   7   19
     1845   61 *b*–62   7   15
     1845   77   7   12
     1845   119   4   17
    Observations on Heresy and Orthodoxy   1843   93   3   20 seq.
     1843   97   5   15
     1843   102 *a*   2   14
     1843   102 *b*   2   last
     1843   113 *a*
     1843   2 IV *t*   4   5
  LETTER to Crabb Robinson   1812   70

WILKINSON, James John Garth
  Human Body, The   1849   78
     1849   80 *a*   1   5

WILKINSON, James John Garth—*contd.*
  Improvisations from the Spirit   1857   20 *a*
  (*War, Cholera, and the Ministry of*
    Health)   1854   76 *b*
                        1855   2 *b*
  LETTERS to Crabb Robinson   1848   27 *b*; 46 *b*–47 *a*; I II 9;
                                  I VIII 13
                        1849   5 *a*; 45 *b*; 78
                        1851   10 *b*
                        1854   26 *b*; 55 *a*; 59 *b*; 76 *b*
                        1855   17 *a* fragment; I II 11;
                                    81 *b*; 85 *a*
                        1856   20 *a*; 30 *a*; 31 *b*; 51;
                                    63 *a*
                        1857   20 *a*; I II 10
                        1859   13 *b*
                        1861   36 *a*
WILKINSON, Sir John Gardner
  Manners and Customs of the Ancient
    Egyptians   1838   19   3   23
WILLIAMS, Helen Maria   1814   108   2   19
                        1815   6 XIII *a*   I   21
                        1817   106   I   5
                [in 1807 vol.]
                        1826   150   2   I
  LETTERS to Crabb Robinson   1814   113 *b*
                        1819   24; 26; 31; 52
WILLIS, Nathaniel Parker
  introduced to Crabb Robinson by
    Landor   1834   80   I   2
  indiscretions   1834   143   4   5 of P.S.
                        1834   146   3   14
                        1836   121   3   16
  'The perfect world by Adam trod.'
    [Published in J. Martineau's
    Hymns]   1849   77   I   last
                        1850   1 *b*–2 *a*   4   15
                        1850   5 *b*   3   12
WILLMOTT, Robert Aris
  Crabb Robinson on   1849   56   4   I
WILSON, John, pseud. Christopher North
  and *Blackwood's Magazine*   1828   85 *b*   2   15
                        1829   91   3   12
  and Elleray   1842   168 *a*–169 *a*   3   9
                        1842   172 *a*   4   3 seq.
  and Quillinan's *Imaginary Conver-*
    sation between W. S. Landor and
    the Editor of Blackwood's Maga-
    zine   1843   8   I   15 seq.
                        1843   28 *a*   2   13
                        1843   27 *b*   3   10
  Crabb Robinson on   1829   97   3   13
  and N. P. Willis   1835   143   4   last
  Wordsworth on   1829   91   3   12
                        1835   143   4   last

WILSON, John—*contd.*
  Wordsworth on — 1844 — 5 XVI 5 — 7 — 4
  and the Wordsworths — 1843 — 79–81 — 6 — 6 seq.
  WORK:
    Trials of Margaret Lyndsay — 1829 — 91 — 3 — 15
WILSON, Walter
  LETTER to Crabb Robinson — 1840 — 147 *a*
WISEMAN, Nicholas Patrick Stephen, Cardinal
  and the establishment of the hier-
    archy in England — 1850 — 69 *b*–70 *a* — 8 — 7
     — 1850 — 74 — 3 — 20
     — 1850 — 81 *b* — 5 — 19
     — 1850 — 82 *a* — 3 — 2
     — 1853 — 30–31 — 5 — 17
  and the Oxford Movement — 1843 — 93 — 6 — 6
  Crabb Robinson's letter of intro-
    duction — 1829 — 131 — 1 — 3
  Crabb Robinson meets — 1829 — 163 — 2 — 33
     — 1829 — 163 — 2 — 46
     — 1830 — 20 — 4 — 21
WOLCOT, John, pseud. Peter Pindar — 1796 — 70 — 4 — marginal note
     — 1801 — 3 A 12 — 1 — 42
     — 1801 — 30 — 2 — 27
     — 1866 — 39 *a* — 4 — 5
WOLLSTONECROFT, Mary. *See* Godwin
WORDSWORTH, Christopher
  Diary in France, Crabb Robinson
    on — 1845 — 132 *b*–133 *b* — 7 — 10
     — 1846 — 1 — 4 — 14
     — 1846 — 10 — 2 — 19
WORDSWORTH, Dorothy
  LETTER from Crabb Robinson — 1825 — 120
WORDSWORTH, Dorothy (Dora). *See* Quillinan
WORDSWORTH, Mary
  Lady Byron on — 1856 — 21 *a* — 4 — 1
  T. Paynter on — 1859 — 3 — 8 — 4
  and Crabb Robinson's gift to H.
    Martineau — 1846 — 57 *a* — 1 — 9
  LETTERS from Crabb Robinson — 1840 — 160 *a*; 164 *a*
     — 1844 — 2 IV K [incomplete]
     — 1846 — [in 1840 vol.] 164 *b*
WORDSWORTH, William
  and American Stocks — 1844 — 5 XVI *b* — 2 — 18
  article by Hutton in the *National
    Review* — 1857 — 6 *b* — 4 — 1
  autograph for Mrs. Barrett — 1831 — 1 II 30 — 1 — 8
  and Josephine Garcia (Beppina) — 1853 — 1 10 *a* — 1 — 5
  imitation by Hancox, Crabb Robin-
    son on — 1838 — 5 IX 13
  handwriting betraying his age — 1842 — 2 IV *o* — 2 — 19
  memorial fund — 1850 — 54 *b* — 1 — P.S.
     — 1850 — 58 *b* — 2 — 5

WORDSWORTH, William—*contd.*

John Miller on. See also *Prelude*	1857	1	1	16 seq.
J. K. Miller on	1852	67–68*a*	9	3
and the Queen	1844	39 *b*–40	5	13
on poet's monuments	1846	164 *b*	8	7

[in 1840 vol.]

and E. Quillinan	1848	2 IV vii (*a–b*)	2	last
J. C. Richmond on	1840	172	4	11
F. W. Robertson's lectures on	1853	17 *b*	2	1
and T. Robinson's investments	1845	12	3	17
T. Robinson on	1845	131 *b*	1	18
Archdeacon Robinson to meet	1845	I VIII 59		
and S. Rogers	1836	126	1	8
	1839	I II 21		
as a schoolboy	1859	21	7	6 seq.
and the Southey family	1841	8 *b*	3	11
	1841	30 *a*	1	6
	1841	19 *a–b*		
other references	1843	I VIII 39	1	8
	1845	8	4	19

WORKS:

writings	1842	2 IV *g*	4	last
	1842	158 *a*	2	21 seq.
	1842	164 *a*	1	31
	1845	2 IV xvii	5	11
	1845	2 IV xvii	7	2
	1850	23 *a*	2	14
Excursion	1845	2 IV xvii	7	8
Female Vagrant	1853	18	3	19
Lyrical Ballads	1850	75	4	14
Prelude	1850	58 *b*	2	19
	1850	75	2	8
	1852	45–46 *a*	3	2
	1852	45–46 *a*	5	23
	1853	18	4	4

LETTERS:

to Crabb Robinson	N.D.	I II 31; I II 34; I II 36
from Crabb Robinson on the Clarkson–Wilberforce controversy	1840	159 *a*; 160 *b*; 161 *a*; 161 *b*; 163; 166 *a*; 177

WORDSWORTH, Mr. and Mrs.

proposed visit to Brinsop and Welsh tour	1843	2 IV iii	4	12
Crabb Robinson's account of, after Dora's death	1848	2 IV vii (*a–b*)		

WORDSWORTHS, the

and Mrs. Clarkson	1845	78 *b*–79 *a*	2	20
and H. Martineau	1845	12	2	6
	1845	132 *a*	2	21

WYNN, The Rt. Hon. Charles Watkyn Williams

and the Southey Family	1841	19 *b*	2	2

WYNN, The Rt. Hon. Charles Watkyn
  Williams—*contd.*

and the Southey Family	1841	26	1	6
	1841	35	1	4
	1841	45 *c*	1	6
	1841	64 *a*	1	6
	1848	29 *b*	2	9

YORKE, Philip, 2nd Earl of Hardwick
Athenian Letters	1801	3 A 9	2	15

II.   TITLES

Published works to which reference under the author may be found.

Abridgment of The Light of Nature Pursued, by Abraham Tucker.
        Hazlitt, W.
Account of Cretinism.   Twining, W.
Adam Bede.   Evans, M. A. (George Eliot)
Adventures of Hugh Trevor.   Holcroft, T.
—— *of Ulysses.*   Lamb, C.
Agrarian Justice.   Paine, T.
Aids to Reflection.   Coleridge, S. T.
Alfred.   Cottle, J.
All in the Wrong.   Murphy, A.
Ambrosio, or the Monk.   Lewis, M. G.
American Notes for General Circulation.   Dickens, C.
Ancient Christianity and the Doctrines of the Oxford Tracts.   Taylor, Isaac.
Ancient Songs.   Ritson, J.
Anna St. Ives.   Holcroft, T.
Antonio.   Godwin, W.
Apologia pro Vitâ Suâ.   Newman, J. H.
Apostacy of the Church Established by Law.   Hinton, G. P.
Armageddon.   Townsend, G.
Ascent to Mount Parnassus.   Buckstone, J. B.
Athenian Captive.   Talfourd, Sir T. N.
Athenian Letters.   Yorke, Philip.
Author's Mind.   Tupper, M. F.
Autobiography of a Dissenting Minister.   Scargill, W. P.

Ball I Live On.   Taylor, E.
Banished Man.   Smith, C.
Barnaby Rudge.   Dickens, C.
Battle of Flodden Field.   Weber, H. W.
Biographia Borealis.   Worthies of Yorkshire and Lancashire.   Coleridge,
        Hartley.
Biographia Literaria.   Coleridge, S. T.
Biographical Dictionary.   Aikin, J.
Bleak House.   Dickens, C.
Book of the Church.   Southey, R.
Botanic Garden.   Darwin, E.
Bothie of Tober-na-Vuolich.   Clough, A. H.
Bridge of Sighs.   Hood, T.

Caleb Williams.   Godwin, W.
Castilian.   Talfourd, Sir T. N.
Causes and Consequences of the War with France.   Erskine, T.
Celebrated Female Sovereigns.   Jameson, A. B.
Characteristics of Goethe.   Austin, S.

Charity Ball, The. Byron, Lord.
Chartism. Carlyle, T.
Childe Harold's Pilgrimage. Byron, Lord.
Christabel. Coleridge, S. T.
Christian Aspects of Faith and Duty. Tayler, J. J.
Church of Christ not an Ecclesiasticism. James, Henry.
Cid, The, appendix. Southey, R.
Citation and Examination of William Shakespeare. Landor, W. S.
Clubs of London. Marsh, C.
Colombe's Birthday. Browning, R.
Commentaries. Blackstone, Sir W.
Commonplace Book. Southey, R.
Comparison of the Institutions of Moses with those of the Hindoos, etc.
          Priestley, J.
Complete Guide to the English Lakes. Martineau, H.
Confessional. Blackburne, F.
Confessions of an English Opium Eater. De Quincey, T.
------ *of an Inquiring Spirit.* Coleridge, S. T.
Conquest of Scinde. Napier, Sir William.
Constitutional History of England. Hallam, H.
Country Neighbours. Burney, S. H.
Crofton Boys. Playfellow, The. Martineau, H.
Curiosities of Literature. Disraeli, I.
Curse of Kehama. Southey, R.

Dark Ages. Maitland, S. R.
David Copperfield. Dickens, C.
Devotional Taste. Barbauld, A. L.
Diary in France. Wordsworth, C.
Diary Illustrative of the Times of George II. Bury, Lady C.
Diogenes' Lanthorn. Taylor, T.
Discourse on Matters Pertaining to Religion. Parker, T.
Discourse on the Study of the Law of Nature and Nations.
          Mackintosh, Sir J.
Disquisitions, Metaphysical and Literary. Sayers, F.
Diversions of Purley. ῎ΕΠΕΑ ΠΤΕΡΟ῾ΕΝΤΑ. Tooke, J. H.
Divine Drama of History and Civilization. Smith, James.
Doctor, The. Southey, R.
Doctrine of Original Sin Defended. Edwards, J.
Don Juan. Byron, Lord.
Dred. Stowe, H. E. B.

Early Recollections chiefly relating to the late S. T. Coleridge. Cottle, J.
Eastern Life, Past and Present. Martineau, H.
Edmund Oliver. Lloyd, C.
Edwin the Fair. Taylor, Sir H.
Elements of the Human Mind. Stewart, Dugald.
Elements of the Philosophy of the Mind. Belsham, T.
Ellen Middleton. Fullerton, Lady.
Eloquence of the British Senate. Hazlitt, W.
Emmeline, or the Orphan of the Castle. Smith, C.
End of Religious Controversy. Milner, J.
Enquirer. Godwin, W.
Enquiry concerning Political Justice. Godwin, W.

Enquiry into our Ideas of the Sublime and Beautiful. Burke, E.
—— *into the State of the Nation at the Commencement of the Present Administration.* Pamphlet. Brougham, H. P.
Eōthen. Kinglake, A. W.
Ernest. Lofft, C.
Errors of Romanism. Whately, R.
Esmond. Thackeray, W. M.
Essay on the Development of Christian Doctrine. Newman, J. H.
—— *on the Freedom of the Will.* Edwards, J.
—— *on the Impolicy of the African Slave Trade.* Clarkson, T.
—— *on Italian Literature.* Hobhouse, Sir J. C.
—— *on Literary Character.* Disraeli, I.
—— *on the Nature and Principles of Taste.* Alison, A.
—— *on the Principles of Human Action.* Hazlitt, W.
—— *on the Principle of Population.* Malthus, T. R.
—— *on the Rate of Wages.* Carey, H. C.
—— *on the Slavery and Commerce of the Human Species,* Clarkson, T.
Essays. Emerson, R. W.
——. Whately, R.
—— *in Criticism.* Arnold, M.
—— *in Ecclesiastical Biography.* Stephen, Sir J.
—— *of Elia.* Lamb, C.
—— *on the Formation and Publication of Opinions and other Subjects.* Bailey, S.
—— *in a Series of Letters to a Friend.* Foster, J.
Essential Principles of the Wealth of Nations. Pamphlet. Gray, J.
Essentials of English History. Littlewood, W. E.
Eugene Aram. Lytton, Lord.
Eve of the Conquest and Other Poems. Taylor, H.
Evelina. D'Arblay, F.
Examination of a Sermon preached at Cambridge by Robert Hall on Modern Infidelity. Robinson, A.
Excursion, The. Wordsworth, W.

Fare thee Well. Byron, Lord.
Farmer's Boy, The. Bloomfield, R.
Feats on the Fjord. *Playfellow, The.* Martineau, H.
Female Biography. Hays, M.
Fleetwood. Godwin, W.
Forest and Game Law Tales. Martineau, H.
Fossils of the South Downs. Mantell, G. A.
Fragment on the Church. Arnold, T.
Frankenstein. Shelley, M. W.
Friend, The. Coleridge, S. T.

Gebir. Landor, W. S.
Genealogies of our Lord and Saviour Jesus Christ. Hervey, A.
General Biographical Dictionary, The. Chalmers, A.
Geraldine. Agnew, E. C.
Geraldine Fauconberg. Burney, S. H.
Geraldine: a Sequel to Christabel. Tupper, M. F.
German Anti-supernaturalism. Harwood, P.
German and English Dictionary. Crabb, G.
German Grammar. Crabb, G.

German Romance. Carlyle, T.
Germany from 1760 to 1814. Austin, S.
Glencoe. Talfourd, Sir T. N.
God in Christ. Bevan.
Great Opportunities. Stanley, A. P.
Gresford Vale and Other Poems. Holford, M.
Grongar Hill. Dyer, J.

Hear Both Sides. Holcroft, T.
Heaven and Earth. Byron, Lord.
Helen. Edgeworth, M.
Herald of Sight. Harris, T. L.
Herman and Dorothea. Holcroft, T.
——. tr. Whewell, W.
High and Low Life in Italy. Landor, W. S.
Hints towards a formation of a more Comprehensive Theory of Life.
      Coleridge, S. T.
Historic Survey of German Poetry. Taylor, W.
Historical Dialogues for Young People. Hays, M.
History of Egypt. Sharpe, S.
—— *of England.* Froude, J. A.
—— ——. Lingard, J.
—— ——. Macaulay, T. B.
—— ——. Mackintosh, Sir J.
—— —— *during the Thirty Years' Peace.* Martineau, H.
—— *of English Dramatic Poetry.* Collier, J. P.
—— *of Europe.* Alison, Sir A.
—— *of Great Britain.* Henry, R.
—— *of Greece.* Thirlwall, C.
—— *of Hallamshire.* Hunter, J.
—— *of Kent.* Hasted, E.
—— *of Latin Christianity, The.* Milman, H. H.
—— *of Rome.* Arnold, T.
—— *of Scotland.* Laing, M.
—— *of Spanish Literature.* Ticknor, G.
—— *of the Abolition of the Slave Trade.* Clarkson, T.
—— *of the British Colonies in the West Indies.* Edwards, B.
—— *of the French Revolution.* Carlyle, T.
—— *of the Hebrew Monarchy.* Newman, F. W.
—— *of the Peninsular War.* Southey, R.
—— *of the Popes.* Austin, W.
—— *of the Speculative Society of Edinburgh.* Ferguson, W.
—— *of the University and Colleges of Cambridge.* Dyer, G.
—— *of Wales.* Warrington, William.
Honington Green. A ballad. Bloomfield, N.
Hour and the Man. Martineau, H.
Household Education. Martineau, H.
Human Body and its Connection with Man. Wilkinson, J. J. G.

Idylls of the King. Tennyson, A.
Illustrations of Northern Antiquities. Weber, H. W.
—— *of Political Economy.* Martineau, H.
Imaginary Conversations. Landor, W. S.

Improvisations from the Spirit. Wilkinson, J. J. G.
Independent Man. Ensor, G.
Ingoldsby Legends. Barham, R. H.
Inheritance. Ferrier, S. E.
In Memoriam. Tennyson, A.
Inquiry into the nature and character of the Possessive Augment. Manning, J.
Introduction to Entomology. Spence, A. W.
Introduction to the Study of the Greek Classic Poets. Coleridge, H. N.
Ion. Talfourd, Sir T. N.
Iphigenia in Tauris. tr. Taylor, W.
Isle of the Sirens. Whewell, W.
Italian. Radcliffe, A. W.
Italian Sonnets. tr. Glassford, J.
Italy. Rogers, S.
Italy Past and Present. Gallenga, A. C. N.

Jack Sheppard. Ainsworth, W. H.
Jane Eyre. Brontë, C.
Joan of Arc. Southey, R.
Job. Blake, W.
Journal in France in 1845. Travels in France. Allies, T. W.
Journal of a Residence in Norway. Laing, S.
Journey throughout Ireland in 1834. Inglis, H. D.
Juridical Essays. Randall, E.
Justice of the Peace. Burn, R.

Lalla Rookh. Moore, T.
Land We Live In. Knight, C.
Last Days of Pompeii. Lytton, Lord.
Latter Day Pamphlets. Carlyle, T.
Lay of the Last Minstrel. Scott, Sir W.
Lazarus and Other Poems. Plumptre, E. H.
Lectures on the Dramatic Literature of the Reign of Queen Elizabeth. Hazlitt, W.
—— *on the History of France.* Stephen, J.
Letter concerning the Two First Chapters of Luke. Taylor, W.
—— *to a Noble Lord.* Burke, E.
—— *to the Duke of Portland.* Burke, E.
—— *to the Rt. Hon. H. Dundas with the sketch of a Negro Code.* Burke, E.
—— *to William Smith, Esq. J.P.* Southey, R.
Letters from Canada. Traill, C. P.
—— *from England by Don Manuel A. Espriella.* Southey, R.
—— *from Italy to a Younger Sister.* Taylor, C.
—— *from the Mountains.* Grant, A.
—— *on Chivalry and Romance.* Hurd, R.
—— *on Mesmerism.* Martineau, H.
—— *on the Laws of Man's Social Nature and Development.* Martineau, H.
—— *on the Poor Law in Ireland.* De Vere, A. T.
—— *to his Son.* Chesterfield, Lord.
Life of Addison. Aikin, L.
—— *of Lorenzo de Medici.* Roscoe, W.
—— *of Napoleon Buonaparte.* Scott, Sir W.
—— *Public and Private, of Lord Eldon.* Twiss, H.
—— *in the Sick-room.* Martineau, H.

Life of Wesley. Southey, R.
Literary Remains. Coleridge, S. T.
Lives of the Lord Chancellors and Keepers of the Great Seal of England.
—— Campbell, J.
—— *of the Most Eminent British Painters.* Cunningham, A.
Locke's Writings and Philosophy. Tagart, E.
Lucretius. Wakefield, G.
Lyric of the Golden Age. Harris, T. L.
Lyrical Ballads. Wordsworth, W.

Mackbeth Travestie. Talfourd, F.
Manfred. Byron, Lord.
Manners and Customs of the Ancient Egyptians. Wilkinson, Sir J. G.
Manners and Customs of the Modern Egyptians. Lane, E. W.
Man's Responsibility. Haldane, J. A.
Mary Barton. Gaskell, E. C. S.
Materialism in Religion. Harwood, P.
Medical Report of the case of Miss H. M. Greenhow, T. M.
Memoirs of Emma Courtney. Hays, M.
—— *of Joseph Grimaldi.* Dickens.
—— *of the Kings of Great Britain of the House of Brunswick.* Belsham, W.
Memorials on French Affairs. Burke, E.
Men and Manners in America. Hamilton, T.
Mesmerism true, Mesmerism false. Forbes, J.
Minstrel, The. Beattie, J.
Mirandola. Procter, B. W.
Miscellanies. Aikin, J.
Mr. H——. Lamb, C.
Mrs. Leicester's School. Lamb, C.
Monk, The. See *Ambrosio, or the Monk.*
Moral Principle of the Atonement. Penrose, J.
More Wonders. Moonshine.
My Last Tour and First Work; or, A Visit to the Baths of Wildbad and Rippoldsau. Vavasour, Lady.

Nathan the Wise. tr. by W. Taylor.
Natural History of Enthusiasm. Taylor, Isaac.
Nemesis of Faith, The. Froude, J. A.
New Testament . . . revised from the Authorized Version. **Taylor,** E.
Nineveh and its Remains. Layard, A. H.
Northern Summer Trip round the Baltic. Carr, Sir John.
Notes and Lectures upon Shakespeare. Coleridge, S. T.
—— *from Life.* Taylor, Sir H.

Observations on Heresy and Orthodoxy. White, J. B.
—— *on the Nature of Demonstrative Evidence.* Beddoes, **T.**
—— *on Zoonomia by Darwin.* Brown, T.
Old Manor House, The. Smith, C.
On Inconsistent Expectations. Barbauld, A. L.
On the Genius and Character of Hogarth. Lamb, C.
On the Natural and Supernatural. Campbell, G. D.
Order and Method of Instructing Children. Crabb, G.
Our Clerks. Taylor, T.

Parliamentary History of England. Cobbett, W.
Parriana. Barker, E. H.

Passages from the Diary of a Late Physician.   Warren, S.
Past and Present.   Carlyle, T.
Pelham.   Lytton, Lord.
Pericles and Aspasia.   Landor, W. S.
Peveril of the Peak.   Scott, Sir W.
Phantasmagoria, or Sketches of Life and Character.   Jewsbury, M. J.
Phases of Faith.   Newman, F. W.
Philip van Artevelde.   Taylor, Sir H.
Philosophy of Comte.   Martineau, H.
Physical Theory of Another Life.   Taylor, Isaac.
Pictorial History of England.   Craik, G. L.
Playfellow, The.   Martineau, H.
Poetical Sketches.   Blake, W.
Poet's Fate.   Dyer, G.
Political Index to the Histories of Great Britain and Ireland.   Beatson, R.
Poor Laws and Paupers Illustrated.   Martineau, H.
Popular Ballads.   Jamieson, R.
Portraiture of Quakerism.   Clarkson, T.
Practical Christianity.   More, H.
Practical Education.   Edgeworth, M.
Prelude, The.   Wordsworth, W.
Princess, The.   Morgan, Lady.
Proofs of a Conspiracy.   Robinson, J.
Proverbial Philosophy.   Tupper, M. F.
Pursuits of Literature.   Mathias, T. J.

Redgauntlet.   Scott, Sir W.
Reflections on the French Revolution.   Burke, E.
Relation between Judaism and Christianity.   Palfrey, J. G.
Religion of the Nineteenth Century.   Stanley, A. P.
Remarks on Mr. J. P. Collier's and Mr. C. Knight's editions of Shakespeare.
     Dyce, A.
Remorse.   Coleridge, S. T.
Representative Men.   Emerson, R. W.
Retrospect of the Religious Life of England.   Tayler, J. J.
Retrospect of Western Travel.   Martineau, H.
Reynard the Fox.   Naylor, S.
Rhetoric.   Blair, Hugh.
Rioters.   Martineau, H.
Road to Ruin.   Holcroft, T.
Rokeby.   Scott, Sir W.
Romance of the Forest.   Radcliffe, A. W.
Romance of Private Life.   Burney, S. H.
Rome in the Nineteenth Century.   Eaton, C. A.
Rural and Domestic Life of Germany.   Howitt, W.
Rural Tales.   Bloomfield, R.
Ruth.   Gaskell, E. C. S.

Sabbation ; Honor Neale and Other Poems.   Trench, R. C.
St. Leon.   Godwin, W.
Sakuntala, or the Fatal Ring.   Jones, Sir W.
Sardanapalus.   Byron, Lord.
Satire upon Satirists.   Landor, W. S.
Saturday Evening.   Taylor, Isaac.
Series of Adventures in the Course of a Voyage up the Red Sea.   Irwin, E.

Sermons. Blair, Hugh.
——. Robertson, F. W.
—— *before the University of Oxford.* Newman, J. H.
Settlers at Home. Playfellow, The. Martineau, H.
Sights and Thoughts in Foreign Churches. Faber, F. W.
Silas Marner. Evans, M. A. (George Eliot).
Sinai and Palestine. Stanley, A. P.
Society in America. Martineau, H.
Son of the Soil. Oliphant, M. O.
Soul: Her Sorrows and her Aspirations. Newman, F. W.
Spirit of the East. Urquhart, D.
Springtime with the Poets. Martin, F.
State in its Relations with the Church. Gladstone, W. E.
Suffolk Bartholomeans: A memoir of John Meadows. Taylor, Edgar.
Sybil. Disraeli, B.

Table Talk. Coleridge, S. T.
Tales. Edgeworth, M.
Tales from Shakespeare. Lamb, C.
Temple of Nature. Darwin, E.
Thaddeus of Warsaw. Porter, J.
Thalaba. Southey, R.
Theodore Cyphon. Walker, G.
Theodore or the Enthusiast. Hare-Naylor, F.
Theological Essays. Maurice, J. F. D.
Thoughts on Man. Godwin, W.
Travels in France. Holcroft, T.
Travels in Turkey. De Vere, A. T.
Travels of an Irish Gentleman in search of a Religion. Moore, T.
Travels to Discover the Source of the Nile. Bruce, J.
Treasure or Storehouse of Similies. Cawdry, R.
Treatise on Prison Discipline. Field, J.
Tremaine. Ward, R. P.
Trials of Margaret Lindsay. Wilson, J.
Triumphs of Temper. Hayley, W.
True Intellectual System of the Universe. Cudworth, R.
Tour through Italy. Eustace, J. C.
Tour in Wales. Pennant, T.
Two Hundred Years Ago. Mountfield, D.
Two Old Men's Tales. Marsh, A. C.

Uncle Tom's Cabin. Stowe, H. E. B.
Unspoken Sermons. MacDonald, G.

Vacation Rambles and Thoughts. Talfourd, Sir T. N.
Vancenza; or the Dangers of Credulity. Robinson, M.
Vanity Fair. Thackeray, W. M.
Vaurien or Sketches of the Times. Disraeli, I.
Vestiges of the Natural History of Creation. Chambers, R.
Vicar of Wakefield. Taylor, T.
View of the Evidences of Christianity. Paley, W.
View of the Scripture Revelations concerning a Future State. Whately, W.
View of Society and Manners in France. Moore, J.
Villette. Brontë, C.
Vision of Judgment. Southey, R.

Walk through Wales.   Warner, R.
Wallenstein.   Tr. Coleridge, S. T.
Wanderings of Warwick.   Smith, C.
War, Cholera, and the Ministry of Health.   Wilkinson, J. J. G.
Way to Keep Him.   Murphy, A.
Werner.   Byron, Lord.
Within and Without.   MacDonald, G.
Wives and Daughters.   Gaskell, E. C. S.
Woman's Mission.   Lewis.
Words of Christ.   Field, C.
Worthies of Yorkshire and Lancashire.   Coleridge, Hartley.

Youth and Age.   Coleridge, S. T.

Zincali ; or an Account of the Gypsies in Spain.   Borrow, G.

GENERAL INDEX

GENERAL INDEX

Since the whole book consists of Crabb Robinson's opinions and criticisms on *Books and Their Writers*, these are not separately indexed under his name. His criticisms of a book he is reading so often lead him from the subject of the book itself to comment on the character of the author, that his more important personal opinions may generally be found among the references to an author's works.

The following signs should be noted:

[ ] indicate information supplied by the editor.

〈 〉 indicate a paraphrase in the text, e.g. '〈*Biographia Literaria*〉' appears on p. 182 as 'two volumes of Miscellanies,' on pp. 200 and 210 as Coleridge's 'Memoirs,' and on p. 213 as 'Coleridge's book.'

‖ indicates a typographical, spelling or other error in the text, e.g. '‖ Lawrence, James Henry, poem,' in the index indicates a correction of 'Laurence, *The Knight of Malta*,' p. 646; '‖ Parken, 55, 85, 87, 88' in the index indicates that 'Parker,' p. 55, and 'Parkin,' p. 85, should read 'Parken' throughout.

〈ABBOTSFORD〉, 266
ABEILLA, 11
ABERDEEN, visited, 433
ABINGER, 1st baron. *See* Scarlett, James
ABINGTON, Frances, 55
ABLETT, Joseph, 495
ABOLITION. *See* Slavery
ADAIR, J. M., 352
ADAMS, Dr. Joseph, 36, 48
ADAMS, Mrs., 36
ADDISON, Joseph
    lecture by Hazlitt, 226
    mentioned by Thackeray, 721, 725
    WORK:
    Cato acted, 26
ADERS, Charles, 56, 58, 106, 119, 122, 307, 310, 392, 442
ADERS, Eliza [Mrs. Charles]
    on Byron's 〈*Question and Answer*〉, 422
    Carlyle and, 825, 828
    and Coleridge, 361, 405, 442
    gifts to Crabb Robinson, 511, 625; letter to Crabb Robinson, 687
    described by Rogers, 422
    and Wordsworth, 361; portrait of Wordsworth, 618
    mentioned, 281, 331, 345, 406, 426

ADERS, The
    introduced by Crabb Robinson to the Flaxmans, the Lambs, and
        the Wordsworths, 256, 257; to Landor, 406
    literary parties, 222, 237, 256, 257, 288, 293, 311, 324, 325, 359,
        404, 497
    pictures, collection of, 228, 236, 237, 292, 325, 406
    —— sale of, 570, 572
    mentioned, 258, 261, 303
ADVOCATE'S LIBRARY, The, 824
AGNEW, Eleanor C., *Geraldine*, 580
AIKIN, Anna Laetitia. *See* Barbauld, A. L.
AIKIN, Anne. *See* Aikin, Mrs. Charles
AIKIN, Arthur, 69 and note, 83, 292
AIKIN, Charles Rochemont, 50, 117, 204, 218, 692, 748
AIKIN, Mrs. Charles, Anne, *born* Wakefield, 24, 57, 74, 265, 275, 847
AIKIN, Mr. and Mrs. Charles, 81, 83, 84, 109, 118, 151, 197
AIKIN, John, M.D., 10, 69, 152, 155, 177, 207, 232, 844, 848
AIKIN, Mrs. John, 78, 144, 232, 320
AIKIN, Lucy
    and Mrs. Barbauld, 512, 634
    and Coleridge's *Christabel*, 155
    and Lamb and his works, 69, 79, 144, 817
    Life and Letters. *See* Le Breton
    relations with Crabb Robinson, 143, 844. *See also* on Wordsworth
    and Rough's *Gowrie*, 38
    and Wordsworth, 83, 462
    on Wordsworth, 232, 710, 711, 740, 817 and note
    —— and the *Excursion*, 152, 155
    mentioned, 167, 182, 320

    WORKS:
    (*Balloon, The*), verses, 49
    edn. *Legacy for Young Ladies*. *See* Barbauld, A. L.
    Lorimer, 143
    Memoir of Mrs. Barbauld, 8, 332
    Memoirs of the Court of King Charles I, 512
    Memoirs of the Court of Queen Elizabeth, 221, 229, 262
    Memoirs of the Court of James I, 229, 287, 512
    review, of Wordsworth's *Poems*, 143
AIKINS, The, 69, 79, 144, 145, 642
AINSWORTH, William Harrison, 317, 497, 654

    WORKS:
    Jack Sheppard, reviews in the *Athenæum*, 578; *Examiner*, 578
    Rookwood, 497, 575
AKENSIDE, Mark, *Works*, ed. *See* Barbauld, A. L.
ALBERT, Prince Consort
    and the Wordsworth monument, 700
    Ode, by Wordsworth, 664
ALDERSON, Amelia. *See* Opie
ALDERSON, Mrs. and Miss, 227
ALEXANDER, William, 170
Alexander the Great, drama, 115
ALISON, Archibald, *Essay on the Nature and Principles of Taste*, review,
    36
'All my Eye and Betty Martin,' derivation, 114

ALLAN [Edinburgh banker], 433
ALLEN, Joseph William, 570
ALLEN, Miss, 40
ALLEN, 734
Allgemeine Zeitung, 529
ALLSOP, Thomas, 315, 344, 814, 815, 818
    and Coleridge's family, 488
    and the Lambs, 315, 344, 453, 468
    (*Letters, Conversations, and Recollections of S. T. Coleridge*), 468 seq.,
        815, 819, 820
|| ALLSTON, Washington, 222
    portrait of Coleridge, 724 seq.
    Monaldi, 605
ALSAGER, Thomas M.
    and Hazlitt, 179, 184
    Lamb's description, 674
    parties, 133, 145, 161, 162, 164, 178, 179
    and Wordsworth, 160, 168, 184, 616
    other references, 166, 167, 170, 215, 217, 814
ALSAGER [son of the above], 725
ALTHORP, Viscount [John Charles Spencer], 431
AMBLESIDE, Wordsworth library, 807
AMBLESIDE CHURCH, window to Wordsworth, 715, 726
AMERICA, 429, 430, 541, 612
    and copyright, 541, 544
    slavery in.   *See* Slavery
    see also under :
        Carlyle, T. [*Latter Day Pamphlets*]
        De Tocqueville, works
        Dickens, C. [*American Notes* and *Martin Chuzzlewit*]
        Emerson, R. W., works
        Hamilton, T., works
        Martineau, H., *Retrospect of Western Travel* and *View of Society
            in America*
        Moore, T. [*Epistles*]
        Stowe, H. E. B., works
AMERICAN edition of *Elia*, 405
AMORY, Thomas, *Life of John Buncle*, 134, 144
AMYOT, Thomas
    and the Camden Society, 548
    and Larpent's plays, 404
    literary taste, 50, 226, 279, 397
    and Southey, 132, 133
    and Windham's Speeches, 54
    other references, 12, 13, 117, 144, 146, 280, 285, 311, 319, 392,
        404, 415, 421, 424, 465, 503
AMYOTS, The, 157
Analytical Review
    ARTICLE :
        Lloyd, C., *Edmund Oliver*, 5
ANDERSEN, Hans
    Emperor's New Clothes, The, 712
    Ugly Duckling, The, 672, 712
ANDERSON, Robert, M.D., 269
    Complete Edition of the Poets of Great Britain, 269 and note

ANDERSON, Robert, M.D.—*contd.*
  Life of Samuel Johnson, 269
ANDREWS, Alexander, *History of British Journalism*, 780
ANDREWS, Mordecai, 36, 51
ANIMAL MAGNETISM, 149
Anniversary, The, article by E. Irving, 363
Annual Register, 497 note, 723, 781
Annual Review
  ARTICLES:
    Godwin, W., *Chaucer*, 28
    Lamb, C., *John Woodvil*, 69, 638, 695
    Wordsworth, W., *Poems*, 143
ANTIBES, visited with Wordsworth, 518
Anti-Jacobin, The, 40
ANTIQUARIES, Society of
    J. P. Collier and, 804
    Emerson dines with, 675, 676
    Crabb Robinson's paper before, 462 and note
Appeal to Dissenters, by a Lay Dissenter, 477
Arabian Nights, 303, 316
ARBLAY, Frances Burney, Mme D'. *See* D'Arblay
ARBUTHNOT, 37
ARCHITECTURE, lecture by G. Street, 781, 782
ARIOSTO, 381, 383
ARISTOCRACY, lecture by Emerson, 678
ARMY, The, 133, 743
ARNDT, Ernst Moritz, 33
    (*Geist der Zeit*), 9, 13
ARNIM, Bettina von, 650
    Briefwechsel mit einem Kind, 495, 531
ARNO VALLEY visited with Wordsworth, 522
ARNOLD, Charles, 661 and note
ARNOLD, Mrs. Charles, 661 and note
ARNOLD, Fanny, 807
ARNOLD, Mary [Mrs. Thomas]
    and Dr. Arnold's death, 621; on Dr. Arnold, 476, 855; ed. of Dr.
      Arnold's *Works*, 476
    and A. H. Clough, 682
    and Hughes, *Tom Brown's Schooldays*, 770
    on H. Martineau, 718
    personal qualities, 476, 604, 838, 854
    and Crabb Robinson, 743, 807; letters from Crabb Robinson, 665,
      767; letter to Crabb Robinson, 666
    and (Whately's) letters, 673
    and Wordsworth, and Dora's last illness, 666, 667
  other references, 473, 628, 637, 638, 648, 683, 684, 835
ARNOLD, Mary [later Mrs. Aldred Twining, then Mrs. Hiley], 565, 566,
    587, 667
ARNOLD, Matthew
    and Lord Lansdowne, 665
    and Louis Napoleon, 790
    and Oxford University, 767
    personal qualities, 806, 822
    and Crabb Robinson, 743, 753, 807
    at Crabb Robinson's, 699

ARNOLD, Matthew—*contd.*
  and schools abroad, 783
  and the *North British Review*, article on Wordsworth, 812
  mentioned, 684, 759, 818
  WORKS:
    Balder Dead, 754
    Essays in Criticism, 810 note, 822
    (*Memorial Verses 1850* 'Goethe in Weimar Sleeps'), 754
(ARNOLD, Mrs. Matthew), 807
ARNOLD, Samuel James, 112
ARNOLD [son of Samuel James], 341
ARNOLD, Thomas, D.D.
  article on, 639
  and Bunsen, 473, 618
  character, 473, 475, 476, 479, 611
  and the Church, 473, 475, 476, 565, 855
  death, 568, 618, 621
  and his family, 476, 588, 611
  and Miss Fenwick, 561, 562
  and Fox How, 428, 476
  and Goethe, 478
  in Hughes, *Tom Brown's Schooldays*, 770
  Life and Correspondence. See Stanley, A. P.
  and Dr. Passavant's book, 486
  personal description, 471
  and Crabb Robinson, 476, 483, 562 and note
  and Southey, 564, 565
  and University College, London, 481, 562 and note
  verses on, 648
  and Wordsworth, 428, 476, 481, 564, 611,
  mentioned, 470 and note, 472, 481 note, 484, 486, 560, 566, 587, 608,
    610, 628
  WORKS:
    Fragment on the Church, 648
    History of Rome, 350, 560 seq., 618
    Inaugural Lecture as Professor of Modern History, 604
    Letters in the *Sheffield Courant*, 639
    Miscellanies, 476
    Sermons, 606, 607
ARNOLD, William Delafield
  and Lady Byron, 743, 746
  death, 783
  and the *Economist*, 753
  and the (Indian Mutiny), 835
  personal qualities, 743, 753
  WORK:
    Oakfield, or Fellowship in the East, 741, 743, 835; review, 740
ARNOLD, 215 and note
ARNOLD, Mrs. [friend of Wilkes], 23
ARNOLDS, The [Fox How Family], qualities as a family, 587, 588, 741
    seq., 812
  mentioned, 483, 485, 605, 661, 670, 681, 685, 754, 806
ARRIAZA, Juan Bautista de, 42

ART
  Exhibitions visited, 34, 304, 358, 359, 492, 571, 769
    Bologna, 524
    Florence, 388
    National Gallery, 491
    Stafford collection, 35
    see also Aders, Collection of Pictures; British Museum; Louvre
ARTS, Society of, 292
ASHBURNER, Dr., 722
ASHLEY, 5
ASPLAND, Robert, 119 and note
ASPLAND, Robert Brook, 670, 705, 728
ATHENÆUM CLUB
    Browning elected, 804
    Carlyle elected, 723
    B. Disraeli and, 575
ATHENÆUM, librarian [Hall], 812
Athenæum, The
  ARTICLES:
    Ainsworth, W. H., *Jack Sheppard*, 578
    De Quincey, T., *Anecdotes of Coleridge*, 456
    Collier, J. P., forgeries, by Dixon, 795
    Gilchrist, A., *Blake*, 810
    Lamb, C., by B. W. Procter, 456
    Lamb and Moore, by Crabb Robinson, 724 seq., 730
    Talfourd, T. N., *Final Memorials*, 679
  mentioned, 351, 714, 715, 758
ATKINS, Mrs. [landlady at Rydal], 469 seq.
ATKINSON, Henry George, 754
    Letters on the Laws of Man's Social Nature and Development. See
    Martineau, H.
ATTERBURY, Francis, article on, 798
ATTIC CHEST, Society of the, 67
ATTORNEY-GENERAL. *See* Gibbs
ATWOOD, Mr. and Mrs., 217
Ausland, 531
AUSTEN, JANE
  WORKS:
    writings, 575, 576, 629, 797
    Emma, 282, 577
    Mansfield Park, 576
    Northanger Abbey, 625
    Persuasion, 625
    Pride and Prejudice, 227, 575, 576, 851
    Sense and Sensibility, 574, 576
AUSTIN, John, 332, 393
    (*Plea for the Constitution, A*), 782
AUSTIN, Sarah, *born* Taylor, 121, 332, 441
  WORKS:
    (*Characteristics of Goethe*), 430, 467; review, 426
    preface to Lady Duff Gordon's *Letters*, 817
    tr. of Ranke's *History of the Popes*, 638, 639
    edn. of Sydney Smith's *Letters*. *See* Holland, Lady
AUSTINS, The, 121

AYRTON, William
   and Lady Blessington, 415
   death, 780
   and Godwin, 285 seq.
   in Hazlitt's *Literary Remains*, 780
   in P. G. Patmore's *My Friends and Acquaintance*, 744
   and Crabb Robinson, 16, 678
  other references, 161, 170, 178, 259, 298, 421, 725
AYRTONS, The, 494

BABBAGE, Charles, 569, 770 and note
BACON, Francis, Lord Verulam
   article on, 533
   Spedding on, 702, 760
BAGE, Robert, *Hermsprong*, 319
BAGEHOT, Walter, 688, 689, 765, 807
  ARTICLES:
   Balzac, 765
   Crédit Mobilier, 765
   Poetry, 813
   Shakespeare, 726, 810
   Shelley, 762, 810
BAILEY, Philip James, *Festus*, review, 669
BAILLIE, Joanna, 84, 86, 91, 105, 546, 547
  WORKS:
   writings, 109, 436, 847
   Beacon, The, 66
   Dream, The, 66
   Hate, 212
   (*Plays on the Passions*, Vol. III), review, 92
BAILLIE, Miss [sister of Joanna], 91, 105
BAKEWELL, Robert, 38, 39, 416
BALA-SALA, 495 note
BALDWIN, Robert [of Baldwin, Cradock, & Joy, publishers]
   and Landor's works, 401, 402
   and H. M. Williams's works, 230 seq.
(BALDWIN, CRADOCK, & JOY), 337
BALDWINS, The, 546
Baldwin's Magazine. See *London Magazine*. [Publishers, Baldwin, Cradock, & Joy]
BALL, 562
BALLANTYNE, James, 826
BALLANTYNE, Thomas, 690 and note
BALZAC, Honoré de, article on, 765
BANIM, John and Michael, *Tales of the O'Hara Family*
   Boyne Watch, 705
   Boyne Water, 348, 349
   Peter of the Castle, 349
BANK ROBBERY, A, 647 and note
BARANTE, Baron de, essay on French Literature, 248 and note
BARBAULD, Anna Laetitia, *born* Aikin
   and L. Aikin, 512, 634
   and G. Dyer, 4, 5
   M. Edgeworth's letter on, 634

Barbauld, Anna Laetitia—*contd.*
  and the Edgeworths, 128, 130
  and C. Lamb, 78, 306
  and the review of Lamb's *John Woodvil*, 69, 638, 695
  and the Lambs, 145, 265
  and Machiavelli, 384
  Memoir of. *See* Aikin, L.
  and H. More, 480
  chess with Crabb Robinson, 25, 49, 118, 229
  and T. N. Talfourd, 198
  and H. M. Williams, 148
  and Wordsworth, 8, 83

  OPINIONS AND CRITICISM:
    literary, 175, 176, 198 seq., 465, 472
    L. Aikin's *The Balloon*, 49
    Byron's works, 69, 142, 223
    Coleridge, 118
    Mme D'Arblay's works, 136
    M. Edgeworth's *Patronage*, 136
    Hayley's *Old Maids*, 177 seq.
    Wordsworth, 118, 176
    —— works, 79, 151, 198

  PERSONAL QUALITIES:
    appearance, 8, 260, 314, 835
    character, 8, 17, 56, 62, 218, 306, 634, 843
    conversation, 179, 218, 260, 844
    health and old age, 176, 197, 207, 229, 230, 264, 302, 314

  mentioned, 147, 182, 617, 642, 848

  WORKS:
    writings, 8, 45, 74, 320, 848, 849; collected edition, 785
    edn. of Akenside, M., *Works*, 74
    (*Civic Sermons to the People*), 23
    lines to Coleridge, 697
    edn. of Collins, W., *Works*, 74
    verses to George III, 45
    Legacy for Young Ladies, ed. Aikin, L., 331
    'Life! We have been long together,' 8 and note, 651
    Ode to Content, 62
    On Inconsistent Expectations, 362, 607, 730
    Sins of the Government, Sins of the Nation, 64
    Year 1811, 63, 64, 86
    —— review, 64

Barbauld, Rochemont, 56, 843
Barham, Richard Harris, 603 and note
Barker, Edmund Henry, 609
Barker, Jemima, 167, 297, 431
Barnes, Thomas, 66 seq., 117, 155, 156, 162, 167, 230, 270 and note, 451, 616
  articles in the *Examiner*, 142
Barnes, Mrs. Thomas, note, 270
Barrett, Charlotte, 585, 586, 601
  see also D'Arblay, Mme., *Diary and Letters*

BARRETT, Eaton Stannard, *Heroine, The*, 181
BARRETT, Elizabeth. *See* Browning, Elizabeth Barrett
(BARRETT, Richard A. F.), 586, 601
BARRETT, 797
BARRETTS, The, 362
|| BARROSA, Battle of, 41
BARROW, Sir John, articles in the *Quarterly Review*, 237
BARRY, James, pictures, 292
BARTON, Bernard, 366, 642, 645
    Life and Letters, 693
BATH, visited, 581, 582, 592 seq., 622, 712, 755, 756, 779
BAUDOUIN, Captain and Mme, *born* Caroline Wordsworth
    visited by Wordsworth, 248, 255, 516
    business arrangements with the Wordsworths, 452, 454, 461 seq., 483,
        623, 697, 699, 703 seq., 710
BAUDOUIN, Mlle, 248
BAYLEY, Miss S., 600, 615, 752, 764, 788, 789, 799
BAYLY, Thomas Haynes, *Musings and Prosings*, 437, 438
BAYNE, Alicia, *born* Pryme, 651, 751, 760, 800
BEACONSFIELD, Lord. *See* Disraeli, B.
BEATTIE, William, M.D., 715, 728
    Life and Letters of Thomas Campbell, 721
BEAUMONT, Sir George Howland, Bart.
    and works of art, 291, 292
    and Haydon, 242
    and Hazlitt, 24
    and Wordsworth, 358, 486; Wordsworth's *Epistle* to, 615; Words-
        worth visits, 78
   other references, 70, 312
BEAUMONT, Lady, 78, 98, 239, 291, 435
BEAUMONT AND FLETCHER, essay by Donne, W. B., 775
BECHER, Alfred, 359
BECHER, 21, 185
BECHER, Mrs., 21, 23, 207
BECHER, Lady. *See* O'Neill
BECKFORD, William
    History of Caliph Vathek, 180 and note, 181, 443, 517 and note
    ⟨*Italy, with Sketches of Spain and Portugal*⟩, 504; review, 443
BECKY [Lamb's old servant], 365
BEDDOES, Thomas Lovell
    Death's Jest Book, 712 and note
    Poems ⟨*with a Memoir*, by Kelsall, T. F.⟩, 711, 713
BEDFORD COLLEGE, 692, 730, 786, 787
BEESLY, Edward Spencer, 804
BEHLEN'S LETTERS, 332
BELL, Andrew, D.D., 484
    Life, by Southey, 484
BELL, Robert, 758
BELLES LETTRES, lecture by Coleridge, 112
BENECKE, William, 356
BENEFIT SOCIETIES, 90, 127
BENGER, Miss, 56, 64, 81, 83, 335, 336
BENJAFIELD, John, 34, 35
BENNETT [vicar of Hatfield], 263
BENSON, 357, 358

BENTHAM, Jeremy
     article on, 301
     interviewed, 397 seq.
     opinions, 22, 320, 742, 744, 750 and note
     mentioned, 311, 314, 378
     WORKS:
          Codification Proposals, 320
          Preuves Judiciaires, 300
          Rationale of Evidence, 170
BENTLEY, Richard, 143
BENTLEY, Thomas, *Life*, 634
BÉRANGER, Pierre Jean de, writings, 517
BERGAMO, visited with Wordsworth, 525
BERNARD, Simon-François, 814
Bernardine, poem, 806
BESSER, Heinrich [partner of Perthes], 206
BETHAM, Matilda, 232
BETTINELLI, l'Abbate (*Lettres de Virgile aux Arcades*), 407
BETTY, William Henry West, 113, 115
BEYLE, Henri. *See* Stendhal, pseud.
BIBLE SOCIETY, The, 59, 131
Bijou, The, 1828
     poems by Coleridge, 350 and note
     contributions by Jameson, A. B., 350
BLACK, Adam, 433
BLACKMORE, Richard Doddridge, 759
BLACKSTONE, 608
(BLACKWOOD, William), 213
Blackwood's Magazine, 696, 808
     article on, by Scott, J., 256, note 262
     attack on Coleridge, 581
     and Lamb's *Letter of Elia to R. S.*, 298
     and E. Quillinan, 272 and note, 273, 630, 635
     and Crabb Robinson's article on *Prussian Reforms*, 318 and note
     attack on Wordsworth, 363

     CONTRIBUTIONS BY:
          Byron, letter, 428
          Coleridge, S. T., articles, 694
          Landor, W. S., *Dialogue*, 626
          Wilson, J., 316
          Wordsworth, sonnets, 229
               see also: Evans, Mary Ann, *Scenes of Clerical Life*; Lamb, C., *The Wife's Trial*; Landor, W. S., *Satire upon Satirists*; Lytton, *The Caxtons*; Warren, S., *Passages from the Diary of a Late Physician, Ten Thousand a Year*

     ARTICLES:
          Dickens, C., 751
          Hunt, J. H. Leigh, *Byron*, 355
BLAIR, Hugh, *Lectures on Rhetoric and Belles Lettres*, 1
BLAKE, Catherine [Mrs. William], 329, 331, 353, 498
(BLAKE, James), brother of William, 15
BLAKE, William
     principal entries, 324 seq., 335, 337, 342, 344

BLAKE, William—*contd.*
  article by Crabb Robinson, 15, 31
  death, 353
  Life. See Cunningham, A., *Lives of the Most Eminent British Painters*
    Gilchrist, A., *Life of Blake*
  state of his mind, 40, 41, 355, 498, 752
  writings and works of art:
    exhibition, 15; sale, 705
    'Canterbury Pilgrims,' 325, 353, 356
    Catalogue, 15, 625, 717
    Chimney Sweeper, 25
    Jerusalem, 41
    Job, 331
    Poems, 85, 117, 625, 717
    Prose, 810
    Songs of Innocence, 669
    (*Songs of Innocence and Experience*), ed. Wilkinson, 675, 676
    songs, 810
    illustrations for Young's (*Night Thoughts*), 25, 117
  mentioned, 20, 361, 550, 706, 799
BLAKESLEY, Joseph Williams, 509
BLANC, Louis, 783
BLESSINGTON, Charles John Gardiner, Earl of, 411
BLESSINGTON, Marguerite, Countess of
  principal entries, 411 seq., 420, 421, 423 seq., 438, 440, 443, 450, 451, 456, 458, 460, 464, 465, 468, 488, 489, 492, 506, 511, 549, 551, 572
  her Book of Beauty, 438, 750
  and Count D'Orsay, 469
  financial position, 426, 469, 689
  leaving for France, 689
  in D. Quillinan's letter, 509
  and Crabb Robinson, 456, 491, 549, 749
  and N. P. Willis, 443, 445, 450, 460, 464
  mentioned, 383, 491, 497, 504, 561, 575, 631, 746
  WORKS:
    writings, 426, 689
    (*Conversations with Lord Byron*), 411, 412, 415, 457
    Memoirs [ed. Madden, R. R.], 749, 750
    Repealer, The, 426
    Two Friends, The, 456
BLEWITT, Octavian, 759
BLOMEFIELD, Francis (*Essay towards a Topographical History of the County of Norfolk*), 645
(BLOMFIELD, Charles James), Bishop of London, 664, 697, 698, 732
BLOOMFIELD, Robert, 28, 202, 394, 409
BLOSSETT, Serjeant, 225
BOADEN, James
  Life of Mrs. Inchbald, 456
  Life of Mrs. Siddons, 354
BOCCACCIO, 407
BODICHON, Mme, note 680
BOEHMEN, Jacob, 88, 108, 327

III—M

[BOGUE, David], (*History of Dissenters*), review, 139
BOLOGNA, visited with Wordsworth, 524
BOOKSELLERS and German books, 826, 828
BOOKSELLERS' ASSOCIATION and cheap books, 716
BOOTH, James, 584, 597, 600, 640, 764 and note
BOOTH, at Godwins, 233
BOOTT, Francis, M.D., 694, 724, 748, 800
BOOTT, Mrs. F., 737, 748
BORROW, George, *Zincali; or An Account of the Gypsies in Spain*, 675
    and note
BOSTOCK, Dr. John, 641, 642
BOSTOCK, Miss, 642
BOSWELL, James, *Life of Samuel Johnson*, 7, 397
    ed. Croker, J. W., 392
BOURGOYNE, Mrs. Montagu, 601, 602
BOWLES, Caroline Anne. *See* Southey
BOWLES, William Lisle, Sonnets, 140, 480
BOWRING, Sir John, 301, 311, 314, 397 seq., 750 note
BOXALL, Sir William
    portrait of Landor, 764
    and the Wordsworth monument, 698 seq., 708, 714, 718, 726,
        747, 748
    other references, 497, 739
(BOYER, the Rev. James) and Coleridge, 197
BRABANT, Dr. R. H., 663 and note
BRANWHITE, Nathan, 500, 502
BRATHAY WOOD, gale damage, 565, 566
BRENT, Miss [Mrs. Morgan's sister], 202
BRENTANO, Clemens, 530
BRENTANO, Elizabeth [Bettina]. *See* Arnim von
BRIDGEWATER HOUSE, library, 643
BRIGHTON
    epigram on, by H. Smith, 635
    visited, 311, 312, 361, 395, 408, 436, 466, 509, 577, 704, 707, 721,
        728, 736, 745, 817
BRIGHTWELL, C. L., *Memorials of Amelia Opie*, 747
BRINSOP, visited with Wordsworth, 537 seq., 634
BRISTOL [Augustus John Hervey, 3rd Earl], 13
BRITISH ASSOCIATION, 504
BRITISH MUSEUM, 170, 257, 494, 645, 759
    librarianship, 536
British Critic, The, 841
British and Foreign Review, The, 493, 639
British Lady's Magazine, article by M. Lamb, 156
British Poets of the Nineteenth Century, German anthology, 366
British Quarterly Review
    ARTICLES:
        Coleridge, 736
        The Crystal Palace, 747
BRITTAIN [Crabb Robinson's clerk], 342, 532
BRITTAINE, George
        Confessions of Honor Delany, 753 and note
        Election, The, 680 and note
        Hyacinth O'Gara, 614
        Irish Men and Irish Women, 613, 614

BRITTAINE, George—*contd.*
Nurse M'Vourneen's Story, 544 and note, 545, 613
BRITTANY, tour with Southey, 552 seq.
BROKEDON, William, 514
BRONTË, Charlotte
Jane Eyre, 684, 686
Shirley, 693, 694
Villette, 723
BRONTË, Patrick Bramwell, 768
BROOKE, Henry, *Fool of Quality, The*, 840
BROOKE [Sir Fulke Greville, 1st Baron], 'tragedies,' 38, 41
BROOKE, Stopford A.
Life and Letters of the late Frederick W. Robertson, 817, 819, 820
BROUGHAM, Henry Peter, Baron Brougham and Vaux
pamphlet by De Quincey, 727
and J. H. Leigh Hunt and Wordsworth, 166
correspondence with Southey, 432
in Warren's *Ten Thousand a Year*, 596
pamphlet by Wordsworth, 567
mentioned, 42, 239, 258, 380, 398, 414, 835
WORKS:
(*Diary illustrative of the Times of George IV*), 557
Historical Sketches of Statesmen, review, 571
Introduction to the Library of Useful Knowledge, 364
BROWN, Charles Armitage, 387, 388, 520
BROWN [son of Charles Armitage], 388
BROWN, Hannah [wife of William Brown, M.D., *born* Meredith], 778, 788
BROWN, John
(*Health; Five Lay Sermons*), 813, 814
Rab and His Friends, 804, 813
BROWN, Robert, 764, 777
BROWNE, Sir Thomas
Inquiry into Vulgar Errors, 673
Religio Medici, 813
BROWNING, Elizabeth Barrett, 613, 657, 719, 752
letter from H. Martineau, 657
WORKS:
poems, 562, 719; review, 654
Aurora Leigh, 790; review, 767
Casa Guidi Windows, 710
BROWNING, Robert, 591, 642, 658, 710, 719, 752, 804
in Bagehot's article on *Poetry*, 813
WORK:
Colombe's Birthday, acted, 724
BROWNINGS, The
to visit Florence, 710
lent Kenyon's house, 760
BRUCE, John, 794
BRUCE, Peter Henry (*Memoirs, containing an account of his Travels*), 632
BRYANT, William Cullen, 653, 654
BRYDGES, Sir Samuel Egerton, 712

BRYDGES, family lawsuit, 613
BUCCLEUCH, Duke of, and Scott, 266
BUCH, Christian Leopold von, 207
BUCHAN, Lord, 266 and note, 267
BUCK, Catherine. *See* Clarkson
BUCK, John, 2, 58, 555
BUCK, Miss, 58
BUCKLE, Henry Thomas, *History of Civilization in England*, review, 775
BULL, George, Bishop, 55
BULLER, Charles, 466, 620
BULLER, Sir Francis, 105, 106
BULLER, Mrs. [widow of J. B. Buller of Downes in Devon], 22
BULWER, E. G. E. *See* Lytton
BULWER, William Henry Lytton Earle, Baron Dalling, 504
    France, 504
BUNBURY, Sir Charles, 9 and note
BUNBURY, Sir Henry Edward
    ed. *Correspondence of Sir Thomas Hanmer, Bart.*, 551, 609, 625
BUNN *v.* Macready, 497 note
BUNSEN, Carl Christian Josias, Baron von, 378, 389, 473, 519 seq., 618,
    690, 791
BUNSEN, Baronin von, 389, 521
BUNYAN, John
    article by Macaulay, 798
    Pilgrim's Progress, 540, 798
BUONAPARTE. *See* Napoleon
BUONAROTTI, Michael Angelo.   *See* Michael Angelo
BURDER, George, 657 and note
BURDETT, Sir Francis, 81 seq.
BURDETT-COUTTS, Baroness, 760, 778, 788
BURGOYNE, Montagu. *See* Bourgoyne
BURKE, Edmund
    anecdotes, 609
    and the *Annual Register*, 723
    critique by Hazlitt, 236
    speech in the Regency Debate, 20
    mentioned in:
        Brougham, H. P., *Historical Sketches*, 571
        Crabbe, G., *Life*, 472
        D'Arblay, Mme, works, 421, 617
        Macaulay, T. B., *Warren Hastings*, 601
        Moore, T., *Sheridan*, 324
        More, H., *Life and Correspondence*, 478
    WORKS:
        Letter to a Noble Lord, 777
        Reflections on the Revolution in France, 313, 386, 744
        Speeches in the House of Commons, 176, 184, 198
BURNETT, George, 24 and note
BURNEY, Charles, Mus.Doc., 216
    Memoirs of. See D'Arblay, Frances
BURNEY, Frances [Fanny].   *See* D'Arblay
BURNEY, James, Captain, later Admiral, 16, 160, 276
    whist parties, 32, 105, 108, 197, 213, 233
    other references, 51, 164, 170, 375

BURNEY, Martin
    and C. Burney's death, 216
    on Mme D'Arblay and her works, 110, 144
    death, 720
    financial affairs, 276, 361, 363, 586, 666
    legal career, 318, 361, 666
    and Lamb, 197, 216, 276, 363
    at M. Lamb's funeral, 666
    personal qualities, 168, 282, 361, 666
    and *The Times*, 361, 666
    other references, 134, 153, 161, 170, 177, 180, 183, 196, 213, 215,
        283, 299, 301, 316, 324, 344
    WORK:
    Parliamentary Index, 318
BURNEY, Mrs. Martin, 277
BURNEY, Sarah. *See* Payne
BURNEY, Sarah Harriet, 375, 376, 581, 582, 593, 594, 723, 853
    and Martin Burney, 361
    legacy from Mme D'Arblay, 580, 586
    WORKS:
    Country Neighbours, 396
    (*Romance of Private Life*)
        Hermitage, The, 579
        Renunciation, 577
BURNEYS, The, 116, 232, 298
BURNS, Robert
    lecture by Carlyle, 584
    —— Hazlitt, 220, 223
    in Kingsley, C., *Miscellanies*, 793
    Letter on. *See* Wordsworth, *Letter to a Friend of R. Burns*
    Life. *See* Lockhart, J. G.
    criticized as a poet, 562, 614
    and G. Thomson, 578, 579
    mentioned, 303, 486, 848, 849
    WORKS:
    Death and Doctor Hornbook, 89
    Holy Willie's Prayer, 106
    Tam o' Shanter, 88, 102, 106
    Vision, The, 106, 367, 368, 370
BURRELL, 60, 91, 115, 134, 152, 160, 178, 179
BURTON, John Hill, ed. of Bentham, 742, 744, 750 and note
Bury Post, article on Wordsworth by Crabb Robinson, 696
BUSK, Henry J. W., 686
BUTLER, Frances Anne. *See* Kemble
BUTLER, Joseph, *Sermons*, 300
BUTTERGILL FORCE: Wordsworth's yew trees, 192
BYLES, Emma, Lady, 739, 768
BYLES, Sir John Barnard [Serjeant, later Judge], 666, 769
BYNG, George, 133
BYRON, George Gordon, Lord
    and Lady Blessington, 412, 413
    and Lady Byron, 198, 199, 306, 441, 737, 746
    and Jane Clairmont, 412, 446, 447

BYRON, George Gordon, Lord—*contd.*
and (Mrs. Clermont), his wife's governess, 199, 737, 746
at Coleridge's lecture, 60
composition, method of, 440
and Dallas, 2, 85, 129, 418
death, 305
and the Don bridge, Aberdeen, 433
and his friends, 412, 413
in Geneva, 224
and Goethe, 224, 373, 631
dedication to Goethe, 369 and note, 371
and Hobhouse, 412
on Hope's *Anastasius*, 419, 420
and Keats's death, 389, 390
retort to Miss Kelly, 396
and the 'Lake Poets,' 167, 199
lecture by Cooper, 666, 667
—— MacDonald, 784, 786
letter: to *Blackwood's Magazine*, 428; on his own death, 413; to Goethe, 371; to Countess Guiccioli, 412; to J. Hogg, 167, 199; to Rogers, 619
literary jealousy, 374, 375, 446, 447
and Medwin, 413
state of his mind, 85, 339, 377, 521, 786
on Moore, 412
accused of plagiarism, 141, 199, 373, 413
on Pope, 415
religion, 521, 751
see also in criticisms of his works
and Rogers, 412, note 428
Satire on Rogers. See *Question and Answer*
and Sir W. Scott, 850
and Shelley, 222, 413, 446, 447
and Mrs. Shelley, 412, 413, 446
and Southey, 280, 286, 412, 428, 463
statue, by Thorwaldsen, 521
on Ward's politics, 377
and W. R. Wright, 2, 85, 129, 336, 418
and Wordsworth, 436, 467, 504, 508, 736; on Wordsworth, 199, 275, 428, 429

BOOKS, ETC., RELATING TO:
Barker, J. [pamphlet], 167, 297
Blessington, Lady, *Conversations with Lord Byron*, 411, 412, 415, 457
Dallas, A. R. C., *Correspondence of Lord Byron*, 362
Hunt, J. H. Leigh, *Lord Byron and some of his Contemporaries*, 353 and note, 412
Kennedy, J., *Conversations on Religion with Lord Byron*, 749 seq.
Medwin, T. (*Journal of the Conversations of Lord Byron*), 413, 737
Moore, T., *Letters and Journals of Lord Byron*, 306, 359, 360, 370 seq., 392, 412, 415, 417, 736 seq.
mentioned in:
Bagehot, W., on *Poetry*, 813

BYRON, George Gordon, Lord—*contd.*
 BOOKS, ETC., RELATING TO—*contd.*
  mentioned in:
   Disraeli, B., *Venetia*, 755, 756
   Gore, C., *Cecil*, 592
   Hazlitt, on the *Poets*, 222
   Irving, W., *Newstead Abbey*, 465
   Kingsley, C., *Miscellanies*, 793
   Lytton, *England and the English*, 435
   Medwin, W., *Shelley*, 668
   Shelley, P. B., *Essays*, 587
   Smith, H. and J., *Rejected Addresses*, 112
   Trelawny, E. J., *Adventures of a Younger Son*, 631, 632
  mentioned, 150, 201, 279, 351, 366, 427, 438, 454, 469, 485, 550, 748
 WORKS:
  writings, 85, 93, 129, 133, 137, 149, 188, 246, 247, 254, 264, 274, 339, 435, 443, 486, 778, 849; sale of, 85, 129, 552
  Beppo, 226
  Bride of Abydos, 137
  Cain, 281, 352
  Childe Harold's Pilgrimage, 2, 69, 85, 129, 136, 198, 222, 223, 339, 367, 377, 390, 418, 587; review, 82
  Corsair, 136, 137, 167, 267
  Darkness, 199
  Deformed Transformed, 305, 369, 373
  Don Juan, 275, 373, 428, 442, 450, 468, 520
   dedication, 463
   review, 624
  Dream, The, 198
  English Bards and Scotch Reviewers, 418
  Giaour, The, 129, 136
  Heaven and Earth, 289, 369 seq.
  Hebrew Melodies, 374
  translations from *Horace*, 2, 129, 418
  Island, The, 296
  Lara, 147, 267
  Manfred, 224, 369, 372 seq.
   acted, 450
   review in the *Critical*, 207; *Edinburgh*, 499
  Marino Falerio, 264
  Occasional Pieces, 418
  Ode to Napoleon Buonaparte, 141, 142
  Parisina, 180
  Prisoner of Chillon, 198
  (*Question and Answer*), satire on Rogers, 380, 383, 412, 420, 421 and note, 422, 440, 458, 467, 506, 547
  Sardanapalus, 281, 374, 375
   acted, 441
   dedication, 369 and note, 371
  Siege of Corinth, 180
  Two Foscari, 367
  Vision of Judgment, 286, 289, 367 seq., 372, 373, 447, 463
  Werner, 287
   acted, 540, 667

BYRON, Lady Noel [Anne Isabella Milbanke]
    principal entries, 729, 736, 737, 746
    and W. D. Arnold, 743, 746
    and Byron's death, 306
    and Byron's *Dream*, 198, 199
    and Byron's *Sardanapalus*, 441
    and Hogg's *Shelley*, 777, 778
    on Kennedy's *Conversations*, 749
    and G. MacDonald, 783, 784, 786
    and Crabb Robinson, 724, 748; letters from, 729, 738, 739, 751, 778
    and F. W. Robertson, 721, 729, 736, 746, 747
BYRON's daughter Ada. *See* Lovelace, Lady
BYRON's grandson. *See* Milbanke

Cabinet, The, Vol. I, 841
CADELL [publisher], 505
CAGLIOSTRO, Count [Joseph Balsamo], in Carlyle's *Miscellanies*, 581, 582
CALDER ABBEY, visited with Wordsworth, 192, 851
CALDERON, de la Barca, don Pedro
    Carlyle and, 830
    Coleridge on, 52
CALDWELL, Anne. *See* Marsh
CALVIN, 328
CALVINISM
    Byron and, 751
    Coleridge and, 671
    T. Graham and, 554
    Southey and, 609, 671
CAMBRIDGE, the Lambs' visit, 243
Cambridge Intelligencer, article by Crabb Robinson, 3, 842
CAMDEN SOCIETY, 548, 582, 639
(CAMPBELL, John, 1st Baron), Lord Chief Justice, 780
    Lives of the Lord Chancellors and Keepers of the Great Seal of England, 660, 674
CAMPBELL, Thomas
    Crabb Robinson meets, 404, 407, 408
    his monument in Westminster Abbey, 836
    mentioned, 88, 618
    WORKS:
    writings, 85, 86, 104, 227, 721
    (*Dramatic Works of William Shakespeare*), 559
    (*Letters from the South*), 466
    Pleasures of Hope, 90 and note
    Specimens of the British Poets, 239
CANNING, George, 304, 305, 436, 437
    (*Friend of Humanity and the Knife Grinder*), 40, 647, 716
CANOVA, Antonio, 208
CARGILL, Richard, 65 and note, 93, 136, 137, 168, 185, 197, 199, 200, 263, 490, 495
    WORKS:
    Poems on the Obeah Superstition, 184
    Sermons, 228

CARGILLS, The, 615
CARLYLE, Jane Welsh, 403, 542, 580, 830
CARLYLE, John Aitken, 521, 580, 597, 819
CARLYLE, Thomas
    articles on: *Christian Reformer*, 726; *Dublin Review*, 558
    elected to the Athenaeum, 723
    character and conversation, 308, 372, 375, 402, 403, 621, note 661,
        688, 690, 745, 805
    at Comeley Bank, 830
    and the *Edinburgh Review*, 375
    and the *Foreign Quarterly*, 552 and note
    and German literature. *See* character, and *German Romance*
    in Hare, J. C., *Mission of the Comforter*, 661 and note
    and E. Irving, 308, 309, 402, 403, 805
    at Lamb's, 310
    lectures, 569, 570, 571, 582 seq.
    leaving London, 318
    marriage, 830
    in Martineau, J., *Personal Influence*, 762
    professorship, 830 seq.
    and Crabb Robinson, 315, 403, 550, 580, 796, 819; correspondence,
        319, 335, 823 seq.; first meeting, 309
    and Spanish literature, 829, 830
    and Tennyson, 651
    in Trollope, A., *Warden*, 791
    in ⟨Westmorland⟩, 829
  OPINIONS AND CRITICISM:
    Americans, 612, 695. *See also* Slavery
    Dr. Channing, 541, 542
    Frederick the Great, 819
    Goethe, 402, 403, 425
    London, 830
    Slavery, 541, 542, 566, 695, 715
  mentioned, 433, 650, 703, 716, 720, 740
  WORKS:
    writings and style, 552, 566, 598 and note, 779
    Chartism, 580, 744
    German Romance, 347, 354
      collecting material for, 319 and note, 335, 823 seq.
    History of the French Revolution, 560 seq., 564, 566, 567, 665,
        690
    Latter Day Pamphlets, 542, 695 seq., 702
    Life of Schiller, 318, 825
    Life of John Sterling, 601, 714
    ⟨*On Heroes, Hero-Worship, and the Heroic in History*⟩, 598
      see also Lectures
    Past and Present, 633
    Sartor Resartus, 440, 552, 556, 557, 593, 594
    Wilhelm Meister's Apprenticeship, 308, 309
  ARTICLES AND REVIEWS:
    Critical and Miscellaneous Essays, 542, 580 seq., 665
    Diderot, 425
    Dr. Francia, 633

CARLYLE, Thomas—*contd.*

   ARTICLES AND REVIEWS—*contd.*

     Goethe, 409, 581
     Mirabeau, 509
     (*Occasional Discourse on the Negro Question*), 695, 715
     Petition on behalf of the Copyright Bill, 542, 582
     Reineke Fuchs, 596
     Sir W. Scott, 550
     Taylor, W., *Historic Survey of German Poetry*, 408, 421; note by
       Crabb Robinson, 408, 638 and note
     Voltaire, 579
CAROLINE, Queen, 124, 242 and note, 243, 258, 379
CARR [surgeon, of Ambleside], 273, 473, 480, 482, 486, 604, 605, 607,
    610, 611, 648, 671, 672, 682
CARR [solicitor], 86, 91
CARRIAGE, A, bought for travelling with Wordsworth, 514 seq., 570
CARRICK, Thomas, portrait of Wordsworth, 674
CARRUTHERS, Richard, portrait of Wordsworth, 217; of Mrs. Wordsworth,
    217
CARTER, John, 473, 604 and note, 697, 712, 722, 743, 753
CARY, Francis Stephen, portrait of Lamb, 776
CARY, Henry Francis, 405, 439, 453, 454, 468, 536, 642

   WORKS:

     translation of Dante, 329
     Life of Dante, 394
CASE, W. A., 738
CASSEL, visited with Wordsworth, 532
CASTLEREAGH, Lord, 286, 299
CATHOLIC Emancipation. *See* Rome, Church of
CATTERMOLE, Richard, 642
CERTOSA visited with Wordsworth, 524
CERVANTES, 313
     lecture by Coleridge, 219
     Don Quixote, 825, 829
CHALMERS, Alexander
     preface to *British Essayists*, 175
     edn. of the *Poets*, 15, 334
CHALMERS, Thomas, D.D., 294
CHAMBERS, Robert
     Encyclopaedia of English Literature, 656
     Vestiges of the Natural History of Creation, 652 and note, 664
Champion, The
     article by Hazlitt, 151, 153
     review of Lamb's works, 231
CHANCE, 308
CHANNING, William Ellery, 541, 542, 606, 816
CHANTREY, Sir Francis Legatt, 279, 395
     bust of Wordsworth, 279, 280, 707, 739
CHANTREY, Lady, 739
CHANTREY MUSEUM, 665
CHAPMAN, 678, 688, 707, 716
CHARLES II (*State Papers*), article, 805
CHARLOTTE, Queen, and Mme D'Arblay, 586
Chartism, 705

CHARTRES CATHEDRAL, visited with Southey, 555
CHATEAUBRIAND, 424
CHATTERTON, Thomas, 134, 610, 611
CHAUCER, 562, 586, 751, 776
CHENIER, Marie Joseph de (*Tableau Historique de l'Etat et des Progres de la Litterature Française*), 292
Chevy Chase, 131
CHIABRERA, Wordsworth and, 378, 518, 719
CHINON, Southey and, 553, 555
CHISHOLM, Dr. and family, 247, 254
CHITTY, Joseph, 119
CHOLERA, 402, 439, 512, 513
CHOLMONDELEY, 415
CHORLEY, Henry Fothergill, 460, 495, 496
    Memorials of Mrs. Hemans, 505
CHORLEY, John Rutter, 495, 496
CHORLEY, 506

Christian Reformer, The
    CONTRIBUTIONS BY:
    Kenyon, 670 and note
    Crabb Robinson:
        Froude, *Nemesis of Faith*, 690 and note
        obituary, F. W. Robertson, 728, 729, 733, 760, 817
        Wordsworth, *Prelude*, 702

    ARTICLES:
        Carlyle, 726
        G. Smith's *Lectures*, 805
        (*State Papers*), of the reign of Charles II, 805
Christian Teacher, article by Blanco White, 658
CHRISTIANITY. *See* various churches, sects, movements, and individual views on religion
CHRISTIE, Jonathan Henry, 262 note
CHRISTIE'S SALES, 359, 796
Chronicle, The.   See Morning Chronicle
CHURCHILL, Charles, 203, 472
CIBBER COLLEY
    pamphlets against Pope, 365
    mentioned, 735
CICERO.   *See* Hallam, A. H., and Heberden, W.
CITY OF LONDON INSTITUTE, 695
CLAIRMONT, Charles, 136, 198, 229, 231, 265, 275, 299
CLAIRMONT, Jane, 299, 412, 413, 446, 447
CLARE, John, 311
CLARKE, Mary [Mme Mohl], 83
CLARKE [auctioneer], 795
CLARKSON, Catherine, *born* Buck
    and Benjafield, 34
    and Coleridge, 42, 45, 110, 122; letters from, 632; and Coleridge and Wordsworth, 47, 67, 84, 123, 130
    and Godwin's *Political Justice*, 3
    and Mrs. Godwin, 123 and note
    and Hazlitt, 116
    and Mrs. Opie, 2
    personal qualities, 2

CLARKSON, Catherine—*contd.*
    gift from Crabb Robinson, 738; influence on Crabb Robinson, 2, 3;
        introductions of Crabb Robinson, 2 and note, 9 seq., 148; letters
        from Crabb Robinson on Coleridge, 687 seq.
    and Tennyson's *In Memoriam*, 707
    and Wordsworth; *see also* Coleridge and Wordsworth, 7, 196;
        letter from, 159, 680; and Wordsworth's *Excursion*, 152, 159, 160,
        680
    D. Wordsworth visits, 16
    Mrs. Wordsworth visits, 730 seq., 834
    other references, 6, 125, 288, 442, 474, 559, 581, 635, 648, 657, 671,
        710, 725, 749
CLARKSON, Thomas
    personal qualities, 35, 468, 601
    and the Wilberforces, 550, 561, 590, 591, 648 and note, 746, 760.
        See also *Strictures on a Life of William Wilberforce*
    H. M. Williams's verses, 152
    and Wordsworth, 551
    mentioned, 12, 86, 168, 725
    WORKS:
        History of the Abolition of the Slave Trade review by Coleridge, 471
        Strictures on a Life of William Wilberforce and Crabb Robinson's
        Supplement, 553, 554, 558 seq., 562, 568, 591
CLARKSON, Thomas [Tom, son], 187, 333, 358, 465
CLARKSONS, The
    and Lamb, 833
    visit H. M. Williams in Paris, 147
    D. Wordsworth visits, 16
CLAUREN, H. pseud. [Heun], 824, 825
(CLERMONT, Mrs.), Lady Byron's governess, 199, 737, 746
CLIVE, Caroline, Mrs. Archer, and her writings, 801 and note, 802
CLIVE, Robert, Lord, article by Macaulay, 580
CLOUGH, Arthur Hugh
    visit to America, 719, 731, 735
    and the Arnolds, 681, 682, 685
    lecture on English Literature, 720
    marriage, 735
    personal qualities, 681, 692, 695, 714
    and Rogers, 695, 696
    and University College, 706 and note, 720
    and University Hall, 682 and note, 684, 686, 692, 693, 713 seq.
    mentioned, 694, 699
    WORKS:
        Bothie of Tober-na-Vuolich, 685
        Letters and Remains, 821
        (*Poems with a Memoir*), 806
CLOUGH, Mrs., 680 note
COAL SCOOP, A, Lamb's letter on, 488
COBBETT, William, 112, 189, 203, 258, 259, 403
COBDEN, Richard, 633
COCHRANE, Thomas, Earl of Dundonald, 61
COCKERMOUTH CHURCH, 490 seq.
COCKERMOUTH, Wordsworth's property, 192, 851

COETLAGON DE, 513
COLBURN, Henry, 231, 337, 401, 414
COLCHESTER, Crabb Robinson leaves, 2
COLERIDGE, Derwent
    and H. Coleridge's death, 683 seq.; and H. Coleridge's works, 685,
        708, 710, 713, 714
    and a portrait of S. T. Coleridge, 724, 726
    personal qualities, 190, 683
    Memoir of Praed, 812
COLERIDGE, Edith, 689
COLERIDGE, Hartley
    and alcohol, 473, 648, 671
    last illness and death, 682 seq.
    and Jameson, 262, 442
    at Monkhouse's, 214
    personal qualities, 44, 190, 280, 636, 671
    at the Wordsworths, 473, 671
  WORKS:
    writings, 685; verses on Dr. Arnold, 648; inscription, 627
    Essays and Marginalia, 710, 713, 714
    Poems with a Memoir, by Coleridge, D., 708
    Worthies of Yorkshire and Lancashire, 634
COLERIDGE, Henry Nelson, 357 and note, 462, 465, 468, 496, 502, 506,
    570, 580, 592, 595, 597, 636
    edns. of S. T. Coleridge's works. *See* Coleridge, S. T.: *Confessions
    of an Inquiring Spirit; Literary Remains; Specimens of Table
    Talk*
COLERIDGE, Colonel James, 442
COLERIDGE, John, the Rev., 105
COLERIDGE, Sir John Taylor, 488, 698, 699, 706, 832
COLERIDGE, Samuel Taylor
    and the Aders, 119, 122, 288, 293, 311, 359, 361, 405, 442
    and Mrs. C. Aikin, 57
    and alcohol, 49, 75, 182
    explains 'All my Eye and Betty Martin,' 114
    and T. Allsop, 315, 344, 814, 818
    anecdotes of himself, 59
    and Benjafield, 34, 35
    and the Bible Society, 59
    borrows books, 106, 150, 184, 185
    and Dr. Brabant, 663
    at the Buck's, 58
    and Burnett's death, 24
    at J. Burney's, 51, 108
    cast by Dawe, 68
    childhood, 44, 105, 106
    and Mrs. Clarkson, 42, 45, 110, 122, 123
    at the Colliers, 16, 48, 60, 116
    and the *Courier*, 32, 33, 35, 37 and note
    death, 446
    De Quincey's gift, 501, 502, 534, 549
    and the *Edinburgh Magazine*, 213
    and the *Edinburgh Review*, 48. *See also*, and Jeffrey, and *Biographia
    Literaria* reviewed
    and Eichhorn's works, 332

COLERIDGE, Samuel Taylor—*contd.*
    epigram on the promises of the great, 92
    and his family, 105, 106, 150, 442, 446
    financial affairs, 118, 128, 413, 442, 506
    and P. Fraser, 50, 51
    and the German language, 207
    moves to Gillman's, 185
    and Godwin, 114
    and J. H. Green, 207, 294, 307, 443
    and Hazlitt, 24; at Hazlitt's, 27
    lecture by Hazlitt, 222
    attacks by Hazlitt. *See* Hazlitt's reviews of Coleridge's works
    health, 179, 200, 288, 292, 413, 442, 443
    and E. Irving, 307 seq., 320, 338, 359, 402, 403
    and Jeffrey, 209, 210, 471
    compared with Joubert, 810
    and C. Lamb, 219, 833
    letters from C. Lamb, 679
    and the Lambs, 24
    at the Lambs, 18, 24, 28, 31, 44, 48, 181, 215
    and W. S. Landor, 413, 414
    and the Marchioness of Lansdowne, 150
    lectures: 1795, 59; 1808, 11, 681; 1811, 49 seq., 60 seq., 847; 1812,
        78, 84, 85, 87, 88, 92, 102, 112 seq., 116, 117; 1813, 121; 1818,
        218 seq.; articles by Crabb Robinson, 51, 53, 54
    letters: to Dr. Brabant, 663; to Mrs. Clarkson, 632; in Cottle's
        possession, 499, 501 seq.; to the editor of the *Eclectic Review*, 55;
        from Germany, 466; to Godwin, 810; given to Frau von Goethe,
        730; to Gooden, 689; in D. Turner's collection, 646; to Wade,
        501, 502, 534, 549, 681
    Letters. See Allsop, T.
    at T. Monkhouse's, 214, 292, 293
    and B. Montagu. *See* breach with Wordsworth
    at the Morgan's, 41
    and music, 288, 293
    and opium, 185, 200
    letter on opium taking. *See* letter to Wade
    plans: to devote himself to the drama, 114; a new *Faust*, 108, 448;
        a Greek grammar, 41; lectures on education, 112; *Michael Scott*,
        448; translations from Richter, 150
    portrait by: W. Allston, 724 seq.; R. Hancock, 500, 502
    pun, 294
    recites: *Christabel*, 49; ⟨*The Rash Conjuror*⟩, 108
    and Richter's works, 26, 106, 150
    at Rickman's, 21
    introduction to Crabb Robinson, 2, 6, 11, 16, 845
    and Crabb Robinson's German translations, 24 seq.
    and R. Southey, 26, 29, 41, 185, 210, 671
    Southey's letter on, 502, 681, 754
    and D. Stuart, 51. *See also*, and the *Courier*
    and Thelwall, 42
    meets L. Tieck, 207, 208
    and Toller, 60 seq.
    and *The Times* and J. Walter, 37, 40, 50 seq.
    and D. Wordsworth, 78

COLERIDGE, Samuel Taylor—*contd.*
    and W. Wordsworth, 26, 73, 97, note 179, 214 seq., 245
    breach with Wordsworth, 40, 67, 68, 70, 72, 74 seq., 84
    to visit Wordsworth, 123 seq., 128
    OPINIONS AND CRITICISM:
    literary:
        Barbauld, A. L., 62, 697; Barbaulds, The, 56
        books for children, 747
        Calderon, 52
        Cottle, J., *Alfred*, 663
        the *Edinburgh Review*, 28, 48
        fancy and imagination, 200
        Godwin, W., 28, 29
        Goethe and his works, 89, 106 seq., 122 seq., 185, 308
        Hazlitt, W., 200
        Herder, 308, 447
        Job, 107
        Junius, 24
        Kant, I., 70, 88, 107
        Klopstock, 42
        Lamb, C., 200; Lamb's conversation, 28; *Hogarth*, 28
        Lessing, G. E., *Laocoon*, 123
        Pasley, C. W., *Essay on Military Policy*, 21
        poetry, 52
        poets, 89
        Reynard the Fox, 123
        Rogers, S., 28
        Schelling, 88, 107, 307
        Schiller, 21, 308; *Wallenstein*, 107
        Schlegel, 21, 123, 200, 307
        Scott, Sir W., poetry, 47, 48
        Shakespeare's fools, 21, 108.   *See also* lectures
        Southey, R., and his works, 26, 29, 48, 52, 96, 288, 359, 632
        Spinoza, 112, 447
        Steffens, 200
        Stolberg's *Felsenstrom*, 107
        Tasso, 89
        Taylor, W., *Letter Concerning the Two First Chapters of Luke*, 31
        Tieck, L., 200
        Vico, G. B., *Principi della Scienza Nuova*, 320, 321
        Wordsworth and his works, 52, 96, 360, 550, 667; (*Borderers*),
            502, 503; *Excursion*, 202, 288
        writings, 26, 48, 185, 413, 632
    miscellaneous:
        art, 34, 214, 215
        (*Boyer, J.*), 197
        Clarkson, T., 35 and note, 468
        Coleridge, Hartley, as a child, 44, 708
        Graham, T., 41, 42
        Hone, W., trial, 214
        incest, 27
        Ireland and Catholicism, 18, 19
        Lancastrian Schools, 53, 59
        law, 22, 214

COLERIDGE, Samuel Taylor—*contd.*

OPINIONS AND CRITICISM—*contd.*

miscellaneous:

lawyers and litigation, 19

his letter writing, 632

malice, 736, 757

Montagu, B.   *See* breach with Wordsworth

Montagu, Mrs. B., 171, 716

music, 122

Napoleon Buonaparte, 114

national character, 28, 29

Peel, Sir R., 360

Perceval's assassination, 81, 82

the loss of his pension, 413

philosophy, 28, 70, 108, 307, 593, 664; influence of German thought, 52, 63, 70, 88, 178, 506, 581, 659

politics, 10, 22, 33, 177

definition of Priest, 469

Queen Caroline's trial, 124, 258

Reform Bill, 405

religion, 61, 108, 112, 308, 320, 321, 447, 481, 482, 501, 503, 505, 663, 671, 694, 727, 736

steam engines, 35, 432

Stuart, D., 170

PERSONAL QUALITIES:

character:

adverse criticism, 41, 53, 55, 76, 78, 80, 81, 92, 114, 127, 267

balanced, 11, 73, 88, 103, 108, 118, 119, 289, 487, 669, 683, 846, 847; favourable criticism, 43, 112, 501

conversation, 16, 17, 51, 55, 114, 132, 209, 288, 292, 320, 321, 338, 372, 413, 429, 763, 775, 847

BOOKS, ETC., RELATING TO:

Allsop, T. (*Letters, Conversations, and Recollections of S. T. Coleridge*), 468 seq., 815, 819, 820

Barbauld, A. L., verses, 697

Cottle, J. (*Early Recollections chiefly relating to the late S. T. Coleridge*), 501, 502, 505, 533, 534, 680, 681, 703, 754

De Quincey, T., *Anecdotes of S. T. Coleridge*, 451, 456, 464

Gillman, J., *Life of S. T. Coleridge*, 549

article:

in *Blackwood*, 581

in the *British Quarterly*, 736

in the *Examiner*, 142

by Lockhart, 447, 448

in *The Times*, 51 and note, 669

mention in:

Carlyle, T., *Life of Sterling*, 714

De Quincey, T., *Autobiography*, 738

Green, J. H., Hunterian Oration, 664

Hazlitt, W., *Literary Remains*, 780; *Spirit of the Age*, 322, 377

Lloyd, C., *Desultory Thoughts*, 297

Martineau, J., on *Personal Influence*, 762

COLERIDGE, Samuel Taylor—*contd.*
  BOOKS, ETC., RELATING TO—*contd.*
    mention in:
      Medwin, T., *Shelley*, 668
      Peacock, T. L., *Nightmare Abbey*, 229
      Smith, H. and J., *Rejected Addresses*, 112
      Wordsworth, D., *Journal of a Scotch Tour*, 432
    mentioned, 20, 130, 312, 332, 375, 387, 565, 746, 778, 784
  WORKS:
    writings, 17, 26, 29, 47, 48, 59, 185, 413, 540, 632, 694, 700, 735;
      excerpts in Chambers's *Encyclopaedia*, 657; in Germany, 366
    article on:
      Clarkson, T., *History of the Abolition of the Slave Trade*, 471
      H.R.H. the Duke of York, 34, 35, 37 and note
    marginalia and notes:
      Browne, T., *Inquiry into Vulgar Errors*, 673
      German philosophy, 511 and note, 514
      Herbert, G., *Works*, 636
      Lightfoot, J., *Works*, 496
      Petvin, J., *Letters Concerning Mind*, 598
      Southey, R., *Life of Wesley*, 671
      Spinoza, *Works*, 469
      Theodor des Zweiflers Weihe, 671, 672

    Poems, in the Bijou, 350 and note
    —— recommended by Crabb Robinson, 772 and note
    —— review, 378
    Aids to Reflection, 322, 335, 336, 829, 853
    Ancient Mariner, 17, 800
    —— German translation, 531
    —— origin of the idea, 481
    (*Biographia Literaria*), 182, 200, 210, 213
    —— review, 209, 499
    —— edn. ed. Coleridge, Sara, 659, 661, 662, 665, 667; dedication to
      Wordsworth, 661, 662
    Christabel, 47 seq., 155, 157, 164, 209, 487
    —— review, 210
    Conciones ad Populum, 701
    Confessions of an Inquiring Spirit, 586, 817
    (*Essays on his own Times*), ed. Coleridge, Sara, 691, 701
    Fire, Famine, and Slaughter, 198, 370
    Foster Mother's Tale, 23
    Friend, 26, 51, 55, 505
    —— review, 55
    —— sonnets by Wordsworth, 846 and note
    Lay Sermon, 200
    —— review in the *Critical*, 202; [in the *Examiner*], 196, 197, 200
    Literary Remains, ed. Coleridge, H. N., 505, 506, 588, 589
    Love, 209, 370
    Lyrical Ballads. See Wordsworth, W.
    (*Notes and Lectures upon Shakespeare*), ed. Coleridge, Sara, 688, 689,
      691, 694
    Omniana, ed. Southey, R., 115, 588
    On the Constitution of Church and State, 400

COLERIDGE, Samuel Taylor—*contd.*

WORKS—*contd.*

    Osorio. See *Remorse*

    (*Rash Conjuror*), 108

    Remorse, 23, 112, 116, 119, 652, 664

    —— first performance, 117, 843

    —— profit on, 118, 128

    —— review, 146

    (*Seven Lectures on Shakespeare and Milton*), ed. Collier, J. P., 761, 763, 839

    (*Sibylline Leaves*), 182

    Sonnet to Lord Stanhope, 501, 503

    Statesman's Manual. See *Lay Sermon*

    Table Talk, ed. Coleridge, H. N., 464, 465, 506, 586

    —— review, 462

    We are Seven, 481

    (*Zapolya*), 182

COLERIDGE, Sara, Mrs. H. N.

    introduction to Dr. Brabant, 663 and note

    and Hartley Coleridge, 686

    and S. T. Coleridge, 669, 680, 681, 697

    editing S. T. Coleridge's works, 636, 659, 661 seq., 687 seq., 691, 701

    and J. Cottle, 680, 681

    death, 716

    personal qualities:

      as a child, 190

      as a girl, 270, 271

    gift from Crabb Robinson, 665

    on Crabb Robinson's *Supplement* to Clarkson's *Strictures*, 568

    and Southey's niece, 693, 694

    and Wordsworth, 661, 662, 681, 697

    on the Wordsworths, 709 and note

    marginalia in Wordsworth's *Life*, 803

    mentioned, 570, 581, 592

    WORKS:

    translation (M. Dobrizhopfer, *Account of the Abipones*), 270

    Phantasmion, 538

COLERIDGE, Sara, Mrs. S. T., *born* Fricker, 27, 189, 271, 297

COLERIDGE, William Hart [Bishop], 446 and note, 488

COLERIDGE FAMILY, 446 and note, 488, 501, 502, 685

COLISEUM, visited with Wordsworth, 520

COLLIER, Jane, 16, 26, 55, 87, 145, 163, 218

COLLIER, John Dyer, 3, 16, 145

COLLIER, John Payne

    articles on: *Athenæum*, 795; *Saturday Review*, 797

    and the Camden Society, 548

    and Coleridge's lectures, 52. *See also* Coleridge, S. T., *Seven Lectures upon Shakespeare and Milton*, ed. Collier, J. P.

    and the Duke of Devonshire, 403

    accused of forgery. *See* his ed. of Shakespeare

    and Gifford's notes on Shirley, 344

COLLIER, John Payne—*contd.*
  and Inigo Jones's drawings, 403, 404
  and Larpent's plays, 404
  at Maidenhead, 761
  and the *Morning Chronicle*, 590
  in Paris, 284
  a party, 288, 424
  personal qualities, 503, 556, 657, 713, 761, 777
  letter from Crabb Robinson, 839
  and Crabb Robinson and Gilchrist's *Blake*, 810
  and H. M. Williams, 150
  other references, 68, 168, 170, 198, 375, 676, 751
  WORKS:
    article in *The Times*, 787
    Ballad of Fridolin, 301
    Life of Spenser, 807, 808
    pamphlet letters, 465
    Poets' Pilgrimage, 289, 290
    preface to Coleridge's *Lectures*, 839
    Roxburghe Ballads, 660
    edns. of Shakespeare, 590, 643, 644, 647, 720, 722, 786 seq., 790, 792,
      794, 795, 797, 804, 815, 839
COLLIER, J. [son of J. P. Collier], 794
COLLIER, Mrs. Joshua, 232, 455
(COLLIERS, The), 16, 20, 48, 60, 79, 103, 142, 146, 147, 153, 163, 165, 167,
    199, 207, 213, 215, 217, 218, 223, 261, 321, 455, 520
COLLINS, William
  poems, 1, 14, 261
  edn. of *Works*. *See* Barbauld, A. L.
COLLINS, William, R.A., 307, 519, 682
  Life. *See* Collins, W. W.
COLLINS, William Wilkie
  After Dark, 758 and note
  Memoirs of the Life of William Collins, R.A., 682
  Woman in White, 799
COLMAN, George [the Younger]
  Blue Beard, acted, 27
(COLQUHOUN, *Inquiry into the Poor Laws*), review, 127
COMBE, William, 12, 13, 142, 203
  and the authorship of the 'Knife-Grinder,' 40, 647
  WORKS:
    German Gil Blas, 12
    Letters of a Nobleman to his Son, 12
    Travels of Dr. Syntax in Search of the Picturesque, 12
COMIC WRITERS, The, lecture by Hazlitt, 225, 236
COMO, visited with Wordsworth, 245, 251, 524
CONDER, Josiah, 849
CONDILLAC, Étienne Bonnot de, 28
CONGREVE (*Memoirs* by Charles Wilson), 364
CONSTABLE, John, 312
CONSTANT, Benjamin, 149
COOK, Captain, 16
COOKE, Lady, 113
COOKSON, Elizabeth, Miss, 806

COOKSON, J., sonnet by Wordsworth, 434, 495
COOKSON, The Misses, 672
COOKSON, Mrs., 473, 486, 560, 672, 806
COOKSON, W. Strickland [son], 495, 595, 597, 604, 616, 635, 644, 653, 661, 697, 698, 703, 778
COOKSONS, The, 477, 605, 683
COOPER, Henry, 311
COOPER, James Fenimore, 377
　WORKS:
　　writings, 348
　　Bravo, The, 393
　　Last of the Mohicans, 347
　　Lionel Lincoln, 343
　　Pilot, The, 498
　　Pioneers, The, 346
　　Red Rover, The, 352, 353
　　Spy, The, 433
COOPER, John, 441
COOPER, Thomas
　　lecture, 666
　　and Wordsworth, 667 and note
　WORK:
　　Purgatory of Suicides, 666
COPLESTON, Edward, 150 and note, 151
COPYRIGHT
　　in America, 541, 544
　　International, 548
　　in letters, 499 and note, 501
COPYRIGHT BILL, 121, 566, 567, 570, 591, 596, 617
　　article by Lockhart, 607
　　petition by Carlyle, 542, 582
　　Petition by Talfourd, 568
Coriolanus, article on, 199
CORNWALL, Barry, pseud.　*See* Procter, B. W.
CORREGGIO, 36, 203 and note, 491
CORRI, Domenico, 133
COSTELLO, Louisa Stuart, 636 and note
COTTLE, Amos Simon, 502, 503, 663
COTTLE, Joseph, 499 seq., 505, 594
　WORKS:
　　Alfred, 500, 663
　　Early Recollections chiefly relating to the late S. T. Coleridge, 505, 533, 534, 703
　　—— preface 501, 502; 2nd revised edn., 680, 681, 754
　　Malvern Hills, 503
COTTON, Charles, *Winter*, 93
COULSON, Walter, 170, 178, 282
Courier, The
　　Coleridge and, 32, 33, 35, 37 and note
　　De Quincey and, 161
　　letter by Southey, note 550
　　Wordsworth's sonnet, 848
　　mentioned, 538

COURTENAY, Philip, 360, 450, 451, 457, 458, 462, 486, 514, 515, 534, 535, 568, 603 and note, 604
COURTENAY [son], 534
COURTENAY, Mrs., 534
COURTENAY, 752
COUTTS. *See* Burdett-Coutts
COWPER, William, 72, 125, 477, 486, 569, 575, 660
    letters, 341, 646, 660
    Life. See Southey, R.
  WORKS:
    Castaway, The, 660
    translation of *Homer*, 72
    John Gilpin, 1
    Sonnet to Romney, 485
    Task, The, 72
CRABBE, George, letter to Sir T. Hanmer, 625
  WORKS:
    writings, 150, 168, 222, 454, 562; article on, 142
    Bachelor's Tale, The, 234
    Dumb Orators, The, 130 and note
    (*Poetical Works with his Letters and Journals and a Life by his Son*), 472
    Village, The, 472
CRANWORTH, Lord. *See* Rolfe, R. M.
CRAWFORD, 541, 542, 566
CRAYON, Geoffrey, pseud. *See* Irving, Washington
CRÉCY, visited with Southey, 554
CRESWELL, 455
CRIMEAN WAR, *The Times* and, 776
Critical Review
    article on Coleridge's *Lay Sermon* by Crabb Robinson, 202, 207
    and Rough, 38
  mentioned, 641
CROKER, John Wilson
    mentioned in:
      Disraeli, B., *Coningsby*, 644
      Morgan, Lady, *Florence McCarthy*, 226
  WORKS:
    edn. of Boswell's *Johnson*, review, 392
    review of Moore's *Life*, 736
    Sketch of the State of Ireland, Past and Present, 127
CROLY, George, 121, 122 and note, 745
CROMWELL, Oliver
    lecture by Carlyle, 584
    in H. Smith's *Oliver Cromwell*, 585
CROSBY, Brass, 73
CROSS, Mary Ann [George Eliot]. *See* Evans, Mary Ann
CROSSE, Andrew, 504, 599 note
  WORKS:
    Apple, The, 599 note
    Black Doctor, The, 599
CROSSE [son], 634
‖ CROW, Eyre Evans, *To-day in Ireland*, 337

CROWE, Catherine, *Night Side of Nature*, 16 and note
CROWE, Lieutenant-Colonel, 16
CROWE, Martha, *Adventures of Susan Hopley*, 770 and note
CROWE, William, *Lewesdon Hill*, 16, 125
CRYSTAL PALACE, The
    pamphlet by Ruskin, 747
    and a bust of Wordsworth, 739
CULLEN, 83
CULLUM, Sir Thomas Gery, 795
CULLUM, Lady, 497, 795
CUMBERLAND, Ernest Augustus, Duke of.   *See* Hanover, King of
CUMBERLAND, Henry Frederick, Duke of, marriage to (Anne Horton), 73
CUMBERLAND, Richard
    and the *London Review*, 9, 13
  WORK:
    Arundel, 840
CUNNINGHAM, Allan, 280, 303
  WORKS:
    Lives of the Most Eminent British Painters, 15, 394
    Sir Michael Scott, 352
CURLL, Edmund, 364
CURRAN, Amelia, 116, 139, 150
CURRAN, John Philpot, 14, 32, 49
CURRAN [son], 139
CURRIE, Dr., *Life of Burns.   See* Wordsworth, *Letter to a Friend of
    Robert Burns*
CURTEIS, 494, 681
CURWEN, Mr. and Mrs., 554
Cyprists, The, 841

Daily News, The, 718, 757, 781, 783
DALLAS, A. R. C., *Correspondence of Lord Byron*, 362
DALLAS, Robert Charles, 2, 85, 129, 418, 501
Dallas's Poetics, article by Masson, 726
DALRYMPLE, Sir Hew, 299
DALRYMPLE [solicitor], 800
DALSTON, 66
    the Lambs at, 259
DANIELL, E. T., 682
DANTE, Alighieri, *Life.   See* Cary, H. F.
  WORKS:
    writings: Blake on, 326 seq.; lecture by Carlyle, 583; Landor on,
        378, 381, 383
    Divine Comedy, 407
    Prophecy, 390
    Vision, 326
D'ARBLAY, Alexandre, sr., 626
D'ARBLAY, Alexandre, jr., 343
D'ARBLAY, Frances [Fanny Burney], 108, 124, 144, 361, 580, 586, 617,
    651
  WORKS:
    writings, 16, 136, 147

D'ARBLAY, Frances [Fanny Burney]—*contd.*
  WORKS—*contd.*
    Camilla, 135, 136, 145
    Cecilia, 110, 135
    Diary and Letters, 611, 612, 617, 623, 626
    —— review, 623
    Evelina, 110, 111, 135, note 428
    Memoirs of Dr. Burney, 421
    Wanderer, sale, 144
    —— review in the *Edinburgh*, 16, 165, 170; *Quarterly*, 146
DARLEY, George, *Thomas à Becket*, 582
DARWIN, Charles, 740, 810
DARWIN, Erasmus, 172, 626
    Zoonomia, 843
DARWIN, Erasmus [grandson], 626, 631, 740, 810
DASHWOOD, Mrs., 410, 413, 415, 514
DAVIS [Crabb Robinson's clerk], 222
DAVIS [partner of Borrodale], 359
DAVY, Sir Humphry, 60, 62, 91, 307
DAVY, Lady, 91, 359
DAVY, John, M.D., 649, 650, 685, 707, 708, 714, 715, 726, 781
DAVY, Mrs. [wife of the Dr.], 650, 660, 672, 694, 718, 807, 854
DAVY, Mrs. S., 52, 88
DAWE, George
    cast of Coleridge's head, 68
    article by Lamb, 404
  mentioned, 11
DAWSON, George, *Lectures on Wordsworth*, 659
DAWSON, 357
DAWSON, Mrs. [sister of Mrs. Walter], 735, 768
DEACON, Mrs., 87
DE LAMMENAIS, 545
DELANY, Mrs. [Mary Granville], *Autobiography and Correspondence*, 802
DELLA CRUSCAN, verse, 112, 841
DE MORGAN, Augustus, 647, 810, 815
DE MORGAN, Sophia Elizabeth, *born* Frend, 799
DENMAN, Lord, 398
DENMAN, Maria, 494, 495, 504, 550, 612, 625, 678
DENMANS, The, 415, 459
DE QUINCEY, Margaret, *born* Simpson. *See* De Quincey, T.
DE QUINCEY, Thomas
    principal entries, 104, 137, 187, 188, 194 seq., 275
    character and conversation, 143, 162, 740
    gift to Coleridge, 501, 502, 534, 549
    on Coleridge, 195. *See also Anecdotes of Coleridge*
    in Hood's *Wordsworth*, 763
    and Jeffrey, 161
    Lamb's joke on, 311
    Crabb Robinson's first meeting, 103
    Crabb Robinson and his books, 238
    and Taylor and Hessey, 275, 276
    and Valpy, 275
    and Wordsworth, 103, 137, 161, 195, 196
  mentioned, 136, 160, 185, 794

DE QUINCEY, Thomas—*contd.*
   WORKS:
      writings, 702, 735, 778, 838
      Autobiography, 273, 738, 767
      Close Comments on a Straggling Speech, 272, 273
      Confessions of an English Opium Eater, 267, 273, 513, 767, 768
      —— payment for, 275, 276
      English Mail Coach, 747, 748
      Klosterheim, 482, 483
      Leaders in Literature, 789
      Miscellanies, 740, 741
      On Murder as a Fine Art, 749
      Revolt of the Tartars, 748
      Selections Grave and Gay, 776 and note, 782
   ARTICLES:
      Anecdotes of Coleridge, 451, 464
      —— review, 456
      Ceylon, 821
      Joan of Arc, 740
      C. Lamb, 789
      Last Days of Kant, 740
      Literary acquaintance, a, 696
      Milton, 776
      Milton v. Southey and Landor, 818
      Modern Superstitions, 740
      Pope, 789, 820
      Shakespeare, 820
      Spanish Military Nun, A, 740

DERBY, Lord. *See* Stanley, E. S.
DE TOCQUEVILLE, *La Démocratic en Amérique*, 477, 478, 481 seq.
DE VERE, Aubrey Thomas, 656, 677, 704, 778
      Poems, review, 741
DEVONSHIRE, Duke of, 403, 786
DE WINT, Peter, 552
DIBDIN, John Bates, 317
DIBDIN, Thomas Frognall, 319, 343
DICKENS, Catherine, 675, 778
DICKENS, Charles
      articles on: *Blackwood*, 751, *Edinburgh Review*, 650
      at the Booksellers' Association meeting, 716
      and Mrs. Dickens, 778
      at the Literary Fund Meeting, 758
      personal description, 543, 573, 675, 678
      readings at St. Martin's Hall, 770, 771, 777
      in Trollope, A., *Warden*, 791
      verses on, 815
   mentioned, 544, 796
   WORKS:
      writings, 543, 592, 593, 598, 652, 676, 758, 786, 812
      articles:
         obituary of Talfourd, 737
         on spirit-rapping, 722
      American Notes for General Circulation, 618, 625

DICKENS, Charles—*contd.*
WORKS—*contd.*
Barnaby Rudge, 598, 599, 612
Bleak House, 379, 715 seq., 721
Christmas Carol, 770
David Copperfield, 751, 754
Dombey & Son, 680 seq.
Great Expectations, 802
Hard Times, 740, 744 seq.
Household Words (ed.), 696, 722
Martin Chuzzlewit, 645 seq.
Master Humphrey's Clock, 585
Nicholas Nickleby, 559, 572
Old Curiosity Shop, 590
Oliver Twist, 542 seq., 558, 578
Pickwick Papers, 546
Sketches by Boz, 577 seq.
DICKENSON, Mary [widow of T. Clarkson, jr.], 732, 733
DICKENSON, Willoughby W., 733
DIDEROT, Denis, article on by Carlyle, 425
WORKS:
Le Neveu de Rameau, review, 15, 33
DIGBY, Kenelm Henry
Broad Stone of Honour, 357
DILKE, Charles Wentworth, 758
DISRAELI, Benjamin, Earl of Beaconsfield, 450, 451, 511, 575, 591, 780
WORKS:
Coningsby, 643 seq., 653
Contarini Fleming, 575
Sybil, 653
Tancred, 664
Venetia, 755 seq.
Vivian Grey, 354, 574
DISRAELI, Isaac, 315, 392, 421, 575
WORKS:
Calamities of Authors, 143, 848
Commentaries on the Life and Reign of Charles I, 358
Curiosities of Literature, 236
Essay on the Literary Character, 238, 281, 300
Quarrels of Authors, 143
DISSENTERS, article by Southey, 139
DISSENTERS' CHAPELS BILL, 644
DIX, John, *Life of Chatterton*, 610
DIXON, James
and Mrs. Quillinan's death, 673, 855
Crabb Robinson's gift to, 639 seq.
mentioned, 475, 488, 637 and note, 640, 655, 682, 690, 712, 744, 753, 806, 835
DIXON, William Hepworth, defence of J. P. Collier, 795
DR. WILLIAMS'S CHARITY TRUST, 813
DODSLEY, Robert, 334; payments to authors, 723
DOMENICHINO, 524
DOMESTIC LIFE, lecture by Emerson, 678
—— men of letters and, 289, 666 seq.

DONALDSON, John William, 699 seq.
DONNE, William Bodham
    epigram on Landor, 813
    literary taste, 691, 702
    mentioned, 660 and note, 696, 699, 700, 716, 748, 768, 800
    WORKS:
      Essays on the Drama, 775
      edn. *Magic and Witchcraft*, 728 and note
DORIGNY, engravings, 261
D'ORSAY, Count, 411, 414, 438, 443, 451, 460, 465, 469, 491, 511, 549
D'ORSAY, Countess, 469
DOU, Gerard, 851
Douglas Jerrold's Shilling Magazine. *See* Jerrold
DOWLING, James, note 272
DOWLING, Miss, 272 and note seq.
DRAMA, The. *See also* Theatre, and particular plays, 36, 377, 450
    Articles by Hazlitt, 133, 182
    Essays by Donne, 775
    Essays by Scott, 394
    Lectures. *See* Schlege
    Specimens. *See* Lamb
DRAMA, Greek, 21, 163, 789
    lectures by Coleridge, 85, 87, 88
DRAMATISTS, 17th c., lecture by Hazlitt, 225
DRUMMOND, Mrs., 559
DRYDEN, John. *Life.* *See* Scott, Sir W.
    writings, 608, 751
    Poetical Works, review by Macaulay, 355
DUBLIN, Archbishop of. *See* Whately
Dublin Review.
    ARTICLE:
      on Carlyle, 558
DUCK, Stephen, 394
DUDEVANT, Baroness. *See* Sand
DUFF GORDON. *See* Gordon
DUGDALE, Sir William. *Monasticon*, Warton's sonnet, 145 note
DUIGENAN, Patrick
    (*Answer to the Address of the Rt. Hon. H. Grattan to his Fellow Citizens*), 19
DUMAS, Alexandre [the elder]
    new play discussed, 493
    Trois Mousquetaires, 696
DUNLOP, John
    History of Fiction, 167
DUPPA, Richard, 91, 92
    letters from Southey, 635, 640 seq.
    WORK:
      (*Life and Literary Works of Michael Angelo Buonarotti*), 91, 92, 641
DURANGO, 11
DÜRER, Albrecht, 572
DURHAM, Lord, 451

DUVAR, 287 and note

DYCE, Alexander
    and J. P. Collier, 424 seq., 786, 815
    as a critic, 424 seq., 760
    at Rogers's, 658, 693, 715, 729
    WORKS:
    Recollections of the Table Talk of Samuel Rogers.   *See* Rogers, S.
    Remarks on Mr. J. P. Collier's and Mr. C. Knight's Edition of Shake-speare, 643 and note seq.

DYER, George, 4 and note, seq., 65, 170, 548, 798 and note
    letter from J. Newton, 575
    WORKS:
    Life and Writings of Robert Robinson, 4
    M.S. autobiography, 595

DYER, Mrs., 5, 595, seq., 798 and note, seq.

EAST INDIA HOUSE
    Lamb's income from, 116, 318
    —— pun on ' Compounds,' 35
    —— retirement, 318
    —— story of, 144
    —— work, 160, 162
    allowance to M. Lamb, 459

EASTLAKE, Sir Charles, 367
    pictures, 492
    article on Ruskin, 759

EASTLAKE, Elizabeth, Lady [*born* Rigby]
    writings, 366 and note, seq., 686, 759

EATON, Daniel Isaac, 513

ECKERMANN, *Gespräche mit Goethe,* 778

Eclectic Review
    Coleridge's letter to the editor [Parken], 55
    review of Southey's *Kehama,* 30
    —— of Wordsworth's poetry by Montgomery, 84 seq., 158 seq.,
        234, 692 seq., 748, 848

Economist, The
    and W. P. Arnold, 753
    and R. H. Hutton, 768

EDGEWORTH, Maria, 128 seq., 634, 642, 712
    WORKS:
    writings, 109, 143, 147, 418, 436, 629
    Absentee, The, 124
    Émilie de Coulanges, 123
    Ennui, 846
    Forester, The, 850
    Harrington, 234
    Helen, 625
    L'Amie Inconnue, 850
    Leonora, 36
    Ormond, 221, 338
    Patronage, 136, 140

EDGEWORTH, Maria—*contd.*

  WORKS—*contd.*

    Tales, Moral and Popular, 850
    Vivian, 109

EDGEWORTH, Richard Lovell, 128 seq.

EDINBURGH visited, 269, 718

Edinburgh Magazine [later *Blackwoods*], 213

Edinburgh Review. See also Jeffrey, Francis
    and Byron's works, 499, 736
    and Lady Byron, 737 seq.
    and Coleridge's poems, 48, 499
    financial affairs, 541
    and German literature, 353, 367
    and Hazlitt, 153
    politics, 434
    position in Scotland, 28
    compared with the *Quarterly,* 63, 210, 237, 833
    and S. Smith, 26
    and Southey's poems, 26, 39, 638
    style, 210, 229
    and Talfourd, 461
    and the works of Wilson and Wordsworth, 82, 140
    and Wordsworth's works, 136, 268, 425, 434, 493, 500, 667, 696,
      833

  CONTRIBUTIONS BY:
    Brougham, 557
    Carlyle, 375, 408
    Chenier, 292
    Hazlitt, 16, 165, 170, 172, 209, 210, 299, 378, 391
    Hogg, T. J., 398
    Macaulay, T. B., 341, 347, 353, 392, 533, 558, 569, 580, 585
    Stephen, J., 582

  ARTICLES:
    Alison, *Essay on Taste,* 36
    Bacon, F., 533
    Byron, *Childe Harold,* 82
    Baillie, J., *Plays on the Passions,* 92
    —— (*Manfred*), 499
    Clive, 580
    Coleridge (*Biographia Literaria*), 209, 499
    —— *Table Talk,* 462
    Croker, Boswell's *Johnson,* 392
    D'Arblay, F., *Wanderer,* 16, 165, 170
    Dickens, C., 650
    Goethe, 702 and note
    Gladstone, W. E., *State in its Relations with the Church,* 569
    The Gorham controversy, 702 and note
    Hayward, A., *Faust,* 425
    Hazlitt (*Round Table*), 210
    Hogg, J., *Queen's Wake,* 160, 850
    Hunt, J. H. Leigh, *Rimini,* 186
    Landor (*Imaginary Conversations*), 390 seq.
    London University, 341

Edinburgh Review—contd.

ARTICLES—*contd.*

Machiavelli, 347

Milton, 341

Niebuhr, *History of Rome,* 398

Periodical Press, 299

Prior, *Goldsmith,* 540

Quillinan, D., *Journal of a few Months' Residence in Portugal,* 667

Ranke, *History of the Popes,* 585

Recent Shakespearean Literature, 584

Ruskin (*Modern Painters*), 760

Sismondi (*De la Littérature du Midi de l'Europe*), 172

Southey, R., *Carmen Nuptiale,* 186

—— *Curse of Kehama,* 26, 29

—— *Madoc,* 30, 638

Taylor, I., 582

Temple, Sir W., 558

Walpole, H. (*Letters from the Hon. Horace Walpole to George Montagu, Esq.*), 229

Wilson, J., *City of the Plague,* 186

—— (*Isle of Palms and other Poems*), 82, 151

Wordsworth, *Excursion,* 159

—— *White Doe of Rylstone,* 178

EDINBURGH REVIEWERS, 39, 48, 82, 136, 140, 150, 151

EDMONTON

M. Lamb at, 454, 455, 463, 492, 506, 536, 567, 576; removal from, 597

The Lambs move to, 434

EDMUND [valet to Rogers], 744

EDWARDS, Edward, 765

EGERTON, Francis, Lord, 465

EGLOFFSTEIN, Countess, 41

EICHHORN, K. F., *Commentarius in Apocalypsem Johannis,* 332

ELDON, Lord, 501

Life. See Twiss, H.

ELIA, pseud. *See* Lamb, C.

ELIOT, George, pseud. *See* Evans, Mary Ann

ELLENBOROUGH, Lord, bust by Chantrey, 279

ELLERAY, 477 seq.

ELLIOTT, Ebenezer

character and writings, 485, 710

epigram, *The Communist,* 767

in Kingsley, C., *Miscellanies,* 793

[ELLIOTT, George], *Life of Wellington,* review, 178

ELLIS, Charles, 40, 54

ELLIS, George, *Specimens of Early English Metrical Romances,* 848

ELLISTON, Robert William, Theatre Memorial, 223

ELTON, Charles Abraham, 311

ELY, Talfourd, 738, 818

ELY, Mrs., 738

ELYS, The, 287

EMERSON, Ralph Waldo

at the Antiquaries' dinner, 675 seq.

article on, 799

leaving England, 679

EMERSON, Ralph Waldo—*contd.*
lectures, 677 seq.
and H. Martineau, 621, 677
mentioned, 773
WORKS:
English Traits, 762 seq.
Essays, 619, 621 seq., 654
Representative Men, 695, 789 seq.
Emigrants, The, 840 and note
EMPSON, William, 534 seq., 662
Encyclopaedia Britannica, The
ARTICLE:
by Hazlitt, 185 seq.
by Macaulay, 798
ENFIELD
a walk with Lamb to, 145
the Lambs at, 347, 351.   *See also* Westwoods, The
ENGLEFIELD, Sir Henry, 76
Englishman's Magazine, 404 and note
ERSKINE, Captain, 266 and note
ERSKINE, Thomas, 674
ESCOBAR, Fray Luys d', *Las Quatro-cientas*, 115
ESSENES, The, article by De Quincey, 776
ETTY, William, pictures, 492, 571
EVANS, Sir George De Lacy, epigram by Wordsworth, 538
EVANS, Joseph, 312
EVANS, Mary Ann, later Cross, pseud. George Eliot
and Lewes, 751, 787 seq.
Crabb Robinson meets, 707, 799
and Wordsworth's works, 799
WORKS:
writings and style, 808, 821
Adam Bede, 782 seq., 787 and note seq.
Felix Holt, 820, 822
Janet's Repentance, 789 seq.
Mill on the Floss, 796 seq.
Romola, 808
Scenes from Clerical Life, 789
Silas Marner, 800 seq.
translation of Strauss's *Leben Jesu*, 707, 787 seq.
EVANS [of Islington], 151
‖ EVANSON, Edward, *Dissonance of the Gospels*, Pitchford's pun on, 35 and note, 197
EVELYN, John, *Memoirs and Diary*, 300
Examiner, The, 67, 127, 755
CONTRIBUTIONS BY:
Barnes, T., 142
Coleridge, S. T., 198
Hazlitt, W., 146, 151 seq., 169, 186, 196 seq.
Lamb, C., 67
Landor, W. S., 488, 571, 581, 713
Willis, N. P., 444

Examiner, The—contd.
  ARTICLES:
    Ainsworth, W. H., *Jack Sheppard*, 578
    Brougham, *Historical Sketches*, 571
    Coleridge, 142
    Commonplace Critics, 198
    Coriolanus, 199
    Crabbe, 142
    Iago, 151
    Landor, *Citation and Examination of William Shakespeare*, 450
    Southey, *Carmen Nuptiale*, 186, 201
    Stoddart, 199
    West, B., picture, 146, 152
    Wordsworth, 697; *Excursion*, 151
  mentioned, 399, 401, 545, 605, 609
EXETER, Bishop of. *See* Phillpott, Henry

FABER, Frederick William, 605, 628, 655
    Education Sermon, 608 and note
FALSTAFF, Sir John. *Essay on*, see Morgann; *Letters*, see White, J.
Family Party, 840 and note
FANSHAWE, Catherine Maria, parodies, 385 seq.
FANSHAWE, Sir Richard, translation of Camön's *Lusiad*, 643
FARADAY, Michael, 707
FARQUHAR, Lady [later Mrs. Hamilton], 478, 639
FARREN, William, 225
FEARON, Mrs., 691
FELL, R., 31
FELLOWES, Robert, 641
FELLOWS, Sir Charles, 597, 615, 653, 700
FENWICK, Mrs. E., 54
FENWICK, Isabella, 401, 560 seq., 581, 587, 589, 592 seq., 604, 610 seq.,
    628 seq., 638 seq., 643 seq., 655 seq., 662 seq., 667 seq., 672, 677,
    689 seq., 703 seq., 708, 712 seq., 719 note, 730 seq., 743, 749 seq.,
    763, 765, 834, 854
FERGUSON, Robert, *Shadow of the Pyramids*, 672
FERRIAR, John, *Essay towards a Theory of Apparitions*, 223
FERRIER, Susan Edmonstone
    Inheritance, 339, 629
    Marriage, 339
FICHTE, Johann Gottlieb, 70
FICTION
    novel reading, 815
    novels of 1765, 840
    novel writing, 409
    article on 18th c. novelists, 165
    essay on classes of novels, 496
FIELD, Barron, 36, 59, 60, 66, 68, 70, 117, 167, 168, 170, 225, 315 and note,
    317, 353, 361, 439, 441, 643
    preface to Vaux's *Life*, 229
FIELD, Edwin Wilkins, 268, 546, 664, 675, 676, 678, 681, 714, 778, 808,
    820, 822
(FIELD, Frederick), brother of B. Field, 70
(FIELD, Mary), Lamb's grandmother, 669

FIELDING, Copley, 459, 509, 597
FIELDING, Henry, 374, 375
FILANGIERI, Gaetano, 397, 399
FILICAJA, 433
FILICHIA, 512
FINCH, Robert, 376 and note seq., 571 note
FISHER, Esther J., 579, 810, 817
FISHER, Mary, 606
FISHER, portrait of Landor, 764 and note
FITZGERALD, Percy, *Charles Lamb, his Friends, his Haunts, and his Books*, 819
FITZGERALD, William Thomas, 48, 110
FITZHERBERT, Mrs., 35
FLACK, George, 58
FLAXMAN, Ann, *born* Denman, 34, 55, 63, 128, 219
FLAXMAN, John, 23, 219, 292 seq., 298, 305, 335, 361
    and his art, 149, 208, 327, 342, 345, 410, 415. *See also* Denman, Maria
    death, 342
    lectures, 121, 367, 847
    library sold, 359
    literary criticisms, 30, 50, 125, 146, 156 seq., 295
FLAXMAN, Mary Ann, 34, 56
    designs for Robin Goodfellow, 69
FLAXMANS, The, 257, 293, 295
    Crabb Robinson and, 102, 106, 155, 282, 314.   *See also* Flaxman, John, literary criticisms
FLAXMAN GALLERY, The, 706, 707, 709, 731, 740
FLEISCHER [German bookseller], 826 seq.
FLEMING, Mrs., 559 seq.
FLETCHER, Angus, 686, 715
FLETCHER, Eliza, Mrs., 434, 638, 648, 650, 661, 672 seq., 684, 693, 714, 754, 835, 838, 854
    lines *Written on leaving Grasmere Churchyard after Mr. Wordsworth's Funeral*, 711
FLETCHER, John, *Two Noble Kinsmen*, 751
FLETCHER, Sir W., 375
FLETCHER, 268 note
FLETCHERS, The, 670, 754
FLORENCE, visited with Wordsworth, 523
FLOWER, Benjamin, 3
FONBLANQUE, Albany, 395 seq., 398 seq., 404, 445, 450, 452, 468, 489, 568, 635
FORBES, Miss, 335
FORD, John, *Dramatic Works* in Lamb's *Specimens*, 63
Foreign Quarterly Review, articles by Carlyle, 409, 425, 552 and note, 581
FORSTER, John, 497, 596, 618, 642, 666, 700, 755, 758, 820
    WORKS:
        Life and Adventures of Oliver Goldsmith, 680, 706
        Statesmen of the Commonwealth, 545 and note
FORSYTH, Joseph, 504
Fortnightly Review, Trollop, A., *Belton Estate*, 818
[FOSBROKE, Thomas Dudley], *British Monachism*, review, 237
FOSS, Edwin, 416
FOSS, Henry, 720

FOUQUÉ, F. H. K. de la Motte, 823 seq., 826
  Sintram and his Companions, 259, 343
FOUQUÉ, K. A. de la Motte, writings, 824 seq.
FOURIER, François Charles, lecture by Emerson, 677
FOX, Charles James, 5, 103, 571, 845
  letters, 619
  letters from Wordsworth, 551, 625
FOX, Henry.   *See* Holland, 3rd Lord
FOX, William Johnson, 574
  letter on Wordsworth's *Excursion*, 849 and note
Fox How Miscellany, 588
FRANCIA, Dr., article by Carlyle, 633 seq.
FRANKLIN, Eleanor Anne, *born* Porden, 67 and note, 301
  WORK:
    Veils, The, 171 seq.
FRANKLIN, Sir John, 301, 305 seq.
FRASER, James, 506
FRASER, Peter, 12 and note, 37, 40, 50 seq., 203, 205, 230, 616, 647, 716
FRASER, Mrs., 647
  and Lady Blessington, 413
Fraser's Magazine
  CONTRIBUTIONS BY
    Byron, *Question and Answer*, 420 and note, seq.
    Carlyle, T., 440, 542, 695, 715
    Kingsley, C., review of Clough, A. H., *Bothie of Tober-na-Vuolich*,
      685; *Yeast*, 705, 837
FREDERICK II of Prussia, 819
  article on, 615
FREE WILL, lecture by Hazlitt, 68
FREEMAN, Edward Augustus, article on *Presidential Government*, 813
FREEMAN, Mrs. [Rydal friend], 480
FREEMAN, Mrs. [friend of M. Lamb], 146
FREEMANS, The, 145
FREILIGRATH, Ferdinand, translations from Coleridge and Wordsworth,
  531
FRENCH
  editions of Byron's works, 362, 369
  character, 291 seq.
  article on Crédit Mobilier, 765
  and Italy, 380 and note, 397 seq.
  literature, 29, 115, 292, 343, 517
  —— essay on, 248
  Ministry, 1837, 397, 399
  novels wanted by M. Lamb, 463
  Revolution, 183, 189, 324, 348, 571, 855
    See also Burke, E., and Carlyle, T., works
  social conditions, 254 seq.
  tour with Wordsworth, 244, 255, 515, 518
FREND, William, 5, 235
FRERE, John Hookham, 122
  *Prospectus and Specimens of an intended National Work by William
    and Robert Whistlecraft, of Stowmarket in Suffolk, Harness and
    Collar Makers, intended to comprise the most interesting particulars
    relating to King Arthur and his Round Table*, 122, 226

FRERE, John Hookham—*contd.*
  review of [Hill, H. D.] (*Essays on the Institutions, Government, and Manners of the States of Ancient Greece*), 237
FRIEDLANDER, Professor, 359
FROUDE, James Anthony, 690 seq.
  WORKS:
    History of England, 771 seq., 779
    Nemesis of Faith, 688; review, 690 and note
    Oxford Essay, 772
    Shadows of the Clouds, 688
FULLER, Margaret, 729
FULLER, Thomas, 20
FUSELI, Henry, 6, 116, 227, 292
  article on, 59
  engravings, 669
  'Macbeth,' 34

GAINSBOROUGH, Thomas, portrait of J. Quin, 144
Galignani, 532
  edn. of Wordsworth, 378
GALLENGA, Antonio Carlo Napoleone, pseud. Mariotti, 814
GALT, John, 406 and note
  WORKS:
    Annals of the Parish, 500
    Steamboat, The, 500
    Tragedies, review, 146
    Witness, The, 137 and note
GAMBA, Count, and Byron's letters, 412
GARRICK, David, 478
GARWOOD, 311 seq.
GASKELL, Daniel, 584
GASKELL, Mrs. Daniel, 574 and note, 583, 584
GASKELL, Elizabeth Cleghorn Stevenson, 688 seq., 768
  WORKS:
    Mary Barton, 685, 722
    Ruth, 722 seq.
GASKELL, Mrs. [friend of H. Martineau], 754
GAWSELL, Sam, 1
GAY, J., inscription, 521
GENEVA, Byron's life in, 224
GENLIS, Comtesse de, 506
Gentleman's Magazine, articles, 110, 716, 795
GEORGE III, 73
  verses by Mrs. Barbauld, 45
  ‖ in Byron's *Vision of Judgment*, 286, 367, 373
  J. Smith's inscription, 543
  Southey, lines on his death, 239
  sonnet by Wordsworth, 135 and note, 136
GEORGE IV, 35, 81, 91, 258, 379
  lecture by Thackeray, 799
GEORGE III and IV, article by Brougham, 557

GERMAN
　editions:
　—— *British Poets*, 366
　—— Byron's works, 369, 370
　—— translations from Coleridge and Wordsworth, 366, 531
　literature, 353, 367, 773
　—— article by: Carlyle, 580; Macaulay, 353
　—— Crabb Robinson and, 4, 25 seq., 33, 146, 245, 374, 426, 546, 634;
　　　advice to Carlyle, 319, 335, 823 seq.; translation from. *See*
　　　Robinson, H. C., works
　philosophy, 70, 191, 307
　See also under particular philosophers and individual opinions
German Playwrights, article by Carlyle, 580
GERMANY
　Coleridge's letters from, 466
　article on *Prussian Reform*, 299, 318 and note, seq.
　—— Religion in, 552
　visited, 224, 366 seq., 446 seq.
　—— with Wordsworth, 528 seq.
GERVINUS, G. G., 658
GIBBON, Edward, 759, 774
　(*History of the Decline and Fall of the Roman Empire*, abridged edn.,
　　1789), 496
GIBBS, Michael, 745
(GIBBS, Sir Vicary), Attorney-General, 77
GIBSON, John, 395
GIBSON, Dr., 740, 794
GIBSON, 692
GIFFORD, William, 63, 225, 311, 344
　notes on Shirley, 344
GILBERT, Miss, 60
GILBERTS, The, 23
GILCHRIST, Alexander, 752, 799
　Life of Blake, 809 seq.
　—— review, 810
GILCHRIST, James, 322 and note, seq.
GILES, essay on E. Elliott, 710
GILLIES, Margaret
　portrait of: M. Wordsworth, 582, 660, 781; W. Wordsworth, 582, 781
GILLMAN, James
　and Coleridge, 185, 200, 506
　and Cottle's letters from Coleridge, 499, 501 seq.
　mentioned, 208, 293, 320, 488
　WORK:
　Life of S. T. Coleridge, 549
GILLMAN, Mrs., 293, 687
GIORDANO, Lucca
　pictures, 711
　sonnet by Wordsworth, 711
GIOTTO, 524
GLADSTONE, William Ewart, 564 seq.
　WORKS:
　(*State in its Relations with the Church*), 563 seq.
　—— review, 569

GLASGOW University rectorship, 659

Globe, The, and Southey, 581

GODDARD, Frederick William, 243 and note, 247, 249 seq., 272, 278, note 512

GODSON, 178

GODWIN, Fanny. *See* Imlay

GODWIN, Mary. *See* Shelley

GODWIN, Mary Jane Clairmont, 14, 32, 55 seq., 63, 105, 111, 118, 123 and note, 129, 150, 162 seq., 199, 206, 211 seq., 229, 235, 264, 297, 299, 441, 549

GODWIN, Mary Wollstonecraft, 5, 6, 209, 235, 569, 629

GODWIN, William
    and F. Abington, 55
    in L. Aiken's *Letters*, 817
    at Alsager's, 179
    article by Hazlitt, 378
    —— Crabb Robinson, 3, 842
    and the bookshop, 14, 136
    and Clairmont, 198
    and Coleridge, 28 seq., 60 seq., 114
    Coleridge's letters to, 810
    and the Commonwealth Judges, 311
    death, 490 seq.
    health, 39, 43, 151
    and Holcroft, 11
    and Miss Jones, 139
    at Lamb's, 178, 259, 307, 345
    and Mackintosh, 132
    personal qualities and financial affairs, 7, 14, 32 seq., 43, 55, 61, 80, 105, 109, 117, 118, 132, 135, 138, 162, 175 seq., 204, 210 seq., 235, 283, 286 seq., 297 seq., 316, 491, 810
    —— in old age, 426
    and Crabb Robinson, 1, 3, 6 seq., 14, 56, 111, 133, 171, 206, 208 seq., 229, 345, 841
    and Shelley and Mary Godwin, 199, 211
    and Shelley's works, 279
    and Southey, 28, 171
    and Wordsworth, 171, 183

  OPINIONS AND CRITICISMS:
    Aikin, L., *Queen Elizabeth*, 221
    Barbauld, A. L., *Year 1811*, 63 seq.
    Betty, W. H. W., 113, 115
    Lord Cochrane, 61
    Coleridge and his lectures, 55, 92, 127, 177
    Hale, Sir M., 105
    Mandeville, B., *Fable of the Bees*, 25
    Napoleon's campaigns, 114 seq., 171
    Crabb Robinson, 25, 105, 114
    Sandeman, R., 847
    Shakespeare, 55, 66
    Slavery, 305
    Mme de Staël, 132
    Wordsworth, *Letter to a friend of R. Burns*, 184

  mentioned, 30, 49, 69, 70, 116, 144, 165, 231, 241, 306, 569

GODWIN, William—*contd.*
WORKS:
writings, 1, 274; influence on the drama, 377; proposed German edition, 206, 208 seq.
Caleb Williams, 2, 215, 345
Deloraine, 423
Enquiry concerning Political Justice, 3, 6, 25, 27, 199, 841
Faulkner, 118
History of the Commonwealth, 338
Life of Geoffrey Chaucer, review, 28
Mandeville, 212, 215, 216. *See also* writings, proposed German edn.
Of Population, in Answer to Mr. Malthus, 263 seq., 587
Pamphlet, 221
St. Leon, 7
Thoughts on Man, 418 seq.
GODWIN, William [son], 241, 299, 307, 316, 317
GODWINIAN notion, a, 806
GODWINS, The, 142, 152, 155, 162 seq., 167, 263, 275, 299, 574
GOESCHEL, Karl Friedrich (*Unterhaltungen zur Schilderung Goetheischer Dicht- und Denkweise*), 495
GOETHE, August von, 751
GOETHE, Johann Wolfgang von
main entry, 367 seq.
on Byron and his works, 224, 339, 438, 450, 746. *See also* Robinson, H. C., letter to Moore
supposed death, 400
death, 405
Lewes inquires concerning, 751 seq.
literary obligations, 776
portrait, 491
on Sir W. Scott, 438
on Vico, 321
other references, 89, 114, 308, 402, 403, 425, 478, 480, 507, 562, 619, 627 seq., 651, 656, 658, 789
BOOKS, ETC., RELATING TO:
Arnold, M., *Essays in Criticism*, 822
—— *Memorial Verses*, 745
Austin, S., *Characteristics of Goethe*, 430, 467; review, 426
Beddoes, T. L., *Poems, with a Memoir*, 713
Goeschel, *Unterhaltungen zur Schilderung Goetheischer Dicht- und Denkweise*
Lewes, G. H., *Life of Goethe*, 495, 756
article:
by Carlyle, 409, 581
by Crabb Robinson, *Goethe's Works*, 408, 415, 416, 426, 430, 638 and note
mentioned, 252, 286, 410, 411, 414, 467, 506, 512, 515, 540, 545, 566, 679, 690, 709, 717, 727
WORKS:
article on English Literature, 438
Braut von Corinth, 180, 628
Briefwechsel mit einem Kind. See Arnim, von
Correspondence with Knebel, 751, 759
Correspondence with Zelter, 374

GOETHE, Johann Wolfgang von—*contd.*
  WORKS—*contd.*
    Cupid as Landscape Painter, Crabb Robinson's translation, 34
    translation of Diderot, *Le Neveu de Rameau* review, 15, 33
    Egmont, 161
    —— Crabb Robinson's translation, 122, 546
    (*Farbenlehre*), 185
    Faust, 45, 107 seq., 208, 224, 372 seq., 425, 448, 689
    —— Hayward's translation, 423 and note, 425
    Gespräche mit Eckermann, 778
    Herman and Dorothea, 628, 677
    —— Whewell's translation, 584
    Iphigenia in Tauris, 294, 628
    Kunst und Alterthum, 359, 360
    Kunst am Rhein, 336
    Melusine, 823
    Reinecke Fuchs, 123
    Tasso, 628
    Wahlverwandschaften, 300
    Wanderer, The, Crabb Robinson's translation, 34
    Werther, 122, 367, 368, 823
    Wilhelm Meister, 124, 402, 403, 790, 825
    —— translation by Carlyle, 308, 309
    Winckelmann, 408
    Zueignung, 106, 107, 367, 368
GOETHE, Ottilie von, 367 seq., 442
GOLDSMID, Sir Francis, 714 note, 723, 804
GOLDSMITH, Oliver, 234, 263
  article by Macaulay, 798 and note
  lecture by Thackeray, 715
  Life. See Forster and Prior
  WORKS:
    Deserted Village, The, 263, 472
    Traveller, The, 517
    Vicar of Wakefield, The, 448
GOOCH, Dr., 240
GOODEN, James, 616
  letter from Coleridge, 689
GOODEN, Mrs., 689
GOODWIN, 60
GORDON, Sir Alexander Duff (*Sketches of German Life*), 742
GORDON, Lady Duff, *Letters from Egypt*, 817 seq.
GORE, Catherine
  Cecil, or the Adventures of a Coxcomb, 592 and note, 602
  Cecil, a Peer, 602 seq.
GORES, The, 58
GÖRRES [father], 448
GÖRRES [son], 448
GOSSON, Stephen, *School of Abuse*, 595
GÖTZENBERGER, 344 seq.
GRAHAM, Fanny. *See* Wordsworth, Mrs. William, jr.
GRAHAM, Thomas, Baron Lynedoch, 41 seq.
GRAHAM, Thomas, 554
GRAHAM, 246 seq.

GRASMERE, epitaph, 627
GRATTAN, Henry, Duigenan's *Letter* to, 19
‖ GRAVES, Captain, 478, 485, 650
GRAY, Thomas, *Correspondence with Mason*, ed. Mitford, 746
    WORKS:
        writings, 1, 144
        Bard, The, 90, 723
        Poems, with a Life, ed. Mason, 178
        Progress of Poesy, 723
GRAY'S INN, 86
GREEK drama.   *See* Drama
GREEN, Bevis E. [partner in Longmans], 359
GREEN, Joseph Henry, 207, 294, 307, 443, 469, 496, 501, 514, 732
        Hunterian Oration, 664
        Introduction to Coleridge's *Confessions of an Inquiring Spirit*, 817
GREEN, Mrs. Joseph Henry, 207, 307
GREENOUGH, on R. Chambers's *Vestiges of the Natural History of Creation*, 652
GREENWOOD, Joseph Gouge, 765
GREENWOOD, 510
GREG, William Rathbone, 650, 672
GREG, Mrs. W. R., 650
GRÉGOIRE, l'Abbé, 150
GREGORY, Mrs., 128
GRENFELL, 233
GRENVILLE, Lord, 42
(GRETA HALL), described, 189
‖ GREY, Charles, 2nd Earl, 42, 304, 431, 451, 620
GREY, The Hon?, 245
GRIMM, Crabb Robinson meets, 446
        Reinecke Fuchs, 510
        Tales, translated by Taylor, J. E., 659
GROTE, George, 743
GUELPHIC ORDER, The, 432
Guerre des Dieux, 14
GUEST, Edwin, 679
GUICCIOLI, Countess, 412
(GUICHARD, M.) and the Lambs, 281, 283, 288
GUIDO, 524
GUILLEMARD, 642
GUIZOT, 121, 780
GÜNDERODE, Karoline von, 531
GURNEY, Hudson, 212, 220, 230
GURNEY, Mrs. Hudson, 220, 228
GURNEY, Joseph John, 336
GURNEY, Russell, 783
GUTENBERG, 521

HADRIAN'S VILLA, visited with Wordsworth, 520
HALE, Sir Matthew, 85, 105
HALIBURTON, Thomas Chandler, writings, 558 and note, 565
HALL, Captain Basil, 540
        (*Journal written on the Coasts of Chili, Peru, and Mexico*), 309

HALL, Mrs. Samuel Carter
    writings, 545 and note
    Ireland, 600 seq.
HALL [librarian at the Athenæum], 633, 812
HALL, 355
HALLAM, Arthur Henry
    (*Essay on the Philosophical Writings of Cicero*), 588
    Remains in Verse and Prose, 588 and note
HALLAM, Henry, 225, 568
    Constitutional History of England, 349 seq., 661
HALLEIN, visited with Wordsworth, 528
HALLETT, 466, 515
    pamphlet against Sydney Smith, 513
HAMILTON, N. E.
    [article in *The Times*] on Collier's *Shakespeare*, 786
    (*Inquiry into the Genuineness of Collier's Annotated Shakespeare*),
        794
HAMILTON, Captain Thomas, 428 seq., 476 seq., 627
    WORKS:
        Cyril Thornton, 476, 577
        Men and Manners in America, 476
HAMILTON, Sir William, 476
HAMILTONS, The, 479 seq., 483
(HAMOND, Charles), brother of Elton Hamond, 87
HAMOND, Elton, 50, 56, 60, 63, 84, 87, 90, 105 and note, 109, 114, 124,
        128, 132, 134, 135, 198, 219, 239, 832
HAMOND, Miss [sister of Elton Hamond], 87, 218
HAMONDS, The, 117
HANCOCK, Robert, portraits of Coleridge, Lamb, Southey, and Words-
        worth, 500, 502
HANMER, Sir John, 618
HANMER, Sir Thomas, Bart., *Correspondence*, 551, 609, 625
HANOVER, King of [Ernest Augustus], 530 seq., 638
HANSARD, 806 and note
HARDCASTLE [of Hatcham], 10
HARDCASTLE, Ephraim, pseud. *See* Pyne
HARDENS, The [of Field Head], 472, 475, 479, 483, 565, 566, 568, 855
        and note
HARDY, Thomas, 3
    Trial of, 586
HARE, Francis, 569
HARE, Julius Charles, Archdeacon, 400 seq., 406, 410, 413, 415, 460, 495,
        514, 600, 675, 697 seq., 723, 732, 815, 817, 837
    WORKS:
        article on Landor's *Imaginary Conversations*, 305
        Essays and Tales of John Sterling with a Memoir of his Life, 674
        Mission of the Comforter, note on Carlyle, 661 and note
HARE, Mrs., *born* Cottle, 502, 594
HARNESS, William, 121, 591, 597, 644, 760, 788
HARRIS, 759
HARRISON, Benson and family, 429, 479, 483, 560, 605, 682, 726,
        739
HARTLEY, David, lecture by Hazlitt, 64
HARVEY, landlord, 521

HARWOOD, Philip
    (*German Anti-supernaturalism ; six lectures on Strauss's 'Lebens Jesu'*), 607
    Materialism in Religion, 607
HARWOOD, M.D. [of Sheffield], 377
HASTINGS, Warren, article by Macaulay, 601
HAWKERS, The, 555
HAWTHORNE, Nathaniel
    WORKS :
        Blithedale Romance, review, 747
        House of the Seven Gables, 765, 766
        Scarlet Letter, 752
        Twice-Told Tales, 722
HAWTREY, Edward Craven, 783
HAY, Will, *Deformity, an Essay*, 334
HAYDON, Benjamin Robert, 121, 170, 217 seq., 222, 286, 316, 520
    'Christ's entry into Jerusalem,' 239 seq.
    portraits of Newton, Voltaire, and Wordsworth, 240
    WORKS :
        Autobiography and Memoirs, ed. Taylor, T., 729 seq.
HAYLEY, William, 23, 102
    (*Philosophical Essay on Old Maids*), 177 seq.
HAYS, Mary, 5 seq., 124 seq., 128, 130 seq., 212, 234 seq., 629, 843
    WORKS :
        Female Biography ; or Memoirs of Celebrated and Illustrious Women, 5
        Memoirs of Emma Courtney, 5
HAYWARD, Abraham, 497, 591
    translation of *Faust*, 423 and note, 425 ; review, 425
(HAZLITT, Isabella), 387
HAZLITT, John, 6, 7
(HAZLITT, Mrs. John), 7
HAZLITT, Sarah, 170, 230, 317
HAZLITT, William
    and alcohol, 161, 178, 179
    at Alsager's, 145, 161, 178, 179
    and art as a career, 6, 30
    and Ayrton, 744
    and Sir George Beaumont, 24
    and C. A. Brown, 387
    and J. Burney, 16, 170
    and Byron, 222
    and Coleridge, 24, 27
    death, 386, 387
    divorce, 281, 286
    and the *Edinburgh Review*, 153
    financial affairs, 65, 110, 116, 386, 424
    W. C. Hazlitt inquires concerning, 807
    and J. Johnson, 6
    at Keswick, 169
    and Knowles, 319
    and C. Lamb, 142, 200, 286, 298
    and J. Lamb, 200
    and the Lambs, 9, 24

HAZLITT, William—*contd.*

at the Lambs', 28, 128, 133, 232, 237, 239, 261, 264, 265, 278, 301

and W. S. Landor, 390, 391

lectures, 54, 57 seq., 218 seq., 222, 223, 225, 226, 237

and the *London Magazine*, 260

and B. Montagu, 424

at B. Montagu's, 60, 200, 211, 258

and the *Morning Chronicle. See* and Perry

introduced to C. Orme, 176, 184

parties, 27, 116

and Perry, 110, 116, 153, 154

portrait of: Hartley Coleridge, 44; T. Robinson, 23, 30, 104 and note, 116; a young man, 30

and A. Robinson, 6

and Crabb Robinson, 6, 15, 66, 201, 211, 237, 239, 261, 264, 301, 386, 449

and J. Severn, 378

at Thelwall's, 65

and Wordsworth, 169

OPINIONS AND CRITICISM:

authors, 421

Blake, W., Poems and illustrations for Young's *Night Thoughts*, 25

Coleridge, S. T., 11, 179 note, 201, 222

German literature, 161

ideas, 28

Lamb, C., puns, 28

Mandeville, B., 179

Montaigne, 179

the publication of private conversations, 201

politics, 6, 133, 142, 161, 164, 386, 391, 744

Crabb Robinson, 6

Rogers, S., 222

Southey, R., 201, 222

Wordsworth, W., 151, 166, 169, 179 and note, 200, 202, 213, 218, 220, 222, 223, 322

PERSONAL QUALITIES: 6, 211, 265, 386, 387

conversation, 178, 179

intellect, 30, 128, 154, 172, 184

BOOKS RELATING TO:

Holcroft, T., *Hazlitt's Last Hours*, 424

Patmore, P. G., *My Friends and Acquaintances*, 342 and note, 744, 819

—— *Personal Recollections of W. Hazlitt*, 651

mentioned in Lytton's *England and the English*, 435

mentioned, 2 note, 50, 88, 117, 134, 145, 221, 374, 375, 814

WORKS:

writings and style, 151, 172, 186, 226, 237, 260, 301, 322, 349

Abridgment of The Light of Nature Pursued, by Abraham Tucker, 844

Characters of Shakespeare's Plays, 217, 223, 226

HAZLITT, William—*contd.*

WORKS—*contd.*

Conversations of James Northcote, Esq., R.A., 397, 399, 457
Eloquence of the British Senate, 6, 387
Lectures on the English Comic Writers, 236, 281
⟨Lectures on the English Poets⟩, 222, 226
Liber Amoris, 296
Life of Napoleon, 356
Literary Remains, 497, 779, 780
Memoir of Thomas Holcroft, 185
Plain Speaker, 347
⟨Political Essays⟩, 236
—— review, 237
Reply to the Essay on Population by the Rev. T. R. Malthus, 844
Round Table, 226
—— review in the Edinburgh, 210; Quarterly, 210
Spirit of the Age or Contemporary Portraits, 317 and note, 322, 377
Table Talk, 260, 276, 302
⟨View of the English Stage⟩, 226

ARTICLES AND REVIEWS:

Allied Powers, 153
improvement of the Arts, 151
the fine arts, 185, 186
Bentham, J., 301
Coleridge, S. T. (Biographia Literaria), 209; Christabel, 210;
    Lay Sermon, 196, 197, 200, 202
Commonplace Critics, 198
Coriolanus, 199
D'Arblay, Mme, Wanderer, 165
Drama, 133
English Students at Rome, 348, 349
Godwin, W., 378
Iago, 151
Illustrations by Vetus, 133
Irving, E., 301, 317 note
Irving Washington, 317 and note
Lamb, C. [Elia and Geoffrey Crayon], 317 and note
Landor, W. S., Imaginary Conversations, 391
in the Liberal, 289
Main Chance, 355
Periodical Press, 299
Rochefoucauld's Maxims, 153
Schlegel, Lectures on the Drama, 182
Sismondi (De la Litterature du Midi de l'Europe), 172
Southey, R., Carmen Nuptiale, 186, 201
Stoddart, Sir J., 199
Sun-Dial, 349
Those we should Wish to have Seen, 331, 780
West, B., 'Rejection of Christ,' 146, 152
Wordsworth, W., Excursion, 151, 202

HAZLITT, William [son], 265, 387
    Memoir of his father, 497
HAZLITT, William Carew, 807

HAZLITT FAMILY visited, 7
HEAUPET, Baron d', 424
HEBER, Richard, 319
HEBERDEN, William, translation *Letters of Cicero to Atticus*, 564
HELIODORUS, *Theagenes and Chariclea*, 840 and note
HELMONT, Johann Baptist, 418, 419 and note
HELVETIUS, Claude Adrien, 29
        in Hazlitt's lectures, 60, 65
HEMANS, Felicia Dorothea, *Memorials of*, 505
HENDERSON, Dr., 598, 658, 693
HENLEY, Samuel, 180 note
HERAUD, John Abraham, 565
HERBERT, George, *Works*, note by Coleridge, 636
HERDER, 308, 447, 628, 776
        preface to *Volksballaden*, 276
HERN, Southey's anecdote, 432
HERODOTUS, article by De Quincey, 789
HERVEY, James, 42
HERVEY, Thomas Kibble, 336 and note, 337
‖ HERVEY family, 142
HESSEY, James Augustus, 310. *See also* Taylor and Hessey
HEUN, K. G. S. *See* Clauren pseud.
HEYNE, Christian Gottlob, article by Carlyle, 580
HEYNE, Christian Lebrecht, pseud. Anton Wall, *Amatonda*, translation
        by Crabb Robinson, 24 seq.
HEYWOOD, Thomas, 595
HIGHGATE, Coleridge at, 185 seq.
HILBURY, 231
[HILDRETH, Richard], *White Slave*, 760
HILL, Bertha, *born* Southey, 587
HILL, Herbert, 587, 609
[HILL, Henry David] (*Essays on the Institutions, Government, and Manners
        of the States of Ancient Greece*), review, 237
HILL, 21, 124, 555
HILLS, 358, 423, 458, 604, 806
HILLS, Mrs., 806
HOADLY, Bishop, 628 note
HOARE, banker, 91
HOARE, Mrs., the Wordsworths' visit, 462, 533, 596, 618, 653, 659, 664
HOBBES, Thomas
        in Hazlitt's lecture, 57
        (*Human Nature and Liberty and Necessity with a Life*), 54
HOBHOUSE, Sir John Cam, 306, 412, 668
HODSON, Margaret, *born* Holford, *Wallace*, 138
HOFFMANN, writings, 824, 826, 828
HOGAN, 109
HOGARTH, William
        'Captain Coram,' 144
        Lamb, C., *On the Genius and Character of Hogarth*, 42, 50, 394
HOGG, James, 167, 434, 849 seq.
        Queen's Wake, 849
        —— review, 160, 850
HOGG, Thomas Jefferson, 237, 314, 315, 398, 406, 421
    WORKS:
        Life of Shelley, 777, 778, 784

HOGG, Thomas Jefferson—*contd.*
  WORK—*contd.*
    review of Niebuhr's *History of Rome*, 398
    Two Hundred and Nine Days, 346 and note, 398 and note
HOLCROFT, Louisa. *See* Kenney
HOLCROFT, Louisa [daughter of Thomas], 360
HOLCROFT, Thomas, 3, 6, 11, 31, 557
  WORKS:
    Adventures of Hugh Trevor, 3
    Anna St. Ives, 3
    Autobiography, ed. Hazlitt, 185
    Letter to the Rt. Hon. W. Windham, 2
    (Plain Narrative of the late Riots in London), 2
    Road to Ruin, 694
    Travels, 425
HOLCROFT, Thomas [Tom, son], 553, 556
    Hazlitt's Last Hours, 424
HOLCROFT, Mrs. Tom, 553
HOLFORD, Margaret. *See* Hodson
HOLLAND, Henry Fox, 3rd Lord, 33, 42, 304, 456
HOLLAND, Lady, *Memoir of the Rev. Sydney Smith by his Daughter, Lady
    Holland, with a selection from his Letters, edited by Mrs. Austin*,
    757 seq.
HOLLAND, Miss, 427
HOLLAND, Wordsworth's tour in, 293, 295, 296, 359
HOLMES, Oliver Wendell, *Elsie Venner*, 802, 803
HOLTZ, 26
HOLYOAKE, George Jacob, letter in the *Examiner*, 767
HOMER, 72, 378, 628
HONE, William, 214, 323, 357, 590
    Parodies, 217
HOOD, Edwin Paxton, *William Wordsworth a Biography*, 762, 763
HOOD, Thomas, 360, 423, 623, 633
  WORKS:
    writings; album verse, 498
    serious poems, 658, 768
    Bridge of Sighs, 721, 746, 749, 832, 833
    Ode to Rae Wilson, 721
    Song of the Shirt, 746
    Tale of a Trumpet, 747
    Whimsicalities, 640 seq.
HOOD, Mrs. Thomas, 360
HOOK, Theodore, 644, 663
  WORKS:
    Gilbert Gurney, 576
    translation of a Sicilian tale, 551
HOPE, Thomas, *Anastasius*, 273, 274, 306, 413, 419, 420, 443 and note
HOPPNER, R. B., 447
HOPPNER, Mrs. R. B., 446, 447
HORACE translated. *See* Byron
HORATIAN SCHOOL, 848
HORN, Franz, 585, 826, 827
HORNBY, 606, 607
HORNE, Richard Henry, *New Spirit of the Age*, 642
HORROCKS, Miss, 246, 248, 304

Household Words
    and C. Dickens, 696, 722
    H. Martineau, articles, 703, 704, 718
    The Raven, pseud., articles, 704, 696
    obituary of Talfourd, 739
HOUSMAN, 39
HOVENDEN, 539
HOWEL, portrait by Hazlitt, 30
HOWITT, William, article on Wordsworth, 657
HUGHES, Thomas, *Tom Brown's Schooldays*, 770
HUGHES, Miss, 663
HUGO, Victor, *Hunchback of Notre Dame*, 442 and note
HULTON, 622
HUME, David, 326, 632, 772
    Treatise of Human Nature, 221
HUME, Joseph, 25, 105 and note, 110
    Lamb's joke on, 197
HUME, Joseph, M.P., 314
HUNDLEBY, George, 238, 242, 295, 330
HUNT, Henry, 203, 236
HUNT, James Henry Leigh
    financial affairs, 121, 236, 406, 408, 520, 569
    in Horne's *New Spirit of the Age*, 642
    and Lamb, 59
    in Medwin's *Shelley*, 668
    and Moore's letters, 414
    personal qualities, 155 seq., 221, 255
    trial, 104
    and Wordsworth, 166, 169, 179, 854
    and Wordsworth's *Excursion*, 156
    on Wordsworth, 138
    mentioned, 66, 70, 198, 239, 390, 409, 465, 814
    WORKS:
        articles: in the *Examiner*, 67; on Fuseli, 59; on Moore's *Byron*, 414
        Autobiography, 700, 701, 796
        Feast of the Poets, 138
        Foliage, 222
        —— review, 223
        Indicator, 255
        London Journal, 440
        Lord Byron and some of his Contemporaries, 353 and note, 412
        —— review, 355
        Poetical Works, 420
        Rimini, 423
        —— review, 186
        Wit and Humour, 659
HUNT, John, 324
HUNT, John Higgs, 641
HUNT, Marianne [Mrs. J. H. Leigh, *born* Kent], 155, 221
HUNT, Thornton, 751, 787
HUNT, William Holman, 812
HUNTS, The, 145
HUNTER, Joseph
    and Collier's *Shakespeare*, 643, 786 seq., 788, 794, 795
    other references, 675, 676, 678, 699, 759, 777, 779

HUNTER, Miss, 787, 794
HURST, Thomas, 67, 335
HURWITZ, Hyman, *Hebrew Tales*, 591
HUSKISSON, William, 436
HUSTLER, 161
HUTCHINSON, George, 634, 690
HUTCHINSON, Mrs. George, 691
HUTCHINSON, Joanna
    death, 634, 635
    poem by Wordsworth, 194
HUTCHINSON, Sarah, 167, 168, 187, 194, 214, 278, 293, 297, 465
HUTCHINSON, Thomas, 570
HUTCHINSON, Mrs. Thomas, 465, 539, 634, 835
HUTCHINSON [son of Thomas], 536, 537
HUTCHINSON, 520
HUTCHINSON family, 835
HUTCHISON, The Misses, 769 and note
HUTTON, Richard Holt, 719, 729, 740 note, 753, 768, 775
    WORKS:
        articles on: Buckle's *History*, 775; Scott's *Novels*, 777; Wordsworth, 764
        edn. of W. C. Roscoe's *Poems*, 796
HUTTON, 546, 584, 600, 620

IAGO, 55; article by Hazlitt, 151
Il Fabro di San Paolo, drama, 377
Illustrated News, 658
IMLAY, Fanny, 203, 234 seq.
IMLAY, Gilbert, 6, 235
IMPEY, Sir Elijah, 601
INCHBALD, Elizabeth
    article on, 435
    Life. See Boaden, James
    WORKS:
        Nature and Art, 160, 366, 435, 806
        Simple Story, 336, 435, 840
INDIA HOUSE. See East India House
INGLIS, Sir Robert, 457, 609, 610, 675
Inquirer, The
    ARTICLES:
        F. W. Robertson, 729
        Talfourd's *Final Memorials*, 679 seq.
        Wordsworth, 696 seq., 857
Inverness Courier
    article on Wordsworth, 699
    Crabb Robinson's letter, 699
IRELAND, Alexander, 678
IRELAND, William Henry, 159
IRELAND, social and religious questions, 18 seq., 434, 475 seq., 478 and note, 481, 486, 545
IRVING, Edward, 294 seq., 304, 307 seq., 312, 315, 318, 320, 328, 331, 332, 338, 359, 402 seq.
    articles by: Carlyle, 805; Hazlitt, 301, 317 note

IRVING, Edward—*contd.*

WORKS:
article in the *Anniversary*, 363
Orations on the Judgment to Come, 300, 316
IRVING, Washington, pseud. Geoffrey Crayon
article by Hazlitt, 317 and note
Crabb Robinson meets, 615

WORKS:
Bracebridge Hall, 284
Newstead Abbey, 464
Sketch Book, 243, 260
IRWIN, Ellen, in Wordsworth's poem, 740
IRWIN, 740
ISAAC, Thomas, 158
Isabella, drama, 157
ISCHL, visited with Wordsworth, 529
ISEO, visited with Wordsworth, 525 seq.
ISLE OF MAN, Wordsworth's tour, 427, 433
ISLINGTON, the Lambs at, 298
ISOLA, Emma [Mrs. Moxon], 360, 404, 406, 408, 410, 455
lines by C. Lamb, 363
Italian Christian Ballads, 510
ITALIAN
Lamb and, 408
literature, 388
—— article on, 805
opera, 789
politics, 804, 815
ITALY
Crabb Robinson's tour, 375 seq., 397, 399, 515, 518 seq.
Wordsworth's tour, 245 seq., 515, 518 seq. *See also* Wordsworth,
plans to visit Italy

'JACK ROBINSON,' 428 and note
JACKSON, Dr., 743
JACOBI, Friedrich, 447
JACOBIN [Jacobinism], 3, 42, 55, 115, 189
JAFFRAY, Robert, 452, 454, 533, 548, 579, 623
JAFFRAY, Mrs. Robert, 553
JAFFRAYS, The, 456, 463, 494, 508, 556, 557, 582, 583
JAMES, Rydal servant. *See* Dixon
JAMES, George Payne Rainsford, 506, 571

WORKS:
Corse de Leon, 607, 608
Mary of Burgundy, 498 seq.
JAMES, Sarah [M. Lamb's nurse], 283, 454, 468, 492, 506, 597
JAMESON, Anna Brownell, 441 seq., 549, 615, 619, 651, 655, 724, 730, 734

WORKS:
writings, 171, 262, 442, 549
(*Characteristics of Women : Moral, Poetical, and Historical*), 442 and
note, 614
Diary of an Ennuyée, 407
Halloran the Pedlar, 350
Sacred and Legendary Art, 702

JAMESON, Robert, 171, 262, 441, 442
JAMESON [merchant in partnership with Aders], 58, 421
|| JAMIESON, Robert, *Illustrations of Northern Antiquities. See* Scott,
    Sir W.
JARDINE, David, 569
JARVIS, Thomas, 539 and note
JEFFREY, Francis, Lord. See also *Edinburgh Review*
    and Coleridge, 209, 210
    letters to Coleridge, 471
    and Hazlitt, 153
    and J. Hogg, 850
    and Lamb, 536
    Crabb Robinson meets, 460, 461
    and Southey's poems, 39
    and Talfourd, 461, 535
    and Wilson, 151
    and Wordsworth, 695, 699; on Wordsworth, 461; and Wordsworth's
        works, 151, 161, 434, 461, 535, 636, 638, 835
JEKYLL, Joseph, 420
JERNINGHAM, Edward, 22
JERROLD, Douglas William
    his paper [April 1849], 689
    || *St. Giles and St. James*, 543
    Shilling Magazine, 651, 652
JESSE, Edward, 554 and note
JOAN OF ARC
    article by De Quincey, 740
    Southey and, 553, 555
JOB, 107
John Bull, article on Hazlitt's *Liber Amoris*, 296
JOHNSON, Joseph, 6, 32, 72
JOHNSON, Samuel, 18, 102, 103, 437 and note, 478, 479, 601, 723, 742
    article by Macaulay, 798
    lecture by: Carlyle, 584; Coleridge, 53, 57, 58
    Life. See Boswell
    mentioned in: Mme D'Arblay's *Diary*, 612, 617; Smith, H. and J.,
        Rejected Addresses, 112
    WORK:
        Rasselas, 841
JOHNSON, William, 355
JOHNSTON, William
    and E. Quillinan's writings, 722
    ed. (*Earlier Poems of William Wordsworth*), 836
JOHNSTONE, Charles, *Sonnets*, 484
JONES, Harry, 817
JONES, Inigo, 404
JONES, John, *Attempts in Verse*, ed. Southey, R., 394
JONES, Robert, 524
JONES, Sir William, translation *Sakuntala, or the Fatal Ring*, 140 and note
JONES, Captain, 552 seq., 602
JONES, Miss, 139
JONSON, Ben, 34, note 473
    Alchemist, The, 225
    Discoveries, 43 and note

III—P

JORDAN, Mrs., 423, 775
JOSEPHUS, Flavius, in De Quincey's *Selections*, 776
JOUBERT, Joseph, article on, 810 and note
JOURNALISM, 780. *See also* Press
JUDAS ISCARIOT, in De Quincey's *Selections*, 776 and note
JUDITH of Borrowdale, 431
JULIUS, Nikolaus Heinrich, 15, 827 and note
JUNIUS
　　in Byron's *Vision of Judgment*, 286, 367, 370
　　letters, 73

KANT, Immanuel
　　philosophy, 28, 70, 88, 92, 107, 150, 309, 727, 831, 844, 845
　　Last Days of. See De Quincey, T.
KAUFMANN, Angelica, 29, 124
KEAN, Edmund, 180
KEAN, Mrs. Charles. *See* Tree, Ellen
KEATINGS, The Misses, 139
KEATS, John
　　principal entries, 389, 390, 520
　　in Hunt, J. H. Leigh, *Lord Byron and some of his Contemporaries*,
　　　354, 355
　　lecture by G. MacDonald, 784
　　in Trelawny, E. J., *Adventures of a Younger Son*, 631, 632
　　mentioned, 302 note, 727
　　WORKS:
　　　Eve of St. Agnes, 259
　　　Hyperion, 258
　　　Isabella, 263
　　　Pot of Basil, 259
KEBLE, John, 803
Keepsake, The, 460 note
KELLEY, Isabella, *Madeline*, 841
KELLY, Fanny Maria, 257, 355 and note, 396, 414
　　Dramatic Recollections and Imitations, 423, 424
KELTY, Mary Ann, *Osmond*, 395 and note seq.
KEMBLE, Charles, 726
KEMBLE, Frances Anne [Mrs. Butler]
　　in the *Hunchback*, 405 seq.
　　MS. Poems, 633
KEMBLE, John Philip, 27, 115, 423, 726
KENDAL, visited with D. Wordsworth, 188, 189
KENNEDY, James, *Conversations on Religion with Lord Byron*, 749 seq.
‖ KENNEY, James, 68, 112, 133, 144, 204, 312, 401, 650
　　WORK:
　　　Raising the Wind, 319 note
‖ KENNEY, Louisa [Mrs. Holcroft], 11, 56, 68, 117
　　and M. Lamb in Paris, 284, 285
‖ KENNEYS, The, 114, 116
KENT, William, 783
KENYON, Edward, 752, 763
KENYON, John
　　letter to Lady Blessington, 750
　　and the Brownings, 760

KENYON, John—*contd.*
death, 763
and W. S. Landor, 491, 494 seq., 511, 626, 766
and Crabb Robinson, 256, 438, 544, 546, 751, 764
and Southey, 357, 550, 644
—— tour 1838, 552 seq.
his will, 764 and note, 766
and Wordsworth, 357, 533, 546
and Wordsworth's memorial, 699, 700, 717, 748
and Wordsworth's sonnets, 433
other references, 241, 491, 492, 497, 503, 514, 556, 557, 570, 572,
  573, 585, 591, 596, 597, 599 note, 600, 603 note, 613, 615, 618,
  629, 630, 632, 634, 642, 650, 651, 658, 681, 687, 697, 700, 710, 719,
  725, 729, 752, 753, 755
WORKS:
Poems, 548, 559
Experimentum Crucis, 670 and note
Rhymed Plea for Tolerance, 670 and note
KER, Mrs. Bellenden, 534
KESWICK
Vicar of, Southey's letter concerning, 551
visited, 189 seq., 270, 339, 431, 432, 483
KETT, epigram by Landor, 382
KEY, Thomas Hewitt, 647
'KIND WIT OF KINGSTON' pseud., *Westward for Smelts*, 811 and note
KINDER, Mrs. and Miss, 78
KING, Lady Arabella, 787
KING, Peter, 7th Lord, 39
KING, Dr. William, 724, 727, 728, 729
KINGLAKE, Alexander William, 662, 714
Eöthen, 647, 774
KING'S BENCH PRISON, Combe and, 12
KING'S COLLEGE, and F. D. Maurice, 732
KINGSLEY, Charles
WORKS:
writings, review, 777
article on Clough's *Bothie of Tober-na-Vuolich*, 685
Alton Locke, 704 seq.
Hypatia, 773 seq., 808
Miscellanies, 793
Phaethon, 773, 785
Saint's Tragedy, The, 683 and note
Two Years Ago, 767, 784, 785
Westward Ho! 779
Yeast, 705, 715
KINGSTON, Elizabeth Chudleigh, Duchess of, 13
KIPPIS, Dr., 148
KIRKUP, Seymour Stocker, 384, 385
KITCHENER, Miss [later Mrs. Habbakuk Robinson], 6, 7
KLOPSTOCK, 42
KNEBEL, Major C. W. von, 224, 368, 369, 373
Correspondence with Goethe, 751, 759
KNIGHT, Charles
and H. Martineau, 684, 703, 708

KNIGHT, Charles—*contd.*
  WORKS:
    London, 642, 643
    (*Passages of a Working Life*), 812
KNIGHT, Ellis Cornelia, *Dinarbas*, 841
KNOWLES, James Sheridan, 319, 424, 425
    Hunchback, 405
    Virginius, 319
    William Tell, 319
KNOWLES, Mrs., and Dr. Johnson, 7
KNOX, John, lecture by Carlyle, 583 seq.
KNOX, Vicesimus, *Elegant Extracts in Verse*, 221
KOCK, Paul de
  WORKS:
    novels, 453, 574
    Bon Enfant, Un, 511
    Cocu, Le, 511
    Moustache, 577
KOHL, 633
KÖLLE, 531
Konversations Lexikon der Gegenwart, 679
KOSSUTH, Louis, 791
KOTZEBUE, A. F. F. von, writings, 14, 231, 374, 375

LA CROIX, 313 note
LADIES' COLLEGE. *See* Bedford College
LAFONTAINE, A. H. J., 823 seq., 829
LAING, David, 266, 267
'LAKE POETS,' in L. Aikin's *Letters*, 817
    in Byron's letter to Hogg, 167, 199
    in Medwin's *Shelley*, 668
LAMB, Charles
    accident, 40
    at the Aders's with Mary, 228, 237, 256, 288
    and Mary, and the Aikins, 144, 145, 265
    and alcohol, 59, 133, 146, 162, 242, 256, 293, 301, 347, 363, 393, 406, 439
    and T. Allsop, 315, 344
    character of Alsager, 674
    at Alsager's with Mary, 133, 145, 162, 178
    at Mrs. Barbauld's, 306
    —— with Mary, 265
    and Mary, and Becky [old servant], 365
    birth, 455
    and Sir C. Bunbury, 9
    and Mary, and G. Burnett, 24
    and M. Burney, 197, 216, 276, 363
    in Cambridge with Mary, 243
    and card playing, 323. *See also* parties
    and H. F. Cary, 405, 439
    visits Coleridge, 185, 307, 308
    at Coleridge's lecture, 53
    and Coleridge's 1818 lectures, 219
    and Mary, affected by Coleridge's company, 24

LAMB, Charles—*contd.*
    and Mary and Coleridge's breach with Wordsworth, 40, 76, 78
    at the (Colliers') with Mary, 20, 54, 104, 146, 288
    at Dalston, with Mary, 259
    death, 452, 453
    and De Quincey, 137
    and G. Dyer, 4 note
    and Mary, and Mrs. Dyer, 799
    and the East India House.   *See also* financial affairs
    —— the cannibal clerk, 144
    —— the 'compounds' and 'simples,' 35
    —— retirement, 318
    —— work, 160, 162
    and Mary, move to Edmonton, 434
    —— at Enfield, 347, 351.   *See also,* and the Westwoods
    —— financial affairs, 116, 318, 323, 452, 453
    —— 457 seq., 511
    —— visit France, 283 seq.
    funeral, 454, 455
    Gifford and, 63, 471
    and Godwin, 123 note, 283, 286
    at Godwin's with Mary, 33, 133, 139, 163, 165, 233, 299
    and Mary, and Mrs. Godwin, 56
    —— and W. Godwin, jnr., 317
    and Goethe, 373
    grave, visited with M. Lamb, 536, 853
    and Hazlitt, 9, 27, 59, 170, 200, 286, 298
    health, 17, 40, 154, 176, 207, 320, 321, 323, 332, 393, 401, 404,
      669
    and T. Holcroft, 11
    and J. H. Leigh Hunt, 59, 298
    and Mary, in Inner Temple Lane, 9
    and E. Irving, 310
    and Mary, move to Islington, 298
    and E. Isola, 360, 408, 455
    and Jeffrey, 536
    and the Kenney marriage, 68
    and Mary, and John Lamb's death, 276
    and Mary Lamb, 27, 157, 160, 162, 176, 256, 407, 452, 453, 455, 457,
      458, 468, 474
    and Mary, visited by W. S. Landor, 410
    letter given to Frau von Goethe, 370
    letters: to Patmore, 744; collection and selection, for publication,
      466, 469, 471, 476, 477, 488, 499, 500, 503, 510, 666, 668, 669,
      673 seq., 853; to Crabb Robinson, 456, 488
    library, 301, 357, 364, 675
    and the use of 'C. L.' by Capel Lofft, 705
    and the *London Magazine*, 301, 324
    and Lytton, 449
    and T. Monkhouse, 315
    at T. Monkhouse's, 222, 242, 256, 292
    —— with Mary, 214, 217, 256, 292, 300, 303
    and Moxon, 455, 579, 709
    and the *New Monthly Magazine*, 331
    and Mrs. Norris, 344

LAMB, Charles—*contd.*

parties: 9, 36, 49, 57, 63, 65, 153, 170, 178, 221, 259

and Perceval's assassination, 81

pictures, 145, 195, 229

portrait by: F. S. Cary, 776; R. Hancock, 500, 502; Meyer, 336

and the Procters, 347

puns and witticisms, 28, 104, 225, 387 and note, 856

―――― Chatterton's forgeries, 134; Chinese 'Sell teas,' 35; compounds and simples, 35; De Quincey's 'Payne and fuss,' 311; Hume's fine family, 197; punsters' ridicules, 36; Crabb Robinson's first brief, 176; Shakespeare and 'panting time,' 18; two puddings, 28

Quarterly Review attack, 63

and reviewers, 69

and Mary, and the Anthony Robinsons, 103, 133, 145, 146, 153, 155, 162

and Crabb Robinson: books lent, 223, 259, 321, 334; books retrieved from Coleridge, 184; friendship, 15, 55, 142, 314; German translations, 24, 26, 33, 34; gift to, 198; gifts from, 184, 198, 212, 217, 229, 316 and note, 356; introduction, 2 and note, 6, 9, 11; at Crabb Robinson's, 295, 356, 405, 407, 439, 441, 443, 444, 446

and Mary, move to Russell Street, 210

and Scargill's *Penelope*, 358

and J. Scott, 262

and S. Sharpe, 344

loses his Sheridan, 9, 10

Smith and Lamb's 'beauty,' 18

introduces Talfourd to Wordsworth, 120

at Talfourd's, 406, 407

―――― with Mary, 287, 316, 356

at the theatre, 9, 26, 27, 28, 157

meets S. Warren, 440, 441

and the Westwoods, 392, 425

and White's *Falstaff's Letters*, 33 note, 410

and Mary, meet N. P. Willis, 443, 444, 488, 489

and W. Wilson, 357

and Mary, D. Wordsworth visits, 16

―――― and Wordsworth, 10, 103, 125, 165 seq., 170, 240, 242, 295, 304, 356

and Wordsworth's *Ecclesiastical Sketches*, 282

and Wordsworth's *Memorials of 1820*, 278

OPINIONS AND CRITICISMS:

literary:

Blake, W., poems, 328

Burke, E., speeches, 20, 198

Byron, *Vision of Judgment*, 289

Cary, H. F., translations, 405

Coleridge, S. T., and his works, 17, 43, 50, 53, 59, 178, 197, 202, 289

Collier, J. P. (*Poet's Pilgrimage*), 289

Godwin, W., *Mandeville*, 212

Goethe, *Faust*, 45, 425

Gray, T., poetry, 144

LAMB, Charles—*contd.*
OPINIONS AND CRITICISMS—*contd.*
literary:
Hazlitt, W., 50
—— review of Coleridge's *Lay Sermon*, 197, 202
humour and satire, 33
Keats, J., 258
Le Sage, *Gil Blas*, 177
Prior writings, 145
Schlegel writings, 44
Shakespeare's characters, 53 seq.
Southey, and Wordsworth, 40
—— writings: early poems, 207; *Kehama and Thalaba*, 17, 173; *Vision of Judgment*, 289
Voltaire writings, 177
Warton, T., sonnet, 145 and note
Wordsworth, 40, 78, 466; and his works, 17, 18, 145, 466; *Excursion*, 154, 156; *Peter Bell*, 103, 230
miscellaneous:
art, 36, 144, 228, 237, 261, 528
Barton, B., 645
Cottles, The, 502, 503
Dawe, G. See *Recollections of a late Royal Academician*
Godwin, Mrs. Mary Jane, 441
Isola, E., 408
Le Grice, C. V., 834
Manning, T., 308
keeping a mistress, 146
Paris, 285
Plumptre, Anne, 15
Procter, B. W., conversation, 437 and note
punning, 35 and note, 197
religion, 125, 302, 546
Crabb Robinson, 298
Wakefield, G., 265
Westwoods, The, 408
PERSONAL QUALITIES: 30, 142, 145, 170, 185, 243, 306, 310, 487, 832
conversation, 28, 43, 56, 67, 155, 178, 225, 233, 289, 306, 410, 487, 775
BOOKS, ETC., RELATING TO:
FitzGerald, P., *Charles Lamb, his Friends, his Haunts, and his Books*, 819
Procter, B. W., *Charles Lamb, a Memoir*, 819, 821
Talfourd, T. N., *Final Memorials*, 9, 142, 679, 711
—— dedication to Wordsworth, 682
—— review in the *Athenæum*, 679; *Inquirer*, 679, 680
Letters with a Life, 533, 534, 546
article by: De Quincey, T., 789; Procter, B. W., 456; Crabb Robinson, 724 seq., 730
dedication, by Wordsworth, 691
epitaph, by Wordsworth, 468, 477

LAMB, Charles—*contd.*

  BOOKS, ETC., RELATING TO—*contd.*

    mentioned in:

      Aikin, L., *Letters*, 817

      Hazlitt, W., *Spirit of the Age*, 317 and note

      Lloyd, C., *Desultory Thoughts*, 297

      Lytton, *England and the English*, 435

      Willis, N. P., *Pencillings by the Way*, 444, 467, 489

    mentioned, 31, 32, 60, 62, 102, 113, 117, 164, 180, 183, 203, 239, 264, 291, 315 note, 319, 324, 330, 342, 371, 403, 421, 512, 513, 581, 582, 703, 715, 746, 780, 814

  WORKS:

    writings, American edn., 405; edn. in three volumes, 454, 456; *Essays of Elia*, 853; manner of composition, 425; MSS., 414; style, 69, 423, 424, 543, 669; review, 231

    separate works:

      Adventures of Ulysses, 711

      Album Verses, 393

      Bachelor's Complaint, 286

      (*Blakesmoor in H——shire*), 314

      Blank Verse with C. Lloyd, 125 seq.

      Chapter on Ears, 262

      Composed at Midnight, 125

      Confessions of a Drunkard, 128

      Guy Faux, 39 and note

      John Woodvil, review, 69, 638, 695

      Letter of Elia to Robert Southey Esq., 298, 300, 312

      —— review, 298

      Life of Liston, 316, 317

      (*Many Friends*), 317

      Mr. H—, 78, 125

      —— first performance, 9

      Mrs. Leicester's School (with Mary Lamb), 156, 283, 454, 712, 833, 845

        Changeling, The, 459

        Witch Aunt, The, 833

        Young Mahometan, The, 833

      Old Familiar Faces, 126, 127

      On Eating and Drinking, 320

      (*On the Custom of Hissing at the Theatres*), 50

      (*On the Genius and Character of Hogarth*), 42, 50, 394

      On the Inconveniences Resulting from being Hanged, 39

      Poor Relations, 294

      Popular Fallacies, 331, 332

      Prince Dorus, 33, 314

      Recollections of a late Royal Academician, 404 and note

      Rosamund Gray, 36

      Sonnet (*To Emma learning Latin*), 363

      —— (*Family Name*), 369, 373

      Specimens of English Dramatic Poets, 36, 63, 625 and note

      (*Tragedies of Shakespeare*), 68

      Triumph of the Whale, 67

LAMB, Charles—*contd.*
  WORKS—*contd.*
    separate works:
      verses, for an album, 350, 378; in *Cœlebs in Search of a Wife* 'If ever I marry a wife,' 471
      (*Wedding, The*), 320
      (*Wife's Trial, The*), 362
      (*Wordsworth's Excursion*), 153, 166, 471
      Written on Xmas Day, 126
(LAMB, Elizabeth), [mother of Charles and Mary]
    death, 666, 669, 781
    in Lamb's *Old Familiar Faces*, 126
LAMB, John, 35, 177, 200, 259, 276
LAMB, Mrs. John, 281
LAMB, Mary Ann. *See also* Lamb, Charles and Mary
    accident, 635
    at Alsager's, 164
    and Mrs. Martin Burney, 277
    and cards, 363, 455, 653, 655
    and the Colliers, 455
    death, 666
    at Edmonton, 454, 455, 463, 492, 506, 536, 567, 576
    move from Edmonton, 597
    and French novels, 463
    and German works, 294
    and Hazlitt's divorce, 281, 282
    health:
      recurrent illness, 24, 27, 32, 64, 128, 157, 160, 162, 176, 177, 207, 256, 276, 290, 298, 321, 323, 324, 404, 408, 410, 443, 449, 452 seq., 457, 464, 466, 482, 488, 514, 536, 567, 576, 600, 611, 623, 635, 853
      in old age, 626, 630, 653 and note, 654, 655, 658, 659
    and C. Lamb. *See* Lamb, C., and Mary
    learning Latin, 156
    and her mother. *See* Lamb, Elizabeth
    on the Moxons, 455
    at Moxons, 468
    move to Regent's Park, 597; removal, 647
    and Crabb Robinson, 18, 132, 142, 301, 314, 845
    —— translation of *Amatonda*, 24
    —— gifts from, 184, 647
    at Crabb Robinson's, 443, 444, 597
    at the theatre, 9, 163, 167, 179, 225, 305
    on the Wordsworths, 455
    Wordsworth visits, 615
    mentioned, 36, 58, 62, 67, 88, 105, 108, 110, 124, 197, 213, 262, 307, 318, 337, 347, 357, 362, 364, 386, 462, 502, 510, 598
  WORKS:
    writings, 123
    difficulties as a writer, 156
    article for the *British Ladies' Magazine*, 156
    Mrs. Leicester's School. *See* Lamb, Charles and Mary
LAMBS, The
    mentioned, 150, 171, 182, 196, 217, 293, 312

LAMBERT, John, 105 and note
LANCASTER, Joseph, educational system, 53, 59, 77, 109, 484
LANDON, Laetitia Elizabeth [Mrs. Maclean], 336
    writings, 336, 366
LANDOR, Arnold, 385, 424, 582
LANDOR, Edward, 524
LANDOR, Julia, 515, 523, 524
LANDOR, Robert Eyres
    Earl of Brecon, 594
    Ferryman, 594
    Fountain of Arethusa, 691, 692
LANDOR, Walter, 403, 596
LANDOR, Walter Savage
    main entry, 378 seq.
    at Bath, 581, 582, 593, 662, 713, 755, 756, 779
    and Lady Blessington, 411, 414, 415, 456, 465, 468, 488, 497, 506, 572
    and S. H. Burney, 581, 582
    visit to Coleridge, 413, 414
    domestic affairs, 380, 381, 385, 440, 465, 491, 515, 523, 524, 550, 582,
        756
    epigram on, 813
    at the Flaxmans, 410, 495
    and T. Forster, 642
    and Miss Hughes, 713
    and J. H. Leigh Hunt, 406, 465
    and E. Isola, 360, 410
    in Italy, 378 seq.
    return to Italy, 497
    visits the Lambs, 410
    and Lamb's MS., 414
    letters to Crabb Robinson, 393, 419, 452, 465, 507, 508, 544, 818;
        sent to Forster, 820
    libel action, 779
    literary judgments, 407, 498, 506, 550, 593
    in London, 406, 409 seq., 491 seq., 549, 551, 571
    and Louis Napoleon, 756
    and T. Manning, 581, 582
    and Morehead, 654
    and Napoleon Buonaparte, 20, 391
    personal qualities, 39, 41, 507, 510, 511, 582, 593, 713, 820
    and pictures, 406, 491, 492, 571, 756
    portrait by: Boxall, 764; Fisher, 764 and note
    and publishers, 39, 393, 400 seq., 406, 424, 443
    on Quill-inanities, 632
    on Crabb Robinson, 389, 444, 488, 489, 514, 515, 662, 749
    and Seymour, 452
    and Mrs. Shelley, 412
    and Southey, 20, 378, 379, 381, 506, 508, 581. See also *Satire on
        Satirists*
    and Talfourd's *Ion*, 494. See also *Satire on Satirists*
    and Trelawny, 409, 410, 631
    in Wales, 406, 481
    and N. P. Willis, 444, 488, 489, 491
    and Wordsworth, 379 seq., 492, 509, 543, 626, 642, 662. See also
        Satire on Satirists and *Ode to Wordsworth*

LANDOR, Walter Savage—*contd.*

BOOKS, ETC., RELATING TO:

De Quincey, T., article, 818

Quillinan, E., *Imaginary Conversation between W. S. Landor and the Editor of Blackwood's Magazine*, 383 and note, 630

mentioned in:

Blessington, M., *Life*, 749, 750

Dickens, C., *Bleak House*, 379, 717

Horne, R. H., *New Spirit of the Age*, 642

mentioned, 398, 438, 734, 815

WORKS:

writings, 659, 691, 692. *See also* and publishers

articles in the *Examiner*, 571, 713; edn. of 1847, 662; ode in the *Examiner*, 581; juvenile poems, 414; poems, 424, 559

Andrea of Hungary, 571 and note, 572

Citation and Examination of William Shakespeare, 448 seq.

—— review, 450

'Cities but rarely are the haunts of men,' 619 note

⟨*Count Julian*⟩, 39, 82, 138

⟨*Ferranti and Giulio*⟩, 39

Fra Rupert, 586

Gebir, 20, 380, 382 and note

—— lines on the shell, 507, 516

⟨*Giovanna of Naples*⟩, 571 and note, 572

Imaginary Conversations, 383 seq., 390 seq., 418, 420, 488, 491, 599, 626, 642

—— sale, 401

—— review in the *Edinburgh Magazine*, 390, 391; *London Magazine*, 305; *Quarterly Review*, 384

Last Fruit off an Old Tree, 771

Ode, to Wordsworth, 440

Pentameron and Pentalogia, 543

Pericles and Aspasia, 444, 488, 489

Popery, British and Foreign, 709

Satire on Satirists, 506 seq., 514 seq.

—— note in the *Quarterly Review*, 513, 514

Terry Hogan, 503

LANDOR, Mrs. Walter Savage. *See* Landor, W. S., domestic affairs

LANDSEER, Sir Edwin, 492, 571

LANGHORNE, John, *Country Justice*, 517

LANSDOWNE, Marquis of, 304, 665

LANSDOWNE, Marchioness of, 150

LAPPENBERG, Johann Martin, 497

LARDNER, Dionysius, 511

LARPENT, Mrs. John, 404

LAS CASAS, Bartolomé de, 601

LAUDERDALE, Earl of, 33

LAURENCE. *See* Lawrence

LAURIE, 294

LAW, William

Letters to Bishop Hoadly, 628 and note

⟨*Works of Jacob Boehmen*⟩, 327

‖ LAWRENCE, James Henry, poem, 646

LAWRENCE, Sir Thomas
as an artist, 240
and Rogers, 395
WORKS:
portrait of Lady Blessington, 412
—— of two boys, 34
'Rural Amusements,' 796 and note
LAWRENCE, Miss, 265, 572
LAWS OF THOUGHT, lecture by Emerson, 677
LAYARD, Sir Austen Henry, 571, 674, 770
Nineveh and its Remains, 688
LEACH, 730
LEADBEATER, Mrs. [Mary Shackleton], letters to Crabbe, 472
LE BRETON, Philip Hemery, 681
ed. Memoirs, Miscellanies, and Letters of L. Aikin, 813, 816, 817
LE BRETON, Mr. and Mrs., 462
LEE, James Prince, 628
LEE, Mr., in Mme D'Arblay's Diary, 617
LEE, Mrs., in De Quincey's Autobiography, 738
LEECH-GATHERER. See Wordsworth, Resolution and Independence
LE GRICE, Charles Valentine, 512, 513, 833, 834
WORKS:
(General Theorem for A—— College Declamations), 513
True and Faithful Account of the Appearance of the Ghost of Mr. de
Coetlagon, 513
LEIGH [retired solicitor], 601, 602
LEIPZIG, Battle of, 133 and note
LEISHMAN, Mrs., 363
LEONARDO DA VINCI, 252, 253
LEOPARDI, Giacomo, 740
LE SAGE, Alain-Réné, Gil Blas, 177, 306, 307
LESLIE, Charles Robert, 615
Autobiographical Recollections, 800 and note
LESSING, Gotthold Ephraim, 604
Laocoön, 123
LEVER, Charles, novels review, 770
LEVESQUE, Peter, 697
LEWES, George Henry
and Mary Ann Evans [George Eliot], 751, 787, 788
inquiries concerning Goethe, 751, 752
WORK:
Life of Goethe, 756
LEWES, Mrs., and Thornton Hunt, 751, 787
LEWIS, Sir George Cornewall, Essay on the Influence of Authority in
Matters of Opinion, 701 seq.
LEWIS, Matthew Gregory, 'Monk,' 37 seq., 111
Letters on the State of Jamaica, 742
LEWIS, Miss, 207
Liberal, The
ARTICLES BY:
Byron, 286, 289
Hazlitt, 289
LIBRARY, the Red Cross, 332

LIGHTFOOT, John (Biblical criticisms), annotated by Coleridge, 496
LIGHTFOOT, 480, 484
LIGHTFOOT, Mrs., 480, 484
LINCOLN, Bishop of [George Pretyman], 131
LINDSEYS, The, 573
LINGARD, John, *History of England*, 605
LINNÆUS, Carl von, 776
LINNELL, John, 324, 328, 353, 498, 820
LISTER, Colonel, 414
LISTON, John, *Life* by Lamb, C., 316, 317
LITERARY FASHIONS, 377, 800, 806
LITERARY FUND, 595, 596
    meeting, 48, 758
[*Literary*] *Gazette*, 336
LITERATURE
    for children, article on, 747
    —— parents' views, 69
    English article by Goethe, 438
LITERATURE, Royal Society of, 641, 642
LITTLE THOMAS, pseud. *See* Moore, T.
LIVERPOOL, Lord, 304, 436
LLANDAFF, Bishop of [Alfred Ollivant], 698
LLANOVER, Lady (*Autobiography and Correspondence of Mary Granville Mrs. Delany*), 802
LLOYD, Charles, 170, 232, 237
    WORKS:
    Blank Verse by Charles Lloyd and Charles Lamb, 125 seq.
    Desultory Thoughts, 297
    Edmund Oliver, 5
LLOYD, Charles [son], 296
LLOYD, Sophia [Mrs. Charles], 187
LLOYD, Gamaliel, 14
LLOYD, Mrs. Gamaliel, 14
LLOYD, William, 14, 642
LLOYD [of Florence], 379, 387
LOBO, 11
LOCKE, John, 329, 845
    lecture by Hazlitt, 60, 62
LOCKHART, John Gibson, 262 note, 267, 506, 570, 635
    WORKS:
    article on Coleridge, 447 and note seq.; on Copyright, 607
    History of Matthew Wald, 360
    Life of Robert Burns, 356
    Memories of the Life of Sir Walter Scott, 302 note, 524, 526, 528, 534, 536, 540, 548
LODGE, Edmund, 357
LOFFT, Capel, 6, 47, 845
LOFFT, Capel [son], 570, 705
    WORKS:
    Ernest, 569, 572, 573
    Self-Formation, 551
LOFFT, Mrs., 573
LOGAN, J., *Braes of Yarrow*, 131
LOIRE VALLEY, visited with Wordsworth, 517

LONDON, Bishop of. *See* Blomfield
London Encyclopaedia, 591, 592
London Journal. *See* Hunt, J. H. Leigh
London Magazine
　　editorship and style, 262 and note, 296 note, 317, 319, 324, 332
　　Hazlitt and, 260
　　Lamb and, 301, 324
　　attack on Southey, 317
　　Talfourd and, 260, 262
　mentioned, 291, 323
　CONTRIBUTIONS BY:
　　Austin, S., 332
　　De Quincey, 267
　　Hare, J. C., 305
　　Hazlitt, 260
　　Lamb, 262, 294, 298, 300, 312, 317, 320
　　Reynolds, J. H., 302
　　Scott, J., 256, 259, 262 note
　　Talfourd, T. N., 260, 262, 318, 319
London Review
　　article by Crabb Robinson, 9, 13, 15
LONDON UNIVERSITY. *See* University College, London
London and Westminster Review [1836 to 1840]. *See also Westminster
　　Review*
　　articles by Carlyle, 509, 550
　　mentioned, 541
LONG, George, 168, 669
LONGDILL, Pynson Wilmot, 222
LONGFELLOW, H. W., *Evangeline*, 677, 678
LONGMAN, Thomas Norton, 67
LONGMAN AND Co., publishers [partners: Green, B. E.; Hurst, T.;
　　Orme, C.; Rees, O.]
　　and Hazlitt, 176, 184
　　and Landor's (*Count Julian*), 39
　　literary dinners, 67, 184
　　and Crabb Robinson's *Amatonda*, 26
　　and H. M. Williams, 224
　　and Wordsworth, 344, 355, 358, 469
　　mentioned, 23, 54, 337, 508, 509
LONSDALE, Lord, 125, 129 note, 457
　　park damaged by a gale, 565, 566
LORD CHIEF JUSTICE. *See* Campbell, John
LORRAINE, Claude, 838
LOUGH, John Graham, 699
LOUIS XVIII, 142
LOUIS NAPOLEON. *See* Napoleon III
LOUIS PHILIPPE, 121
LOUVRE
　　visited, 148 seq., 284, 559
　　with M. Lamb, 284
　　Mrs. Siddons visits, 148
LOVELACE, Lord, 721, 737 note, 746
LOVELACE, Lady, 721, 737, 746
LOVELL, Mary, Mrs. Robert, 27, 189, 297
LOVER, Samuel, 460, 800

LOWNDES, 268, 403
LOWTHER CASTLE, Wordsworth's sonnet, 435 and note
LUFF, Mrs. [of Patterdale], 428, 560, 587, 627, 639
LUGANO, visited with Wordsworth, 251 and note
LUSHINGTON, Edmund Law, 650, 651
LUTHER, Martin, lecture by Carlyle, 570, 583, 584
LUTTRELL's sister [Anne Horton], 73
LUTTRELL, Henry, *Letters to Julia*, 804 and note, 805
‖ LUTWYDGES, The, 479, 483, 485
LYELL, Sir Charles, 493, 539
LYNDHURST, Lord, 450, 451, 462
    in Warren's *Ten Thousand a Year*, 596
LYTTELTON, Lord, 12
LYTTON, Edward George Earle Lytton Bulwer, Lord, 413, 499, 500, 502, 504, 511, 780
    WORKS:
        Alice, 548
        Caxtons, The, 706, 710
        Disowned, 496
        England and the English, 435
        Ernest Maltravers, 541, 548
        Eugene Aram, 401, 402, 496
        notes in Hazlitt's *Literary Remains*, 779
        Last Days of Pompeii, 456, 496, 797
        Last of the Barons, 632
        Pelham, 362
        Rienzi, 496
        Zanoni, 623, 624

MACAULAY, Thomas Babington, Lord, 341 seq., 349, 393, 590 seq., 772, 795, 801
    WORKS:
        History of England, 686 seq., 757, 854
        —— sale of, 704, 757
    ARTICLES AND REVIEWS:
        Atterbury, 798 and note
        Bacon, 533
        Bunyan, 798 and note
        Clive, 580
        Croker, J. W., edn. of Boswell, *Life of Johnson*, 392
        Dryden, J., *Poetical Works*, 355
        Frederick the Great, 615
        German Literature, 353
        Gladstone, *State in its Relation with the Church*, 569
        Goldsmith, 798 and note
        Johnson, 798
        London University, 341
        Machiavelli, 347
        Milton, 341
        Pitt, the Younger, 798 and note
        Ranke, *History of the Popes*, 585
        Temple, Sir W., 558
        Warren Hastings, 601

(MACAULAY, Zachary), 591
MacDONALD, George
  and Bedford College, 786, 787
  lectures, 783, 784, 798
  WORKS:
    Adela Cathcart, 812
    Annals of a Quiet Neighbourhood, 821 and note
    David Elginbrod, 807
    Within and Without, 783
MACHIAVELLI, Nicolo
  article by Macaulay, 347
  Discorsi, 384
  Life, 473
MACKARNESS, Mrs.
  Trap to Catch a Sunbeam, 689 and note
MACKENZIE, the Hon. Frances C., 388 seq., 391, 519, 520, 522, 801
MACKINTOSH, Sir James, 132, 135, 136, 219, 297, 436
  WORKS:
    Dissertation on the Progress of Ethical Philosophy, 589
    Discourse on the Study of the Law of Nature and Nations, 842
MACKINTOSH, Lady, 97, 153
[MACKNIGHT, T.] (*Right Hon. Benjamin Disraeli*), 742
MACLISE, Daniel, 571
MACREADY, W. C., 242, 287, 296, 497 note, 700
  acting in Byron's *Sardanapalus*, 441; *Werner*, 540, 667
  —— Talfourd's *Ion*, 494
  —— Taylor's *Philip van Artevelde*, 670
MADGE, Thomas, 88, 120, 130, 135, 147, 160, 196, 616, 699
MAGINN, William, 413
MAHOMET, lecture by Carlyle, 583, 584
MAHON, Lord, 675
MAITLAND, Samuel Roffey, *Dark Ages, The*, 648
MALDEN, Henry, 481
MALING, Sarah Jane, 6, 574 note
MALKIN, Benjamin H. (*A Father's memoirs of his Child*), 15
MALKIN [barrister], 86, 356
MALLET, Philip, ed. of Hobbe's Works, 54
MALLETT, John, 724
MALTBY, W., 658
MALTHUS, Thomas Robert, *Reply to*, by Hazlitt, 844
MALVERN, visited with the Wordsworths, 690 seq.
MANCHESTER FREE LIBRARY, 765
MANDEVILLE, Bernard, 179, 532
  Fable of the Bees, 25
MANNING, Anne
  Cherry and Violet, 761
  Household of Sir Thomas More, 761
  Maiden and Married Life of Mistress Mary Powell, 599, 760
  Old Chelsea Bun House, 748, 761
MANNING, James, 48, 54, 56, 599
MANNING, Thomas, 213, 215, 225, 302 and note, 308, 581, 582
  letters from Lamb, 466, 469
MANNING, Mrs. [mother of James], 599
MANNING, Miss [sister of James], 599

MANSFIELD, Lord, 13
MANZONI, Alessandro, 393
MARCET, Mrs. Jane, writings, 436
MARIOTTI pseud.   *See* Gallenga
MARLOWE, Christopher, *Faustus*, 369 and note, 371, 425
MARRYAT, Frederick
   Jacob Faithful, 466
   Peter Simple, 448, 466
MARS, Mlle, 775
MARSH, Mrs. Anne Caldwell, 600, 640
   Admiral's Daughter, The, 724
   Two Old Men's Tales, 600
MARSH, Arthur Cuthbert, 600
MARSH, Charles
   article in the *Cabinet*, 841
   Clubs of London, 352 and note
MARSHALL, William, 745
MARSHALLS, The, 570 seq., 595
MARTIN, John, 459
MARTIN [brother-in-law of Irving], 320
MARTIN, 571
MARTINS, The [of Liverpool], 427
MARTINEAU, Harriet
   principal entries, 416 seq., 619 seq.
   life at Ambleside, 417, 650 and note, 655, 683, 684, 854
   and the *Daily News*, 718
   financial affairs, 541, 620, 631, 655
   health, 619, 622, 650 and note, 655, 754, 757
   judgment, 546, 621, 718
   in Ireland, 718
   letter to E. B. Browning, 657
   a party, 569
   poem by R. M. Milnes, 619 seq.
   and S. Smith, 651
   and Mrs. Wordsworth, 677, 781 and note
  OPINIONS AND CRITICISM:
    Americans, 540 seq.
    Carlyle, 542, 621
    copyright, 548
    Emerson, 621, 677
    human nature, 638
    Mrs. Jameson, 549, 655
    politics, 548, 656
    Wordsworth, 657, 658, 781
  mentioned, 673, 680, 682, 712, 725
  WORKS:
   writings, 436
   writing for Knight's *Pictorial History*, 684, 703
   articles:
    Foreign Policy of England, 736
    Rydal Mount sale, 783
    Sanitary tales, 703, 704, 718
    Mrs. Wordsworth, obituary, 781 and note

MARTINEAU, Harriet—*contd.*
  WORKS:
    Autobiography, 754
    Deerbrook, 576
    Eastern Life, Past and Present, 675
    (*Factory Controversy*), 757
    For Each and For All, 654
    Forest and Game Law Tales, 654
    French Wine and Politics, 654
    History of England during the Thirty Years' Peace, 718
    Illustrations of Political Economy:
      Brook Farm, 416
      Demerara, 417
      Hill and Valley, 415
      Life in the Wilds, 416
      Manchester Strike, 417
      Vanderpost and Suvek, 438
    Letters on the Laws of Man's Social Nature and Development, 707 and note seq., 713
    Life in the Sickroom, 636, 637, 655
    Martyr Age of Abolitionists, 623
    Peasant and the Prince, 814
    Playfellow, The, 621, 622
        Crofton Boys, 621
        Feats on the Fjord, 621
        Settlers at Home, 621
    Retrospect of Western Travel, 547 and note
    View of Society in America, 539, 547 and note
(MARTINEAU, Henry), letter on his death by Emerson, 621
MARTINEAU, James, 729, 737, 775
  WORKS:
    articles:
      (*Personal Influences on Present Theology*), 762
      Rationale of Religious Enquiry, 542
      Religion, 735
    Collection of Hymns, 445
MARVELL, Andrew, 407
(MARY, Queen of Scots), 583
MASKELL, Miss, 151, 152
MASON, William
    in Southey's *Doctor,* 563
  WORKS:
    Correspondence with Gray, ed. Mitford, 746
    edn. of Gray's *Works,* 178
MASQUERIER, James, 230, 292, 312, 362, 395, 396, 408, 426, 466, 509, 572, 578, 579, 707, 745
MASQUERIER, Rachel, 466, 595
MASQUERIERS, The, 335, 355, 574
MASSA, visited with Wordsworth, 518
MASSINGER, Philip, *New Way to Pay Old Debts,* acted, 180
MASSON, David, 720, 727
  WORKS:
    articles:
      Dallas's Poetics and A. Smith's Poems, 726 and note seq.
      Milton, 720
      Three Devils, The, 720

MASSON, David—*contd.*
WORKS—*contd.*
British Novelists and their Styles, 786
Life of Milton, 780
MATURIN, Charles Robert
writings, 274, 374
Bertram, 183
MAULE, Sir William Henry, 497
MAURICE, John Frederick Denison, 692, 731 seq., 776, 815, 837
WORKS:
Eustace Conway, 568, 817, 818
Subscription no Bondage, 545, 732
Theological Essays, 727 seq.
MAWMAN [publisher], 231
MAYER, Enrico, 441, 571 and note, 572, 749
MAZZINI, Guiseppe, 814
MECKLENBURG, Prince Paul of, 224
MEDWIN, Thomas
(*Journal of the Conversations of Lord Byron*), 413, 737
Life of Shelley, 668
MEGGISSON, 51
MELBOURNE, Lord, 458, 570, 620
MERIVALE, John Herman, 211
MESMERISM, 623, 650 and note, 655
MEYER, Henry, portrait of Lamb, 336
MEYER, Dr., 520
MICHAEL Angelo Buonarotti, *Life*. *See* Duppa
paintings, 793
Sonnets. *See* Wordsworth, *Sonnets from the Italian of Michael Angelo*
MICKIEWICZ, Adam, 374
MIGNET, *History of the French Revolution*, 316
MILAN
visited with Wordsworth, 251 seq., 524 seq.
Wordsworth's poems, 252, 525
[MILBANKE, Ralph Gordon Noel] Lady Byron's grandson, 737 and note, 743, 746
MILL, James or John Stuart, 314
MILL, John Stuart
Crabb Robinson meets, 404
mentioned, 716, 720
WORK:
On Liberty, 782
MILLAIS, Sir John Everett, 769
MILLER, Hugh
writings, 747
First Impressions of England, 774
MILLER, John, letters from Crabb Robinson, 832 seq.
MILLER [three brothers, John, Joseph Kirkman, and Thomas Elton], 89, 114, 711 and note, 725
MILLER, Thomas, and his writings, 575
MILMAN, Henry Hart, 493, 496, 568, 584, 698, 788
article on Lofft's *Ernest*, 573
History of the Jews, 585

MILNE, 545 and note, 557
MILNES, Annabel, *born* Crewe, 723
MILNES, Richard Monckton
    and Blake's works, 717, 752
    breakfast parties, 591, 688
    on Carlyle's *Latter Day Pamphlets*, 697
    in Disraeli's *Tancred*, 664
    on A. Landor, 582
    and H. Martineau, 619
    personal qualities, 545, 551
    Crabb Robinson first meets, 545 and note
    and Wordsworth, 697, 700
  mentioned, 549, 550, 583, 584, 596, 612, 618
  WORKS:
    Christian Endurance, 619 and note
    'For honest men . . .,' 619 note
    Memorials of a Tour in Greece, 547, 548
    Memorials of Foreign Travel, 551
    Poems, 549, 559
MILTON, John
    article by: De Quincey, 776; Macaulay, 341
    lecture by: Coleridge, 57, 58, 60, 62; Hazlitt, 218
    Life. See Masson, D.
    receipt for *Paradise Lost*, 795
  WORKS:
    writings, 169, 329 seq., 486, 628, 776
    Comus, 506
    Paradise Lost, 330, 479, 484
    Paradise Regained, 479
    Samson Agonistes, 371, 373, 374, 479
MINCE, Miss, 207
MIRABEAU, Gabriel, Comte de, 29, 404
    article by Carlyle, 509
MITCHELL, 70, 145
MITFORD, George, 365, 445, 544, 629
MITFORD, John, 693, 729, 760
    ed. *Correspondence of Gray and Mason*, 746
MITFORD, Mary Russell, 315, 316, 365, 445 seq., 449, 494, 495, 544 seq.,
    585, 629
  WORKS:
    Our Village, 544 seq.
    Recollections of a Literary Life, 545 and note, 715
MOIR, George, *Magic and Witchcraft*, 728 and note
MONKHOUSE, John, 463, 537, 634 seq., 706, 753
MONKHOUSE, Mary, 254
MONKHOUSE, Thomas
    last illness, 314, 315
    literary dinner, 292
    —— article by Crabb Robinson, 292 note, 724 seq.
    marriage tour with the Wordsworths, 248 seq.
    parties, 214, 217, 222, 241, 242, 256, 278, 287, 291 seq., 300, 302 seq.
  other references, 215, 279, 281, 283, 295, 340, 524, 635

MONKHOUSE, Mrs. Thomas, *born* Horrocks, later Mrs. Dick, 248, 254, 287, 293, 303, 314
    sonnet by Wordsworth, 336 and note
MONKHOUSE family, 743
MONTAGU, Basil
    and Blake's *Job*, 331
    and Coleridge's breach with Wordsworth, 40, 70 seq.
    visits Coleridge, 307 seq., 320, 338
    death, 716
    and Godwin, 210, 211
    and Hazlitt, 424
    and E. Irving, 331, 402, 403
    and Jameson, 171, 442
    personal qualities, 170, 171, 178, 206
    and the Shelleys, 211
    and Wordsworth, 210, 211, 358, 505
    and Wordsworth's works, 464
  other references, 60, 176, 198, 200, 201, 233, 234, 258, 291, 296, 332, 435
MONTAGU, Mrs. Basil, 77, 80, 81, 171, 178, 201, 206, 211, 224, 286, 332, 338, 505, 518, 716
MONTAGU, Elizabeth, 478
MONTAGU, Lady Mary Wortley, *Letters*, 527
MONTAGUE, Miss, 670
MONTAIGNE, M. de, writings, 179, 463
MONTEAGLE, Lord, 401, 656, 763
MONTGOMERY, James, 83 seq., 642, 692, 693
    Life [Holland, J., and Everett, J.], 748
  WORKS:
    article on: Wordsworth's *Poems*, 84, 85, 692, 693, 748
    The Excursion, 158, 159, 849
    Lectures on Poetry, 589
    Prose by a Poet, 339
Monthly Magazine, 481, 565
Monthly Register, translations from Goethe by Crabb Robinson, 34
Monthly Repository, articles, [Goethe's Works] by Crabb Robinson, 408, 415, 416, 426, 638 note
MOODY, 801
MOORE, John, M.D., *Zeluco,* 465
MOORE, Thomas
    and Byron and Wordsworth, 504
    death, 716
    letters to Hunt, 414
    Crabb Robinson meets, 291 seq., 550, 630, 632, 633; letter from Crabb Robinson, 630, 631. See also *Letters and Journals of Byron*
  BOOKS, ETC., RELATING TO:
    article:
      in the *Prospective Review,* 722
      by Crabb Robinson, 724 seq., 730
      in *The Times,* 722
    Life. See Russell, Lord John
    mentioned in:
      Medwin, T., *Shelley,* 668
      Smith, H. and J., *Rejected Addresses,* 111

MOORE, Thomas—*contd.*
mentioned, 129 note, 222, 366, 424, 619 note
WORKS:
Epicurean, The, 347, 348
Epistles, Odes and other Poems, 45 seq., 49
Fudges in England, The, 466 and note, 790
Lalla Rookh, 223
(*Letters and Journals of Lord Byron*), 306, 359, 360, 370 seq., 392, 412, 415, 417, 736 seq.
Life of Sheridan, 324
Memoirs of Captain Rock, 316
Odes upon Cash, Corn, Catholics . . ., 790
Poetical Works of the late Thomas Little, 49
Political Squibs, 392, 624, 634, 716, 722, 790
Tom Cribb's Memorial to the Congress, 230
Twopenny Post Bag, The, 128, 131
MOORE, 521
MORE, Hannah, 503
Life. See Roberts
WORK:
Cœlebs in Search of a Wife and Lamb's verses, 471
MOREHEAD, 654
MORGAN, Sir Charles, 309 seq.
MORGAN, Lady, pseud., Sydney Owenson, 309 seq.
WORKS:
writings, 310 and note
Florence Macarthy, 225, 226
Italy, 282
O'Donnel, 500
MORGAN, John, 18, 128, 132, 184, 198
MORGAN, Mrs. John, 202
MORGANS, The, John and Coleridge, 41, 71, 105 seq., 119, 182
[MORGAN, J. M.], *Revolt of the Bees,* 420
MORGANN, Maurice, *Essay on the Dramatic Character of Sir John Falstaff,* 316
MORIER, J. J.
Hajji Baba, 306, 307, 316
Hajji Baba in England, 358
Morning Chronicle
and J. P. Collier, 590
and Fonblanque, 468
attack on Crabb Robinson, 217
mentioned, 451
CONTRIBUTIONS BY:
Clairmont, 229
Hazlitt, 133
Crabb Robinson, 53, 54
Morning Herald, 553
Morning Post, 34, 35, 112
MOTTRAM, J., letter from Crabb Robinson, 771 and note, 772 and note
MOXON, Edward
on the book trade, 603
and J. Cottle, 503, 505

Moxon, Edward—*contd.*
death, 779
indebtedness to friends, 579, 709
sells Lamb's books, 675
at Lamb's funeral, 453
and Lamb's letters, 469, 488, 510, 679
and Lamb's works, 454, 466
and M. Lamb, 454 seq., 492, 506, 510 seq., 666
and Landor's works, 403, 424, 642
marriage, 455
and H. Martineau's works, 655
party, 497, 618
personal qualities, 355, 403, 455
and the *Quarterly Review*, 534
and Talfourd, 510, 511
and Talfourd's works, 739
in France with Wordsworth, 516
and Wordsworth's works, 449, 495, 496, 603, 612 seq., 654, 657, 674
and Wordsworth's *Life*, 705, 706, 708, 709
the Wordsworths' visit, 533 seq., 653
visits the Wordsworths at Malvern, 690, 691; at Rydal, 656
    mentioned, 341, 365, 462, 464, 512, 514, 515, 572, 573, 586, 591,
    596, 605, 621, 636, 650, 659, 664, 693, 697, 700, 704, 710, 711, 719,
    724, 726, 729, 739, 740, 743
PUBLICATIONS:
Campbell, T., *Shakespeare*, 559
Layard, A. H., *Nineveh and its Remains*, 688
Crabb Robinson, *Exposure of misrepresentations contained in a Life of
    William Wilberforce*, 585
Southey and Wordsworth, *Selections*, 403
Tieck, *Tales*, 403
edn. of Wordsworth's *Works*, 489
Moxon, Emma. *See* Isola
Moxon [brother of Edward], 497
Moxons, The, 611
Mudie's Library, 783
Muir, 520
Müller, Maler, 826 seq.
Mulock, Dinah Maria, 802
    John Halifax Gentleman, 793
Mulock, Thomas Samuel, 246, 247, 253, 254
Murch, The Rev. —, 820 and note
Murchison, Sir Roderick, 539, 642
Murillo, Bartolome-Esteban, 'Elizabeth tending the wounded,' 149, 150
Murray, John
and Byron and his works, 129, 306, 390, 467, 552
and Coleridge and *Faust*, 448
and copyright, 607
finances, 337
and Godwin, 297, 298
and Landor's MS., 403, 406
and the *Quarterly Review*, 64
and Crabb Robinson's *Egmont*, 122
—— letter to Moore, 370, 371, 392

MURRAY, John—*contd.*
    and Wordsworth, 344
    and Wordsworth's *Life*, 705
  mentioned, 616, 687, 759
MURRAY, 157
MURRAYS, The, 595
MUSÄUS, Johann August, 823, 826
MUSIC
    Coleridge and, 122, 288, 293
    Crabb Robinson on, 115
    Wordsworth and, 293
    and Wordsworth's poetry, 718
MUSSET, Louis Alfred de, article by Palgrave, 773
MYLIUS, 221

NAPOLEON I [Buonaparte], 5, 13, 14, 19, 20, 114, 115, 133 and note,
    142, 147, 148, 150, 154, 161, 164, 169, 171, 177, 313, 367, 368,
    403, 756
    Byron, *Ode to*, 141
    Carlyle, lecture, 584
    Channing, *Essay on*, 541, 542
    Life. See Hazlitt, W., and Scott, Sir W.
    in Scott's *Vision of Don Roderick*, 40
NAPOLEON III [Louis], 720, 756, 790, 791, 804, 814, 815
NARNI, visited with Wordsworth, 522
NASH, Hester, 321, 331
NASH, Wedd, 236
NASH [friend of Southey], 217, 218
NASHES, The, 164, 239, 363
NATIONAL GALLERY
    visited with Landor, 491
    —— Wordsworth, 357, 359
NATIONAL PORTRAIT GALLERY, 776 note, 881 and note
National Review
    foundation, 753 and note, 754
    new series, 813
  CONTRIBUTIONS BY:
    Arnold, M., 810 and note
    Bagehot, W., 762, 765, 810, 813
    Freeman, E. A., 813
    Hutton, R. H., 764, 775
  ARTICLES ON:
    Browning, E. B., *Aurora Leigh*, 767
    Kingsley, C., writings, 777
    Lever, S., Novels, 770
    Patmore, C. K. D., writings, 775
    Rossetti, D. G., *Early Italian Poets*, 805
    Scott, Sir W., novels, 777
    Social Innovators, 783
    Tennyson, A., writings, 775
    Tupper, M. F., writings, 777 seq.
NAYLOR, Samuel, 364, 426, 439
    letters from Crabb Robinson, 837 seq.

NAYLOR, Samuel—*contd.*
  WORKS:
    Charles, 401
    Reynard the Fox, 364, 613, 647
    —— dedication, 647
NAYLOR [unspecified whether the father or uncle of S. Naylor], 262, 294
'NEEDY KNIFE GRINDER.' *See* Canning, G.
New Monthly Magazine
    and H. Smith, 317
  CONTRIBUTIONS BY:
    Blessington, M. (*Conversations with Lord Byron*), 411
    Campbell, T., 466
    Coleridge, S. T., 466
    Hazlitt, W., 301, 302, 331, 348, 355
    Lamb, C., 331, 332
    Poole, J., 576
    Talfourd, T. N., 259
New Times, The, article by Lamb, 317
New York Mirror, articles by Willis, 444 and note
NEWMAN, Francis William, 692, 737
    Appeal to the Middle Classes, 675
NEWMAN, John Henry, Cardinal
    in Martineau, J., *Personal Influences on Present Theology*, 762
  WORKS:
    Apologia pro Vitâ Suâ, 812
    Sermons, 631
NEWMAN, 691
NEWTON, Isaac, portrait by Haydon, 240
NEWTON, John, 72
    letter to Dyer, 575
NEWTON [of Witham], 13, 131
NICCOLINI, Giovani Battista, 380, 393, 523
NICHOLSON, 11
NICOLAI and Philisters, Carlyle's note, 829
|| NICOLAY, the Rev. C. G., 730
NIEBUHR, B. G., *History of Rome*, review by T. J. Hogg, 398
NÎMES, visited with Wordsworth, 517
NONCONFORMITY. *See* Dissent, Unitarians
NORMANDY, tour with Southey, 552 seq.
NORRIS, Randal, death, 344
    Lamb's letter on, 456
NORRIS, Mrs., 344
NORTH, Christopher, pseud. *See* Wilson, John
NORTH, Lord, 234
North British Review
  ARTICLES ON:
    Children's Books, 747
    Hawthorne's works, 747
    Ruskin, 747
    Wordsworth, 812

North British Review—contd.
  CONTRIBUTION BY:
    Masson, 720, 726
NORTHCOTE, James, 65, 105
  Conversations of, 397, 399, 457
NORTHMORE, Thomas, 65
  (*Washington on Liberty Restored*), review, 65
NORTON, Caroline Elizabeth Sarah
  and Lord Melborne, 458
  and Tennyson, 650, 651, 797
  WORK:
    Breton Mother, The, 618, 619 and note
NOTTAGE, George Swan, 695
NOVELS. *See* Fiction

OASTLER, 688
O'BRIEN, Henry, *Round Towers of Ireland*, 464
O'CONNELL, Daniel, 426, 589, 633
OEHLENSCHLÄGER, Adam, *Correggio*, 203 and note
OGLE, Mrs., 601
OLDENBURG, 531
OLIPHANT, Margaret O., *Salem Chapel*, 807 and note seq.
OLLIVANT, Alfred. *See* Llandaff, Bishop of
O'NEILL, Eliza, 157, 163, 789
OPIE, Amelia, *born* Alderson, 2, 8, 147, 227, 311, 312, 317, 335, 336, 544, 550, 840
  Illustrations of Lying, 317
  Memorials of. See Brightwell, C. L.
OPIE, John, 2, 8
ORME, Cosmo [partner in Longmans], 176, 184
ORSINI, Felice, 814, 818
OSBORNE, Francis, *Advice to His Son*, 340
OSOLIMSKI, Count, 633
OSSIAN, poems, 367, 368, 842
OSSIAN'S HALL, 269
OSTADE, 851
OTWAY, Thomas, *Venice Preserved*, 264
OUTRAM, Dr., 509
OUVRY, Frederic, 786, 792, 794, 804
OWEN, Robert, 269, 270, 783
  lecture by Emerson, 677
  WORK
    New View of Society, 196
OWEN, Professor, 716
OWEN'S COLLEGE, 765
OWENSON, Sydney, pseud. *See* Morgan, Lady
OXENSTERN, 725
OXFORD, Bishop of. *See* Wilberforce, Samuel
Oxford Essays, 772, 773
(OXFORD MOVEMENT), 562, 636, 639, 648, 655
OXFORD TRACTS, 576
OXFORD UNIVERSITY, 382 note, 398, 690, 805
  New College glass, 539
  Poetry professorship, 767

PAGET, 800
PAINE, Thomas, 842
PALGRAVE, Sir Francis, 306, 646
PALGRAVE, Francis Turner
    Alfred de Musset, 773
    Golden Treasury, 806
    (*Poems of Arthur Hugh Clough with a Memoir*), 806
PALGRAVE, Lady, 306, 646
PALGRAVE [son of Sir Francis], 646
PALMER, Charles, Major-General, 532
PALMER, Samuel, 498, 752
PALMER, 268 note
PALMERSTON, Lord, 431
Pamphleteer, The, 120, 127
PANIZZI, Sir Antony, 536, 700
PAPWORTH, Edgar, 739
PARACELSUS, Philippus, 418, 419
PARDOS'S *Sonnets*, 41
PARIGI, Landor's dog, 391
PARIS, John Ayrton, 543
PARIS
    C. Lamb on, 285
    Southey on, 553
    visited, 147 seq., 209
    —— with M. Lamb, 284, 285
    —— with Southey, 553, 555 seq.
    —— with Wordsworth, 248, 255, 515 seq.
PARKE, Sir James, 503
‖ PARKEN, 55, 85, 87, 88
PARKER, J. W., 837
PARKER, Theodore, 773
PARKES, Joseph, 590 and note
PARR, Samuel, 13, 159, 376, 382, 411
PARRY, 481, 483, 485
PARSONS, Mrs., 600
PASCAL, Blaise, *Lettres Provinciales*, 152
PASLEY, Charles William, *Essay on the Military Policy and Institutions
    of the British Empire*, 21
PASLEY, Sir Thomas, 428, 429, 562, 565
PASSAVANT, Dr., 486
PATMORE, Coventry Kersey Dighton, article on, 775
PATMORE, Peter George
    My Friends and Acquaintances, 342 and note, 744, 819
    Personal Recollections of W. Hazlitt, 651
PATTISON, M., *Essay on Oxford Studies*, 772
PATTISSON, Jacob, 169, 785, 786, 833
PATTISSON, Miranda, 111
PATTISSON, William, 13, 157, 158
PATTISSON, Mrs. William, 84, 111, 131, 157, 158, 169, 172, 174, 206,
    219, 234, 263, 833, 845
PATTISSON, William, jr., 169, 295, 296, 396, 450, 451, 596 note, 833
PATTISSONS, The, 36, 37, 172, 186, 784, 796
    letters from Crabb Robinson, 840 seq.
PAULUS, Heinrich E. G., 663
PAYNE, John Howard, 284, 285

PAYNE, John, 287, 298, 343
PAYNE, Sarah, *born* Burney, 276, 298, 343, 617
    marriage, Lamb's article on, 320
PAYNE and Foss, Lamb's pun, 311
PAYNTER, Thomas, 407, 512, 532, 777
PEACOCK, Thomas Love
    Headlong Hall, 226
    Nightmare Abbey, 229
PEARSON, 703
PEEL, Sir Robert, 360, 456, 596, 625, 655 note, 656, 696, 699
PEEL, son of Sir Robert, 623
PENN, Granville, 307
PENN, William, 795
PENROSE, Charles, 729
PEOPLE'S JOURNAL, article by Howitt, 657
PERCEVAL, Spencer, assassination, 81, 83, 436
PERCY, Thomas, 276
PERCY SOCIETY, publications, 595, 811
PERRY, Sir Erskine, 456
PERRY, James, 110, 116, 153, 154
PERTHES, Friedrich Christoph, 15, 31, 206
PETOS, The [Crabb Robinson's housekeepers], 730, 731
PETRACH, 407, 517
    and Laura, 253
PETVIN, John, *Letters Concerning Mind*, marginalia by Coleridge, 598
PHILIPPS, Richard Nathaniel, 692, 748
PHILLIPS, Sir Richard, 5
PHILLIPS, Samuel, 739
PHILLIPS, Professor, 531
PHILLIPS, friend of Lamb, 16, 170, 259
PHILLIPS, friend of Wilkinson, 676, 678
PHILLPOTT, Henry, Bishop of Exeter, 507, 513, 651
PHILOSOPHY, lecture by Hazlitt, 57
PHOTOGRAPHIC SOCIETY, lecture by G. E. Street, 781
PICKERING, William
    edn. of G. Herbert's *Works*, with notes by Coleridge, 636
    and a portrait of Wordsworth, 715
PICKERSGILL, Henry Hall, portrait of Wordsworth, 457 seq.
PICKERSGILL, Henry William, portraits of Wordsworth, 426, 715
(PICKERSGILL, Joshua), *Three Brothers, The*, 413
PICTET, H., 224
PINDAR, Peter, pseud. *See* Wolcot, John
PINKERTON, John, introduction to *Ancient Scottish Poems*, 265
PIRANESI, Giovanni Battista, 230
    Rome, 219
PITCHFORD, 135
    and a 'lukewarm Christian,' 35 and note
PITT, William [the Younger], 22
    article by Macaulay, 798
PLACE, Francis, 109, 198
PLANCHÉ, James Robinson, 493
PLAYFORD visited. *See* Clarkson, C.
PLUMER, William, 314, 669
PLUMPTRE, Anne, 14, 15
    Lamb on, 15

PLUMPTRE, family of Edward Hayes, 791
PLYMLEY, Peter, *Letters.* *See* Smith, Sydney
POE, Edgar Allan, *Poems* and *Tales*, 768 seq.
POETRY, article by Bagehot, 813
POLAND, Society of the Friends of, 404, 407
POLITIAN, Poems, 378
POLITICS, 14, 74, 161, 164, 171, 177, 183, 655
POLLOCK, Sir Jonathan Frederick, 87, 91, 286
POLLOCK, Lady, 286, 287
POLLOCK, Fred, 734
POOLE, John, 144
    Little Pedlington, 576, 577
POOLE, Thomas, 443, 501, 503, 599
POOR LAW, *Tales* by H. Martineau, 654
POOR LAW Amendment Bill, note by Wordsworth, 458, 459, 510
POPE, Alexander
    article by De Quincey, 789, 820
    lecture by Thackeray, 725, 799
    pamphlets by Byron, 415
    —— Cibber, 365
  WORKS:
    writings, 143, 172, 538, 608, 845
    Dunciad, The, 537, 780
    [*Moral Essay III*], 'And lo! two puddings . . .,' quoted by
      Lamb, 29
    Rape of the Lock, 364
POPLE, W., 31, 118
PORDEN, Eleanor Anne. *See* Franklin
PORDEN, William, 67, 138, 157
PORDEN, Mrs., 129
PORDENS, The, 125, 155, 180
PORSON, Richard, 376
    in Landor's *Imaginary Conversations*, 626
PORTER, Anna Maria, *Recluse of Norway*, 162
PORTER, Henry, *Two Angry Women of Abingdon*, 625
PORTER, Jane, 81 seq., 88, 136, 179, 336, 337, 692
  WORK:
    Thaddeus of Warsaw, 146, 162, 453, 454
PORTUGAL, visited by the Quillinans, 653, 659
POTTER, 441
POWELL, Mary, *Life.* *See* Manning, A.
POWELL, 414
PRAED, Winthrop Mackworth, 393
  WORKS:
    Poems, ed. Coleridge, D., 812
    Red Fisherman, The, 499
    Vers de Société, 715
PRANDI, Fortunato, 407 and note, 426, 452, 461, 569, 662
    translation of Matteo Ripa, 742 and note
PRATI, 310, 320
PREEDY, 690
PRE-RAPHAELITES, 755, 760, 769
PRESCOTT, William H., 700

PRESIDENTIAL GOVERNMENT, article on, 813
PRESS, The, 86, 127, 189, 435, 614, 626, 773, 777
    article by Hazlitt, 299
PRICE, Sir Robert, 538, 539
PRICE, Dr., 313
PRICE, 287, 406
PRIESTLEY, Joseph, 546, 727
PRIOR, Sir James, *Life of Oliver Goldsmith*, review, 540
PRIOR, Matthew, 219
    Down Hall, 145
PROBY, 21
PROCTER, Adelaide Anne, 804
    Poems, 804, 806
PROCTER, Bryan Waller, pseud. Barry Cornwall
    at Lamb's funeral, 453, 454
    Lamb's *mot*, 437
    and M. Lamb, 597
    literary opinions, 819
    personal qualities, 238, 242, 548, 755
  mentioned, 171, 257, 258, 591, 658, 710, 719
    WORKS:
    writings, 238; articles on Lamb, 546
    (*Charles Lamb, a Memoir*), 819, 821
    Mirandola, 261
    Poems:
        Fall of Saturn, 294
        Flood of Thessaly, 294
        Maid of Provence, 294
        Tartarus, 294
PROCTER, Mrs. B. W. [Anne Skepper], 171, 238, 591, 725, 821
PROCTERS, The, story of Lamb, 347
PROCTOR, George, 331
PROCTOR, Robert, 761, 790
PROCTOR, Mrs., 455, 795
Prospective Review
    ARTICLES:
        Arnold W. D., *Oakfield*, 740
        Bailey, P. J., *Festus*, 669
        Browning, E. B., *Poems*, 654
        Leopardi, 740
        Moore, T., 722
        Religious Fiction, 726
        Shakespeare, 726
        Tennyson, *In Memoriam*, 704
        Thackeray, 734
PRUSSIA politics, 605, 638, 791
Prussian Reform, article by Crabb Robinson, 299, 318 and note
PRYME, George, *Poems*, 559
Punch, 643
PURCELL, 122
PURITANS, The, in Carlyle's lecture, 583, 584
    in Southey's *Doctor*, 483
PUSEYISM. *See* Oxford Movement

Pye, Henry James, 110
Pyne, William Henry, *Wine and Walnuts*, 346 and note

Quarterly Review
    compared with the *Edinburgh*, 63, 210, 237, 833
    finances, 541
    and Keats, 389, 390, 520
    attack on Lamb, 63
    and Lamb's review of (the *Excursion*), 153, 471
    attack on Moxon, 534
    Crabb Robinson and, 17, 41
    and Wordsworth, 390, 535, 624, 833
  CONTRIBUTIONS BY:
    Barrow, 237
    Croker, J. W., 736
    Eastlake, Lady, 366, 367, 686
    Frere, J. H., 237
    Lamb, C., 153, 166, 471
    Lockhart, J. G., 447 and note seq., 607
    Crabb Robinson, 299, 318 and note
    Scott, Sir W., 30, 39
    Southey, R., 127, 139, 178, 192, 237, 431, 432
    Taylor, Sir H., 452, 606, 741
  ARTICLES:
    Barbauld, A. L., *Year 1811*, 64
    Beckford, W., *Italy*, 443
    Brontë, C., *Jane Eyre*, 686
    Cathedral Establishment, 513
    Coleridge, S. T., 447, 448
    —— *Remorse*, 146
    Copyright, 607
    Cottle, J., *Early Recollections chiefly relating to the late S. T. Coleridge*, 534
    D'Arblay, F., *Diary*, 623
    —— *Wanderer, The*, 146
    De Vere, A., *Poems*, 741
    Galt, J., *Tragedies*, 146
    Gothic Architecture, 607
    Hazlitt, W., *Characteristics of Shakespeare's Plays*, 223
    —— *Round Table*, 210
    Hunt, J. H. Leigh, *Byron*, 355
    —— *Foliage*, 223
    Landor, W. S., *Imaginary Conversations*, 384
    —— *Satire upon Satirists*, 513, 514
    Lofft, E., *Ernest*, 573
    Northmore (*Washington or Liberty Restored*), 65
    Quillinan, D., *Journal of a few Months Residence in Portugal*, 667
    Ruskin, J. (*Modern Painters*), 759
    Russell, Lord John, *Memoirs, Journals and Correspondence of T. Moore*, 736
    Scott, Sir W. (*Forester's Guide and Profitable Planter*), 353
    Shelley, P. B., *Prometheus and other Poems*, 279
    Southey, C. C., *Life and Correspondence of Robert Southey*, 706

Quarterly Review—contd.
  ARTICLES—*contd.*
    Southey, R., *Kehama*, 30, 39
    Tennyson, A., *Poems*, 624
    Weber, H. W., ed. *Dramatic Works of John Ford*, 63
    Wordsworth, W., *Excursion*, 153, 166, 471
    —— *Poetical Works*, 452, 741
    —— Sonnets, 606, 607
    —— *White Doe of Rylstone*, 181
QUAYLE, Thomas, 289
QUAYLE, William, 407, 680
QUEEN'S COLLEGE for Women, 730
QUEVEDO, y Villegas, 825, 830
QUILLINAN, Dorothy, *born* Wordsworth.   *See also* Quillinan, E.
  as a child, 188, 272
  health, 462, 463, 465, 470, 471, 487, 499, 505, 539, 562, 615, 652, 653
  last illness and death, 664 seq., 670 seq., 682, 685, 781, 835, 854, 855
  Herefordshire Tour, 536, 537, 539
  letter: on Lady Blessington, 509; to Crabb Robinson, 446, 513
  gifts from Crabb Robinson, 443 and note, 591, 592, 594 seq.
  and Wordsworth, 16, 474
  and Mrs. Aders's portrait of Wordsworth, 618
  to have a portrait of Wordsworth, 457
  mentioned, 533, 587, 603 and note, 606, 611, 613, 614, 625, 629, 637, 648, 655, 660, 668, 703, 712
  WORKS:
  Journal of a few Months' Residence in Portugal, review in the *Edinburgh*, 667; *Quarterly*, 667
QUILLINAN, Edward
  proposed work in a bank, 573
  and the Baudouins, 623, 699
  and Camoën's *Lusiad*, 643
  and Dr. Davy, 685
  death, 710, 712, 838
  and Dora's death, 665, 667
  and Miss Fenwick, 668, 712, 713
  lawsuit, 613, 614
  attack on Landor.   See *Imaginary Conversation between W. S. Landor and the Editor of Blackwood's Magazine*
  in London, 300, 302, 355 seq., 497, 568, 573
  —— with Dora, 580, 592, 596 seq., 615 seq., 652, 653, 659
  marriage to Dora, 559, 568, 570, 573, 580, 581, 592, 594, 711, 715
  visits Portugal with Dora, 653, 659
  religion, 504, 505
  and John Wordsworth, 568
  and Wordsworth.   *See* marriage
  breach with Wordsworth, 671, 672, 674, 681
  informs Wordsworth of Landor's *Satire*, 516
  and Wordsworth's *Life*, 708, 709, 713, 856
  and Wordsworth's monument, 698, 699, 700, 707
  and Miss Fenwick's notes to Wordsworth's poems, 668, 713
  and the Wordsworths, 712

QUILLINAN, Edward—*contd.*
mentioned, 579, 603 and note, 627, 636, 637, 660, 661, 677, 679, 680, 682, 686, 693, 694, 696, 697
WORKS:
writings for private publication, 722
Conspirators, The, 588, 589
Dunluce Castle, review, 272 note, 635
Imaginary Conversation between W. S. Landor and the Editor of Blackwood's Magazine, 383 and note, 630 seq.
Retort Courteous, 272 and note, 273, 635
QUILLINAN, Mrs. Edward, *born* Egerton Brydges, 1st wife, 272
QUILLINAN, Jemima, 504, 671, 710, 712
portrait [Wordsworth, *Lines Suggested by a Portrait from the Pencil of F. Stone*], 512
QUILLINAN, Rotha, 504, 710, 712
QUILLINAN, brother of Edward, 497, 504, 712
QUILL-INANITIES, 632
QUIN, James, portrait by Gainsborough, 144

RADCLIFFE, Ann Ward
writings, 122, 124, 130, 163, 173, 538
Mysteries of Udolpho, 366, 843
Sicilian Romance, 202
RAHEL. *See* Varnhagen von Ense
RAILWAYS, Wordsworth on, 435 and note, 539, 648
RANBY, John, 795
RANKE, Leopold von, 768
History of the Popes, translation by Austin, S., 638, 639
—— article by Macaulay, 585
RAPER, Colonel, 691
RAPHAEL, Sanzio, 793
'Planets,' 261
RAVEN, The, pseud., articles in *Household Words,* 696, 704
RAVENGLASS, Wordsworth's property, 192, 851
RAWLINSON, Mr. and Mrs., 472
RAYMOND, George, 766
READ, Godwin's landlord, 298
READ, Miss, 201
READE, Charles
[*Course of True Love never did run Smooth*], 774
Peg Woffington, 734, 735
Two Loves and a Life, acted, 738
READE, John Edmund, *Record of the Pyramids, A,* 615
REAL DEL MONTE mines, article by S. Austin, 332
RÉCAMIER, Mme de, 411
REDDING, Cyrus, *Fifty Years' Recollections,* 776
REECES, The, 293
REES, Owen, 67
Reflector, The
verses by L. Aikin, 49
articles by Lamb, 39 and note, 50, 68
REGENT, The Prince. *See* George IV
Register, The, 127
III—R

REID, Elizabeth Jesser, *born* Sturch, 4 note, 569, 600, 615, 620, 622, 626, 634, 637, 680, 724, 725, 730, 740, 786
REID, John, M.D., 4 and note, 62, 221
    review of Lloyd's *Edmund Oliver*, 5
REID, Mary, 332 and note
RELIGION, article by J. Martineau, 735
Religious Fiction, article on, 726
RELPH, Cuthbert, 357, 408, 410
Retrospective Review, 296 note, 302, 316
REVOLUTIONS, lecture by Carlyle, 569 seq.
REYNOLDS, Frederick, 460
REYNOLDS, John Hamilton, and his writings, 302 and note, 424, 425
REYNOLDS, Sir Joshua, 478, 539, 731
RICARDO, David, 509 note
RICARDO, Moses, 509 and note, 728, 745
    epigram on H. Smith, 577, 578
RICHARDSON, Mary, Lady, *born* Fletcher, 684, 854
    article on Wordsworth, 723 and note
RICHARDSON, Samuel, 42, 374, 375
    WORKS:
        Clarissa, 7
        Sir Charles Grandison, 284
RICHMOND, James C., 377 and note, 378, 443, 603 and note, 609, 610, 612, 694, 695
    Memorial to the Bench of Bishops, 607
RICHTER, Jean Paul
    WRITINGS:
        article by Carlyle, 580, 823 seq.
        studied by Coleridge, 26, 106, 150, 689
        Crabb Robinson's translations, 24, 26
RICKARDS, Miss, 564
RICKMAN, John, 16, 18, 21, 22, 134, 363, 364, 510
RIDGWAY, James Leech, 231
RIGBY, Elizabeth. *See* Eastlake, Lady
RIGBYS, The, 366
RIO, A. F., *La Petite Chouannerie*, 618, 619 and note
RIOU, 595
RIPA, Matteo, *Memoirs during Thirteen Years at the Court of Peking*, 742 and note
RITSON, Joseph, *Robin Hood*, 283
ROBBERDS, John Warden, *Memoir of the Life and Writings of William Taylor of Norwich*, 638 and note
ROBERTS, William, *Memoirs of the Life and Correspondence of Mrs. Hannah More*, 477 seq.
ROBERTSON, Frederick William, 721, 724, 727 seq.
    obituary articles in the *Inquirer*, 729; by Crabb Robinson, 728, 729, 733, 760, 817
    Life, 729, 736, 747. *See also* Brooke, Stopford A.
    Sermons, 746, 753, 760
    verses by Lady Byron, 747
ROBERTSON, 541
ROBESPIERRE, 404, 571
ROBINSON, Anthony, 4 note, 6, 31, 72, 92, 103, 105, 109, 112, 133, 138, 157, 162, 204, 205, 317, 344
    letter to Wordsworth, 74

ROBINSON, Anthony [son], 163
ROBINSON, Mrs. Anthony, 455
ROBINSONS, The Anthony, 133, 145, 146, 153, 155, 168
ROBINSON, Habbakuk, 414, 767 note
ROBINSON, Henry Crabb
  and alcohol, 56, 113
  book of anecdotes, 512 and note
  and works of art, 201, 212, 228, 230, 261, 571, 572, 705, 838
  bust, 459
  dedication: Naylor, S., 647; Wordsworth, 1, 592, 603, 608 and
    note, 611 seq.
  diary and reminiscences, 79, 189, 317, 470, 480, 627, 748, 751, 777,
    778, 784, 785, 800 note, 812; the diary begun, 17 note; quoted in
    Blake's *Life*, 809, 810; lent to Sara Coleridge, 687 seq.; account
    of Holstein journey, 684; mentioned, 637 note, 640 note
  financial affairs, 450, 451, 489
  and German literature. *See* German Literature
  gifts, subscriptions and applications for money: Blake, 331;
    Bloomfield, R., 202; Coleridge, Sara, 665; Dixon, James, 639,
    640; Ely, T., education, 738; Godwin, 33, 162, 175, 283, 285;
    Goethe, Ottilie von, 370; Gurney, 212; Hazlitt, 110; Holcroft's
    widow, 11; Hone, 590; Lamb, C., 198, 212, 217, 229, 316 and note,
    356; Lamb, M., 184, 647; Landor, 403; Martineau, H., 631;
    National Review, 753 note; Quillinan, Dora, 443 and note, 591
    seq.; Robinson, Mrs. T., 221; Southey, 443 and note, 510;
    Southey memorial, 644; Wordsworth, Dorothy, 257; Wordsworth,
    M., 488 and note, 610, 613, 688; Wordsworth, W., 572, 591, 592,
    639; Wordsworth, W. [son], 640, 651, 659, 660; Wordsworth
    memorial, 698, 700
  letters to Carlyle (*see* Carlyle, *German Romance*); Mrs. Clarkson,
    681, 687 seq.; from Germany, 546 and note; to Lewes, 752; to
    Moody, 801; to Moore, 359, 370 seq., 392, 630, 631, 736; to
    Mottram, 771 and note, 772 and note; to the Wordsworths,
    685, 686
  library, 750
  portrait by Schmeller, 373
  winnings at whist, 197
  purchases a bust of Wordsworth, 280
  classification of Wordsworth's sonnets, 496
  recommendations of Wordsworth's works, 771 and note, 772 and
    note, 801
  PERSONAL QUALITIES: 14, 29, 103, 115, 171, 197, 270, 276, 389, 674, 715,
    781
  contribution to F. Sharpe's album, 775
  conversation, 39, 466, 540
  friendships, 8, 10, 15, 116, 536, 556, 832, 844, 845
  health: accident, 637 and note seq.; carbuncle, 694; deafness, 812
    death, 822; old age, 662, 758, 777, 808
  legal career, 3 note, 26, 33, 104, 114, 116, 121, 217, 234; Lamb on
    the first brief, 176; retirement, 355, 381, 444, 489
  and letters, 111
  reading, 1 seq., 6, 225, 234, 300, 302, 316, 548, 654, 815, 816, 837
  religion, 3, 479, 482, 490, 741
  hope of reputation, 276
  as a speaker and writer, 13, 114, 746

ROBINSON, Henry Crabb—*contd.*

  PERSONAL QUALITIES—*contd.*
    appreciation by the Wordsworths, 288, 466, 471, 485, 534, 604, 628, 629
    enthusiasm for Wordsworth's works, 14, 65 and note, 84, 111, 133, 134, 230, 247, 268 and note, 295, 330, 368, 370, 374, 447, 466, 539, 540, 834, 845, 848
  MENTION IN BOOKS:
    Austin, S., *Characteristics of Goethe*, 430
    —— review, 426
    Blessington, Marguerite, *Life*, 749
    Clough, A. H., *Letters and Remains*, 821, 822
    Coleridge, S. T., *Notes and Lectures on Shakespeare*, 688, 689
    FitzGerald, P., *Charles Lamb*, 819
    Gilchrist, *Blake*, 810
    Goethe, *Correspondence with Knebel*, 751, 759
    —— *Correspondence with Zelter*, 374
    Lamb, C., *Letter of Elia to R.S.*, 298, 312
    Landor, W. S., note to *Pericles and Aspasia*, 444, 488, 489
    Montgomery, T., *Life*, 748
    Patmore, P. G., *My Friends and Acquaintances*, 342 and note, 744, 819
    Procter, B. W., *Charles Lamb, a Memoir*, 821
    Russell, Lord John, *Life of Moore*, 723
    Schlosser, *History of the Eighteenth Century*, 532
    Southey, R., *Life*, 699
    —— *Selections from the Letters of*, 761
    Talfourd, Sir T. N., *Final Memorials*, 9
    Taylor, Sir H., *Notes on Life*, 401, 687
    Willis, N. P., *Pencillings by the Way*, 444, 445, 467, 488
    Wordsworth, C., *Memoirs of W. Wordsworth*, 709
  WORKS:
    translation, *Amatonda*, 24 seq.
    Brief Reply [to arguments against the Dissenters' Chapels Bill], 644
    Exposure of Misrepresentations contained in a Life of William Wilberforce, 585
    translations from Goethe on Byron. *See* letter to Moore
    —— *Egmont*, 122, 546
    —— Poems, *Cupid as Landscape Painter*, 34; *Wanderer*, 34
    Introduction to Wordsworth's *Elegiac Stanzas*, 249, 250, 272, 278, 512 and note
    Richter, J. P., *Works*, notes on, 24, 26
    Supplement to Clarkson, T., *Strictures on a Life of William Wilberforce*, 553, 554, 558 seq., 568, 591
  ARTICLES AND REVIEWS:
    Blake, W.,[1] 15, 31
    Byron, *Manfred*, 207
    Coleridge, S. T., *Lay Sermons*, 202, 207
    —— *Lectures*, 51, 53, 54
    Etymology of the Word 'Mass,' 462 and note
    Froude, J. A. (*Nemesis of Faith*), 690 and note
    Godwin, W., tenets (*Philo-Godwin*), 3, 842
    Goethe, *Le Neveu de Rameau*, 15, 33

        [1] K. A. Esdaile. Cf. *The Library*, 3rd series, vol. v.

ROBINSON, Henry Crabb—*contd.*

ARTICLES AND REVIEWS—*contd.*
  Goethe, *Works*, 415, 416, 426, 430; note in defence of W. Taylor,
    408, 638 and note
  Lamb and Moore, 724 seq., 730
  Prussian Reforms, 299, 318 and note, 319
  Robertson, F. W., *Obituary*, 728, 729, 733, 760, 817
  contributions to *The Times*, 10
  Wordsworth, W., 696, 699, 700, 811
  —— *Convention of Cintra*, 9, 13, 15, 74
  —— *Prelude*, 702
ROBINSON, Henry Hutchison [great-nephew], letter with Wordsworth's
    autograph, 684
ROBINSON, Jemima [mother], 662
ROBINSON, Marmaduke, 515
ROBINSON, Mary [Mrs. Thomas Robinson], gift from Crabb Robinson,
    221
ROBINSON, Robert, 4, 5
  Life, by Dyer, G., 4
ROBINSON, Samuel [uncle], 7, 31
(ROBINSON, Sarah), [wife of Thomas Robinson, jr.], 779, 821
ROBINSON, Thomas [brother], 15, 168, 202, 474, 494, 539, 540, 618, 624,
    649, 660, 795, 856
  portrait by Hazlitt, 23, 30, 104 and note
ROBINSON, Thomas, jr. [nephew], 405, 593 and note, 594, 596
ROBINSON [Rydal friend], 428, 588, 605, 672
ROBINSONS, The, 629
Robinson Crusoe, 630
ROBLEY, 152
ROCHE, Sophie de la, 617
ROCHEFOUCAULD'S *Maxims*, article by Hazlitt, 153
ROCHEJAQUELEIN, Mme la Marquise de la, *Memoirs*, review, 192
ROCHESTER, Lord, 247
ROEBUCK, John Arthur, 532
ROGERS, Henry, 295, 405
ROGERS, Samuel
    accident, 700, 701, 703, 704
    at the Aders's, 292, 293
    article, *Daily News*, 757
    autograph, 370
    and Bloomfield, 28
    breakfasts on Tuesdays, 693
    in Brighton, 395, 436, 704
    at Broadstairs, 504
    and Byron, 133
    and Byron and Wordsworth, 428 note, 429, 436, 467, 504
    Byron's satire.   *See* Byron, *Question and Answer*
    and Chantrey, 395
    and Clough, 695, 696
    at Coleridge's lecture, 60
    death, 757
    at Miss Fenwick's, 644
    and Gibson, 395
    house described, 458
    and Landor, 550

ROGERS, Samuel—*contd.*
  and Sir T. Lawrence, 395
  library treasures, 586, 619, 723
  Memoir by S. Sharpe, 792
  and T. Miller, 575
  at Monkhouse's, 292
  and Moore and Byron's *Life*, 306
  and Moxon, 579, 709
  and Moxon and Talfourd, 510, 511
  in Paris, 284, 556
  and the Quillinans, 559
  robbed by a servant, 462
  robbery at the bank, 647 and note
  and Crabb Robinson, 511, 533, 556, 728
  Crabb Robinson first meets, 102
  and Wellington, 662
  letter from Blanco White, 717
  and Wordsworth, 293, 296, 458, 462, 488, 490, 547, 626, 709. *See also* and Byron and Wordsworth
  and Wordsworth's memorial, 698, 724
  OPINIONS AND CRITICISM:
    Aders, E., 422
    Aikin, L., 512
    Barbauld, A. L., 651
    Beaumont, Lady, 435
    Blessington, Lady, and Count D'Orsay, 469
    Canova and Flaxman, 208
    Goethe, 467, 619, 658
    Lamb's *Letters*, 711
    literary women, 436
    Crabb Robinson, 466
    Scott's finances, 295
    Shakespeare's sonnets, 552
    Southey, 512, 565
    Southey's monument, 659
    Tennyson, *In Memoriam*, 704
    Wordsworth, 467, 512, 533, 586, 611, 711, 715, 728
    Wordsworth's works, 94, 335, 435, 436, 437 and note, 612, 614
  PERSONAL QUALITIES:
    character and conversation, 28, 102, 227, 424, 440, 467, 468, 488, 504, 511, 534, 556, 557, 598, 728, 729
    literary taste, 557, 630, 633, 636
    faculties in old age, 557, 579, 693, 698, 736, 739, 743, 744, 749, 838
    as a poet, 85, 133, 149, 222, 757
  mentioned, 129 and note, 130, 247, 303, 357, 372, 457, 469, 595, 602, 615, 616, 650, 653, 654, 661, 674, 681, 707, 729
  WORKS:
    Italy, 512, 586
    Jacqueline, 147
    Pleasures of Memory, 458
    Recollections, ed. Sharpe, W., 785
    Table Talk, ed. Dyce, A., 758, 760
    —— review, 758

ROGERS, Miss, 284, 436, 493, 534, 546, 547, 595, 615, 619, 644, 681, 704, 739, 749
ROLFE, Robert Monsey [later Lord Cranworth], 324, 404, 460, 461, 547, 643, 657, 677, 689, 698
ROLFE, Lady, 655, 668, 677, 698, 699
ROLT, Sir John, 678
ROME, visited with Wordsworth, 519 seq.
ROME, Church of, 18, 19, 42, 183, 208, 230, 357, 475, 476, 545, 558, 563, 585, 605, 608, 609, 778, 806
ROMILLY, Samuel, 143, 225, 404
ROMNEY, George, sonnet by Cowper, 485
ROOPER, 509, 669
ROSCOE, William, 177 and note, 696
ROSCOE [son of William], 83, 84, 118, 427
ROSCOE, William Caldwell, 688
    Poems and Essays, ed. Hutton, R. H., 796
ROSE, William Stewart, 436
    Letters from the North of Italy, 230, 422 and note
ROSSETTI, Dante Gabriel, 405
    Early Italian Poets, review, 805
ROUGH, Harriet, Lady, *born* Wilkes, 23, 161, 165
ROUGH, Sir William, 16 and note, 20, 23, 37 seq., 41, 55, 60, 61, 63, 74, 79, 82, 84, 93, 102, 113, 131, 135, 161, 165, 168, 178

    WORKS:
        Conspiracy of Gowrie, 36 seq., 41
        (*Letters from the Year 1774 to the Year 1796 by John Wilkes, Esq.*), 23
        Lorenzino, 37
ROUGHSEDGES, The, 604, 606, 608, 609
ROUSSEAU, Jean Jacques, 296, 584
    Émile, 7
    La Nouvelle Héloïse, 2
ROYAL SOCIETY, The, 143
ROYAL SOCIETY OF LITERATURE. *See* Literature
ROYSTON book club, 14
RUSH, James Blomfield, 689
RUSKIN, John, 706, 707, 709, 733, 739, 765, 769, 770, 775, 781 seq., 838
    article on, 747

    WORKS:
    article on the *Crystal Palace*, 747
    Lectures, 755
    Modern Painters, 760
    —— review in the *Edinburgh*, 760; *Quarterly*, 759
    Notes on the Construction of Sheepfolds, 710
    Two Paths, 792, 793
RUSKIN, Mrs., nullity suit, 739
RUSKIN, John James, 733
RUSSELL, Lord John, 431, 570, 655 note, 656, 659, 743, 754
    Memoirs, Journals, and Correspondence of T. Moore, 721 seq., 735, 759
    —— review, 736
RUSSELL, John, *Tour in Germany*, 318 and note
RUSSELL, Thomas, *Poems*, 293 and note
RUSSELL Institution, Hazlitt's lectures, 58
RUTT, Anne, 356
RUTT, John Towil, 63, 119, 120

RUTT, Mrs. J. T., 53, 855
RUTT, Rachel. *See* Talfourd, Lady
RUTTS, The, 355
RYDAL MOUNT, 187, 806
 article on, 783
 sale, 785
 servants:
  Anne, 730
  'cook,' 657
  James. *See* Dixon
  Jane, 635
  Mary, 604
 the Wordsworths to leave, 781
RYLE, 453, 492, 666

SADLER's balloon ascent, poem by L. Aikin, 49 and note
St. Davids, Bishop of. *See* Thirlwall, C.
ST. GOAR, scenery, 223, 224
ST. GOTTHARD, 250, 270
ST. JOHN's GOSPEL, Landor elucidates, 383
|| ST. MARSAULT, Countess de, 411, 414, 420
ST. MARTIN's HALL, readings by Dickens, 770, 771, 777
ST. PAUL's, Dean of. *See* Milman,
SAINT-SIMON, Claude, Comte de, 783
SALZBURG, visited with Wordsworth, 528, 529
SAM SLICK, pseud. *See* Haliburton, T. C.
SAND GEORGE, pseud. [Baroness Dudevant], 545, 574, 673
SANDEMAN, Robert, 847
SASS, Henry, 426
Satanic School, 297
Saturday Review, 789, 800 and note
 ARTICLES ON:
  Collier, J. P., 796
  Dickens, C., *Great Expectations*, 802
  Emerson, R. W., 799
  Irving, E., 805
SAUNDERS [of Saunders and Ottley], 508
SAVAGE, Marmion, *Falcon Family, The*, 658 and note
SAVONA, visited with Wordsworth, 518
SAWBRIDGE, John, 73
SAYERS, Frank, 146
 Disquisitions Metaphysical and Literary, 146
SCAFE, John, *King Coal's Levée*, 369 and note, 373
SCARGILL, William Pitt, 130
 WORKS:
  Penelope, 358
  Rank and Talent, 363
SCARLETT, James, 1st Baron Abinger, 258, 259, 380, 451, 535, 596
SCHARF, Sir George, 664, 739, 776 and note
SCHELLING, Friedrich von, 70, 88, 107, 108, 307, 521, 581, 659
 Crabb Robinson and, 375, 776
 WORK:
  Freiheit, 108

SCHILLER, J. C. Friedrich von, 21, 77, 145, 245, 308, 315, 316, 566, 651, 687, 776
  article by Carlyle, 580
  Life. See Carlyle, T.
  WORKS:
  translation of *Macbeth*, 369 and note
  Wallenstein, 107
SCHLABENDORF, Count, 209
SCHLEGEL, August Wilhelm von
  Crabb Robinson meets, 149, 298
  WORKS:
  writings, 21, 44, 123, 823
  Critiken, 717
  Lectures on the Drama, 178
  —— review, 182
  Lectures on Shakespeare, 63
SCHLEGEL or The Schlegels [August Wilhelm von and Karl Wilhelm Friedrich von], 200, 208, 307, 324, 394, 584, 629, 776
SCHLICHTEGROLL, 207
SCHLOSSER, Friedrich Christoph, 447
  History of the Eighteenth Century, 532
SCHLOSSERS, The, visited with Wordsworth, 531
SCHMELLER, portrait of Crabb Robinson, 373
SCHMIDT, 224
SCHUNCK, Martin, 659
SCOTCH, The, criticized, 28, 29, 170, 406, 437
SCOTLAND, 433
  Memorials of a Tour. See Wordsworth, W.
  visited, 265 seq.
  —— with Wordsworth, 427, 433
  itinerary of Wordsworth's 1803 tour, 274
SCOTT, Alexander John, 683, 698, 706 and note, 720, 765, 783
SCOTT, John, 171 and note, 262 and note
  article on *Blackwood's Magazine*, 256, 262 note
  —— Wordsworth, 259, 260
SCOTT, Michael. *See* Coleridge, S. T., and Cunningham, A.
SCOTT, Russell, 820 note
SCOTT, Sir Walter
  article by Carlyle, 550
  and the Duke of Buccleuch, 266
  and Coleridge's *Christabel*, 47
  on S. E. Ferrier's *Marriage*, 339
  financial affairs, 266, 295, 548
  and Godwin, 286
  and Hazlitt's lecture, 222
  and the laureateship, 132
  lecture by MacDonald, 783
  letter to Southey on W. Smith, 550 and note, 551
  letters to Crabbe, 472
  Life. See Lockhart, J. G.
  in Lytton's *England and the English*, 435
  monument, 718
  Crabb Robinson's introductions, 266 and note
  in Smith, H. and J., *Rejected Addresses*, 111

SCOTT, Sir Walter—*contd.*
  on Southey's poetry, 132
  mentioned, 30, 222, 345, 363, 366, 442, 454, 486, 498, 557, 570, 680
  WORKS:
    writings:
      article on Southey's *Kehama*, 30, 39
      novels, 295, 313, 348, 438, 646
        article on, 777
      poetry, 22, 32, 39, 47, 48, 82, 85, 168, 534, 536, 718, 849
    Abbot, 255
    Anne of Geierstein, 365
    Antiquary, 290
    Betrothed, 321 and note
    Black Dwarf, 201, 202, 645
    Bridal of Triermain, 139 and note, 164, 192 and note
    Bride of Lammermoor, 233, 311, 498
    Chronicles of the Canongate, 349
    Count Robert of Paris, 466
    Essay on the Drama, 394
    Fair Maid of Perth, 356
    Field of Waterloo, 176
    (*Forester's Guide and Profitable Planter*), review, 353
    Fortunes of Nigel, 283
    Guy Mannering, 172, 173, 277
    Harold the Dauntless, 220
    Heart of Midlothian, 228, 851
    —— acted, 231
    Kenilworth, 262, 316
    Illustrations of Northern Antiquities, 214
    Introduction to the Waverley Novels, 457
    Ivanhoe, 238, 598
    Lady of the Lake, 265, 268
    Lay of the Last Minstrel, 124, 266
    Legend of Montrose, 232, 312, 316
    Life of Dryden, 203
    Life of Napoleon, 348, 351
    Lives of the Novelists, 341, 438
    Lord of the Isles, 176, 850
    Marmion, 550
    Minstrelsy of the Scottish Border, 44, 45, 107, 265
    Miscellaneous Prose Works, 354, 548
    Monastery, 241
    Old Mortality, 204, 265, 647
    Paul's Letters to his Kinsfolk, 180
    Peveril of the Peak, 289, 290, 300, 435, 438, 449
    Pirate, 280
    Quentin Durward, 296, 499
    Redgauntlet, 309, 310
    Rob Roy, 219
      acted, 718
    Rokeby, 130
    St. Ronan's Well, 300, 316
    ed. Somers's *Tracts*, 174

SCOTT, Sir Walter—*contd.*
WORKS—*contd.*
  Surgeon's Daughter, 349
  Tales of a Grandfather, 353, 362
  Tales of my Landlord, 201, 204, 221, 232, 233, 851, 852
  Talisman, 321 and note
  Vision of Don Roderick, 39, 40, 850 and note
  Waverley, 152, 163, 164, 173, 277, 539, 850
  Woodstock, 338
SCOTT, Lady [Walter], 91
SCOTT, Dr., 234
SCOTT, William. *See* Stowell
SEA-SHELL image [in *Gebir* and *Excursion*], 507, 516
SEDGWICK, Adam, 539
SENHOUSE [friend of Southey], 552 seq.
SENIOR, Nassau William, 401
Serjeants' Wife, The, 350
SERVIÈRE, Charlotte, 366
SEVERN, Joseph, 377, 378, 552
  and Keats, 390, 520
  portrait of Wordsworth, 521
SEWARD, Anna, letters from Southey, 646
SEWELL, Elizabeth Missing, 790
SEYMOUR, 452
SHAKESPEARE, William
  anachronism, 18
  criticisms, 14, 21, 54, 55, 66, 93, 108, 216, 584, 652; *Comedy of Errors,* 625; *Hamlet,* 21, 54, 57; *Love's Labour's Lost,* 706, 811; *Julius Caesar,* 66; *King John,* 55; *King Lear,* 21, 55, 108; *Macbeth,* 54; *Midsummer Night's Dream,* 56; *Othello,* 102; *Rape of Lucrece,* 52; *Richard II,* 55, 57, 167; *Romeo and Juliet,* 53, 54, 56; *Sonnets,* 53, 552; *Taming of the Shrew,* 625; *Tempest,* 56; *Troilus and Cressida,* 811; *Venus and Adonis,* 52; *Winter's Tale,* 102, 694
  forgeries. *See* Collier, J. P. and Ireland, W. H.
  lectures by:
    Carlyle, 583
    Coleridge, 52, 53, 55, 56, 102, 117, 218
    Hazlitt, 218
  mentioned, 466, 486, 727, 776, 810
  BOOKS, ETC., RELATING TO:
    Coleridge, S. T., *Notes and Lectures upon Shakespeare,* 688, 689, 691, 694
    Collier, J. P. *See* Collier, J. P., edns. of Shakespeare
    Hazlitt, W., *Characters of Shakespeare's Plays,* 217, 223, 226
    —— on the character of *Iago,* 151
    Jameson, A. B., *Characteristics of Women,* 442 and note, 614
    Lamb, C., *Specimens of English Dramatic Poets,* 36, 63, 625 and note
    —— (*Tragedies of Shakespeare*), 68
    Landor, W. S., *Citation and Examination of William Shakespeare,* 448 seq.
    Schlegel, A. W. *See* Schlegel, A. W., writings

SHAKESPEARE, William—*contd.*
　　BOOKS, ETC., RELATING TO—*contd.*
　　　　Stendhal, pamphlet, *Racine et Shakespeare*, 343 and note
　　　　articles: by Bagehot, 810; by De Quincey, 820; in the *Prospective Review*, 726
SHAKESPEARE SOCIETY, 595, 689, 722
SHARP, Richard, 261, 343
SHARP, 452
SHARPE, F., his album entry by Crabb Robinson, 775
SHARPE, M., 546
SHARPE, Samuel, 693, 749
　　　Memoir of Samuel Rogers, 792
SHARPE, Sutton, 295, 297, 309, 335, 344
SHARPE, W., ed. *Recollections by S. Rogers*, 785
SHARPE, Miss, 295, 335, 596
SHARPE or SPARKE.　*See* Sparke
SHARPES, The, 547, 550, 662
Sharpe's London Magazine, article on Wordsworth, 723 and note
SHEE, Sir William, 440
[SHEEHY, William J. A.], *Reminiscences of Rome*, 587
Sheepfolds, Notes by Ruskin, 710
Sheffield Courant, letters by Dr. Arnold, 639
SHELLEY, Harriet, *born* Westbrook, 199, 211
SHELLEY, Jane, Lady, 784
　　　Shelley Memorials, 791
SHELLEY, Mary Wollstonecraft, *born* Godwin, 199, 203, 204, 211, 212, 235, 299, 316, 412, 413, 446, 447, 552, 569, 574, 654, 777
　　WORKS:
　　　writings, 274
　　　Frankenstein, 418, 419
　　　—— review, 223
　　　Lodore, 464
　　　Rambles in Germany and Italy, 648
SHELLEY, Percy Bysshe
　　article by Bagehot, 762, 810
　　and Byron, 222, 412, 446, 447
　　on Byron, 587
　　and Jane Clairmont, 446, 447
　　in De Quincey, T., *Selections Grave and Gay*, 782
　　in Disraeli, B., *Venetia*, 775, 776
　　domestic affairs and Godwin, 199, 203, 211, 212, 413, 446
　　grave visited, 389, 390
　　in Hunt, J. H. Leigh, *Lord Byron and Some of his Contemporaries*, 353, 355
　　lecture by MacDonald, 784
　　Life. See Hogg, T. J., and Medwin, T.
　　in Lytton's *England and the English*, 535
　　Memorials.　See Shelley, Jane, Lady
　　and Oxford University, 398
　　personal qualities, 212, 222, 446, 485
　　place as a poet, 762, 778
　　politics, 587
　　religion, 211, 279, 354, 398, 479, 587, 597
　　Crabb Robinson meets, 212

SHELLEY, Percy Bysshe—*contd.*
   and H. Smith, 361
  mentioned, 204, 237, 408, 569
  WORKS:
    writings, 274, 631, 632
    Posthumous Poems, 409
    Prometheus Unbound and other Poems, 279, 354
    Prose Works, 587, 589
    separate works:
      Adonais, 704
      Cenci, 409, 652
      Epipsychidion, 654
      Hymn to Mercury, translated, 409
      Lines written among the Euganean Hills, 351
      Sensitive Plant, 351, 368
      Skylark, 351 and note, 704, 779
      Queen Mab, 597
      notes to *Queen Mab,* 479
      Witch of Atlas, 575
SHELLEY, Sir Percy Florence, 235, 236, 299, 569
SHELLEY FAMILY and T. J. Hogg, 778, 784
SHENSTONE, William, 106
SHEPHERD, William, 318 and note, 356
SHERIDAN, Richard Brinsley
    Lamb mistakes Bunbury for, 9, 10
    Life of. See Moore, T.
    Memoir of. See Smyth, W.
  WORK:
    Rivals, acted, 225
SHERIDAN, Tom, 629
SHIRLEY, notes by Gifford, 344
SHOBERL, Frederic, 355
SHUTT, 407, 439
SHUTTS, The, 361, 396
SIDDONS, Sarah
    death, 391
    and Edgeworth, 129, 130
    Miss Kelly's recollections of, 423
    Life. See Boaden, J.
    retirement, 104, 105
    Crabb Robinson meets, 148
  other references, 9, 70, 365, 617, 674, 726, 775, 789
Siege of Belgrade, drama, acted, 28
SIEVEKING, 319
SIMPLON PASS, 250, 270
SIMPSON, Margaret. *See* De Quincey
SINGLETON, Henry, portrait of Southey, 510
SISMONDI, Simonde de, 247, 254
    (*De la Litterature du Midi de l'Europe*), review, 172
SISMONDIS, The, 519
SKEPPER, Anne. *See* Procter
SLATER, portrait of Wordsworth, 509
SLAVERY and Slavery Abolition, 305, 428, 468, 477, 541, 542, 566, 625,
    646, 695, 717, 742, 769

Slave Trade Abolition Minute Books, 759
Sly, 178
Smiles, Samuel, *Self-Help*, 796
Smirke, 83
Smith, Adam, 512
Smith, Alexander
  mentioned in Kingsley's *Miscellanies*, 793
  Poems, 727
  —— article on, 726, 727
Smith, Goldwin
  Lectures on Modern History, 804
  —— review, 805
Smith, Horatio [Horace]. *See also* Smith, James and Horace
  conversation, 361, 396, 437, 466, 635
  Brighton epigram, 635
  epigram by Ricardo, 577, 578
  health, 635
  and the *New Monthly Magazine*, 317
  and Shelley, 361
  Crabb Robinson first meets, 317
  mentioned, 408, 422, 543
  works:
  writings, 348, 361
  Brambletye House, 334, 345
  Gale Middleton, 437
  Nympholept, 409
  Oliver Cromwell, 585
  Tor Hill, 345
Smith, James, 317, 361, 421, 422, 543, 549
Smith, James and Horace, 113, 127
  Rejected Addresses, 48, 113, 167
Smith, James, *Divine Drama of History and Civilisation*, 745
Smith, John Thomas, *Nollekens and his Times*, 361
Smith, Julia, 680 and note, 730
Smith, Martha Frances [Patty], 680 note
  letter on the *Excursion*, 159, 680
Smith, Sydney
  main entry, 493
  last illness and death, 651
  and the *Edinburgh Review*, 26
  Life and *Letters*. *See* Holland, Lady
  story of Rogers, 227
  and Southey's joke, 433
  and Ward's *Tremaine*, 616
  epigram on Whewell, 584
  works:
  Letter on the Americans, 635
  pamphlet on Deans and Chapters, 513, 757
  collected articles, 624, 625
  Plymley's Letters, 624, 845
Smith, Sydney [friend of J. C. Richmond], 377
Smith, Thomas Southwood (*Illustrations of the Divine Government*), 711

SMITH, William, 32, note 680
    Scott's letter to Southey concerning, 550 and note, 551
    Southey's *Letter*, 206, 431, 550 note
SMITH, and Lamb's 'beauty,' 18
    other references, 27, 28, 237
SMITH, Mrs., 18, 27, 28, 220, 228, 237
SMITH [picture dealer], 304
SMITH, Mrs. [of Cambridge], 243
SMOLLETT, Tobias George, 28
    Peregrine Pickle, 374, 375
    Travels through France and Italy, 321
SMYTH, William, *Memoir of Mr. Sheridan*, 629
SOANE, Sir John, 342
    lectures, 121
Social Innovators, article on, 783
SOLLY, The Misses, 662 and note
|| SOMERS's *Tracts*, ed. Scott, Sir W., 174
SOMERSET, Duchess of, 563
SOPHOCLES, *Antigone*, 789
SORTAIN, Joseph, 704, 728, 745
SOTHEBY, William, 30 and note, 129 and note, 130
SOTHEBY's, sale of Southey's library, 643
SOUCHAY, Dr., 366
SOUTHERN, Henry, 296 and note, 301, 302, 313 seq., 319, 324
    review of Austin, S., *Characteristics of Goethe*, 426
SOUTHEY, Bertha. *See* Hill
SOUTHEY, Caroline Anne, *born* Bowles, 556, 595
SOUTHEY, Charles Cuthbert, 590, 595, 706 and note
    tour with Southey, 552 seq.
    WORKS:
    ⟨*Life and Correspondence of Robert Southey*⟩, 555, 694, 695, 699, 701
    ———— review, 706
    Notes to Southey's *Wesley*, 671
SOUTHEY, Edith, *born* Fricker, 27, 189, 271, 297, 555
SOUTHEY, Edith. *See* Warter
SOUTHEY, Henry Herbert, M.D., 240, 299, 595
SOUTHEY, Mrs. Henry Herbert, 595
SOUTHEY, Kate, 564
SOUTHEY, Robert
    and an acrostic, 214
    at Dr. Aikin's, 10
    in L. Aikin's *Letters*, 816
    at Amyot's, 132, 133
    Miss J. Barker and, 297
    and Sir J. Bowring, 301
    bust by Weekes, 658
    and Byron, 280, 412, 428
    ——— in *Don Juan*, 463; *Vision of Judgment*, 286, 370
    and Coleridge, 26, 41, 59, 210, 671
    and Cowper's letters, 660
    and the *Edinburgh Review*, 26, 39
    at Miss Fenwick's, 561, 564
    financial affairs, 31, 484
    and the Hawkers, 555

00

SOUTHEY, Robert—*contd.*
  and M. Hays, 124
  and Hazlitt, 210, 222
  health, 553 seq., 565, 579, 581
  story of the Herns, 536
  and Lamb, 239, 833
  at Lamb's, 40
  Lamb's *Letter of Elia to Robert Southey, Esq.*, 298, 300, 312
  and Landor, 20, 378, 379, 381, 581
  —— *Imaginary Conversations*, 626
  —— *Satire on Satirists*, *passim*
  and the laureateship, 132, 142, 212
  letter to Brougham, 432
  letter on Coleridge, 502, 681
  letter to: Duppa, 635, 640 seq.; Miss Seward, 646; W. Taylor,
    638 note
  Selections from the Letters. See Warter, J. W.
  library, 189 and note
  —— sale, 643
  Life and Correspondence. See Southey, C. C.
  in London, 10, 38 seq., 132, 206, 239, 299, 300, 357, 509, 510
  and the *London Magazine*, 317
  monument, 644, 659
  and Moxon, 579
  personal qualities, 39, 132, 190, 212, 297, 359, 378, 512, 564, 565,
    759, 762
  and T. Poole, 599
  portrait by: [Hancock], 500; Singleton, 510
  at Quillinan's, 357
  and A. F. Rio, 619 note
  and Crabb Robinson: gifts from, 443 and note, 510; introduction to,
    6, 10, 845; letter from, 25; visited at Keswick by, 189, 190, 193,
    270, 339, 431, 432
  and Sir W. Rough, 38, 41
  and Scott's letter on W. Smith, 550 and note, 551
  in Smith, H. and J., *Rejected Addresses*, 111
  and Talfourd, 510
  and Sir H. Taylor, 401
  at Thelwall's, 38
  and *The Times*, 204 seq., 634, 699
  tour in France, 1838, 550, 552 seq.
  and Voss, 213
  and Blanco White, 42, 65
  and the Wilberforces, 551
  and Wordsworth, 40, 179.   *See also* Wordsworth, W., on Southey
    and his works.
  and Wordsworth's poems, 93, 193
  OPINIONS AND CRITICISM:
    Blake, W., 40, 41
    Coleridge, S. T., 10, 41, 754
    Coleridge's poetry, 29
    Cottle, J., *Early Recollections*, 505
    Fellowes, R., 641
    Goethe, 374
    the Guelphic Order, 432

SOUTHEY, Robert—*contd.*

OPINIONS AND CRITICISMS—*contd.*

Hunt, J. H., 641

Landor, W. S., 39, 41, 510

Paris, 553

the press, 127, 189, 193

politics and foreign affairs, 10, 31, 39, 41, 42, 133, 142, 177, 189, 193, 206, 239, 288, 299, 357, 431, 448, 510, 567, 646

religion, 174, 336, 357, 490, 567, 609, 762

—— Calvinism, 561, 671

—— Catholic Emancipation, 18

—— Puritans, 303, 483

Scott's works, 39

Taylor, W., 39, 701

Thelwall, J., 42

Wordsworth and his works, 10, 41, 132

his writings, 193

mentioned, 50, 149, 195, 213, 240, 364, 499, 814

WORKS:

writings, 22, 26, 29, 48, 52, 82, 87 and note, 96, 132, 169, 190, 193, 207, 378, 428, 467, 504, 506 seq., 516, 566, 567, 632

editions:

Poetical Works, 566, 634

German edn. of *Selections*, 366

Selections [Moxon], 403

separate works:

album verse, 589

ed. *Attempts in Verse of John Jones a Servant; Introductory Essay*, 394

Book of the Church, 301, 303

Carmen Nuptiale

review in the *Edinburgh*, 186; *Examiner*, 186, 201

‖ *Carmen Triumphale* [stanzas published as *Ode Written during the Negotiations with Buonaparte*], 142

couplet for a child, 427

ed. Cowper W., *Works, comprising his Poems, Correspondence, and Translations. With a life of the Author*, 470 seq.

Curse of Kehama, 17, 21 seq., 25, 30, 36 seq., 43, 131, 172, 173, 193, 224, 561, 847

—— review in the *Eclectic*, 30; *Edinburgh*, 26, 29, 30; *Quarterly*, 30

Doctor, 483, 537, 538, 560 seq., 663, 744

Essays, Moral and Political, 431, 432

lines on the death of George III, 239

History of Brazil, 759

(*History of the Peninsular War*), 11

Letter to William Smith, Esq., M.P., 206, 431, 550 note

Life of the Rev. Andrew Bell, 484

Life of Wesley, 263, 264, 671

—— *Observations on. See* Watson, R.

Lives of the British Admirals, 553

Madoc, 25, 27, 29, 173

—— review, 30, 638

Omniana, 114, 115

SOUTHEY, Robert—*contd.*
　WORKS—*contd.*
　　separate works
　　　(*Poet's Pilgrimage to Waterloo*), 186
　　　Roderick the last of the Goths, 172 seq., 193, 850 and note
　　　Sir Thomas More, or Colloquies on the Progress and Prospects of Society, 608 seq.
　　　Tale of Paraguay, 634
　　　Thalaba, 17, 20, 36 seq., 42, 43, 847
　　　Vision of Judgment, 289
　　　Wat Tyler, 204 seq., 510
　　ARTICLES AND REVIEWS:
　　　[Bogue] (*History of Dissenters*), 139
　　　[Colquhoun] (*Inquiry into the Poor Laws*), 127
　　　[Elliott], *Life of Wellington*, 178
　　　[Fosbroke], *British Monachism*, 237
　　　Godwin, *Chaucer*, 28
　　　Memoires of Mme la Marquise de la Rochejaquelein, 192
　　　(*Report of the Society for Bettering the Conditions of the Poor*), 192
SOUTHEY, Miss [niece], 693, 694
SOUTHEY FAMILY, 270, 271, 339, 556, 587, 590 and note, 595
SPAIN, current events, 39, 42, 74, 133, 177, 208, 229
——, poetry, 26
——, refugees, 11
SPARKE or SHARPE, 246, 252
SPARROW, Mrs., 312
Spectator, The
　article on S. Austin's *Characteristics of Goethe*, 426
　and Southern, 426
　and N. P. Willis's writings, 444
SPEDDING, James, 588, 589, 650, 651, 702, 760
SPENCE, William, 678
SPENCER, John Charles. *See* Althorp
SPENCER, Lord, library, 343
SPENDER, J. C., M.D., 593
SPENSER, Edmund, 626, 776
　Faerie Queene, 7
　Life. See Collier, J. P.
SPINOZA, Baruch, writings
　Coleridge and, 112, 447; marginalia, 469
　Goethe and, 776
　Wordsworth and, 20
SPIRIT-RAPPING, article in *Household Words*, 722
STABLE, Mr. and Miss, 91
STAËL, Mme de, 2, 17, 128, 132, 133, 135, 149, 150, 208, 298, 310, 411, 424, 626, 848
　WORK:
　　(*De l'Allemagne*), review, 135
STAFFORD, Marquis of, art collection, 35
STANHOPE, Lord, 5, 811 and note
　sonnet by Coleridge, 501, 503

STANLEY, Arthur Penrhyn, 697, 760
    Life and Correspondence of Thomas Arnold, 644
STANLEY, Edward Smith, 13th Earl of Derby, 431
STANLEY, Miss, 615
STANSFELD, Thomas, and son, 688
STANSFELDS, The, 832
Star, The, 275
STEELE, Sir Richard, in Thackeray's *Esmond*, 720, 721
STEEVENS, George, 643
STEFFENS, 200
STENDHAL [pseud. of Beyle, Henri], *Racine et Shakespeare*, 343 and
    note
STEPHEN, Sir James, 104, 242, 341, 349, 401, 439, 492, 561, 698, 699,
    732, 768, 778
    article on Isaac Taylor, 582
(STEPHENS, Alexander), *Memoirs of John Horne Tooke*, 131
STERLING, Edward, 582
    and *The Times*, 205
STERLING, John, *Life. See* Carlyle, T., and Hare, J. C.
    Arthur Coningsby, 600
STERNE, Laurence
    lecture by Thackeray, 715
    payment for *Tristram Shandy*, 723
    mentioned, 374, 375
STEWART, Charles Samuel, 430
STEWART, Dugald, 831
STEWART [Scotch landlord], 268
STILLING, Heinrich, 531, 552
STIRLING, Maxwell, Lady. *See* Norton, Caroline
STISTED, Mrs. Henry, 391
STODDART, Sir John, 110, 142, 177, 199, 243, 257, 292
STOLBERG, *Felsenstrom*, 107
STONE, F., portrait of J. Quillinan, 512
STONE, Hurford, 147, 148, 232
STONE, Mrs., 635, 640
STORKS, Henry, 309
STOTHARD, Thomas, 11
STOWE, Harriet Elizabeth Beecher, 724
    WORKS:
        Dred, 762
        Key to Uncle Tom's Cabin, 741, 742
        Uncle Tom's Cabin, 717, 760
STOWELL, Lord [William Scott], 510
STRAUSS, D. F.
    Lectures on. See Harwood, P.
    translation of *Leben Jesu. See* Evans, M. A. (George Eliot)
STREET, George Edmund, 730, 794, 812
    lecture, 781, 782
    WORK:
        Brick and Marble, 775
STREET, Mrs. George, 804
STREET, Thomas George, 33, 37 and note
STREETS, The, 765
STRICKLAND, Agnes, *Lives of the Queens*, 632

STRUTT, Benjamin, 459
    ed. Collins's *Poetical Works*, 1
STUART, Daniel, 37 and note, 51, 170
STUMPF, 414
STURCH, Miss, 651
SURR, T. S., *Splendid Misery*, 174, 175
|| SURRY INSTITUTION, 180, 198, 217, 223
    see also Coleridge, lectures; Hazlitt, lectures
SUSSEX, Duke of, 414
SWANWICK, Anna, 689, 716, 735, 784, 787
    translation of *Faust*, 689
SWANWICK, Mrs., 689, 737
SWEDEN, Crabb Robinson in, 9
SWEDENBORG, Emanuel, 675
    Blake on, 327, 328
    New Jerusalem, 316
SWIFT, Jonathan, 633, 851
    in Thackeray's *Esmond*, 721, 725
    (*Gulliver's Travels*), 630
SWIFT, and Miss Kelly, 414
SWINBURNE, Algernon Charles, Poems, 821
SWITZERLAND, tour with the Wordsworths, 243 seq.
SYKES, Lady, 450
SYMONDS [of Bury], 795

TAGART, Edward, 675, 687
TAGGART, Cynthia, *Poems*, 443 and note
TAIT, C., 335, 828
TAIT, William, 823, 825, 828
Tait's Magazine
    article on Mrs. Inchbald, 435
    contributions by De Quincey, 273, 451, 456, 464, 696
TALFOURD, Edward and Mrs., 455
TALFOURD, Sir Thomas Noon
    and Mrs. Barbauld, 198
    on J. P. Collier, 556
    and T. Cooper, 666
    and copyright, 121, 566, 568, 596
    death, 738, 739
    and De Quincey, 276
    and the *Edinburgh Review*, 461
    and Jeffrey, 461, 535
    and Lamb, 120, 406, 407
    and Lamb's death, 453
    at Lamb's, 167, 170, 177, 179, 197, 215, 216, 221, 231, 257, 259, 302, 315, 345, 365
    and Lamb's letters. *See* Lamb, C., letters
    and the care of M. Lamb, 510, 511, 567
    and Landor. *See* Landor, W. S., *Satire upon Satirists*
    legal career, 119 seq., 345, 692, 851
    and the *London Magazine*, 260, 262
    and M. R. Mitford, 544, 585
    and Moxon, 510, 511, 675, 739
    in Parliament, 121, 461
    parties, 287, 316, 356, 445, 494, 496, 497, 603, 611

TALFOURD, Sir Thomas Noon—*contd.*
  personal qualities, 119 seq., 259, 535
  and Crabb Robinson, 119 seq., 549, 552, 579, 724
  and Southey, 510
  and *The Times*, 120, 227
  and Alaric Watts, 679
  and Wordsworth, 120, 121, 215, 216, 221, 295, 356, 461, 491, 497,
    569, 682, 697.   *See also* Landor, W. S., *Satire upon Satirists*
  mentioned, 229, 242, 297, 328, 452, 459, 462, 482, 492, 493, 642, 726
  WORKS:
    writings, 378, 579, 739
      articles: for the periodicals, 120, 260; on the *Profession of the Bar*,
        318, 319; Wordsworth, 120, 259
      notes in Hazlitt's *Literary Remains*, 779
    separate works:
      Athenian Captive, 120, 549, 551, 552
      Castilian, 724
      Final Memorials of Charles Lamb, 9, 142, 679, 711
      —— dedication to Wordsworth, 682
      —— review in the *Athenæum*, 679; *Inquirer*, 679, 680
      (*Glencoe*), 120
      Ion, 120, 464, 544, 545, 549, 552, 724
      —— first performance, 494, 507
      —— letters of congratulation on, 855
      Letters of Charles Lamb with a Sketch of his Life, 533, 534, 546, 853
      Vacation Rambles and Thoughts, 735, 738
TALFOURD, Rachel, Lady, *born* Rutt, 120, 121, 302, 315, 459, 495, 508,
    512, 544, 579, 635, 738, 739
TALLEYRAND, 550
TASSO, Torquato
  WRITINGS:
    Coleridge on, 89
    Landor on, 381, 383
    Wordsworth and, 89, 519, 528
Tatler, The, article by J. H. Leigh Hunt, 414
TAYLER, John James, 770, 775, 785
TAYLOR, Adam, 772 note
TAYLOR, Emily, 813
TAYLOR, George and Mrs., 691
TAYLOR, Sir Henry
  account of, 401, 439
  visit to Coleridge, 307, 308
  and Landor's *Satire upon Satirists*, 513, 514
  and Southey's letters, 634, 635
  letters from Southey, 701
  mentioned, 560, 568, 765
  WORKS:
    articles on: De Vere, A., *Poems*, 741; Wordsworth, *Poetical Works*,
      452, 741; *Sonnets upon the Punishment of Death*, 606
    Edwin the Fair, 622
    Eve of the Conquest and other Poems, 671
    Notes on Books, 741
    Notes on Life, 401, 685, 687

TAYLOR, Sir Henry—*contd.*
  WORKS—*contd.*
    Philip van Artevelde, 401, 446, 452, 622
    —— acted, 669, 670
    —— reviews, 670
TAYLOR, Sir Henry and Lady
    visited by Miss Fenwick, 668, 677, 704, 730
    visited by Mrs. and Miss Wordsworth, 731, 834
TAYLOR, Isaac, article on, 582
  WORKS:
    Natural History of Enthusiasm, 563
    Physical Theory of Another Life, 563, 564
TAYLOR, Jeremy, *Life.* *See* Willmott
    Dissuasive from Popery, 83
TAYLOR, John [printer], 171 and note
TAYLOR, John [of Taylor and Hessey], 311
TAYLOR and Hessey, 275, 276
TAYLOR, John [the Water Poet], 394
TAYLOR, John Edward, *Fairy Ring, from the German of Grimm*, 659
TAYLOR, Richard, 171 and note, 669, 846
TAYLOR, Tom, 700, 716, 774
  WORKS:
    Diogenes' Lanthorn, acted, 694
    ed. Haydon, B. R., *Autobiography*, 731
    ed. Leslie, C. R., *Autobiography*, 800 note
    Two Loves and a Life, acted, 738
TAYLOR, William, 4, 123, 135, 146, 168, 169, 196, 323, 415
  BOOKS, ETC., RELATING TO:
    Aikin, L., *Letters*, 816
    Robberds, J. W., *Memoir of the Life and Writings of William Taylor of Norwich*, 816
    Crabb Robinson, *Goethe's Works*, footnote in defence of Taylor against Carlyle, 408, 638 and note
    Southey, C. C., *Life and Correspondence of Robert Southey*, 701
  WORKS:
    article on Mme de Staël's (*De l'Allemagne*), 135
    Historic Survey of German Poetry, 415, 421
    —— review, 408, 421
    Letter Concerning the Two First Chapters of Luke, 31, 39
TAYLOR, Mrs., *born* Fletcher, 754
TAYLOR, 509
TEGG, Thomas, 591
TEMPLE, Sir William, article by Macaulay, 558
TENNYSON, Alfred, 1st Lord, 591, 650, 797
    article on, 755
    in Bagehot on *Poetry*, 813
    in Kingsley, C., *Miscellanies*, 793
    lecture by MacDonald, 798
  mentioned, 727
  WORKS:
    Poems, 425, 705
    —— review in the *National*, 755; *Quarterly*, 624

TENNYSON, Alfred, 1st Lord—*contd.*
  WORKS—*contd.*
    separate works:
      Gardener's Daughter, 651
      Idylls of the King, 791
      In Memoriam, 704, 707
      —— review, 704
      Locksley Hall, 649
      Maud, 755, 820, 821
      Princess, 706
      Two Voices, 649
      Vision of Sin, 649, 651
TERNI, visited with Wordsworth, 522
TERRY, Daniel, 144
TEXAS, annexation, 541, 542
THACKERAY, William Makepeace
    article on, 734
    lectures, 715, 796
    Crabb Robinson meets, 700, 800
    verses on, 815
  WORKS:
    writings, 786, 813
    English Humourists, 725, 779, 780
    Esmond, 720, 721
    Four Georges, 799, 804
    Notes of a Journey from Cornhill to Grand Cairo, 665
    Pendennis, 812 seq.
    Vanity Fair, 674, 676, 677, 679, 816
    —— review, 686
THACKERAY [cousin of W. M. Thackeray], 509, 681
THEATRES visited by Crabb Robinson
    Adelphi, 738
    Covent Garden, 115, 231, 405, 450, 540
    —— with C. Lamb, 26, 27, 157
    —— M. Lamb, 163, 225
    —— The Lambs, 9
    —— Wordsworth, 494
    Drury Lane, 117, 441
    —— with M. Lamb, 179
    —— M. Lamb and the Wordsworths, 167
    French Theatre, with M. Lamb, 305
    —— Wordsworth, 359
    Haymarket, 551, 724
    (King's), [Edinburgh], 718
    Lyceum, with Lamb, 28
    Princess's, 667, 669
    Strand, 694
THEED, Mrs., 519
THELWALL, John, 11, 32, 38, 42, 65, 177, 231
Theodor des Zweiflers Weihe, marginalia by Coleridge, 671, 672
THIERS, Louis Adolphe, 780
THIRLWALL, Connop, Bishop of St. Davids, 698, 800
THOM, John Hamilton, 658, 717
THOMAS, Mr. and Mrs., 499

THOMPSON, Dr. [Thomson ?], 465, 571, 572
THOMSON, George, 578, 579
THOMSON, James
    Castle of Indolence, 42
    Winter, 206
THOMSON, Miss, 749
THORNTHWAITE, Mrs., 847
THORNTON, Henry, *Family Prayers*, 647, 648
THORNTON, Robinson, 767 and note
THORWALDSEN, Bertel
    statue of Byron, 521
    —— of Gutenberg, 521
THRALE, Mrs., 601, 602
THRUPP, Frederick
    bust of Wordsworth, 739
    statue of Wordsworth, 717, 724, 731, 748
THURTELL, John, trial, 302 and note
TIARKS, T. L., 300
TICKNOR FAMILY, 524, 528, 531, 719
TIECK, Ludwig, 207 seq., 374, 375, 446
    Carlyle and, 823, 824, 826
  mentioned, 200, 585, 776
  WORKS:
    Tales, selected by Moxon, 403
    Vorschule von Shakespeare, 307
TILLBROOK, Samuel, 151, 187, 214, 339
Times, The [ed. Walter, John], 205, 451, 616
    and T. Barnes, 66, 67
    and M. Burney, 361, 666
    circulation, 718
    and S. T. Coleridge, 37, 40, 50 seq.
    and Combe, 11, 12
    and the Crimean War, 776
    and Croly, 121, 745
    and Hazlitt, 110
    and Crabb Robinson, 10, 122, 777
    and Southey, 204, 205, 634, 699
    special correspondents, 776
    and Talfourd, 120, 277
    in Trollope's *Warden*, 768, 791
  mentioned, 774, 799 note, 814
  ARTICLES ON:
    Canton prisons, 776
    Catholic Emancipation, 230
    Coleridge, S. T., 669
    —— lectures, 51 and note
    Collier's Shakespeare forgeries, 787
    Moore, T., 722
    Queen Caroline, 243
    Rogers, S., *Table Talk*, 758
    Sonnets, 461, 462
    Wordsworth, 697
TINDAL, Sir Nicholas Conyngham, 121
TINDAL, 127

TIPPER, Samuel, 13, 15, 16
TITIAN 'Seasons,' 36
TITIAN'S HOUSE, visited, 528
TITMARSH, pseud. *See* Thackeray, W. M.
TOBIN, James, and *We are Seven*, 93
TOBIN, John, *Honey Moon*, 36
TOCQUEVILLE. *See* De Tocqueville
TOLLER, 60 seq.
TOMALIN, J., 54, 204
TOMBLESON, William, *Views on the Rhine*, 443 and note
TOOKE, John Horne, 31, 73, 122
    books, 586
    lecture by Hazlitt, 69
    Life. *See* Stephens, A.
   WORKS:
    Diversions of Purley, 69, 846
    political writings, 261
TORLONIA, Count, 186 and note, 850
TOTTENHAM, the Rev. Mr., 593
‖ TOWNSEND, George, 570, 643
    Armageddon, 643
TOWNSHEND, Chauncey Hare, *Facts in Mesmerism*, 608
TOYNBEE, *Tracts*, 677
TRACTARIANS. *See* Oxford Movement
TRAVERS, Miss, 799
TREE, Ellen [Mrs. Charles Kean], 441, 494, 552, 724
TRELAWNY, Edward John, 409, 410, 489, 511
    Adventures of a Younger Son, 631, 632
TROLLOPE, Anthony
   WORKS:
    writings, 816, 817
    Barchester Towers, 787, 788, 791
    Belton Estate, 818, 819
    Bertrams, 794
    Doctor Thorne, 798
    Rachael Ray, 809
    Warden, 768, 791
TROLLOPE, Frances Milton, 430, 541
TROTTER, 243 note, 247, 250, 615
TUCKER, Abraham, *Light of Nature*, abridged by Hazlitt, 844
TULK, 550
TUPPER, Martin Farquhar
    works, review, 778
TURNER, Dawson, 306, 319, 456
    library treasures, 341, 645, 646, 795
TURNER, Miss Dawson, 795
TURNER, Joseph Mallord William, 602
    art, 34, 240, 459, 571, 602, 755, 796
TURNER, Sharon, 67, 168
TURNER, 20
TWINING, Mrs. Aldred. *See* Arnold, Mary
TWISS, Horace, 113 and note
TWISS, Mrs. Horace, 258
TWISTLETON, 492

TWOPENNY, 630
TYRRELL, 463

ULRICI, Hermann, 584
UNDERDOWNE, T., 840 note
UNITARIAN NEW COLLEGE, Hazlitt and, 6
UNITARIANS and Unitarianism, 87, 480, 727, 852, 854, 857
UNIVERSITY COLLEGE, London, 398, 562 and note, 675, 689, 690, 706,
    720, 738, 830, 831
    Senate address to the Council, 841
    article by Macaulay, 341
UNIVERSITY HALL, 268, 682 and note, 684, 686, 692, 713 seq., 731
UPTON, 421
USHER, James, *Clio; or a Discourse on Taste*, 468
UWINS, Thomas, 571

VALLON, Annette, 248
VALPY, Abraham John, 120, 127, 275
VALPY, Dr. Richard, 119 and note
VARNHAGEN VON ENSE, *Sketches of German Life*, translation by Gordon,
    A. D., 742
VARNHAGEN VON ENSE, Rahel, 495
Vaterländisches Museum, 15, 31
VAUCLUSE, visited with Wordsworth, 517, 519
VAUX [Botany Bay convict], *Life*, 229
VENICE, visited with Wordsworth, 527, 528
VERE. *See* De Vere
VERONA, visited with Wordsworth, 527
VETUS. *See* Sterling, E.
VICO, Giovanni Battista, *Principi della Scienza Nuova*, 320, 321
VICTOR Emmanuel, entry into Naples, 799 and note
VICTORIA, Queen
    accession, 529
    and Wordsworth, 653, 657, 700, 748, 836
VOLTAIRE, François Marie Arouet de
    Blake on, 333
    article by Carlyle, 579
    in Haydon's picture, 240
  WORKS:
    Candide, 51
    L'Ingénu, 806
    Tales, 177, 280
VOSS, Johann Heinrich, 208
  WORKS:
    Luise, 447
    translation of *Virgil*, 443
VOSS [son of the above], 213

WADE, letter from Coleridge on opium, 501, 502, 534, 549, 681
WAGNER, George, 817
WAINEWRIGHT, Thomas Griffiths, 679
WAKEFIELD, Gilbert, 265, 275
WALDENS, The, of Edmonton. *See* Lamb, M., at Edmonton

WALES, visited, 7, 498
    lines by T. Hood, 498
WALKER, 203
WALL, Anton, pseud.   *See* Heyne.
WALLIS, Lord [Wallace, Thomas Baron Wallace, sometime M.P. for
    Cockermouth?], letter from Wordsworth, 609
WALLIS, Trajan [son of the artist], 400
WALLIS, artist, 388, 440
WALPOLE, Horace, 4th Earl of Orford
    and Chatterton, 610
    (*Letters from the Hon. Horace Walpole to George Montagu, Esq.*),
        review, 229
WALTER, John the 2nd.   See *Times, The*
    other references, 139, 142, 157, 203
WALTER, Mrs. John, 449, 768
WALTER, John the 3rd, 544
WALTERS, The, visited at Bear Wood, 365, 449, 544
WALTER, W. J., 186 and note, 850
WARBURTON, William, 143
    Alliance between Church and State, 475
WARD, Lord Dudley, 395
WARD, Robert Plumer, *Tremaine*, 616
WARD, Byron's joke on, 377
WARD, Mrs. and son, 638
WARNER, Susan, pseud. Elizabeth Wetherell, *Wide Wide World*, 726
WARREN, Samuel, 439 seq., 666
    Passages from the Diary of a Late Physician, 439, 440, 453
    Ten Thousand a Year, 440, 592, 596, 598
WARREN, Mrs. Samuel, 439
WARREN, Mrs., actress, 552
WARTER, Edith, *born* Southey, 271
WARTER, John Wood, *Selections from the Letters of Robert Southey*, 758,
    759, 761, 762
WARTON, Thomas, the younger, sonnet written in *Monasticon*, 145 and
    note
WATERLAND, Daniel, 55
WATERLOO, Battle of
    in the writings of:
        Scott, Sir W., 176, 180
        Southey, R., 178, 186
        Wordsworth, 182
WATERLOO BRIDGE, 212
WATSON, Richard (*Observations on Mr. Southey's ' Life of Wesley'*), 264
WATSON, barrister, 257
WATSON, Dr., 743
WATSON, 733
WATTS, Alaric Alexander, 334, 335, 337, 679
    poetry, 803
WATTS, Isaac, writings, 477
WAWD.   *See* Wodd
WEBER, Henry William
    ed. *Dramatic Works of John Ford*
    —— review, 63
    Illustrations of Northern Antiquities.   *See* Scott, Sir W.
WEBSTER, Daniel, 430, 573

WEBSTER, Mrs. Daniel, 573
WEDD, Joseph, 315
WEDGWOOD, Josiah
    Coleridge and, 71
    and Godwin's finances, 32, 33, 175, 176, 211
WEDGWOOD, Mr. and Mrs., 724
WEEKES, Henry, bust of Southey, 658
Weird Sisters, The, 841
WELLESLEY, Arthur, Duke of Wellington, 450, 530, 543, 571, 647, 648, 662
    Life, by Elliott reviewed, 178
WELLESLEY, Richard, Marquis of, 625
WENTWORTH, William Charles, 336 note
WESLEY, John, 1
    Life. See Southey, R., and Watson, R.
WESLEY, Miss, 692
WEST, Benjamin, P.R.A.
    Coleridge on, 34
    article by Hazlitt, 146, 152
WESTMINSTER ABBEY, 521
    see also Southey memorial, and Wordsworth memorial
Westminster Review, 296 note
    articles by H. Martineau, 623, 736
Westminster Review, 1836–40.   See *London and Westminster Review*
WESTMORELAND, LADY, 519
Westward for Smelts, 811 and note
WESTWOOD, Thomas, jr., 392
WESTWOODS, The, 392, 408, 425
WETHERELL, Elizabeth, pseud.   *See* Warner, Susan
WHALLEYS, The Misses, 634
WHATELY, Richard, Archbishop of Dublin, 658, 673, 776
WHATELY, 669
WHATELY, Miss, 669
WHEWELL, William, 536, 584, 595, 651, 697, 747
    translation, *Herman and Dorothea,* 584
WHISTON, William, 768
WHITBREAD, Samuel, 32, 112
WHITE, Ferdinand, 717
WHITE, Henry Kirke, 82
WHITE, James, 33 and note, 170, 175, 185, 568
    Falstaff's Letters, 33 note, 410
WHITE, Joseph Blanco, 42, 65
    letter to Rogers, 717
    and Wordsworth's sonnets, 658
    WORKS:
    on the *Caraquenos,* 53
    on *Sonnets,* 658
WHITE, Orme, 179, 363
WHITE [American acquaintance], 528
WHITECOMB, 356
WHITTIER, John Greenleaf, poems, 769
WIELAND, 421, 426, 480, 776, 823 seq.
    Crabb Robinson's bust, 706
WILBERFORCE, Samuel, Bishop of Oxford, 698, 725, 746, 801
WILBERFORCE, William, 104, 468

WILBERFORCES, The, 551
    and Clarkson. *See* Clarkson and the Wilberforces
WILD, 21
WILKES, John, 23, 73, 512
    in Byron's *Vision of Judgment*, 286, 367, 370
WILKES, Mary, 23, 73
WILKINSON, James John Garth, 675 seq., 705
    Human Body, The, 761 and note
WILKINSON, Joseph (*Select Views in Cumberland, Westmorland, and Lancashire*), with an introduction by W. Wordsworth, 47, 111
WILLIAM IV, death, 529
WILLIAMS, Helen Maria, 147, 148, 150, 182, 209, 217, 224, 225, 230 seq., 248, 255, 283, 848
    WORKS:
      writings, 147, 148, 176
        verses to T. Clarkson, 152
      (*Letters on the State of Politics in France*), 230 seq.
      Narrative of the Events that have taken place in France, 176
WILLIAMS, Sir Roger, narrative in *Tracts of the Somers Family*, 174
WILLIAMS, The Rev. —, 360
WILLIS, Nathaniel Parker, 443 seq., 450, 460, 464, 488, 489, 491, 540
    WORKS:
      Hymn, 'The perfect world by Adam trod,' 445
      Pencillings by the Way, 444 and note, 445, 467
WILLMOTT, Robert Aris
    WORKS:
      Bishop Jeremy Taylor, 692
      Journal of Summertime in the Country, 692
WILSON, John, pseud. Christopher North
    and Jeffrey and Wordsworth, 151, 160, 161, 196, 256, 467, 486, 699
    other references, 188, 195, 267, 478, 635
    WORKS:
      writings, 82, 83, 130, 140
      City of the Plague, 186
      Isle of Palms and other Poems, 130, 140
      —— review, 82, 151
      Noctes Ambrosianae, 316
WILSON, Sir Robert, 438
WILSON, Walter, 357
WILSON [barrister], 398, 400
WIMBRIDGE, 574 and note
WINCKELMANN, Johann Joachim, 410
WINDHAM, William, 12, 54
WINDSOR, visited by M. Lamb, 128
WIRGMAN, Thomas, 92, 107
WISEMAN, Nicholas Patrick Stephen, Cardinal, 605
WODD, Henry, 40
WOLCOT, John, pseud. Peter Pindar, 32
WOLFE, Charles, *Memoirs*, 339
WOLLSTONECRAFT, Mary. *See* Godwin
WOOD, Dr., 597
WOOD, 112

WOODFALL, Henry Sampson, 261
WOODS, Joseph, *Letters to an Architect*, 646
WOOLMAN, John (*Journal*), 316, 336
WOOLNER, Thomas, medallion for Wordsworth's monument, 707, 708
WORDSWORTH, Anne [mother of William Wordsworth], 487
WORDSWORTH, Catherine, death, 103
WORDSWORTH, Christopher, D.D. [brother of William Wordsworth], 81 seq., 93, 131, 212, 239 seq., 484, 596, 618, 641, 644, 657
WORDSWORTH, Mrs. Christopher [wife of the above], 131
WORDSWORTH, Christopher [nephew of William Wordsworth]
    Mrs. Wordsworth visits, 734
    Wordsworth visits, 665
    prepares a memoir of Wordsworth, 697, 699, 703, 705, 708, 713, 832, 856
  mentioned, 700, 768
  WORK:
    Memoirs of W. Wordsworth, 709, 711, 712
WORDSWORTH, Mrs. Christopher [wife of the above], 699, 700, 768
WORDSWORTH, Dorothy
    visits the Clarksons, 16
    and Mrs. Clarkson, 474
    and Coleridge, 78
    death, 749
    health, 339 seq., 356, 405, 427 seq., 440, 463, 465, 470, 472 seq., 477, 487, 499, 505, 559, 587, 588, 655, 703, 741, 743
    visits the Lambs, 16
    letter to: De Quincey, 103; Crabb Robinson, 377
    in London, 16, 213, 239 seq., 256 seq., 300, 303, 356
    personal qualities, 16, 166, 271
    excursion with Crabb Robinson, 188, 189
    gift from Crabb Robinson, 257
    tour of the Continent with the Wordsworths, 1820, 243 seq.
    and Wordsworth, 257, 474
    and Mrs. Wordsworth, 455
  mentioned, 296, 297, 314, 358, 524, 606, 609
  WORKS:
    poems, 505, 559
    Journal of a tour on the Continent, 271, 272, 303 seq., 429, 430
    Recollections of a tour made in Scotland, 305, 345, 346, 432
WORDSWORTH, Dorothy [Dora]. *See* Quillinan, E.
WORDSWORTH, Edward [grandchild], death, 656
WORDSWORTH, Jane [grandchild, later Kennedy], 661, 683, 730 seq.
WORDSWORTH, John [father of William Wordsworth], 189
WORDSWORTH, John [son of William Wordsworth]
    as a child, 188
    and E. Quillinan, 568
    and Wordsworth's *Life*, 708, 709
    and W. Wordsworth, jr., 689 and note
  other references, 291, 427 note, 428, 430 seq., 660, 668, 763, 710, 711, 743, 780, 781
WORDSWORTH, John [nephew of W. Wordsworth], 459, 463, 484 seq., 488, 492, 493, 574, 633, 664, 665
WORDSWORTH, Mary, *born* Hutchinson. *See also* Wordsworth, William
    article by H. Martineau, 781

WORDSWORTH, Mary—*contd.*
  and the Baudouins, 248, 454, 697, 699, 705, 710
  and J. Carter, 743
  visit to Mrs. Clarkson, 729 seq., 834
  daguerreotype, 660
  death, 780, 781
  and De Quincey, 195, 196
  and James Dixon, 640, 835
  eyesight, 739, 749, 753
  visits Miss Fenwick, 834
  and Mrs. Greg, 650
  and S. Hutchinson's death, 465
  Journal of a tour on the Continent, 271, 272, 299
  visits to London, 730, 731, 734
  and H. Martineau, 677, 684
  personal qualities, 166, 168, 474, 475, 627, 680, 709 and note;
    faculties and health in old age, 662, 681, 719, 743, 834, 835
  portrait by: Carruthers, 217; Miss Gillies, 582, 660, 781
  and preachers, 593
  and Robertson's *Sermons*, 753
  and Crabb Robinson: bequest to, 781; gifts from, 488, 610, 613,
    688; knits stockings for, 760; letters from, 685, 725, 763, 760; and
    his reminiscences, 684; and visits to Rydal, 428, 432, 466, 470,
    471, 473, 559, 600; visited by, 702, 703, 711, 712, 719, 743, 753,
    778, 834, 837, 838
  visit to Sir H. Taylor, 731, 834
  and D. Wordsworth, 455
  Wordsworth's poems to, 616
  and Wordsworth's *Life*, 705, 708, 709, 832
  —— statue, 731, 834
    mentioned, 103, 497, 505, 520, 538, 595, 614, 630, 644, 654, 668,
      679, 704, 854, 857
WORDSWORTH, Richard [brother of William Wordsworth], administration
    of his estate, 191, 192, 480, 484, 497, 657
WORDSWORTH, Thomas, death, 124 and note
WORDSWORTH, William
  accident, 283 and note, 437
  at the Aders's, 292, 359, 361, 497
  —— with Mrs. Wordsworth, 256, 293
  and Mrs. C. Aikin, 74, 81
  at the C. Aikin's, 83, 84
  L. Aikin attacks, 232, 710, 711, 740, 817 and note
  and Allsop's *Letters, Conversations, and Recollections of S. T. Cole-
    ridge*, 468 seq.
  and Alsager, 616
  and Mrs. Wordsworth, and R. Anderson, 269
  anecdotes, 458
  and Dr. Arnold, 428, 476, 481, 611
  and J. Baillie, 84, 86, 91
  meets Mrs. Barbauld, 83
  in Bath with Mrs. Wordsworth, 592 seq., 662 seq.
  and the Baudouins. *See* Baudouin
  and Sir George and Lady Beaumont, 78, 98, 291, 358, 486
  and Dr. Bell's legacy, 484
  and *Blackwood's Magazine*, 363

WORDSWORTH, William—*contd.*
  and C. Brentano, 530
  at Brinsop with Mrs. Wordsworth, 634
  at the British Museum, 170, 257, 494
  and Bunsen, 520, 521
  bust by: Chantrey, 279, 280, 707, 739; Fletcher, 715; Thrupp, 739
  and Byron, 188, 428, 429, 436
  and the Camden Society, 582, 639
  and card-playing, 559, 560, 648, 671, 684
  and R. Cargill, 228
  at Carr's, 91
  and Catholicism in Ireland, 18
  and the Church as a career, 103
  and C. Clarkson, 7
  and T. Clarkson, 551, 648
  and Cockermouth Church, 490 seq.
  and H. Coleridge's death, 685, 686
  and S. T. Coleridge, 123, 124, 179 note, 214 seq., 245, 359
  breach with S. T. Coleridge. *See* Coleridge, S. T., breach with Wordsworth
  and S. T. Coleridge's lecture, 84
  and S. T. Coleridge's plagiarisms, 581
  S. Coleridge's dedication, 661, 662
  at the Colliers', 79, 167
  and Constable, 312
  and T. Cooper, 667 and note
  and copyright, 121, 541, 544, 566, 567, 570, 596, 607, 617
  and J. Cottle, 594
  death, 696, 835, 838
  and De Quincey, 103, 137, 161, 187, 195, 196
  and R. Duppa, 91, 92
  and the *Edinburgh Magazine*, 213
  and the *Edinburgh Review*. See *Edinburgh Review*
  eyesight, 240, 426, 537, 565, 653
  and Faber, 628, 655
  family prayers, 647, 648
  and Miss Fenwick, 560 seq., 611, 662, 697, 719 note
  and C. Fielding, 459
  financial affairs, 358 seq., 450, 451, 486, 600, 603 note, 617, 618, 625, 626, 758
  at Mrs. Fletcher's, with Mrs. Wordsworth, 661
  funeral, 697, 856, 857
  in Germany, 359, 528 seq.
  and Glasgow University, 659
  and Goethe, 374, 480, 562
  handwriting, 658
  and Haydon, 241
  and Hayward's *Faust*, 423 and note
  and Hazlitt, 169
  and Hazlitt's (review of Coleridge's *Lay Sermon*), 202
  attacked by Hazlitt, 151, 169, 200, 202
  health, 563, 565, 621, 650, 681
  at the Hoares' with Mrs. Wordsworth, 462, 533, 596, 618, 653, 659, 664
  Holland visited with Mrs. Wordsworth, 293, 295, 296

GENERAL INDEX 1107

Wordsworth, William—*contd.*
  and Leigh Hunt, 166, 169, 854
  and E. Irving, 304
  Isle of Man and Scotland visited, 427, 430, 433
  Italian tours: plans, 324, 355, 358, 492, 496, 497, 501, 505, 510,
    512 seq., 607, 618; 1820 tour, 243 seq.; 1837 tour, 515 seq.
  and Jeffrey, 151, 161, 461, 535, 699
  and J. Kenyon, 443, 546
  at J. Kenyon's, 494, 570
  and C. Lamb, 103, 295, 356, 833
  dedication to Lamb, 691
  dedication of C. Lamb's *Final Memorials*, 682
  epitaph and verses on Lamb, 468, 477
  letters from C. Lamb, 469, 471 seq., 476, 477
  and C. Lamb's *Letters*, 671, 853
  visits M. Lamb, 615
  at the Lambs', 10, 215, 216, 242
  —— with Mrs. Wordsworth, 165 seq., 240, 257, 304
  and a landlord at Kendal, 186
  and W. S. Landor, 379, 380, 492, 509, 543, 581
  letters by Landor, 749, 818, 820
  see also Landor, W. S., *Satire on Satirists*
  and the laureateship, 631, 653
  lectures by Dawson, 659, 660
  letters to: Mrs. Clarkson, 159, 680; C. J. Fox, 551, 625; J. Monk-
    house, 463; Crabb Robinson, 581; Sir W. Scott introducing
    Crabb Robinson, 266 and note; Lord Wallis [Wallace, Thomas,
    Baron Wallace?], 609
  library, 785, 807
  and Lightfoot, 480
  and Lofft's *Ernest*, 573
  in London, 73, 78, 303 seq., 492 seq., 514, 533 seq., 653
  —— with Mrs. Wordsworth, 165 seq., 212, 240 seq., 256 seq.,
    291 seq., 355 seq., 457, 569 seq., 595 seq., 615 seq., 664 seq.
  and Miss Mackenzie, 389, 519, 522, 801
  at Malvern with Mrs. Wordsworth, 690, 691
  memorial, 697, 698, 700, 706 seq., 710, 714, 718, 726, 747, 748, 752,
    832, 835, 836, 856
  and T. Monkhouse's last illness, 314
  and the Monkhouses, 256, 635. *See also* tour 1820
  at T. Monkhouse's, 214, 217, 241, 242, 256, 291 seq., 303
  and the B. Montagus, 170, 210, 211, 358, 505. *See also* Coleridge,
    S. T., breach with Wordsworth
  and J. Montgomery, 83, 84, 693, 748
  monument. *See* memorial
  and T. Moore, 291, 723
  and Moxon, 495
  at Moxon's, 497, 533, 653
  and music, 293
  and Niccolini, 523
  and Mrs. Ogle, 601
  in Paris, 248, 255, 515 seq.
  pictures, 572, 711
  and Poole, 599
  and the Poor Law Amendment Bill, 458, 459

III—T

WORDSWORTH, William—*contd.*

portrait by: Mrs. Aders, 618; T. Carrick, 674; R. Carruthers, 217; Miss Gillies, 582, 781; (Hancock), 500, 502; Haydon, 239 seq.; H. H. Pickersgill, 457 seq.; H. W. Pickersgill, 426, 715; J. Severn, 521; Slater, 509; T. Woolner, 707, 708; L. C. Wyon, 664, 665, 674; W. Wyon, 572

and Sir R. Price, 538, 539

and D. Quillinan. *See* Quillinan, Dorothy, last illness and death; Quillinan, E., marriage

breach with E. Quillinan, 671, 672, 674, 681

at Quillinan's with Mrs. Wordsworth, 357

and F. Reynolds, 460

and J. C. Richmond, 694, 695

and Rio's book, 618, 619 note

and Anthony Robinson, 74, 92, 103

and Crabb Robinson, 189, 287, 288, 438, 523, 531, 533 seq., 670, 697

Crabb Robinson an amanuensis for, 459, 460, 528, 649

dedication to Crabb Robinson, 1, 592, 603, 608 and note, 611 seq.

Crabb Robinson as an executor, 457, 495, 604

gift to Crabb Robinson, 849

gifts from Crabb Robinson, 442, 443, 591, 639, 640, 643, 651, 653

introduction to Crabb Robinson, 2 and note, 6, 10, 11, 845

Crabb Robinson's visits to Rydal: 1816, 186 and note seq., 850; 1821, 271 seq.; 1826, 339 seq.; 1833, 427 seq.; 1835, 469 seq.; 1838, 559 seq.; 1840, 587 seq.; 1841, 603 seq.; 1842, 621 seq.; 627 seq.; 1843, 637 seq.; 1844, 647 seq.; 1845, 655 seq.; 1846, 660 seq., 854; 1847, 670 seq., 854; 1848, 682 seq., 854; 1849, 693, 694

and Rogers, 488

at Rogers's, 293, 300, 458, 462, 534, 535, 570, 595

at Miss Rogers's, 493

and the Royal Society of Literature, 641 and note, 642

in Rome, 519, 520

and a Sarnen coachman, 244, 245, 249

and Schiller, 245

and Schlosser, 531

in Scotland, 1803 itinerary, 274 and note; 1833 tour, 427, 430, 433

and J. Severn, 520, 521

shipwreck, 256

at the Society of Arts, 292

and the Misses Solly, 662

and R. Southey, 40, 41, 179, 579

and Southey's *Doctor*, 563

and Southey's niece, 693

and the Southey family troubles, 590

stamp office appointment, 125, 358, 457, 486, 570, 617

statue by Thrupp, 717, 724, 731, 834 seq.

call on D. Stuart, 170

and C. Taggart's *Poems*, 443 and note

and T. N. Talfourd, 120, 121, 491, 682, 697

at Talfourd's, 295, 296, 356, 494, 496, 497, 569

WORDSWORTH, William—*contd.*
  and Talfourd's *Ion*. *See* Landor, W. S., *Satire on Satirists*
  at Sir H. Taylor's, 514
  at the theatre, 167, 356 seq., 494
  and disaster to trees, 565, 566
  tour on the Continent, 1820, with Mrs. Wordsworth, 240, 243 seq., 852
  —— 1837, 515 seq.
  and Wakley, 762
  and Whately, 658
  will, 457 seq., 472, 480, 486, 604, 697
  and Wilson, 160, 161, 196, 256, 467, 486, 699
  at Dr. Christopher Wordsworth's with Mrs. Wordsworth, 217
  and Dorothy Wordsworth, 257, 473, 477
  and Richard Wordsworth's estate. *See* Wordsworth, Richard
  at the Zoological Gardens with Mrs. Wordsworth, 460
  OPINIONS AND CRITICISM:
  literary:
    Ancient Mariner, 481
    Austin, S., *Characteristics of Goethe*, 430
    Baillie, J., 86, 547
    —— *Plays on the Passions*, 92
    Barbauld, A. L., and her writings, 8, 74
    Béranger's works, 517
    Blake, W., poems, 85, 328
    Browning, E. B., poems, 562
    Burns, R., poetry, 88, 102, 486, 562
    Byron and his works, 85, 93
    —— *Corsair*, 167
    —— poetry, 351, 428, 486, 736
    Campbell, T., 85, 86, 90
    Carlyle, T., writings and style, 542, 560, 561, 563, 564, 566, 567, 582
    Chambers's *Encyclopaedia*, 656
    Chatterton, T., 610, 611
    Clarkson, T., *Strictures on a Life of William Wilberforce*, 558, 559
    Coleridge, Hartley, 648
    Coleridge, S. T., 73, 103, 481, 487. *See also* Coleridge, S. T., breach with Wordsworth
    —— *Biographia Literaria*, 213
    Cowper, W., poetry, 486
    —— sonnet to Romney, 485
    Crabbe, G., 168
    Crowe, W., *Lewesdon Hill*, 16
    Darwin, Erasmus, 626
    Dryden, J., 608
    Dyer, G., *Life of Robert Robinson*, 4
    Edinburgh Review, 736, 833
    Elliott, E., 485, 710
    Ferguson, R., sonnets, 672
    Gladstone, W. E., *State in its Relations with the Church*, 564
    Goethe, 478, 507, 627 seq.
    Goldsmith, O., *Traveller*, 517

WORDSWORTH, William—*contd.*
  OPINIONS AND CRITICISMS—*contd.*
    literary:
      Gray, T., poetry, 90
      Hallam, H., *Constitutional History of England*, 661
      Hazlitt, W., 169, 170
      Heberden, W., *Letters of Cicero to Atticus*, 564
      Heraud, J. H., 565
      Hogg, J., 850
      Jeffrey, F., 695
      Johnson, S., 103
      Keble, J., poetry, 803
      Lamb, C., 453, 487
      Landor, W. S., 82, 516
      Langhorne, T., works, 517
      Longfellow, H. W., 678
      Martineau, H., *Life in a Sick Room*, 636
      men and books, 565
      Milton, J., 479, 484 seq., 628
      the Oxford *Tracts*, 576
      his own poetic faculty, 466, 776
      poets and domestic life, 667
      fancy and imagination in poetry, 784
      styles in poetry, 562, 608
      Quarterly Review, 534, 833
      Crabb Robinson
      —— articles on: *Convention of Cintra*, 74; *Goethe*, 430; *Prussian Reform*, 319
      —— memoirs, 480, 627
      —— *Supplement* to Clarkson's *Strictures on a Life of William Wilberforce*, 558, 559, 568
      Rogers, S., as a poet, 85
      Russell, T., sonnets, 293
      Scott, Sir W., *Harold the Dauntless*, 220 and note
      —— poetry, 82, 85, 429, 486, 850
      —— *Life*, by Lockhart, 534
      Shakespeare, W., 93, 466, 486, 628, 776
      Shelley, P. B., 351, 485
      —— *Cenci*, 409
      sonnet, 484, 485
      Southey, R., and his works, 82, 87 and note, 93, 169, 193, 428, 467, 504, 507, 508, 510, 516, 565
      —— *Doctor*, 537, 538
      Tasso, 89
      Talfourd, T. N., *Letters of Charles Lamb*, 853
      Taylor, I., writings, 563, 564
      Voss, J. H., *Luise*, 447
      Watts, A., poetry, 803
      Whewell, W., hexameters, 584
      White, H. Kirke, 82
      Wilson, J., poetry, 82
      writings, 10, 11, 41, 73, 89, 93, 94, 96, 101, 166, 167, 170, 188, 190, 191, 240, 339, 535, 608, 616, 628, 680

WORDSWORTH, William—*contd.*

  OPINIONS AND CRITICISMS—*contd.*

    miscellaneous:

      Dr. Arnold, 473, 476

      works of art, 215, 253, 257, 270, 357, 459, 494, 517, 519

      the Church, 83, 90, 434, 475, 478, 486, 571

      definition of a good churchman, 815

      Dissenters' Chapels Bill, 644, 645

      Fox, C. J., 103

      friendship, 80

      Harden, J., 566

      houses and natural surroundings, 622

      language, 359

      the Maynooth question, 654

      pensions on the civil list, 310

      Perceval's assassination, 83, 84

      politics, 74, 103, 158, 169, 177, 183, 292, 304, 305, 405, 429 seq., 448, 450, 459, 510, 531, 597, 656

      preaching, 593

      the press, 86

      the Queen's trial, 242 and note, 243

      religion, 65, 87, 158, 246, 304, 326, 327, 331, 332, 335, 363, 469, 479, 481 and note, 482, 490, 550, 559, 565, 628, 647, 648, 655, 711, 855

      Crabb Robinson, 197, 534

      Crabb Robinson's legal career, 355

      Roebuck, 532

      Lady Walter Scott, 91

      sensibility, 77

      slavery, 428

      social conditions, 90, 127

      solitude, 537

      Yorkshire scenery, 340

  PERSONAL QUALITIES:

    appearance, 493, 500, 502, 531, 596

    character: adverse criticism, 17, 85, 87, 118, 127, 135, 176, 179, 190, 195, 196, 212, 213, 218, 220, 223, 245, 361, 432, 467, 512, 530, 531, 563, 586, 618, 644, 653, 668, 681, 709 and note, 781; balanced criticism, 143, 158, 159, 166, 234, 516, 522, 533, 535, 564; favourable criticism, 80, 241, 242, 256, 472, 597, 845

    as a child, 487, 488

    conversation, 169, 429, 481, 521, 614

    relations with his family, 16, 131, 166, 188, 257, 297, 474, 487, 611, 616, 657

    demands on his friends, 490 seq., 523, 531, 633

    condition of his mind, 85, 102, 234, 563, 659, 660, 682, 685, 854

    and money matters, 125, 248, 505, 521, 657

    as a poet, 47, 52, 73, 76, 136, 138, 184, 188, 467, 567, 657, 775, 857

    as a writer on politics, 184, 567

    as a sightseer and traveller,   *See* his various tours

  BOOKS, ETC., RELATING TO:

    Fletcher, E., lines to, 711

    Hood, E. P., *William Wordsworth, a Biography*, 762, 763

WORDSWORTH, William—*contd.*
  BOOKS, ETC., RELATING TO—*contd.*
    Landor, W. S., *Ode* to, 440
    Wordsworth, C., *Memoirs of W. Wordsworth*, 709, 711, 712
    articles:
      in the *Examiner*, 697
      by Howitt, W., 659
      by Hutton, R. H., in the *National Review*, 764
      in the *Inquirer*, 696, 857
      in the *Inverness Courier*, 699
      by Jeffrey, F., 636 note, 638
      in the *North British Review*, 812
      by Richardson, Lady, 723 and note
      by Crabb Robinson, 697; for the National Portrait Gallery catalogue, 811
      by Talfourd, T. N., 120, 259
      by Scott, J., 259, 260
      in *The Times*, 697
    mentioned in:
      Arnold, M., *Essays in Criticism*, 822
      Bagehot, W., on *Poetry*, 813
      Chorley, H. F., *Memorials of Mrs. Hemans*, 505
      Coleridge, S. T., *Biographia Literaria*, 210, 213, 667
      De Quincey, T., *Autobiography*, 738
      Hazlitt, W., *Literary Remains*, 780
      —— *Spirit of the Age*, 322, 377
      Horne, R. H., *New Spirit of the Age*, 642
      Hunt, J. H. Leigh, *Lord Byron and some of his Contemporaries*, 354
      —— *Feast of the Poets*, 138
      Landor, W. S., *Imaginary Conversations*, 626, 642
      —— *Satire upon Satirists*, 506 seq., 514 seq.
      Lloyd, C., *Desultory Thoughts*, 297
      Martineau, H., *Obituary* of Mrs. Wordsworth, 781
      Moore, T., *Memoirs, Journal, and Correspondence*, 759
      Crabb Robinson, *Supplement to Strictures on a Life of William Wilberforce*, 553
      Rogers, S., *Table Talk*, 758
      Smith, H. and J., *Rejected Addresses*, 112
    mentioned, 48, 51, 68, 88, 110, 130, 133, 134, 148, 150, 174, 185, 201, 205, 232, 238, 259, 262, 308, 381, 383, 386, 387, 401, 409, 411, 511, 545, 550, 574, 679, 727, 746, 775, 778, 800, 806, 819
  WORKS:
    writings, 14, 17, 50, 79, 82 seq., 93, 94, 104, 106, 129, 130, 140, 144, 146, 181, 188, 268 and note, 369, 390, 464, 467, 566, 638, 639, 735, 799, 834. *See also* opinions and criticisms; *Annual Review* and, 143; *Edinburgh Review* and, 161, 268, 425, 434, 493, 500, 696; Galignani's edn., 378; read in Germany, 224, 366, 368, 370, 531; notes to the poems, 668, 672; parodies, 302 and note, 388, 389, 424, 425, 801; plans for editions, 213, 674, 697; sonnets, 17, 149, 150, 229, 443, 567, 658; *Quarterly Review*, by H. Taylor, 452; Taylor, H., article in *Notes on Books*, 741; poems to Mrs. Wordsworth, 616

WORDSWORTH, William—*contd.*

WORKS—*contd.*

collected poems:

Lyrical Ballads, 1798, 6, 23, 93, 152, 190, 224, 625, 835

—— 1800, preface, 10

Poems, 1815, 161, 164 seq., 241, 263, 849, 850

—— preface, 191, 200, 281, 461

Memorials of a Tour on the Continent, 1822, 249 seq., 272, 278, 281, 282, 525

(*Ecclesiastical Sketches*), 1822, 65, 282, 335, 628 and note, 855 and note

Poetical Works, 1827, 334 seq., 344

Selections, 1832, 403

Poetical Works, 1832: 422 and note, 469

(*Yarrow Revisited and other Poems*), 1835: 434, 435, 449, 459, 463, 469, 495, 539 and note

Poetical Works, 1837: 482, 489, 496, 505

(*Sonnets of W. Wordsworth*), 1838: 551

(*Poems, Chiefly of Early and Late Years*), 1842: 592, 603, 612 seq.

—— *Memorials of a Tour in Italy,* 592, 612, 614

—— (*Sonnets upon the Punishment of Death*), 636; review in the *Quarterly,* 606 and note, 607

Poems in one volume, 1845: 654, 655, 657

Poetical Works, 1857: 765, 766

(*Earlier Poems*), ed. Johnston, W., 1857: 836

separate poems:

'And is it among rude untutored Dales?' 846 and note

Beggars, 10

'Behold an emblem of our human mind,' 711

(*Borderers*), 502, 503

Brothers, 79, 106, 188, 551

Brownie, 267 and note

Brownie's Cell, 240, 267 and note

Character of the Happy Warrior, 89

Chiabrera, translations from, 378, 719

('Clarkson! it was an obstinate hill to climb:'), 551

Composed on the Eve of the Marriage of a Friend, 336 and note

('Companion by whose buoyant spirit cheered'), 1, 592, 603, 608 and note, 611 seq.

Cuckoo-clock, 718, 719 and note

Cuckoo at Laverna, 528, 533

Cumberland Beggar, 84

Daffodils, 145, 166

['Deign, Sovereign Mistress to accept a lay'], 656 and note

Eagle and the Dove, 619 note

Eclipse of the Sun, 252, 525

Effusion in the Pleasure-Ground on the Banks of the Bran, 269 and note

Elegiac Stanzas, 249, 250, 278, 512 and note

Ellen Irwin, 740 and note

epigram on Evans, 538

Epistle to Sir George Howland Beaumont, 615

Excursion, 65, 147, 152 seq., 195 and note, 212, 275, 288, 327, 332 and note, 490, 530, 680, 849 and note

—— lines on the Shell, 507, 516

WORDSWORTH, William—*contd.*
  WORKS—*contd.*
    separate poems:
      Excursion, review in the: *Eclectic,* 158, 159, 849; *Edinburgh,* 159;
          Examiner, 151, 202; *Quarterly,* by C. Lamb, 153, 166, 471
      Fidelity, 191, 224, 628
      ['Five years have past'], 20, 93
      'Giordano, verily thy Pencil's skill,' 711
      ⟨*Guilt and Sorrow*⟩, 169, 615 and note
      Hart Leap Well, 18
      'How beautiful the Queen of Night on high,' 711
      'How sweet it is when Mother Fancy rocks,' 94 and note
      ⟨*Intimations of Immortality*⟩, 330, 331
      'It was a *moral* end for which they fought,' 846 and note
      Kitten and the Falling Leaves, 89, 93, 191
      Laodamia, 167
      Leech gatherer.   See *Resolution and Independence*
      'Let other bards of angels sing,' 616
      Lines left upon a seat in a Yew Tree, 221 and note
      Lucy Gray, 190
      Matron of Jedborough, 346, 799
      Michael, 551
      Night-piece, 166
      Norman Boy, 590, 601
      'Now that all hearts are glad,' 135 and note, 136, 848
      ('O Nightingale! thou surely art'), 166
      Oak and the Broom, 190
      [Ode on the Installation of H.R.H. Prince Albert], 664
      'O'er the wide earth on mountain and on plain,' 846 and note
      'Once in a lonely hamlet I sojourned,' 10
      'Our walk was far among the ancient trees,' 616
      Peter Bell, 94 seq., 111, 230, 241, 636, 801
      —— review, 233, 234
      'Praised be the Art whose subtle power could stay,' 709 and note, 838
      Prelude, 41, 602, 711, 778, 856
      Recluse, 132, 339, 832
      ⟨*Resolution and Independence*⟩, 18, 84, 85, 90, 190, 289
      Rob Roy's Grave, 718
      Russian Fugitive, 632 and note
      Ruth, 107, 247
      'She dwelt among the untrodden ways,' 191
      'She was a Phantom of delight,' 616
      Somnambulist, 437 and note
      Sonnets from the Italian of Michael Angelo, 92, 378
      Stepping Westward, 346
      ⟨*Suggested by a portrait from the pencil of F. Stone*⟩, 512
      Thanksgiving Ode, 182, 212
      'The Land we from our fathers had in trust,' 846 and note
      Thorn, 661 and note
      [*Tintern Abbey*], 20, 93
      To a Highland Girl, 89
      To Joanna, 193, 194
      To a Painter, 616
      To the Cuckoo, 89
      Two Thieves, 145 and note

WORDSWORTH, William—*contd.*
  WORKS—*contd.*
    separate poems:
      'Two Voices are there;' 10
      Waggoner, 93, 101, 102, 636, 691
      —— dedication to C. Lamb, 691
      Wansfell, 628
      We are Seven, 93, 481
      'Where lies the land to which yon ship must go,' 94 and note
      ['While poring Antiquarians search the ground'], 521
      White Doe of Rylstone, 168, 170, 636
      —— review in the *Edinburgh*, 178; *Quarterly*, 181
      'Why should we weep or mourn,' 711
      (*Written after the death of Charles Lamb*), 468, 477
      Yarrow Unvisited, 346
      'Ye Lime-trees ranged before this hallowed Urn,' 312 and note
      Yew Trees, 166, 192, 370
      'Young England,' 577, 649 and note, 651, 856
    prose works:
      Convention of Cintra, 20, 41, 74, 115, 127
      —— review, 9, 13, 15, 74
      (*Description of the Scenery of the English Lakes*), 47, 111
      Letter to a friend of Robert Burns, 182, 184, 220, 223, 356, 433
      Letter on Railroads, 648
      On Epitaphs, 30
      note on the Poor Law Amendment Bill, 458, 459, 510
      political pamphlets, 184, 567
      preface to Hayward's *Faust*, 423 note, 425
WORDSWORTH, William [son of W. Wordsworth]
    at Charterhouse, 281
    as a child, 188
    Miss Fenwick's gift, 663
    health, 562
    in London, 615, 657, 811
    marriage, 659 seq.
    and Mary Monkhouse, 254
    personal qualities, 431, 712, 713
    and J. C. Richmond, 695
    gift from Crabb Robinson, 659, 660
    gift to Crabb Robinson, 660
    and the stamp-office appointment, 457, 615, 617
    and D. Wordsworth's death, 749
    and J. Wordsworth, 689 and note
    executor to W. Wordsworth, 604
    and W. Wordsworth's statue, 717
    and Mrs. Wordsworth's death, 781
  mentioned, 559, 587, 603, 639, 668
WORDSWORTH, Mrs. William, Fanny, *born* Graham, 660, 661, 681
WORDSWORTH, William [grandson of W. Wordsworth], 661, 683, 753
WORDSWORTH FAMILY
    and the Coleridges, 803
    and home comfort, 733
World, The, 175
WORSLEY, 410, 411, 414, 492, 509

WRANGHAM, Francis, 320
WRIGHT, John, 258, 259
WRIGHT, Thomas
    Essays on the Literature of the Middle Ages, 658
    introduction to the *Seven Sages of Rome*, 811
WRIGHT, Waller Rodwell, 2, 36, 60, 62, 85, 129, 336, 418
    WORKS:
    Horae Ionicae, 2, 129, 336
    Inaugural Ode [*on the Duke of Gloucester's installation at Cambridge*],
        663
WYE, Wordsworth's verses on ['Five years have past'], 20, 93
WYON, Leonard Charles, medallion of Wordsworth, 664, 665, 674
WYON, William, 664, 674
    portrait of Wordsworth, 572

YATES, 83
YEW TREES, the original of Wordsworth's verse, 192
YONGE, Charlotte Mary, *Heir of Redclyffe*, 803 seq.
YORK, Duke of, essay by Coleridge, 35, 37 and note
YORKSHIRE, Wordsworth recommends an itinerary, 340
YORKSHIRE HOUSES, 622
YOUNG, Arthur, 284
YOUNG, Charles Mayne, 167, 284, 287
YOUNG, Edward, 42
    [*Night Thoughts*], illustrated by Blake, 25
YOUNG, George, 582

ZOOLOGICAL GARDENS
    visited with Landor, 494
    —— the Wordsworths, 460

TITLES

Titles and first lines to which reference under the author may be found. Biographical works and the works of Shakespeare and Milton are not included.

Abbot, The. Scott, Sir W.
Abridgment of the Light of Nature Pursued, by Abraham Tucker. Hazlitt, W.
Absentee, The. Edgeworth, M.
Adam Bede. Evans, M. A. (George Eliot)
Adela Cathcart. MacDonald, G.
Admiral's Daughter, The. Marsh, A. C.
Adonais. Shelley, P. B.
Adventures of a Younger Son. Trelawny, E. J.
—— *of Susan Hopley.* Crowe, M.
—— *of Ulysses.* Lamb, C.
Advice to His Son. Osborne, F.
After Dark. Collins, W. W.
Aids to Reflection. Coleridge, S. T.
Album Verses. Lamb, C.
Alchemist, The. Jonson, B.
Alfred. Cottle, J.
Alfred de Musset. Palgrave, F. T.
Alice. Lytton, Lord.
Alliance between Church and State. Warburton, W.
Alton Locke. Kingsley, C.
Amatonda. tr., Robinson, H. C.
American Notes for General Circulation. Dickens, C.
Anastasius. Hope, T.
Ancient Mariner, The. Coleridge, S. T.
—— *Scottish Poems.* Pinkerton, J.
'And is it among rude untutored Dales?' Wordsworth, W.
Andrea of Hungary. Landor, W. S.
Anna St. Ives. Holcroft, T.
Annals of a Quiet Neighbourhood. MacDonald, G.
—— *of the Parish.* Galt, J.
Anne of Geierstein. Scott, Sir W.
Answer to the Address of the Rt. Hon. H. Grattan to his Fellow Citizens. Duigenan, P.
Antigone. Sophocles.
Antiquary, The. Scott, Sir W.
Apologia pro Vitâ Suâ. Newman, J. H.
Appeal to the Middle Classes. Newman, F. W.
Apple, The. Crosse, A.
Armageddon. Townsend, G.
Arthur Coningsby. Sterling, J.
Arundel. Cumberland, R.
Athenian Captive. Talfourd, Sir T. N.
Attempts in Verse. Jones, J.
Aurora Leigh. Browning, E. B.

Bachelor's Complaint. Lamb, C.
Balder Dead. Arnold, M.
Ballad of Fridolin. Collier, J. P.
Balloon, The. Aikin, L.
Barchester Towers. Trollope, A.
Bard, The. Gray, T.
Barnaby Rudge. Dickens, C.
Beacon, The. Baillie, J.
Beggars. Wordsworth, W.
'Beguiled into forgetfulness of care.' *Suggested by a Portrait.*
    Wordsworth, W.
'Behold an emblem of our human mind.' Wordsworth, W.
Belton Estate. Trollope, A.
Beppo. Byron, Lord.
Bertram. Maturin, C. R.
Bertrams, The. Trollope, A.
Betrothed, The. Scott, Sir W.
Biographia Borealis. Worthies of Yorkshire and Lancashire.
    Coleridge, Hartley.
Biographia Literaria. Coleridge, S. T.
Black Doctor, The. Crosse, A.
Black Dwarf, The. Scott, Sir W.
Blakesmore in H——-shire. Lamb, C.
Blank Verse, by Charles Lloyd and Charles Lamb. Lamb, C.
Bleak House. Dickens, C.
Blithedale Romance. Hawthorne, N.
Blue Beard. Colman, G.
Bon Enfant, Un. Kock, Paul de.
Book of the Church. Southey, R.
Borderers, The. Wordsworth, W.
Bothie of Tober-na-Vuolich. Clough, A. H.
Boyne Watch. Banim, Michael.
Boyne Water. Banim, John.
Bracebridge Hall. Irving, W.
Braes of Yarrow. Logan, J.
Brambletye House. Smith, H.
Braut von Corinth. Goethe.
Bravo, The. Cooper, J. F.
Breton Mother, The. Norton, Caroline.
Brick and Marble. Street, G. E.
Bridal of Triermain. Scott, Sir W.
Bride of Abydos. Byron, Lord.
—— *of Lammermoor.* Scott, Sir W.
Bride's Tragedy. Beddoes, T. L.
Bridge of Sighs. Hood, T.
Briefwechsel mit einem Kind. Arnim, B. von.
British Essayists, The. Ed., Chalmers, A.
—— *Novelists and Their Styles.* Masson, D.
Broad Stone of Honour. Digby, K. H.
Broken Heart. Ford, J.
'Broken in fortune . . .' Wordsworth, W.
Brothers, The. Wordsworth, W.
Brownie, The. Wordsworth, W.
Brownie's Cell, The. Wordsworth, W.

Cain. Byron, Lord.
Calamities of Authors. Disraeli, I.
Caleb Williams. Godwin, W.
Camilla. D'Arblay, F.
Candide. Voltaire.
Carmen Nuptiale. Southey, R.
—— *Triumphale.* Southey, R.
Casa Guidi Windows. Browning, E. B.
Castaway, The. Cowper, W.
Castilian, The. Talfourd, Sir T. N.
Castle of Indolence. Thomson, J.
Catiline. Croly, G.
Cato. Addison, J.
Caxtons, The. Lytton, Lord.
Cecil, or the Adventures of a Coxcomb. Gore, C.
—— *a Peer.* Gore, C.
Cecilia. D'Arblay, F.
Cenci, The. Shelley, P. B.
Ceylon. De Quincey, T.
Changeling, The. Mrs. Leicester's School. Lamb, C.
Chapter on Ears, A. Lamb, C.
Character of the Happy Warrior. Wordsworth, W.
Characteristics of Women : Moral, Poetical, and Historical.
    Jameson, A. B.
Charles. Naylor, S.
Chartism. Carlyle, T.
Cherry and Violet. Manning, A.
Childe Harold's Pilgrimage. Byron, Lord.
Chimney Sweeper. Blake, W.
Christabel. Coleridge, S. T.
Christian Endurance. Milnes, R. M.
Christmas Carol. Dickens, C.
Chronicles of Carlingford. Oliphant, M.
—— *of the Canongate.* Scott, Sir W.
Church of St. Salvador. Memorials of a Tour on the Continent.
    Wordsworth, W.
Citation and Examination of William Shakespeare. Landor, W. S.
'Cities but rarely are the haunts of men.' Landor, W. S.
City of the Plague. Wilson, J.
Civic Sermons to the People. Barbauld, A. L.
Clarissa. Richardson, S.
'Clarkson! it was an obstinate hill to climb.' Wordsworth, W.
Clio, or a Discourse on Taste. Usher, J.
Close Comments on a Straggling Speech. De Quincey, T.
Clubs of London, Marsh, C.
Cocu, Le. Kock, Paul de.
Codification Proposals. Bentham, J.
Cœlebs in Search of a Wife. More, H.
Colloquies. Sir Thomas More. Southey, R.
Colombe's Birthday. Browning, R.
Commentaries on the Life and Reign of Charles I. Disraeli, I.
Commentarius in Apocalypsem Johannes. Eichhorn, K. F.
Communist, The. Elliot, E.
Compensation. Essays. Emerson, R. W.
Complete Edition of the Poets of Great Britain. Anderson, R.

Composed on the Eve of the Marriage of a Friend. Wordsworth, W.
Conciones ad Populum. Coleridge, S. T.
Confessions of a Beautiful Soul. Goethe.
—— *of a Drunkard.* Lamb, C.
—— *of an English Opium Eater.* De Quincey, T.
—— *of an Inquiring Spirit.* Coleridge, S. T.
Coningsby. Disraeli, B.
Conspiracy of Gowrie. Rough, Sir W.
Conspirators, The. Quillinan, E.
Constitutional History of England. Hallam, H.
Contarini Fleming. Disraeli, B.
Convention of Cintra. Wordsworth, W.
Conversations of James Northcote, Esq., R.A. Hazlitt, W.
Corn Law Rhymes. Elliott, E.
Correggio. Oehlenschläger, A.
Corsair, The. Byron, Lord.
Corse de Leon. James, G. P. R.
Count Julian. Landor, W. S.
Count Robert of Paris. Scott, Sir W.
Country Justice. Langhorne, J.
Country Neighbours. Burney, S. H.
Course of True Love never did run Smooth. Reade, C.
Crofton Boys. Playfellow, The. Martineau, H.
Cuckoo-clock. Wordsworth, W.
Cuckoo at Laverna. Wordsworth, W.
Cumberland Beggar, The. Wordsworth, W.
Cupid as Landscape Painter. Goethe.
Curiosities of Literature. Disraeli, I.
Curse of Kehama. Southey, R.
Cyril Thornton. Hamilton, T.

Daffodils. Wordsworth, W.
Dark Ages. Maitland, S. R.
Darkness. Byron, Lord.
David Copperfield. Dickens, C.
David Elginbrod. MacDonald, G.
Death and Doctor Hornbook. Burns, R.
Death's Jest Book. Beddoes, T. L.
Deerbrook. Martineau. H.
Defaulter, The. Whimsicalities. Hood, T.
Deformed Transformed. Byron, Lord.
Deformity, an Essay. Hay, W.
'Deign, Sovereign Mistress to accept a lay.' Wordsworth, W.
Deloraine. Godwin, W.
Démocratie en Amérique. De Tocqueville.
Descent into the Maelstrom. Poe, E. A.
Description of the Scenery of the English Lakes. Wordsworth, W.
Deserted Village, The. Goldsmith, O.
Desultory Thoughts. Lloyd, C.
Diamond Necklace. Carlyle, T.
Diary Illustrative of the Times of George IV. Brougham, H. P.
—— *of an Ennuyée.* Jameson, A. B.
Dinarbas. Knight, E. C.
Diogenes' Lanthorn. Taylor, T.
Discorsi. Machiavelli.

Discourse on the Study of the Law of Nature and Nations. Mackintosh, Sir J.

Disowned. Lytton, Lord.

Dissertation on the Progress of Ethical Philosophy. Mackintosh, Sir J.

Dissuasive from Popery, A. Taylor, Jeremy.

Diversions of Purley. Tooke, J. H.

Divine Comedy. Dante, A.

—— *Drama of History and Civilization.* Smith, James.

Doctor, The. Southey, R.

Doctor Thorne. Trollope, A.

Dombey and Son. Dickens, C.

Don Juan. Byron, Lord.

Down Hall. Prior, M.

Dramatic Works of William Shakespeare. Campbell, T.

Dream, The. Baillie, J.

Dream, The. Byron, Lord.

Dreams of the Intercourse of Souls. Epistles. Moore, T.

Dred. Stowe, H. E. B.

Dumb Orators. Crabbe, G.

Dunciad. Pope, A.

Dunluce Castle. Quillinan, E.

Eagle and the Dove. Wordsworth, W.

Earl of Brecon. Landor, R. E.

Early Recollections chiefly relating to the late S. T. Coleridge. Cottle, J.

Eastern Life, Past and Present. Martineau, H.

Ecclesiastical Sonnets. Wordsworth, W.

Eclipse of the Sun. Wordsworth, W.

Edmund Oliver. Lloyd, C.

Edwin the Fair. Taylor, Sir H.

Effusion in the Pleasure Ground. Wordsworth, W.

Egmont. Goethe.

Election, The. Brittaine, G.

Elegant Extracts in Verse. Knox, V.

Elegiac Stanzas. Wordsworth, W.

Ellen Irwin. Wordsworth, W.

Eloquence of the British Senate. Hazlitt, W.

Elsie Venner. Holmes, O. W.

Émile. Rousseau, J. J.

Émilie de Coulanges. Edgeworth, M.

Emma. Austen, J.

Emperor's New Clothes. Andersen, Hans.

Encyclopaedia of English Literature. Ed., Chambers, R.

England and the English. Lytton, Lord.

English Bards and Scotch Reviewers. Byron, Lord.

—— *Humourists.* Thackeray, W. M.

—— *Mail Coach.* De Quincey, T.

—— *Traits.* Emerson, R. W.

Ennui. Edgeworth, M.

Enquiry concerning Political Justice. Godwin, W.

Eöthen. Kinglake, A. W.

Epicurean, The. Moore, T.

Epipsychidion. Shelley, P. B.

Epistle to Sir George Howland Beaumont, Bart. Wordsworth, W.
Epistles, Odes and other Poems. Moore, T.
Ernest. Lofft, C.
Ernest Maltravers. Lytton, Lord.
Esmond. Thackeray, W. M.
Essay on the Dramatic Character of Sir J. Falstaff. Morgann, M.
—— *on the Influence of Authority.* Lewis, G. C.
—— *on the Literary Character.* Disraeli, I.
—— *on the Military Policy and Institutions of the British Empire.* Pasley, C. W.
—— *on the Nature and Principles of Taste.* Alison, A.
—— *on the Philosophical Writings of Cicero.* Hallam, A. H.
—— *on the Philosophy of Composition.* Poe, E. A.
—— *towards a Theory of Apparitions.* Ferrier, J.
—— *towards a Topographical History of the County of Norfolk.* Blomefield, F.
Essays in Criticism. Arnold, M.
—— *Moral and Political.* Southey, R.
—— *of Elia.* Lamb, C.
—— *on his own Times.* Coleridge, S. T.
—— *on the Drama.* Donne, W. B.
—— *on the Literature of the Middle Ages.* Wright, T.
Eugene Aram. Lytton, Lord.
Eustace Conway. Maurice, J. F. D.
Evangeline. Longfellow, H. W.
Eve of St. Agnes. Keats, J.
Eve of the Conquest and other Poems. Taylor, Sir H.
Evelina. D'Arblay, F.
Excursion, The. Wordsworth, W.
Exposure of Misrepresentations. Robinson, H. C.

Fable of the Bees. Mandeville, B.
Factory Controversy. Martineau, H.
Facts in the Case of M. Valdemar. Poe, E. A.
—— *in Mesmerism.* Townshend, C. H.
Faerie Queene. Spenser, E.
Fair Maid of Perth. Scott, Sir W.
—— *Rosamond.* Miller, T.
Fairies of Popular Superstition. Minstrelsy. Scott, Sir W.
Fairy Ring. Taylor, J. E.
Falcon Family. Savage, M.
Fall of Saturn. Procter, B. W.
Falstaff's Letters. White, J.
Family Name. Lamb, C.
—— *Prayers.* Thornton, H.
Farbenlehre. Goethe.
Father's Memoirs of his Child. Malkin, B. H.
Faulkner. Godwin, W.
Faust. Goethe, trs. Hayward, A., and Swanwick, A.
Faustus. Marlowe, C.
Feast of the Poets. Hunt, J. H. L.
Feats on the Fjord. Playfellow, The. Martineau, H.
Felix Holt. Evans, M. A.
Felsenstrom. Stolberg.

Female Biography. Hays, M.
Female Vagrant. Guilt and Sorrow. Wordsworth, W.
Ferranti and Giulio. Landor, W. S.
Ferryman. Landor, R. E.
Festus. Bailey, P. J.
Fidelity. Wordsworth, W.
Field of Waterloo. Scott, Sir W.
Fifty Years' Recollections. Redding, C.
Fire, Famine, and Slaughter. Coleridge, S.
First Impressions of England. Miller, H.
Flood of Thessaly. Proctor, B. W.
Florence Macarthy. Morgan, Lady.
Foliage. Hunt, J. H. L.
Fool of Quality. Brook, H.
For Each and For All. Martineau, H.
'For honest men of every blood and creed.' Milnes, R. M.
Forest and Game Law Tales. Martineau, H.
Forester. Edgeworth, M.
Forester's Guide and Profitable Planter. Scott, Sir W.
Forge. Whimsicalities. Hood, T.
Fortunes of Nigel. Scott, Sir W.
Foster Mother's Tale. Coleridge, S. T.
Fountain of Arethusa. Landor, R. E.
Four Georges. Thackeray, W. M.
Fra Rupert. Landor, W. S.
Fragment on the Church. Arnold, T.
Frankenstein. Shelley, M. W.
Freiheit. Schelling.
French Wine and Politics. Martineau, H.
Friend, The. Coleridge, S. T.
Friend of Humanity and the Knife Grinder. Canning, G.
Fudges in England. Moore, T.

Gale Middleton. Smith, H.
Gardener's Daughter. Tennyson, A.
Gebir. Landor, W. S.
Geist der Zeit. Arndt, E. M.
General Theorem for A—— College Declamations. Le Grice, C. V.
Geraldine, Agnew, E. C.
German Anti-supernaturalism. Harwood, P.
German Gil Blas. Combe, W.
German Romance. Carlyle, T.
Giaour. Byron, Lord.
Gil Blas. Le Sage.
Gilbert Gurney. Hook, T.
'Giordano, verily thy Pencil's skill.' Wordsworth, W.
Giovanna of Naples. Landor, W. S.
Glencoe. Talfourd, Sir T. N.
'Goethe in Weimar sleeps.' Arnold, M.
Gold-Bug. Poe, E. A.
Golden Treasury. Palgrave, F. T.
Grace Connell. Ireland. Hall, S. C.
Great Expectations. Dickens, C.
Guilt and Sorrow. Wordsworth, W.

Gulliver's Travels.   Swift, J.
Guy Faux.   Lamb, C.
Guy Mannering.   Scott, Sir W.

Hajji Baba.   Morier, J. J.
Hajji Baba in England.   Morier, J. J.
Halloran the Pedlar.   Jameson, A. B.
Hard Times.   Dickens, C.
Harold the Dauntless.   Scott, Sir W.
Harrington.   Edgeworth, M.
Hart Leap Well.   Wordsworth, W.
Hate.   Baillie, J.
Headlong Hall.   Peacock, T. L.
Health, Five Lay Sermons.   Brown, J.
Heart of Midlothian.   Scott, Sir W.
Heaven and Earth.   Byron, Lord.
Hebrew Melodies.   Byron, Lord.
—— *Tales.*   Hurwitz.
Heir of Redclyffe.   Yonge, C. M.
Helen.   Edgeworth, M.
Herman and Dorothea.   Goethe.   tr., Whewell.
Hermsprong.   Bage, R.
Heroine, The.   Barrett, E. S.
Historic Survey of German Poetry.   Taylor, W.
Historical Sketches of Statesmen.   Brougham, H. P.
History of Brazil.   Southey, R.
—— *of British Journalism.*   Andrews, A.
—— *of Caliph Vathek.*   Beckford, W.
—— *of Civilization in England.*   Buckle, H. T.
—— *of Dissenters.*   Bogue, D.
—— *of England.*   Froude, J. A.
—— *of England.*   Hallam, H.
—— *of England.*   Lingard, J.
—— *of England.*   Macaulay, T. B.
—— *of Fiction.*   Dunlop, J.
—— *of Matthew Wald.*   Lockhart, J. G.
—— *of Rome.*   Arnold, T.
—— *of Rome.*   Niebuhr, B. G.
—— *of the Abolition of the Slave Trade.*   Clarkson, T.
—— *of the Commonwealth.*   Godwin, W.
—— *of the Decline and Fall of the Roman Empire.*   Gibbon, E.
—— *of the Eighteenth Century.*   Schlosser, F. C.
—— *of the French Revolution.*   Carlyle, T.
—— *of the French Revolutian.*   Mignet.
—— *of the Jews.*   Milman, H. H.
Holy Willie's Prayer.   Burns, R.
Honey-Moon.   Tobin, J.
Honor Delany.   Brittaine, G.
Horae Ionicae.   Wright, W. R.
House of the Seven Gables.   Hawthorne, N.
Household of Sir Thomas More.   Manning, A.
Household Words.   Dickens, C.
'How beautiful the Queen of Night on High,'   Wordsworth, W.
'How sweet it is, when Mother Fancy rocks.'   Wordsworth, W.

Hugh Trevor. Holcroft, T.
Human Body, The. Wilkinson, J. J. G.
Hunchback, The. Knowles, J. S.
Hunchback of Notre Dame. Hugo, V.
Hyacinth O'Gara. Brittaine, G.
Hymn to Mercury. Shelley, P. B.
Hypatia. Kingsley, C.
Hyperion. Keats, J.

Idylls of the King. Tennyson, A.
Illustrations of Lying. Opie, A.
—— *of Political Economy.* Martineau, H.
—— *of the Divine Government.* Smith, T. S.
*Imaginary Conversation between W. S. Landor and the Editor of Black-
    wood's Magazine.* Quillinan, E.
Imaginary Conversations. Landor, W. S.
In Memoriam. Tennyson, A.
Indicator, The. Hunt, J. H. L.
Inheritance, The. Ferrier, S. E.
Inquiry into the Genuineness of Collier's Annotated Shakespeare.
    Hamilton, N. E.
—— *into Vulgar Errors.* Browne, Sir T.
Intimations of Immortality. Wordsworth, W. Ode.
Introduction to the Library of Useful Knowledge. Brougham, H. P.
Ion. Talfourd, Sir T. N.
Iphigenia in Tauris. Goethe.
Ireland. Hall, S. C.
Irish Men and Irish Women. Brittaine, G.
Isabella. Keats, J.
Island, The. Byron, Lord.
Isle of Palms and other Poems. Wilson, J.
'It was a *moral* end for which they fought.' Wordsworth, W.
Italy. Morgan, Lady.
Italy. Rogers, S.
Italy with Sketches of Spain and Portugal. Beckford, W.
Ivanhoe. Scott, Sir W.

Jacob Faithful. Marryat, F.
Jane Eyre. Brontë, C.
Janet's Repentance. Evans, M. A. (George Eliot)
Jaqueline. Rogers, S.
Jerusalem. Blake, W.
John Gilpin. Cowper, W.
John Halifax, Gentleman. Mulock, D. M.
John Woodvil. Lamb, C.
Johnny Armstrong. *Minstrelsy.* Scott, Sir W.
Journal of a few Months' Residence in Portugal. Quillinan, D.
—— *of a Tour made in Scotland.* Wordsworth, D.
—— *of a Tour on the Continent.* Wordsworth, D.
—— *of John Woolman.* Woolman, J.
—— *of Summertime in the Country.* Willmott, R. A.
—— *on the Continent.* Hogg, T. J.
—— *written on the Coasts of Chile, Peru, and Mexico.* Hall, B.
Journey to the Coast of the Polar Sea. Franklin, Sir J.

Kendal and Windermere Railway. Wordsworth, W.
Kenilworth. Scott, Sir W.
Key to Uncle Tom's Cabin. Stowe, H. E. B.
King Coal's Levée. Scafe, J.
Kitten and the Falling Leaves. Wordsworth, W.
Klosterheim. De Quincey, T.
Kunst am Rhein. Goethe.
—— *und Alterthum.* Goethe.

L'Amie Inconnue. Edgeworth, M.
Lady Jane Grey. Miller, T.
Lady of the Lake. Scott, Sir W.
Lalla Rookh. Moore, T.
Laodamia. Wordsworth, W.
Lara. Byron, Lord.
Las Quatro-cientas. Escobar, Fray Luys d'.
Last Days of Pompeii. Lytton, Lord.
—— *Fruit off an Old Tree.* Landor, W. S.
—— *of the Barons.* Lytton, Lord.
—— *of the Mohicans.* Cooper, J. F.
Latter Day Pamphlets. Carlyle, T.
Lay Sermon. Coleridge, S. T.
Leaders in Literature. De Quincey, T.
Lectures on Modern History. Smith, G.
—— *on Poetry.* Montgomery, J.
—— *on Rhetoric and Belles Lettres.* Blair, H.
—— *on the English Comic Writers.* Hazlitt, W.
—— *on the English Poets.* Hazlitt, W.
Legacy for Young Ladies. Barbauld, A. L.
Legend of Montrose. Scott, Sir W.
Leonora. Edgeworth, M.
'Let other bards of angels sing.' Wordsworth, W.
Letter concerning the Two First Chapters of Luke. Taylor, W.
—— *of Elia to Robert Southey, Esq.* Lamb, C.
—— *to a Friend of R. Burns.* Wordsworth, W.
—— *to a Noble Lord.* Burke, E.
—— *to the Right Hon. W. Windham.* Holcroft, T.
—— *to William Smith, Esq., M.P.* Southey, R.
Letters concerning Mind. Petvin, J.
—— *from Egypt.* Gordon, Lady Duff.
—— *from Italy.* Shelley, P. B. *Prose works.*
—— *from the Hon. Horace Walpole to George Montagu, Esq.* Walpole, H.
—— *from the North of Italy.* Rose, W. S.
—— *from the South.* Campbell, T.
—— *from the Year 1774. . . . by John Wilkes, Esq.* Rough, Sir W.
—— *of a Nobleman to his Son.* Combe, W.
—— *of Cicero to Atticus.* Heberden, W.
—— *on the Laws of Man's Social Nature and Development.* Martineau, H.
—— *on the State of Politics in France.* Williams, H. M.
—— *to an Architect.* Woods, J.
—— *to Julia.* Luttrell, H.
Lettres de Virgile aux Arcades. Bettinelli.
—— *Provinciales.* Pascal, B.
Lewesdon Hill. Crowe, W.

Liber Amoris. Hazlitt, W.
Life in the Sickroom. Martineau, H.
'Life! we have been long together.' Barbauld, A. L.
Lines left upon a seat in a Yew Tree. Wordsworth, W.
Lines written among the Euganean Hills. Shelley, P. B.
Lionel Lincoln. Cooper, J. F.
Literary Remains. Coleridge, S. T.
Literary Remains. Hazlitt, W.
Little Peddlington. Poole, J.
Lives of the Admirals. Southey, R.
—— *of the Lord Chancellors and Keepers of the Great Seal of England.*
   Campbell, J.
—— *of the Most Eminent British Painters.* Cunningham, A.
—— *of the Novelists,* Scott, Sir W.
—— *of the Queens.* Strickland, A.
Locksley Hall. Tennyson, A.
Lodore. Shelley, M. W.
London. Knight, C.
Lord of the Isles. Scott, Sir W.
Lorenzino. Rough, Sir W.
Lorimer. Aikin, L.
Love. Coleridge, S. T.
Lucy Gray. Wordsworth, W.
Luise. Voss, J. H.
Lyrical Ballads. Wordsworth, W.

Madeline. Kelly, I.
Magic and Witchcraft. Donne, W. B.
Maid of Provence. Procter, B. W.
Main Chance. Hazlitt, W.
Malvern Hills. Cottle, J.
Mandeville. Godwin, W.
Manfred. Byron, Lord.
Mansfield Park. Austen, J.
Marino Falerio. Byron, Lord.
Marmion. Scott, Sir W.
Marriage. Ferrier, S. E.
Martin Chuzzlewit. Dickens, C.
Mary Barton. Gaskell, E. C. S.
Master Humphrey's Clock. Dickens, C.
Materialism in Religion. Harwood, P.
Matron of Jedborough. Wordsworth, W.
Maud. Tennyson, A.
Melusine. Goethe.
Memoirs, containing an account of his Travels. Bruce, P. H.
—— *during thirteen years at the Court of Peking.* Ripa, M.
—— *of Captain Rock.* Moore, T.
—— *of Emma Courtney.* Hays, M.
—— *of the Court of King Charles I.* Aikin, L.
—— *of the Court of King James I.*   ,,
—— *of the Court of Queen Elizabeth.*   ,,
Memorial to the Bench of Bishops. Richmond, J. C.
Memorials of a Tour in Greece. Milnes, R. M.
—— *of a Tour in Italy, 1837.* Wordsworth, W.

Memorials of a Tour on the Continent. Wordsworth, W.
—— *of Foreign Travel.* Milnes, R. M.
Men and Manners in America. Hamilton, T.
Michael. Wordsworth, W.
Michael Scott. Coleridge, S. T.
Michael Scott. Cunningham, A.
Mill on the Floss. Evans, M. A. (George Eliot)
Milton v. Southey and Landor. De Quincey, T.
Mirandola. Procter, B. W.
Mission of the Comforter. Hare, J. C.
Mr. H—. Lamb, C.
Mrs. Leicester's School. Lamb, C.
Modern Painters. Ruskin, J.
Modern Superstition. De Quincey, T.
Monaldi. Allston, W.
Monastery, The. Scott, Sir W.
Monasticon. Dugdale, Sir W.
Moustache. Kock, Paul de.
Murders in the Rue Morgue. Poe, E. A.
My Friends and Acquaintances. Patmore, P. G.
Mysteries of Udolpho. Radcliffe, A. W.
Mystery of Marie Roget. Poe, E. A.

Narrative of the Events that have taken place in France.
    Williams, H. M.
Natural History of Enthusiasm. Taylor, I.
Nature and Art. Inchbald, E.
'Needy knife grinder.' Canning, G.
Nemesis of Faith. Froude, J. A.
New Jerusalem. Swedenborg.
—— *Spirit of the Age.* Horne, R. H.
—— *Way to Pay Old Debts.* Massinger, P.
Newstead Abbey. Irving, W.
Nicholas Nickleby. Dickens, C.
Night Side of Nature. Crow, C.
Night Thoughts. Young, E.
Nightingale, The. Wordsworth, W.
Nightmare Abbey. Peacock, T. L.
Night-piece. Wordsworth, W.
Nineveh and its Remains. Layard, A. H.
Noctes Ambrosianae. Wilson, J.
Nollekens and His Times. Smith, J. T.
Norman Boy. Wordsworth, W.
Northanger Abbey. Austen, J.
Northern Antiquities. Scott, Sir W.
Notes and Lectures upon Shakespeare. Coleridge, S. T.
—— *of a Journey from Cornhill to Grand Cairo.* Thackeray, W. M.
—— *on Books.* Taylor, Sir H.
—— *on Life.* Taylor, Sir H.
—— *on the Construction of Sheepfolds.* Ruskin, J.
Nouvelle Héloïse. Rousseau, J. J.
'Now that all hearts are glad.' Wordsworth, W.
Nurse M'Vourneen's Story. Brittaine, G.
Nympholept. Smith, H.

Oak and the Broom.   Wordsworth, W.

Oakfield.   Arnold, W. D.

Occasional Discourse on the Negro Question.   Carlyle, T.

Occasional Pieces.   Byron, Lord.

Ode on Intimations of Immortality.   Wordsworth, W.

—— *on the Duke of Gloucester's Installation at Cambridge.*   Wright, W. R.

—— *on the Popular Superstitions of the Highlands.*   Collins, W.

—— *to Content.*   Barbauld, A. L.

—— *to Rae Wilson.*   Hood, T.

Odes upon Cash, Corn, Catholics, and other Matters.   Moore, T.

O'Donnel.   Morgan, Lady.

'O'er the wide earth.'   Wordsworth, W.

Of Population in answer to Mr. Malthus.   Godwin, W.

Old Chelsea Bun House.   Manning, A.

Old Curiosity Shop.   Dickens, C.

Old Mortality.   Scott, Sir W.

Oliver Cromwell.   Smith, H.

Oliver Twist.   Dickens, C.

Omniana.   Southey, R.

On a Sun-dial.   Hazlitt, W.

— *Eating and Drinking.*   Lamb, C.

— *Epitaphs.*   Wordsworth, W.

— *Hearing the Ranz des Vaches.   Memorials of a Tour of the Continent.*   Wordsworth, W.

— *Heroes, Hero-worship, and the Heroic in History.*   Carlyle, T.

— *Inconsistent Expectations.*   Barbauld, A. L.

— *Liberty.*   Mill, J. S.

— *Murder as a Fine Art.*   De Quincey, T.

— *the Custom of Hissing at the Theatres.*   Lamb, C.

— *the English Students at Rome.*   Hazlitt, W.

— *the Genius and Character of Hogarth.*   Lamb, C.

— *the Inconveniences Resulting from being Hanged.*   Lamb, C.

— *the probable effects of the Gunpowder Treason.   Guy Faux.*   Lamb, C.

'Once in a lonely hamlet I sojourned.'   Wordsworth, W.

Orations on the Judgment to Come.   Irving, E.

Ormond.   Edgeworth, M.

Osmond.   Kelty, M. A.

Osorio.   Remorse.   Coleridge, S. T.

Our Lady of the Snow.   Memorials of a Tour on the Continent.   Wordsworth, W.

Our Village.   Mitford, M. R.

'Our walk was far among the ancient trees.'   Wordsworth, W.

Palamon and Arcite.   Dryden, J.

Parisina.   Byron, Lord.

Parliamentary Index.   Burney, M.

Passages from the Diary of a Late Physician.   Warren, S.

Passages of a Working Life.   Knight, C.

Past and Present.   Carlyle, T.

Patronage.   Edgeworth, M.

Paul Ferrol.   Clive, C.

Paul's Letters to his Kinsfolk.   Scott, Sir W.

Peasant and the Prince. Martineau, H.
Peg Woffington. Reade, C.
Pelham. Lytton, Lord.
Pencillings by the Way. Willis, N. P.
Pendennis. Thackeray, W. M.
Penelope. Scargill, W. P.
Pentameron and Pentalogia. Landor, W. S.
Peregrine Pickle. Smollett, T.
Pericles and Aspasia. Landor, W. S.
Personal Influence on Present Theology. Martineau, J.
Persuasion. Austen, J.
Peter Bell. Wordsworth, W.
Peter of the Castle. Banim, J. and M.
Peter Simple. Marryat, F.
Peveril of the Peak. Scott, Sir W.
Phaethon. Kingsley, C.
Phantasmion. Coleridge, S.
Philip van Artevelde. Taylor, Sir H.
Philo-Godwin. Robinson, H. C.
Philosophical Essay on Old Maids. Hayley, W.
Physical Theory of Another Life. Taylor, I.
Pickwick Papers. Dickens, C.
Pictorial History. Knight, C.
Pilgrim's Progress. Bunyan, J.
Pilot, The. Cooper, J. F.
Pioneers, The. Cooper, J. F.
Pirate, The. Scott, Sir W.
Plain Narrative of the late Riots in London. Holcroft, T.
Plain Speaker, The. Hazlitt, W.
Playfellow, The. Martineau, H.
Plays on the Passions. Baillie, J.
Plea for the Constitution. Austin, J.
Pleasures of Hope. Campbell, T.
—— *of Memory.* Rogers, S.
Poems on the Obeah Superstition. Cargill, R.
Poet's Pilgrimage. Collier, J. P.
Poet's Pilgrimage to Waterloo. Southey, R.
Poor Relations. Lamb, C.
Popery, British and Foreign. Landor, W. S.
Popular Fallacies. Lamb, C.
Pot of Basil. Keats, J.
'Praised be the Art whose subtle power could stay.' Wordsworth, W.
Prefaces, Biographical and Critical to the Works of the Most Eminent English Poets. Johnson, S.
Prelude, The. Wordsworth, W.
Premature Burial. Poe, E. A.
Presidential Government. Freeman, E. A.
Pride and Prejudice. Austen, J.
Prince Dorus. Lamb, C.
Princess, The. Tennyson, A.
Prisoner of Chillon. Byron, Lord.
Progress of Poesy. Gray, T.
Prometheus. Shelley, P. B.
Prophecy. Dante, A.
Prose by a Poet. Montgomery, J.

Prospectus and Specimen of an Intended National Work. Frere, J. H.
Purgatory of Suicides. Cooper, T.
Purloined Letter. Poe, E. A.

Quarrels of Authors. Disraeli, I.
Queen Mab. Shelley, P. B.
Queen's Wake. Hogg, J.
Quentin Durward. Scott, Sir W.
Question and Answer. Byron, Lord.

Rab and His Friends. Brown, J.
Rachael Ray. Trollope, A.
Rambles in Germany and Italy. Shelley, M. W.
Rameau's Nephew. Le Nevu de Rameau. Diderot.
Rank and Talent. Scargill, W. P.
Ranter. Elliott, E.
Rape of the Lock. Pope, A.
Rash Conjurer. Coleridge, S. T.
Rasselas. Johnson, S.
Rationale of Evidence. Bentham, J.
—— *of Religious Inquiry.* Martineau, J.
Raven. Poe, E. A.
Recluse, The. Wordsworth, W.
Recluse of Norway. Porter, A. M.
Recollections of a Literary Life. Mitford, M. R.
Record of the Pyramids. Reade, J. E.
Red Fisherman. Praed, W. M.
Red Rover. Cooper, J. F.
Redgauntlet. Scott, Sir W.
Reflections on the Revolution in France. Burke, E.
Reinecke Fuchs. Carlyle, T.
Reinecke Fuchs. Goethe.
Reinecke Fuchs. Grimm.
Reinecke Fuchs. Naylor, S.
Rejected Addresses. Smith, H. and J.
Reminiscences of Rome. Sheehy, W. J. A.
Remorse. Coleridge, S. T.
Repealer. Blessington, M.
Representative Men. Emerson, R. W.
Retort Courteous. Quillinan, E.
Retrospect of Western Travel. Martineau, H.
Review of the English Stage. Hazlitt, W.
Revolt of the Bees. Morgan, J. M.
Revolt of the Tartars. De Quincey, T.
Reynard the Fox. See *Reinecke Fuchs.*
Rhymed Plea for Tolerance. Kenyon, J.
Rienzi. Lytton, Lord.
Rimini. Hunt, J. H. L.
Rivals. Sheridan, R. B.
Road to Ruin. Holcroft, T.
Rob Roy. Scott, Sir W.
Rob Roy's Grave. Wordsworth, W.
Robin Hood. Ritson, J.
Roderick the Last of the Goths. Southey, R.

Rokeby. Scott, Sir W.
Romance of Private Life. Burney, S. H.
Rome. Piranesi.
Romola. Evans, M. A. (George Eliot)
Rookwood. Ainsworth, W. H.
Rosamund Gray. Lamb, C.
Round Table. Hazlitt, W.
Round Towers of Ireland. O'Brien, H.
Roxburgh Ballads. Collier, J. P.
Royston Gower. Miller, T.
Russian Fugitive. Wordsworth, W.
Ruth. Gaskell, E. C. S.
Ruth. Wordsworth, W.

Sacred and Legendary Art. Jameson, A. B.
St. Giles and St. James. Jerrold, D. W.
St. Leon. Godwin, W.
St. Ronan's Well. Scott, Sir W.
Saint's Tragedy. Kingsley, C.
Sakuntala or the Fatal Ring. Jones, Sir W.
Salathiel. Croly, G.
Salem Chapel. Oliphant, M.
Sardanapalus. Byron, Lord.
Satire on Satirists. Landor, W. S.
Scarlet Letter. Hawthorne, N.
Scenes of Clerical Life. Evans, M. A. (George Eliot)
Scottish Chiefs. Porter, J.
Self-Formation. Lofft, C.
Self-Help. Smiles, S.
Self-Reliance. *Essays*. Emerson, R. W.
Sense and Sensibility. Austen, J.
Sensitive Plant. Shelley, P. B.
Settlers at Home. *Playfellow, The*. Martineau, H.
Seven Lectures on Shakespeare and Milton. Coleridge, S. T.
Seven Sages of Rome. Wright, T.
Shadow of the Pyramids. Ferguson, R.
Shadows of the Clouds. Froude, J. A.
'She dwelt among the untrodden ways.' Wordsworth, W.
'She was a phantom of delight.' Wordsworth, W.
Shirley. Brontë, C.
Sibylline Leaves. Coleridge, S. T.
Sicilian Romance. Radcliffe, A. W.
Siege of Corinth. Byron, Lord.
Silas Marner. Evans, M. A. (George Eliot)
Simple Story. Inchbald, E.
Sins of the Government, Sins of the Nation. Barbauld, A. L.
Sir Charles Grandison. Richardson, S.
Sir Thomas More, or Colloquies on the Progress and Prospects of Society.
    Southey, R.
Sketch Book. Irving, W.
Sketch of the State of Ireland, Past and Present. Croker, J. W.
Sketches by Boz. Dickens, C.
Sketches of German Life. Varnhagen v. Ense.
Skylark, The. Shelley, P. B.

Somnambulist. Wordsworth, W.
Song of the Shirt. Hood, T.
Songs of Innocence. Blake, W.
Spanish Military Nun. De Quincey, T.
Specimens of Early English Metrical Romances. Ellis, C.
—— *of English Dramatic Poets.* Lamb, C.
—— *of the British Poets.* Campbell, T.
Spirit of the Age. Hazlitt, W.
Spiritual Laws. Essays. Emerson, R. W.
Splendid Misery. Surr, T. S.
Spy, The. Cooper, J. F.
State in its Relations with the Church. Gladstone, W. E.
Statesman, The. Taylor, Sir H.
Statesman's Manual. Coleridge, S. T.
Statesmen of the Commonwealth. Forster, J.
Steamboat. Galt, J.
Strictures on a Life of William Wilberforce. Clarkson, T.
Study from the Antique. Epistles. Moore, T.
Subscription no Bondage. Maurice, J. F. D.
Suggested by a Portrait. Wordsworth, W.
Surgeon's Daughter. Scott, Sir W.
Sybil. Disraeli, B.

Table Talk. Coleridge, S. T.
Table Talk. Hazlitt, W.
Table Talk. Rogers, S.
Tale of a Trumpet. Hood, T.
—— *of Paraguay.* Southey, R.
Tales of a Grandfather. Scott, Sir W.
—— *of my Landlord.* Scott, Sir W.
—— *of the Hall.* Crabbe, G.
—— *of the O'Hara Family.* Banim.
Talisman, The. Scott, Sir W.
Tamlane. Minstrelsy. Scott, Sir W.
Tam o' Shanter. Burns, R.
Tancred. Disraeli, B.
Tartarus. Procter, B. W.
Task, The. Cowper, W.
Tasso. Goethe.
Ten Thousand a Year. Warren, S.
Terry Hogan. Landor, W. S.
Thaddeus of Warsaw. Porter, J.
Thalaba. Southey, R.
Thanksgiving Ode. Wordsworth, W.
'The Land we from our fathers had in trust.' Wordsworth, W.
Theagenes and Chariclea. Heliodorus.
Theological Essays. Maurice, J. F. D.
Thomas à Becket. Darley, G.
Thomas the Rhymer. Minstrelsy. Scott, Sir W.
Thorn. Wordsworth, W.
Those we should wish to have seen. Hazlitt, W.
Thoughts on Man. Godwin, W.
Three Brothers. Pickersgill, J.
Three Cottage Girls. Memorials of a Tour on the Continent.
    Wordsworth, W.

Three Devils. Masson, D.
Tintern Abbey. 'Five years have past.' Wordsworth, W.
To a Highland Girl. Wordsworth, W.
— *Miss Susan B—ekf—d on her Singing. Epistles.* Moore, T. E.
— *Mrs. Bl——. Written in her Album. Epistles.* Moore, T. E.
— *the Cuckoo.* Wordsworth, W.
— *the Lord Viscount Forbes. Epistles.* Moore, T.
To-day in Ireland. Crow, E. E.
Tom Brown's Schooldays. Hughes, T.
Tom Cribb's Memorial to Congress. Moore, T.
Tor Hill. Smith, H.
Tour in Germany. Russell, J.
Tragedy of a Minor. Beddoes, T. L.
Trap to Catch a Sunbeam. Mackarness.
Traveller. Goldsmith, O.
Travels of Dr. Syntax in Search of the Picturesque. Combe, W.
Travels through France and Italy. Smollett, T.
Treatise of Human Nature. Hume, D.
Tremaine. Ward, R. P.
Tristram Shandy. Sterne, L.
Triumph of the Whale. Lamb, C.
Trois Mousquetaires. Dumas, A.
True and Faithful Account of the Appearance of the Ghost of Mr. de Coetlogon. Le Grice, C. V.
Twice-told Tales. Hawthorne, N.
Two Angry Women of Abingdon. Porter, H.
Two Foscari. Byron, Lord.
Two Friends. Blessington, M.
Two Hundred and Nine Days. Hogg, T. J.
Two Loves and a Life. Reade, C.
Two Old Men's Tales. Marsh, A. C.
Two Paths. Ruskin, J.
Two Thieves. Wordsworth, W.
Two Voices. Tennyson, A.
'Two voices are there.' Wordsworth, W.
Two Years Ago. Kingsley, C.
Twopenny Post-Bag. Moore, T.

Ugly Duckling. Andersen, H.
Uncle Tom's Cabin. Stowe, H. E. B.
Unterhaltungen zur Schilderung Goetheischer Dicht- und Denkweise. Goeschel.

Vacation Rambles and Thoughts. Talfourd, Sir T. N.
Vanity Fair. Thackeray, W. M.
Vase. Epistles. Moore, T.
Vathek. Beckford, W.
Veils. Franklin, E. A.
Venetia. Disraeli, B.
Venice Preserved. Otway, T.
Vestiges of the Natural History of Creation. Chambers, R.
Vicar of Wakefield. Goldsmith, O.
View of Society in America. Martineau, H.
Views on the Rhine. Tombleson, W.
Village. Crabbe, G.
Villette. Brontë, C.

Virginius.   Knowles, J. S.
Vision.   Burns, R.
Vision of Don Roderick.   Scott, Sir W.
Vision of Judgment.   Byron, Lord.
Vision of Judgment.   Southey, R.
Vision of Sin.   Tennyson, A.
Vivian.   Edgeworth, M.
Vivian Grey.   Disraeli, B.

Waggoner, The.   Wordsworth, W.
Walhlverwandschaften.   Goethe.
Wallace.   Hodson, M.
Wallenstein.   Schiller.
Wanderer.   D'Arblay, F.
Wanderer.   Goethe.
Wansfell.   Wordsworth, W.
Warden, The.   Trollope, A.
Washington, or Liberty Restored.   Northmore, T.
Wat Tyler.   Southey, R.
Waverley.   Scott, Sir W.
We are Seven.   Wordsworth, W.
Wedding, The.   Lamb, C.
Werner.   Byron, Lord.
Westward Ho !   Kingsley, C.
'Where lies the Land to which yon Ship must go.'   Wordsworth, W.
'While poring Antiquaries search the ground.'   Wordsworth, W.
Whimsicalities.   Hood, T.
Whistlecraft Poems.   Frere, J. H.
White Doe of Rylstone.   Wordsworth, W.
White Slave.   Hildreth, R.
'Why should we weep or mourn . . .'   Wordsworth, W.
Wide Wide World.   Warner, S.
Widow of Kilcrea.   Ireland.   Hall, S. C.
Wife's Trial.   Lamb, C.
Wilhelm Meister.   Carlyle, T.
Wilhelm Meister.   Goethe.
William Tell.   Knowles, J. S.
Winckelmann.   Goethe.
Wine and Walnuts.   Pyne, W. H.
Winter.   Cotton, C.
Wit and Humour.   Hunt, J. H. L.
Witch Aunt.   *Mrs. Leicester's School.*   Lamb, C.
Witch of Atlas.   Shelley, P. B.
Within and Without.   MacDonald, G.
Witness.   Galt, J.
Woman in White.   Collins, W. W.
Woodstock.   Scott, Sir W.
Worthies of Yorkshire and Lancashire.   Coleridge, Hartley.
Wreath and Chain.   *Epistles.*   Moore, T.
Written after the Death of Charles Lamb.   Wordsworth, W.
—— *on leaving Grasmere Churchyard after Mr. Wordsworth's Funeral.*
    Fletcher, E.

Yarrow Revisited.   Wordsworth, W.
'Ye Lime-trees ranged before this hallowed Urn.'   Wordsworth, W.

Year 1811. Barbauld, A. L.
Yeast. Kingsley, C.
Yew Trees. Wordsworth, W.
'Young England.' Wordsworth, W.
Young Mahometan. Mrs. Leicester's School. Lamb, C.

Zanoni. Lytton, Lord.
Zapolya. Coleridge, S. T.
Zeluco. Moore, J.
Zincali, or an Account of the Gypsies in Spain. Borrow, G.
Zoonomia. Darwin, E.
Zueignung. Goethe.

MADE AT THE
TEMPLE PRESS
LETCHWORTH

GREAT BRITAIN